Helen Baker
Endowment

Presented to
Juniata College Library
by Her Family

AFRICAN HISTORICAL DICTIONARIES
Edited by Jon Woronoff

1. *Cameroon,* by Victor T. Le Vine and Roger P. Nye. 1974. *Out of print. See No. 48.*
2. *The Congo,* 2nd ed., by Virginia Thompson and Richard Adloff. 1984. *Out of print. See No. 69.*
3. *Swaziland,* by John J. Grotpeter. 1975.
4. *The Gambia,* 2nd ed., by Harry A. Gailey. 1987.
5. *Botswana,* by Richard P. Stevens. 1975. *Out of print. See No. 70.*
6. *Somalia,* by Margaret F. Castagno. 1975. *Out of print. See No. 87.*
7. *Benin (Dahomey),* 2nd ed., by Samuel Decalo. 1987. *Out of print. See No. 61.*
8. *Burundi,* by Warren Weinstein. 1976. *Out of print. See No. 73.*
9. *Togo,* 3rd ed., by Samuel Decalo. 1996.
10. *Lesotho,* by Gordon Haliburton. 1977.
11. *Mali,* 3rd ed., by Pascal James Imperato. 1996.
12. *Sierra Leone,* by Cyril Patrick Foray. 1977.
13. *Chad,* 3rd ed., by Samuel Decalo. 1997.
14. *Upper Volta,* by Daniel Miles McFarland. 1978.
15. *Tanzania,* by Laura S. Kurtz. 1978.
16. *Guinea,* 3rd ed., by Thomas O'Toole with Ibrahima Bah-Lalya. 1995.
17. *Sudan,* by John Voll. 1978. *Out of print. See No. 53.*
18. *Rhodesia/Zimbabwe,* by R. Kent Rasmussen. 1979. *Out of print. See No. 46.*
19. *Zambia,* 2nd ed., by John J. Grotpeter, Brian V. Siegel, and James R. Pletcher. 1998.
20. *Niger,* 3rd ed., by Samuel Decalo. 1997.
21. *Equatorial Guinea,* 3rd ed., by Max Liniger-Goumaz. 2000.
22. *Guinea-Bissau,* 3rd ed., by Richard Lobban and Peter Mendy. 1997.
23. *Senegal,* by Lucie G. Colvin. 1981. *Out of print. See No. 65.*
24. *Morocco,* by William Spencer. 1980. *Out of print. See No. 71.*
25. *Malawi,* by Cynthia A. Crosby. 1980. *Out of print. See No. 84.*
26. *Angola,* by Phyllis Martin. 1980. *Out of print. See No. 52.*
27. *The Central African Republic,* by Pierre Kalck. 1980. *Out of print. See No. 51.*
28. *Algeria,* by Alf Andrew Heggoy. 1981. *Out of print. See No. 66.*
29. *Kenya,* by Bethwell A. Ogot. 1981. *Out of print. See No. 77.*
30. *Gabon,* by David E. Gardinier. 1981. *Out of print. See No. 58.*
31. *Mauritania,* by Alfred G. Gerteiny. 1981. *Out of print. See No. 68.*

63. *Ghana,* 2nd ed., by David Owusu-Ansah and Daniel Miles McFarland. 1995.
64. *Uganda,* by M. Louise Pirouet. 1995.
65. *Senegal,* 2nd ed., by Andrew F. Clark and Lucie Colvin Phillips. 1994.
66. *Algeria,* 2nd ed., by Phillip Chiviges Naylor and Alf Andrew Heggoy. 1994.
67. *Egypt,* 2nd ed., by Arthur Goldschmidt Jr. 1994.
68. *Mauritania,* 2nd ed., by Anthony G. Pazzanita. 1996.
69. *Congo,* 3rd ed., by Samuel Decalo, Virginia Thompson, and Richard Adloff. 1996.
70. *Botswana,* 3rd ed., by Jeff Ramsay, Barry Morton, and Fred Morton. 1996.
71. *Morocco,* 2nd ed., by Thomas K. Park. 1996.
72. *Tanzania,* 2nd ed., by Thomas P. Ofcansky and Rodger Yeager. 1997.
73. *Burundi,* 2nd ed., by Ellen K. Eggers. 1997.
74. *Burkina Faso,* 2nd ed., by Daniel Miles McFarland and Lawrence Rupley. 1998.
75. *Eritrea,* by Tom Killion. 1998.
76. *Democratic Republic of the Congo (Zaire),* by F. Scott Bobb. 1999. (Revised edition of *Historical Dictionary of Zaire,* No. 43)
77. *Kenya,* 2nd ed., by Robert M. Maxon and Thomas P. Ofcansky. 2000.
78. *South Africa,* 2nd ed., by Christopher Saunders and Nicholas Southey. 2000.
79. *The Gambia,* 3rd ed., by Arnold Hughes and Harry A. Gailey. 2000.
80. *Swaziland,* 2nd ed., by Alan R. Booth. 2000.
81. *Republic of Cameroon,* 3rd ed., by Mark W. DeLancey and Mark Dike DeLancey. 2000.
82. *Djibouti,* by Daoud A. Alwan and Yohanis Mibrathu. 2000.
83. *Liberia,* 2nd ed., by D. Elwood Dunn, Amos J. Beyan, and Carl Patrick Burrowes. 2001.
84. *Malawi,* 3rd ed., by Owen J. Kalinga and Cynthia A. Crosby. 2001.
85. *Sudan,* 3rd ed., by Richard A. Lobban Jr., Robert S. Kramer, Carolyn Fluehr-Lobban. 2002.
86. *Zimbabwe,* 3rd ed., by Steven C. Rubert and R. Kent Rasmussen. 2001.
87. *Somalia,* 2nd ed., by Mohamed Haji Mukhtar. 2002.
88. *Mozambique,* 2nd ed., by Mario Azevedo, Emmanuel Nnadozie, and Tomé Mbuia João. 2003.
89. *Ancient and Medieval Nubia,* by Richard A. Lobban, Jr. 2003.

Historical Dictionary of Mozambique

Second Edition

Mario Azevedo
Emmanuel Nnadozie
Tomé Mbuia João

African Historical Dictionaries, No. 88

The Scarecrow Press, Inc.
Lanham, Maryland, and Oxford
2003

SCARECROW PRESS, INC.

Published in the United States of America
by Scarecrow Press, Inc.
A Member of the Rowman & Littlefield Publishing Group
4501 Forbes Boulevard, Suite 200
Lanham, Maryland 20706
www.scarecrowpress.com

PO Box 317
Oxford
OX2 9RU, UK

British Library Cataloguing in Publication Information Available

Library of Congress Cataloging-in-Publication Data

Azevedo, Mario Joaquim.
    Historical dictionary of Mozambique / Mario Azevedo, Emmanuel Nnadozie,
Tomé Mbuia Joao.—2nd ed.
        p. cm.—(African historical dictionaries ; no. 88)
    Includes bibliographical references (p.).
    ISBN 0-8108-3792-7 (alk. paper)
        1. Mozambique–History–Dictionaries. I. Nnadozie, Emmanuel U. II. Mbuia-
Joao, Tombe Nhamitambo. III. Title. IV. Series.

DT3337.A94 2003
967.9'003–dc21

                                                                    2003045794
First edition: Historical Dictionary of Mozambique by Mario Azevedo, Scarecrow
Press, Metuchen, NJ, 1991. African Historical Dictionaries, No. 47
ISBN 0-8108-2413-2

Contents

Editor's Foreword

Mozambique is one of Africa's larger countries and also has the potential to become one of its more important countries. It possesses many natural resources and has an active population that could again develop agriculture and commerce and then create an industrial base. It is located along the coast and provides a natural outlet for several landlocked neighbors. It is also strategically placed next to South Africa, the regional powerhouse. Regrettably, over the first decade of independence, it did not take advantage of those assets, partly because of a destructive civil war and partly because of its ideological orientation. Now that the war is over and it has reverted to a market economy, Mozambique should be able to make better progress.

When the first edition of the *Historical Dictionary of Mozambique* appeared, I pointed out that Mozambique was one of the least-known African states. Little has happened to change that situation. Thus, there are few enough sources of information even today, which is particularly deplorable now that a fresh start is being made. Fortunately, this second edition can fill more of the gaps and bring the story up-to-date. This is done through an extension of the chronology, which recounts the more significant events, and an expanded dictionary section, which contains new and updated entries on persons, places, events, and institutions of note as well as crucial aspects of the economy, society, and culture. The bibliography has also been revised, with more new titles, many of them in English, but also in Portuguese.

This second edition builds on the first, and the lead author is still Mario Azevedo, who wrote the first edition. Dr. Azevedo, who was born in Mozambique, is presently chair of the African-American and African Studies Department at the University of North Carolina at Charlotte. He has written extensively on Africa, much of this on Mozambique, including a book on Mozambique refugees. This time he is joined by Tomé Mbuia João, also a Mozambican by origin, who works as a broadcaster in Portuguese at the Voice of America, and Emmanuel Nnadozie, who is professor of economics at Truman State University. Together they have produced a very helpful and insightful work on a country that deserves to be better known.

Jon Woronoff
Series Editor

Acknowledgments

Mario J. Azevedo

I wish to thank the University of North Carolina at Charlotte, the Southern Regional Education Board, and the African Studies Center at the University of Florida at Gainesville, all of which provided me with funds for the completion of this manuscript. Likewise, I acknowledge the contribution of Dr. Gwendolyn Spencer Prater, dean and professor of the School of Social Work at Jackson State University, who assumed some of my academic responsibilities while I was doing research at the University of Florida, and the work of Jon Coyle, history major at the University of North Carolina at Charlotte, who assisted me with the research and the drafting of part of this project. Other persons to whom I owe thanks include Carol Albert, of Gainesville, Florida, who helped me with the preparation of the bibliography; Roberta Duff, Eleanor Stafford, and David Landrum, my dedicated office assistants at the University of North Carolina; and Yvette Bratton, education major at the University of North Carolina, who typed parts of the manuscript.

I cannot neglect mentioning my family—Ernestine, Margarida, and Linda Azevedo—for the understanding, patience, and unconditional support they showed while I was preparing the manuscript. Last but not least, I wish to express my gratitude to the personnel and staff of the Overseas Historical Archives and the Biblioteca da Sociedade de Geografia de Lisboa, in Lisbon, for their assistance during my three research periods related to the completion of the first edition of this volume.

Tomé Mbuia João

I am indebted to so many people for the position I hold and the successes I have had throughout my academic life both in Mozambique and the United States that I cannot mention them all in this work. Most of all, however, I wish to thank the Missionaries of Africa (otherwise known as the White Fathers) for providing me with a solid basis that guided me during my entire education and academic career; Dom Sebastião Soares de Resende, the late Bishop of Beira, Mozambique, for facilitating my studies in Europe, especially Spain; and the late Dr. Manuel Cardozo, chairman of the History Department at Catholic University. He was instrumental in my securing of an academic fellowship that allowed me to continue my studies and supported me unconditionally as I pursued my Ph.D. in the Department of History at Catholic University.

Emmanuel Nnadozie

I am indebted to Natasha Jones, Kristina Toshova, Sara Durham, and Tudor Stavrev for their contributions at various stages of the preparation of the economic contributions to this manuscript. Without them, my work would have been much more difficult.

Note on Spelling

For the benefit of the English reader, the book maintains the English spelling except where a translation from the Portuguese or Mozambican languages does not yet exist. However, in the case where recognizable terms or expressions such as Companhia do Niassa (Nyasa Company) and Companhia de Moçambique (Mozambique Company) are used, the corresponding English or Portuguese spelling is kept. Following independence, which occurred on June 25, 1975, the FRELIMO government altered several of the geographic designations as well as street names to reflect African tradition, history, and culture. To avoid confusion in the reader's mind, the authors use the old designations—for example, Lourenço Marques (now Maputo) and Vila Pery (now Chimoio)—whenever reference is made to the period previous to independence, while usage of the new terminology alerts the reader that the discussion refers to the postindependence era, particularly after 1976. Finally, the Portuguese spelling of the colony's former capital, Moçambique (1815–1907), is maintained throughout the book as a way to easily differentiate the city from the colony itself.

Former Names	Present Names
Lourenço Marques	Maputo
Porto Amélia	Pemba
Cidade de Sofala	Chiloane Town
Vila Cabral	Vila Lichinga
Vila Gouveia	Vila Catandica
Vila Pery	Chimoio City
Vila João Belo	Xai-Xai

Acronyms and Abbreviations

AGRO-ALFA	Empresa Estatal Maquinária Agrícola
ALIMO	Aliança Independente de Moçambique
AMODEFA	Associação Moçambicana do Desenvolvimento da Família
ANC	African National Congress
ANFRENA	Agência Nacional de Frete e Navegação
ANM	Associação Nacional de Moçambique
AP	Assembleia Popular
AVICOLA	Empresa Nacional Avícola
BNU	Banco Nacional Ultramarino
CAIL	Complexo Agro-Industrial do Limpopo
CAJU	Empresa Nacional de Caju
CARBOMOC	Empresa Nacional de Carvão de Moçambique
CC	Central Committee
CCM	Conselho Cristão de Moçambique
CEI	Casa dos Estudantes do Império
CFM	Empresa dos Caminhos de Ferro de Moçambique
CHCH	Companhia Hidroeléctrica de Cahora Bassa
CIA	Central Intelligence Agency
CICOMO	Companhia Industrial de Cordoarias de Moçambique
CIFEL	Companhia Industrial de Fundição e Laminagem
CITM	Centro de Informação e Turismo de Moçambique
CNE	Comissão Nacional Eleitoral
CODEMO	Confederação Democrática de Moçambique
COGROPA	Comércio Grossista de Produtos Alimentares

CONCP	Conferência das Organizações Nacionalistas das Colónias Portuguesas
CONIMO	Congresso Independente de Moçambique
COREMO	Comité Revolucionário de Moçambique
COSERU	Comité Secreto da Restauração
CTT	Correios, Telégrafos e Telefones
CUNIMO	Comité para a União Nacional de Moçambique
DEM	Direcção e Exploração de Moçambique
DETA	Divisão de Exploração de Tranportes Aéreos
DGS	Direcção Geral de Segurança
DIMAC	Distribuidora de Materiais de Construção
ECOME	Empresa de Construções Metálicas
EMMA	Empresa Moçambicana de Malhas
EMOCHA	Empresa Moçambicana de Chá
EMOSE	Empresa Moçambicana de Seguros
ENACOMO	Empresa Nacional de Exportação
ENCATEX	Empresa Nacional de Calçado e Têxteis
ENHM	Empresa Nacional de Hidrocarbonetos de Moçambique
ENT	Empresa Nacional de Turismo
EQUIPESCA	Empresa Moçambicana de Apetrechamento da Indústria Pesqueira
FADM	Forças Armadas de Defesa de Moçambique
FASOL	Fábricas Associadas de Óleos
FICO	Frente Independente para a Continuidade do Oeste
FNLA	Frente Nacional de Libertação de Angola
FPLM	Forças Populares de Libertação de Moçambique
FRAIN	Frente Revolucionária Africana para a Independência Nacional (das Colónias Portuguesas)
FRAINA	Frente Africana de Independência Nacional
FRELIMO	Frente de Libertação de Moçambique
FRESAMO	Frente de Salvação de Moçambique
FUMO	Frente Unida de Moçambique
GD	Grupos Dinamizadores (Dynamizing Groups)
HIDROMOC	Empresa Estatal de Hidraúlica

HIPC	Highly Indebted Poor Country
HIV/AIDS	Human Immunodeficiency Virus/Acquired Immunodeficiency Syndrome
IMA	Indústria Moçambicana de Aço
IMBEC	Importadora de Bens de Consumo
IMF	International Monetary Fund
INTERELCTRA	Empresa Distribuidora de Equipamento Eléctrico e Electrónico e Componentes
INTERFRANCA	Lojas Francas de Moçambique
INTERMAQUINA	Empresa de Comércio Externo de Equipamentos Industriais
INTERMECANO	Empresa Nacional de Importação e Exportação de Veículos Motorizados
INTERMETAL	Empresa Distribuidora e Importadora de Metais
INTERQUIMICA	Empresa Moçambicana de Importação e Exportação de Productos Químicos e Plásticos
IPADE	Instituto para a Paz e Desenvolvimento
KANU	Kenya African National Union
LA	Liga Africana
LAM	Linhas Aéreas de Moçambique
LNA	Liga Nacional Africana
MAC	Movimento Anti-Colonialista
MAGMA	Empresa Nacional de Minas
MANCO	Mozambique African National Congress
MANU	Mozambique African National Union
MCD	Movimento de Convergência Democrática
MFA	Movimento das Forças Armadas
MLSTP	Movimento de Libertação de São Tomé e Príncipe
MNR	Mozambique National Resistance (*see* RENAMO)
MOCARGO	Empresa Moçambicana de Cargas
MONAMO	Mozambique National Movement
MONAMO-PMSD	Movimento Nacionalista de Moçambique — Partido Moçambicano da Democracia Social
MORECO	Mozambique Revolutionary Council
MPLA	Movimento Popular da Libertação de Angola

MOZAL	Mozambique Aluminum
MT	*Metical*
NATO	North Atlantic Treaty Organization
NESAM	Núcleo de Estudantes Secundários Africanos de Moçambique
OJM	Organização da Juventude Moçambicana
OMM	Organização da Mulher Moçambicana
ONUMOZ	Organização das Nações Unidas em Moçambique
OTM	Organização dos Trabalhadores de Moçambique
PACODE	Partido de Congresso Democrático
PACOMO	Partido Communista de Moçambique
PADELIMO	Partido Democrático para Libertação de Moçambique
PADEMO	Partido Democrático de Moçambique
PADMO	Partido Democrático de Moçambique
PAIGC	Partido Africano de Independência da Guiné e Cabo Verde
PALDMO	Partido Liberal e Democrático de Moçambique
PAM	Partido Agrário de Moçambique
PANADE	Partido Nacional Democrático
PANAMO	Partido Nacional de Moçambique
PARTONAMO	Partido de Todos os Nativos de Moçambique
PB	Politburo
PCN	Partido de Convenção Nacional
PDC	Partido de Convergência Democrática
PESCOM	Empresa Internacional Moçambicana de Importação e Exportação de Produtos Pesqueiros
PIDEMO	Partido Internacionalista Democrático de Moçambique
PIMO	Partido Independente de Moçambique
PPIMO	Partido Patriótico Independente de Moçambique
PPLFCRM	Partido Progressivo e Liberal Federalista das Communidades Religiosas de Moçambique
PPPM	Partido de Progresso do Povo Moçambicano
PRD	Partido Renovado Democrático

PRE	Programa de Reabilitação Económica
PREPSUMO	Partido Revolucionário do Povo Socialista Unido de Moçambique
PSD	Partido Social Democrático
PT	Partido do Trabalho
PUM	Partido da Unidade de Moçambique
PUN	Partido de Unidade Nacional
PVM	Partido Verde de Moçambique
RCM	Rádio Clube de Moçambique
RECAMO	Regedores e Camponeses de Moçambique
RENAMO	Resistência Nacional Moçambicana (see MNR)
RENAMO-UDE	Resistência Nacional Moçambicana-União Democrática
SADC	Southern African Development Community
SAF	Structual Adjustment Facility
SAP	Structural Adjustment Program
SOLD	Partido Social e Democrático
SONAREP	Sociedade Nacional de Refinação de Petróleos
SONEFE	Sociedade Nacional de Estudos e Financeamento de Empreendimentos Ultramarinos
SWAPO	South-West African People's Organization
TAP	Transportes Aéreos Portugueses
TTA	(Empresa Nacional de) Transporte e Trabalho Aéreo
UD	União Democrática
UDEMO	União Democrática de Moçambique
UDENAMO	União Democrática Nacional de Moçambique
UDI	Unilateral Declaration of Independence
UDMO	União Democrática de Moçambique
UMCA	University Mission of Central Africa
UMO	União de Moçambique
UNAM	União Nacional Moçambicana
UNAMI	União Africana de Moçambique Independente
UNAR	União Nacional Africana da Rombézia
UNDP	United Nations Development Program

UNHRC	United Nations High Commissioner for Refugees
UNIPOMO	União Nacional de Independência Popular de Moçambique
UNITA	União Nacional para a Independência Total de Angola
WNLA (WENELA)	Witwatersrand Native Labour Association
ZANU	Zimbabwe African National Union
ZAPU	Zimbabwe African People's Union
ZIN	Zona de Intervenção do Norte

A land of geographic and demographic diversity, Mozambique is a vast and strategically important country. Once the pride of Portugal in East Africa along with Angola, Mozambique is now a country struggling to overcome its past marked by a devastating war of liberation against Portugal (1964–1974) and a crippling civil war (1977–1992).

Chronology

4000 B.C. Mozambique inhabited

100–1000 A.D. Bantu migrations to Mozambique

1450 Death of King Mutota of Makaranga

1480 Death of Matope, king of Mwenemutapa

1490 Changamire, king of Mwenemutapa

1494 Death of Changamire, king of Mwenemutapa, who had broken away from Zimbabwe, at the hands of Kakuyo Komungyama who dominated Sena country

March 2, 1498 Vasco da Gama's arrival at Mozambique Island

1502 First Portuguese trading center at Mozambique island

1506 Degredado António Fernandes's penetration of interior of Manica e Sofala in search of gold; contact with the Makaranga established

1509 António de Saldanha appointed captain of Sofala and Mozambique (until 1512)

1513 End of dynastic war between ruling Changamire and Makaranga in ancient Zimbabwe; victory of Changamire who is allied to the Quiteve, Torwa, and Manica

1521 Diogo de Sepúlveda appointed captain of Sofala and Mozambique (until 1525)

1530 Arabs expelled by Portuguese from Sena (trading center built)

1541 Francis Xavier disembarks at Mozambique Island, where he stays for six months (until 1542)

1544 First Portuguese trading center at Quelimane; it becomes a center for slave trading to Brazil; Lourenço Marques explores Sofala coast up to Baía do Lago

1549 The Portuguese build forts at Mombasa, Moçambique Island, Quelimane, Sena, Tete, Catembe, and Inhambane

1550 Dominicans establish themselves at Sofala, Mombasa, and Zambezia

February 5, 1560 Jesuit priests Gonçalo da Silveira, André Fernandez, and Brother André da Costa arrive at Moçambique Island from India

1563 Pope Pius VI creates the Ecclesiastical Administration of Mozambique and Sofala

1571 Failure of Francisco Barreto's expedition

1573 Death of Francisco Barreto; defeat and massacre of António Cardoso and his expedition by the Abarue in Chicoa; end of first expedition to Mwenemutapa

1574 Second Portuguese defeat by Mwenemutapa at Manica

1593 Portuguese troops from Tete and Sena defeated by the Zimba; construction of Fort Jesus at Mombasa; punitive expedition against the Zimba from Moçambique Island totally decimated by the Zimba; free gold commerce in Mozambique

1595 The Captain of Sofala and Mozambique receives monopoly over all commerce

1599 First *prazos* acquired by individual soldiers and merchants along the Zambezi

1607 Battle between Matuzianha of Barue and Mwenemutapa Gatse Ruese, who enjoys Portuguese assistance; Barue victory, and gold mines still elusive

1610 Matuzianha, Barue king, defeated by the Portuguese Expedition from Moçambique Island and Sofala at Magide Cochena

January 21, 1612 Dismemberment of the Church in Mozambique from the jurisdiction of the Archdiocese of Goa by Pope Paul V with see at Sena

1614 Two forts built at Chicoa by Diogo Madeira

1623 Death of Gatse Ruese, who had allowed the Portuguese to enter his reign and establish commercial strongholds

1641 First ships from Brazil to Mozambique in search of slaves

1660 Mombasa taken by Oman Arabs

1671 Mombasa, Quelimane, Sofala, Inhambane, and Zambezia open trade to all Portuguese (closed again in 1683)

1684 Portuguese victory over Mwunemutapa at Maungo; monarch's children take refuge at Tete

1685 Establishment of the Companhia de Moçambique (Real Companhia do Comércio de Moçambique) limited to commerce between India and Moçambique (dissolved in 1699)

1716 Establishment of Zumbo *feitoria*

March 16, 1728 Fort Jesus, Mombasa, occupied by the Portuguese (last time until April or November 1729)

1732 The Dutch are forced out of Lourenço Marques

1736 The Dutch expelled from Lagoa Bay by Africans

1750 Fifteen crown *prazos* exist in Quelimane, 29 in Sena, and 59 in Tete

1754 Slaves destined for French islands: Macua, 370; Mujao, 150; Sena, 250; Sofala, 80; Inhambane, 150

April 5, 1758 Suicide of Captain-General of Mozambique João Manuel de Mello (embezzlement suspected cause)

1759 Jesuits expelled from Portugal by Marquês de Pombal; nine Jesuits leave Mozambique

1775 Revolt of Arabs at Inhambane (Portuguese execution of several mutineers)

1782 Lourenço Marques Praesidium destroyed by fire

1807 Mozambique provisional government presided by Bishop de Olia (until 1809)

1813 Execution of António José da Cruz (or Joaquim Vicente da Cruz) for betrayal of a Portuguese expedition to Mwenemutapa

1818 Fifth provisional government of Mozambique presided by the bishop of Mozambique (until 1819)

1822 Praesidium assaulted by Africans in Lourenço Marques, assisted by the Nguni and Swazi; Cardona, its governor, is killed

1824 Establishment of the Companhia Comercial de Lourenço Marques with monopoly over the slave trade in the area

1830 Revolt and defeat of Soliman Agi, cheick of Quitangonha

1832 *Prazos* abolished (in theory)

1833 Lourenço Marques assaulted by "Landins" and Nguni

May 31, 1834 Law abolishing religious orders; Nguni paid chiefs of Machana, Moambe, Maputo, Matola, and Encolene to attack Lourenço Marques Praesidium

December 10, 1836 Slavery abolished by decree of Sá da Bandeira

1841 Caetano Pereira's (Choutam's) rebellion against the Portuguese in Zambezia

1844 Inhaude (Joaquim José da Cruz) builds headquarters at Massangano

1849 The governor of Inhambane District, Captain Pereira Chaves, killed in combat with the Africans

1853 Beginning of war against the Pereiras by the Portuguese (Portuguese defeat)

1856 Death of Soshangane; his son Mawewe, succeeds him; capital transferred to Bilene, further south

November 27, 1857 Charles et Georges incident

1863 Return of Sultan Mussa Quanto from exile; he had been defeated by the Portuguese at the mouth of Angoche in 1861

1869 Fourth expedition against the Bonga

July 24, 1875 French president Edme Patrice MacMahon renders a favorable decision to Portugal on the Lagoa Bay dispute

May 1877 Sheikhs and other African authorities told by Governor-General Carvalho de Menezes of end of slavery and slave trade

1878 Revolt of Chiefs Nhabide, Zavala, Mindu, and Quissico, allied to Muzila

1879 First telegraphic lines laid in Mozambique between Tangalene, Moçambique Island, and Lourenço Marques

October 27, 1880 *Prazos* declared Crown property

1881 Jesuits return to Mozambique

1884 Revolt of Massingire against the Portuguese

1885 Death of Muzila, who had moved the Nguni capital back to Chaimite; Gungunhana installed king; his headquarters moved to Manjacaze

1887 Portuguese victory (assisted by the people of Massinga, Yinguane, Hlavanguane, and Zunque of Inhambane) over Gungunhana at the battle of Chicunquesa

December 8, 1889 Macololo subdued by Serpa Pinto and João de Azevedo Coutinho

January 11, 1890 British ultimatum to Portugal

February 12, 1891 Concession to *Companhia de Moçambique;* Franciscans arrive in Mozambique

1892 Introduction of the hut tax

May 20, 1892 Concession to *Companhia da Zambézia*

1893 Concession to *Companhia do Niassa*

July 1, 1895 Inauguration of first rail line in Mozambique (Lourenço Marques-Pretoria); first telephone line in Mozambique (Lourenço Marques)

December 28, 1895 Arrest of Gungunhana by Albuquerque at Chaimite

July 20, 1897 Maguiguana, Gungunhana's successor, defeated and killed by Mouzinho de Albuquerque

April 1, 1898 Concession to *Companhia do Búzi*; Lourenço Marques declared the capital of Mozambique

August 8, 1898 Concession to *Companhia do Boror*

1902 João de Azevedo Coutinho, accompanied by 4,000 troops, subdues the Barue resistance

1904 Sociedade Agrícola do Madal given a chart

1907 Salesian priests arrive in the colony

1909 The Witwatersrand Native Labor Association (WNLA, WENELA) receives monopoly over worker recruitment in Mozambique; the company recruits 75,000 miners

May 24, 1910 Angoche Arab Cheick defeated by Captain Massano de Amorin

1911 Ministry of Colonies created in Lisbon

1912 Creation of first secondary school in Mozambique, called Licéu Nacional in 1919

1913 Lay "Civilizing" Brigades introduced

1916 Portuguese troops recover Quionga from the Germans

1919 Monfortin priests arrive in Mozambique; identity cards for nonassimilated male Africans of over 14 years of age; restrictons on movement and residence in the cities

January 1, 1920 Sena Sugar Estates gets concession

1921 Law forbidding sale of liquor to Africans north of Save River

1922 Organic Statutes for Mozambique; inauguration of Trans-Zambezia-Sena Railway to Malawi

December 6, 1928 Code of Work for "*Indígenas*" promulgated

September 11, 1928 Approval of the Mozambique Convention in Pretoria

1929 Companhia do Niassa extinct

1930 Concessions to monopolistic companies abolished

1933 Establishment of Negrophile Institute, later known as Centro Associativo dos Negros de Moçambique

1935 Administrative division of the colony into three provinces, Sul do Save, Zambezia, and Niassa

1936 Creation of the Direcção de Exploração de Transportes Aéreos (DETA)

1937 First technical school in Lourenço Marques

September 4, 1940 Bula *Solemnibus Conventionibus* of Pius XII terminates Mozambique Prelacy and institutes the Dioceses of Beira and Nampula (Tete, Inhambane, Quelimane, Vila Cabral, and Porto Amelia became dioceses in the 1950s and 1960s)

1946 Mozambique divided into the Provinces of Manica e Sofala (Beira and Tete districts), Sul do Save (Lourenço Marques, Gaza, Inhambane districts), Zambezia, and Niassa (Nampula, Lago, and Cabo Delgado districts)

1947 Strikes at the Lourenço Marques docks

1948 Xinavane massacre of Africans by the Portuguese; strike at Lourenço Marques harbor: 200 Africans arrested, most deported to São Tomé

1949 Eduardo Mondlane and Mozambique students establish the Núcleo dos Estudantes Secundários Africanos de Moçambique (NESAM)

1954 Mozambique has three deputies in the Portuguese National Assembly; Mozambique is divided into nine provinces: Lourenço Marques, Gaza, Inhambane, Manica e Sofala, Tete, Zambézia, Moçambique, Cabo Delgado, and Niassa; União Maconde de Moçambique is founded, precursor of the União Nacional de Moçambicanos Africanos (UNAMO)

1955 Establishment of the Institute of Tropical Medicine of Mozambique; adoption of the Organic Portuguese Overseas Law making the colonies Provinces of Portugal

1956 President General Craveiro Lopes visits Mozambique; strikes at Lourenço Marques docks

1959 Marvin Harris criticizes forced labor in the Portuguese colonies

June 16, 1960 Mueda massacre

October 2, 1960 Establishment of União Democrática Nacional de Moçambique (UDENAMO)

June 25, 1962 Frente de Libertação de Moçambique (FRELIMO) founded in Dar-es-Salaam

September 23–28, 1962 FRELIMO First Congress in Dar-es-Salaam

September 25, 1964 Armed struggle begins

July 20–25, 1968 FRELIMO Second Congress (at Machedje)

February 3, 1969 Assassination of Eduardo Mondlane

May 9–14, 1970 Fourth Session of FRELIMO's Central Committee chooses Samora Machel as new party president

March 4, 1973 Organização da Mulher Moçambicana (OMM): First Conference

April 25, 1974 Military coup in Portugal

September 7, 1974 Lusaka agreement between Portugal and FRELIMO; settlers take over national radio in Maputo

September 25, 1974   FRELIMO leads transitional government

June 25, 1975   Independence day

July 24, 1975   Nationalization of health, education, law practice, funeral service establishments

February 3, 1976   Nationalization of rented property; capital city renamed Maputo

February 11–27, 1976   Eighth Session of Central Committee sets policy for transition to socialism

March 3, 1976   Sanctions against Rhodesia imposed

October 3–12, 1976   Cooperatives seminar

November 10–17, 1976   Organização da Mulher Moçambicana (OMM): Second Conference

February 3–7, 1977   FRELIMO Third Congress: Marxism-Leninism officially embraced in the country

November 1977   Elections for People's Assemblies

February–November 1978   FRELIMO Party membership drive

August 1978   Joaquim de Carvalho dismissed as agriculture minister

August 1–4, 1979   Council of Ministers declares 1980–90 the "decade of victory over underdevelopment"

December 4, 1979   President Machel's speech on health

December 17, 1979   Lancaster House Agreement ends Zimbabwe (Southern Rhodesia) liberation war

1980   First national census

March, April 1980   Government reshuffle: two party secretaries to work full-time for party; new health minister

March 26–31, 1980   Organização da Mulher Moçambicana (OMM): Third Conference

April, May 1980   Elections

June 16, 1980   The *metical* introduced as new currency

August 1980   First postindependence census

November 27–28, 1980   First Southern African Development Coordination Conference (SADCC) meeting, Maputo

January 30, 1981   South African commandos raid the Maputo suburb of Matola

March 4, 1981   Alleged Central Intelligence Agency (CIA) spies expelled from Mozambique

October 6–9, 1981   People's Assembly approves 10-year plan

October 14, 1981   White man, later identified as South African soldier, killed trying to mine railway.

October 29, 1981   Bridges carrying road and railway freight and the oil pipeline from Beira to Zimbabwe sabotaged

March 4, 1982   President Machel appoints provincial military commanders to strengthen fight against Mozambique National Resistance (MNR) members

May–June 1982   Meetings with "the compromised" (collaborators)

August 17, 1982   Ruth First, South African antiapartheid journalist, assassinated

January 11, 1983   Resumption of summary public executions of captured Mozambique National Resistance (MNR) men

April 10, 1983   First public floggings

April 26–30, 1983   FRELIMO Fourth Congress; socialism relaxed

May 21, 28, 1983   Government reshuffle, including new agriculture minister; two politburo members given additional tasks; other changes in security and economic ministries

May 23, 1983   South African planes bomb Maputo suburbs

July–September 1983   "Operation Production" expels the unemployed from cities

December 20, 1983   Ministerial-level talks between Mozambique and South Africa in Switzerland

February 1, 1984 Floods displace thousands of people, 100 people killed

February 20, 1984 Mozambique and South Africa sign Security Pact

March 16, 1984 Nkomati Accord signed

October 3, 1984 Pretoria Declaration

March 8, 1985 Front-line leaders call Nkomati Accord a failure, blaming South Africa

March 11, 1985 FRELIMO announces a series of economic liberalization measures

March 16, 1985 International Monetary Fund (IMF) first loan (U.S.$45 million) to Mozambique

August 28, 1985 Zimbabwe and FRELIMO troops assault Gorongoza

September 19, 1985 President Samora Machel's first visit to the United States

October 19, 1986 Machel dies in Tupelov airplane crash

November 3, 1986 Joaquim Chissano selected president of Mozambique by Central Committee

March 23, 1987 Paulo Barbosa, official of the Mozambique Resistance Movement (MNR), defects to FRELIMO

October 13–16, 1987 Mozambique officials attend Vancouver, Canada, Commonwealth meeting

November 6, 1987 Mozambique downs Malawi airline over Ulongue, killing two senior Malawi Congress Party officials

June 24, 1988 FRELIMO announces return of expropriated property to Catholic Church

September 11–12, 1988 Pieter B. Botha, South Africa's president, visits Mozambique

September 18–20, 1988 Pope John Paul II visits Mozambique

1989 Fifth FRELIMO Congress

November 1990 New constitution ratified; government announces democratic reforms

December 1990   Partial cease-fire announced by FRELIMO and REN-AMO; an International Commission is established to oversee partial cease-fire; sixth FRELIMO Congress: concept of multipartyism adopted

January 10, 1991   Fighting resumes

March 1992   Agreement on electoral process, stipulating that, within a year, presidential and legislative elections would be held

August 7, 1992   Joaquim Chissano and Afonso Dhlakama sign cease-fire agreement to begin October 1, 1992

October 4, 1992   Peace accord between FRELIMO and RENAMO signed in Rome

December 15, 1992   Donors agree to donate $330m for demobilization of troops and surrender of weapons to the United Nations (UN) within six months for the establishment of a new national force to be called Forças Armadas de Defesa de Moçambique (FADM)

February 1993   Organização das Nações Unidas em Moçambique (ON-UMOZ) troops, observers, and relief agents arrive in Mozambique

September 22, 1994   Electoral campaign begins: 12 presidential candidates and 14 political parties join in the process

October 26, 1994   Afonso Dhlakama announces RENAMO's boycott of the elections

October 27–29, 1994   First multiparty presidential and legislative democratic elections in Mozambique

October 28, 1994   Afonso Dhlakama renounces his elections boycott

December 8, 1994   First session of the multiparty Assembly of the Republic

1995   Adoption of first municipal laws

March 1995   The United Nations (ONUMOZ) completes its mission and withdraws from Mozambique

June 1995   Some 1.7 million returning refugees resettle in Mozambique

May 1996   Farmland Agreement with South Africa, Mozambique leasing 2,000 hectares in Niassa Province

1997   Constitutional amendment on nature of local organs of government

May 1997 Antigovernment riots spread from Beira to Quelimane, Chimoio, and Inhambane; FRELIMO's Seventh Congress reelects Joaquim Chissano party chairman

June 30, 1998 Municipal elections: only 14.6 percent of registered voted; elections boycotted by the opposition

December 29–30, 1999 Second multiparty democratic elections; Afonso Dhlakama refuses to recognize Joaquim Chissano as president

February–March 2000 Floods displace thousands of people mainly in the south and parts of Central Mozambique

September 22, 2000 Raul Domingos expelled from RENAMO

November 9, 2000 Some hundred demonstrators die allegedly asphyxiated in jail in Montepuez, Cabo Delgado Province

December 19, 2000 Joaquim Chissano and Afonso Dhlakama hold first postelection meeting, they agree to meet in January 2001

January 2001 Joaquim Chissano and Afonso Dhlakama hold second meeting

February–March, 2001 Floods in Central Mozambique

March 2001 Joaquim Chissano and Afonso Dhlakama meet: nothing is resolved on vote recounting and RENAMO's request to appoint governors in the provinces it won

May 2001 Afonso Dhlakama breaks off further talks with Joaquim Chissano

August 11, 2001 Murder of António Siba-Siba Macuacua, interim manager of Banco Austral; investigation under way

October 2001 RENAMO's First Post-War Congress Divisions within the party became obvious at the Congress

June 2002 FRELIMO's Eighth Congress: Armando Guebuza is selected as secretary-general of the party, effectively as the next presidential candidate

July 2002 Afonso Dhlakama removes Secretary-General Joaquim Vaz and assumes the position himself

August 8, 2002 Almeida Tambara, RENAMO's Deputy in the Assembly of the Republic, resigns from the party

August 29, 2002 Kofi Annan, UN general-secretary, visits Mozambique

February 2003   Stiff court sentences rendered on those implicated in Cardozo's assassination

May 19–24, 2003   Dhlakama visits Washington to shore up his candidacy in the coming 2004 presidential elections

October 2003   Municipal (autarchic) elections expected

Introduction

A land of geographic and demographic diversity, Mozambique is a vast and strategically important country. Once the pride of Portugal in East Africa along with Angola, Mozambique is now a country struggling to overcome its past marked by a devastating war of liberation against Portugal (1964–74) and a crippling civil war (1977–92) between the ruling party—the Frente de Libertação de Mocambique (FRELIMO)—and the Resistência Nacional Moçambicana (RENAMO). Although still a land of great promise, Mozambique is listed by the United Nations (UN) as one of the 25 poorest countries in the world, whose future has been hampered by a series of natural disasters, such as the droughts of the early 1980s and the floods of the early 2000s. Once a land of clean beaches that attracted thousands of white South Africans a year, Mozambique is now reduced to a country of untreated sewage; abandoned beaches and resorts; overwhelmed hospitals catering to people infected with HIV/AIDS, malaria, cholera, and polio; overcrowded and dilapidated school buildings; and its roads laced with mines, with a national budget that depends 40 percent or more on foreign assistance. Yet, the people are vibrant and determined to succeed and live in harmony, notwithstanding the civil war from which they just emerged. The leaders appear more serious in consolidating the democratic reforms than is the case in other parts of Africa. Indeed, the present and the near future are gloomy, but Mozambique's long-term prospects appear bright, as long as the policies remain progressive, the vast resources are managed wisely, and corruption is curtailed if not altogether eliminated.

LAND AND CLIMATE

In its naturally strategic location in East Africa, the Republic of Mozambique shares borders with the following countries: South Africa and Swaziland in the south, Tanzania in the north, Malawi and Zambia in the northwest, and

Zimbabwe in the west. Mozambique has an area of 303,037 square miles (799,390 square kilometers), is 1,120 miles (1,867 kilometers) long, and has a coastline of some 1,737 miles (2,470 kilometers). Its longest distance from east to west is 380 miles (633 kilometers). Located south of the Equator, it encompasses the area between latitude 10 degrees north and 26 degrees south, and longitudes 30 degrees west and 42 degrees east. Its westernmost area comprises the region where Luganga River intercepts parallel 15 degrees on the Zimbabwe border, while in the east it includes the area between Meridian 30 degrees and 40 degrees east of Greenwich. Its easternmost point is found at Ponta Jana, on the Mozambique Channel.

The climate of Mozambique is tropical, but its temperatures and rainfall vary from region to region. Mozambique has essentially two seasons, wet and dry. The wet season begins around October and ends in March, while the dry season occurs between April and September. The rainy season experiences an average rainfall of 16 to 48 inches (38 to 115 centimeters), 80 percent of which occurs between November and March. The temperatures remain at an average of 68 degrees Fahrenheit (20 degrees Celsius) during the dry season, although in the months of July and August temperatures may fall below 30 degrees Fahrenheit (−1 degree Celsius). During the wet season, particularly in January, the temperatures, averaging 80 degrees Fahrenheit (27 degrees Celsius), may go as high as 100 degrees Fahrenheit (38 degrees Celsius) in Tete Province. The interior highlands experience cooler temperatures. As one moves toward the coast, the rainfall decreases. Mozambique's tropical climate is responsible for its various endemic diseases, including trypanosomiasis (sleeping sickness) in the central and northwestern part of the country, malaria, schistosomiasis (bilharziasis), leprosy, tuberculosis, and hepatitis.

The coastal areas tend to be warmer due to the warm current of Mozambique Channel, which flows south from the vicinity of the Equator. The central coastal line, from Quelimane to Beira, experiences high humidity and heavy rainfalls, with an annual average of 55 inches (132 centimeters) at Beira and 48 inches (115 centimeters) at Quelimane. South and north of this central line, the rains and humidity decrease, the southern coast averaging 35 inches of rain and the northern coast about 24 inches (58 centimeters) to 48 inches (115 centimeters) annually.

The inland areas, because of their varied geographic conditions, do not have a uniform climate and rainfall. In general, the north experiences what is called a tropical monsoon climate, which has relatively high temperatures. While the Zambezi Basin and Zambesi Valley experience a drop in rain averaging between 16 and 24 inches (38 and 58 centimeters) annually,

Manica and Sofala Provinces bordering Zimbabwe have the highest rainfalls, averaging 64 inches (154 centimeters) a year, and are endowed with a cool climate. Both here and at other highlands, such as those found in Angonia, Vila Cabral (Lichinga), and former Vila Pery (Chimoio), the temperatures turn cold during the wet season and, therefore, constitute an ideal habitat for people and animals. Malarial mosquitoes and tsetse flies are unable to breed in these high-altitude regions.

The south has been characterized as a subtropical anticyclonic zone. It is drier than the rest of the country, averaging 12 inches (29 centimeters) of rain a year. Droughts are common here, although cyclones have caused the rivers to flood outlying areas. Temperatures vary between 65 degrees Fahrenheit (18 degrees Celsius) and 80 degrees Fahrenheit (27 degrees Celsius), the latter constituting the most common. Mozambique is a moderate high plateau, decreasing in altitude from the hinterland to the Indian Ocean. The Great Rift Valley passes through the southern portion of the country, creating lowland swamps south of Beira. Two-thirds of the country are coastal low-lying fertile areas, while the remainder is intersected by a series of highlands. In the north, some portions of the plateau reach an average of 7,890 feet, the highest peak being the Namuli Mountain (8,200 feet). In the northwest, Angonia District has sharp highlands, while the Manica Plateau highlands near the Zimbabwean border reach the height of 3,000 feet. The central Gorongoza highlands climb up to 6,125 feet above sea level. The southwest is dominated by the Libombo Mountains, marking the frontier between Mozambique and Swaziland.

The physical environment of Mozambique is endowed with some 25 rivers, almost all running from north to south and emptying into the Indian Ocean. The largest and longest, and therefore the most known, rivers are the Rovuma, Lurio, Ligonha, Zambezi, Pungue, Buzi, Save, Limpopo, Nkomati, and Espírito Santo (Lourenço Marques). These rivers provide fertile land for farming, which constitutes the most important occupation of the people of Mozambique, who produce corn, millet, cassava, cashew nuts, coconuts, sugarcane, copra, tea, tobacco, sisal, rice, and citrus fruits. Also, the long coastline has several ports, three of which—Maputo, Beira, and Nacala—have acquired international importance. Mozambique has several lakes (particularly in Gaza and Inhambane), although the most significant, Niassa, Chiuta, and Shirwa are located on the border with Malawi.

Generally speaking, Mozambique has fertile soil, particularly on the highlands and along the river valleys. Yet, some areas, such as Tete Province, are so arid that people struggle continuously to survive. While occasional flooding, particularly along the Zambezi and Limpopo Valleys, displaces thousands of people, it is the drought that has intermittently caused severe famine during the last 20 years. While swamps abound along the coast, most of the interior holds tropical forests and extensive grasslands that support many species of wild animals (elephants, lions, leopards, rhinoceroses, crocodiles, hippopotamuses, giraffes, zebras, and gazelles) and domesticated livestock (cows, pigs, goats, and donkeys).

Timber is abundant in the country, and coal in central Mozambique is the most extracted mineral. Other minerals that have been tapped include beryl, columbo-tantalite, microlite, bauxite, montmorillonite, asbestos, gold, mica, copper, bismuth, lepidolite, and tourmaline. Prospecting for petroleum has continued since the late 1940s, but so far no major finds have been made.

PEOPLE AND SOCIETY

The population of Mozambique grew by leaps and bounds during the second half of the 20th century. Official figures show its progression: 5,738,911 in 1950; 7,300,000 in 1967; 8,168,933 in 1970; 11,673,725 in 1980; 13,426,604 in 1984; 14,516,000 in 1987; 15,696,000 in 1990; and an estimated 19,000,000 by 2001. It is estimated that, at the present growth of 2.2 to 2.7 percent per year, the Mozambican population will reach 33 million by 2025. From a density of fewer than 22 inhabitants per square mile in 1967, the population reached a density of almost 47.8 per square mile in 1987. In early 2001, unofficial figures (World Vision) claimed that the population density was 61 per square mile.

The densely populated areas are found in the northern and southern coastal flatlands, where people live in farming villages. As expected, cities have always been natural points for the convergence of people, lured by educational and employment opportunities and activities accelerated by the existence of railways, harbors, and roads. During the colonial period, urban centers also constituted the focal point of the European population. Lourenço Marques (Maputo), the colonial capital, for example, was and still is the largest population center, with over one million inhabitants. The city's growth has been stimulated by an excellent harbor, a railway system, and a number of paved roads. Beira, with its once dwindling port and railroad system now being rehabilitated, has seen its population grow more than tenfold, from 25,000 in 1964 to 300,000 in 2001. The population of Quelimane, a swampy area but an important trading center, more than doubled, from 20,000 in 1964 to 50,000 in 1988 to 100,000 in 1997. The population of Nampula, because of rail facilities linking the city to the port of Nacala, grew from 103,985 in 1964 to 182,000 in 1988 and 200,000 in 2001. Similar accelerated growth has occurred in the Tete-Moatize area, whose economic activities were once spurred by coal mines and the railroad that links it to the port of Beira.

Presently, the rural population is estimated at 85 percent, even though some sources claim that presently 31 percent live in the cities. During the 1970s, FRELIMO attempted to slow the tide of urban migration by setting up communal villages and moving unproductive and unemployed people and settling them in the so-called green zones away from the cities. (Similar policies were implemented unsuccessfully in Tanzania.) The female population outnumbers the male population at the ratio of 51.19 percent to 48.81 percent, respectively. These numbers must be taken cautiously, because they are most likely an underestimation. For example, thousands of males, some of whom are unaccounted for, cross the frontiers annually to seek employment in the South African mines (an average of 45,000 to 50,000 each year during the 1980s) and in Zimbabwe and Zambia. Furthermore, large numbers of refugees, forced by civil war and famine (two million in 1980–92), have fled into neighboring Zimbabwe, Tanzania, and Malawi and Swaziland.

Most Mozambicans, especially women, never find time to retire and therefore work in some form or another until their death. Those who are fortunate enough may work for the government, the largest source of employment, for the few private companies, or for themselves in the fields or selling all kinds of products and artifacts. Presently, the percentage of the male workforce in the country is 53 percent and that of female 47 percent.

Linguistically, Mozambique societies belong to the Bantu-speaking group and comprise at least 10 distinct languages, besides Portuguese. Anthropologist António Rita-Ferreira has so far provided the best classification of the country's ethnic composition, which includes the following major groups and subgroups: Yao (Ajau), Barue, Chope, Chuabo, Dema, Indian, Maconde, Maravi, Ndau, Nguni, Portuguese, Rhonga, Shona, Swahili, Swazi, Tawara, Tewe, Tonga, and others. Of course, Portuguese remains the country's official language.

Mozambique is a secular state that has, as recently as 1990, reaffirmed freedom of religion. Traditionalists still constitute the majority of the population (50 to 60 percent according to some sources), whereas the actual number of Muslims (20 percent, perhaps) and Christians (30 percent, most likely) is still disputed. Muslims are mainly located in the north, and

Catholics, stemming from the colonial past, constitute the majority among the Christians. A few Hindus can be found in the major cities.

HISTORY

Early History

Knowledge of the history of Mozambique prior to the 15th century is based mainly on circumstantial evidence derived from archaeological discoveries in East Africa and the scarce written sources indirectly related to that part of the continent. From these anthropological and archaeological sources, it appears that the area, later to be known as Mozambique, was inhabited as far back as 4000 B.C.

Most of the Bantu-speaking populations of Mozambique, however, reported to have originated in the Cameroon-Congo-Nigerian plateaus and forests, had settled permanently in this area by the first millennium A.D. They brought with them superior technology based on iron and the lifestyle of settled farmers. Their superior weapons and agricultural tools enabled them to overcome any resistance offered by the original settlers (who were pastoralists and fruit gatherers) and to maintain a prosperous life of agriculturalists.

As was common in East Africa before European arrival, Mozambicans lived in relatively small communities led by a chief or kinglet who theoretically owned all land and exacted from his people tribute in the form of crops, weapons, ivory, elephant tusks, and work. In most cases, however, his authority was not absolute. The chief made his decision in consultation with counselors who represented their villages. At the time the Portuguese arrived in Mozambique, central Mozambique was loosely linked to two major political entities: the kingdom of Mwenemutapa in present-day Zimbabwe and the Confederation of Malawi. Ever since the seventh century, Arab and Swahili aristocrats and traders, who had mingled with the Bantu-speaking population and adapted to the area's prevailing culture, controlled the coastal area, including Sofala. While the north by and large accepted Islam, the rest of Mozambique remained predominantly traditional until the Portuguese introduced Christianity.

Portuguese Arrival and Early Colonization

The overall social and political evolution of Mozambican societies was drastically altered by the arrival of the Portuguese during the 15th century.

The Mozambique we know today began as a series of trading centers (*feitorias*), administrative posts, and military forts at the onset of the Portuguese encounter with the Africans. Braving the winds and the high seas and defying peoples of unknown lands, the Portuguese embarked on their maritime voyages on small caravels and began, sometimes inadvertently, carving a future empire that would alter their own position in the international arena.

For over 50 years, Portuguese seamen navigated all along the west coast of Africa but did not reach East Africa and India, the major target of their voyages, until 1498. Indian spices (cloves, nutmeg, and pepper) appealed to all Europeans at the time. In 1447, Dom João II sent Pero da Covilhã and Afonso de Paiva on a sea and land mission not only to reach India but also to look for the legendary Christian king erroneously known as Prester John. While Afonso de Paiva died en route, Pero de Covilhã traveled through the Middle East on the Mediterranean Sea, the Persian Gulf, and reached India and then Sofala, completing his mission in Ethiopia, home of the centuries-sought Prester John—Alexander IV.

Dom João II also sent seaman Bartolomeu Dias in July 1487 in search of the promising *caminho marítimo para a Índia* (sea route to India). Dias sailed past the Cape of Good Hope (previously known as the Cape of Torments) and returned to Lisbon to announce the good news to the king. Apparently, Dom João II was not impressed with this accomplishment. Unsure as to whether his envoy had touched the Indian Ocean at all, the king did not reward Dias. In fact, no major expedition to India was organized as a result of Dias's voyage until 10 years later, when Dom Manuel I commissioned Vasco da Gama to lead a crew of three ships—*São Gabriel, São Raphael,* and the *Bérrio.* For almost nine months, Vasco da Gama navigated the African coast and, on March 1, 1498, disembarked at Inhambane in East Africa, which he called *terra de boa gente* (land of good people), and continued his voyage to Quelimane and Mozambique Island. Proceeding to Mombasa, Vasco da Gama became hostile to the Arabs, bombarded the city port, and sailed off to India where he arrived in May 1498.

At first, the king of Portugal was not interested in an economic exploration of the entire coast of Africa but wanted to open immediately a profitable *feitoria* at Sofala. For that purpose, he sent the two brothers, Bartolomeu Dias and Diogo Dias, who had previously served as captains of two of Pedro Álvares Cabral's ships. To strengthen the ties with the Orient, Vasco da Gama was once again sent to India in 1502, a trip that enabled the Portuguese to continue to open the Mozambique coast and further advance their economic and religious interests.

Vasco da Gama had to fight, however, to control the Indian trade. Francisco de Almeida's expedition of 20 heavily armed ships established Portuguese control, at least temporarily, over the Indian Ocean. To strengthen their presence in East Africa, the Portuguese built a fort at Sofala in 1505, which by 1752, with its lucrative *feitoria*, had a settled African and Portuguese (military) population of 10,000 and some 800 Indians. This settlement was strong enough to defend itself in 1506 against an attack by the Arabs, who attempted to prevent the Portuguese from dominating the gold trade. Sofala elicited so much hope of economic gain that it became known in Portugal as *a porta do ouro* (the door to gold), and its first captain, Pero de Anaia, promised that Portuguese commercial interests would be safeguarded even through the force of arms.

In 1505, Duarte de Mello occupied the island of Mozambique, while, in 1508, Vasco de Abreu built a fort there (replacing the old *fortaleza* Dom João de Castro). In 1558 and 1694, the forts of São Sebastião and São Lourenço were added to the island and then reinforced by the establishment of a dispensary, a church, and a warehouse, all of which designed to demonstrate to the Arab traders that henceforth the Portuguese would be lords of the sea and masters of the gold, silver, and ivory trade of East Africa and India. By 1598, the Portuguese had reached and controlled Quelimane (where they built *feitorias* in 1544), Sena (1530), Tete (1537), Angoche (1511), Quirimba (1520), Mombasa (1528)—where Francisco da Gama built Fort Jesus in 1569—and Lourenço Marques (1544), although its famous *praesidium* was not erected until 1791. Angoche, conquered in 1511 by a force of three ships under António de Saldanha, boomed, attracting some 12,000 inhabitants and "frontiersmen," usually called *sertanejos* in other Portuguese colonies.

In general, by 1540, the Portuguese had wrested the control of the trade away from the Arabs and established several trading centers, Tete and Sena being the most important. Even though they had driven their Muslim competitors out of the region, the Portuguese did not enjoy the anticipated abundance in the flow of gold from the interior to the coast. Elsewhere, adventurers, such as *degredado* António Fernandes, for the first time penetrated the Zambezi interior up to Zumbo in search of gold. Consequently, no power or merchant, including the Dutch, could challenge Portuguese supremacy in East Africa and India during the 16th and early 17th centuries. To encourage conquest and trade, Mozambique captains received a three-year monopoly over commerce from the metropolis, although they could bestow similar privileges on others.

The captains paid a certain amount of trade items to the viceroy of India, who in turn, at least until 1752, forwarded them to the king of Portugal. The captains enjoyed nominal control over the *feiras* or trading centers, to which a *confeitor* (a trader or supervisor) and an *escrivão* (a scribe) were assigned either by the metropolis or by the viceroy of India himself. The captain had the power over the whole coast as far south as the Cape of Good Hope and, beginning in 1600, he could forbid any merchant from trading. (Nonlicensed Muslims were barred from trading along the Zambezi.) Likewise, the captain was authorized to search and confiscate licenses and goods. An attempted revolt by coastal merchants to prevent this monopolistic control of trade in 1593–94 ended in failure. Besides gold, items of trade exchanged at the *feitorias* (trading centers) included clove, ivory, silver, cotton cloth, glass, porcelain, beads, and brassware, with guns and gunpowder becoming more common during the 16th century.

In 1635, the government developed a colonization scheme to protect the *feitorias* and improve commerce. Two hundred households with craftsmen, farmers, priests, doctors, and pharmacists from Portugal would leave for Mozambique. The plan did not quite materialize as it was earlier conceived, but several settlers, soldiers, craftsmen, and engineers left for Mozambique and founded the town of Quelimane in 1640. In 1677, five ships loaded with farmers, artisans or craftsmen, miners, court judges, treasury officials, soldiers, engineers, one physician and a surgeon-mor, along with eight female orphans destined to be married, left Lisbon for Mozambique and settled in Sena. Although the colonists received complete freedom of commerce, the experiment did not succeed due to settler inexperience and the hostile climate.

Tete turned out to be an important town (*vila*) with its rivers, especially the Cuama (Zambezi) River in 1761, when it registered a population close to a hundred Portuguese and African Christian families. The successful establishment of Tete led to the creation of the *vila* of Zumbo, entrusted to Captain João Pedro da Silva Baía. In Zumbo, too, the Portuguese established an important *feira* on the right bank of the Zambezi. Likewise, Manica flourished as an important *feira*, although it soon declined because of the "selfish profit motives" of the captain-mores and the soldiers. During the 1650s, slaves slowly took precedence over the other trade commodities of the *feitorias*. In 1673, the government announced that only the captain could control the flow of gold in the colony. This development contributed to the demise of the *Companhia do Comércio da Índia* established in 1633 and the weakening of other mercantilist enterprises in the colony.

Portuguese control over the East African coast was short-lived. In fact, by the end of the 17th century, the Portuguese commercial "empire" had declined, unable to defend itself against African and Arab incursions in areas such as Angoche, Inhambane, and (*Alta*) Zambezia, while the Dutch caused havoc along the coast. Eric Axelson notes that Mozambique remained the only captaincy intact, but with a reduced population, as trade activity began to decline. Quelimane was left with "156 thwarted houses at most with six or seven whites, living mostly from coconut plantations," whereas Luabo had no civilian or military Portuguese residents "except two Jesuits and a few mulattoes." A few priests traded in Sena, but the town's population was reduced to 30 people (20 whites), while Tete had no more than 15 to 20 residents "all living from trade." In Sofala, 15 white residents did their "utmost to survive, while Inhambane, without a single Portuguese resident, was visited once a year by a ship with soldiers who would jump ashore to do some trading in ivory and amber." In spite of this deplorable state of affairs, however, "South-East Africa was still the brightest jewel in Portugal's Indian Crown."

Defying the odds, however, the Portuguese believed that they had found an institution that would eventually vindicate their colonial experiment—the *prazos*. Prazos were landholdings or estates authorized during the 17th century by the Portuguese Crown. Vast properties along the Zambezi Valley, from Quelimane to Tete, were entrusted to Portuguese settlers. The government expected that the *prazeros* (prazo owners), who had to be Portuguese citizens, would guarantee Portuguese sovereignty in the area, cultivate the land, pay a quitrent (*foro*) to the national treasury, and facilitate the task of the few Portuguese troops stationed in places such as Tete, Quelimane, Sena, and Sofala. The prazo system was expected to be an economic success that would assist toward the establishment of a cluster of trading posts, and revitalize the whole valley through the exchange of silver, ivory, gold, animal skins, corn, salt, rice, millet, and other tropical products and commodities.

According to law, a prazo was to last for three generations or three lives, passing from the first prazero family to a daughter who could only marry a white Portuguese citizen. Following the death of the third prazero heiress, the estate would revert to the state, although renewal was an option often granted to the applicant. The prazo institution dominated the Zambezi Valley for more than 200 years (1650 to 1888). In most cases, the prazeros became extremely active in every aspect of daily life, especially in local African polities. Most acquired power through manipulation of traditional authorities, sometimes allying themselves with one of the local warring factions or leaders, at other times simply overpowering militarily a chief or king. Thus, they slowly increased their domain and sphere of influence. Ultimately, the prazo system failed due to several factors including climatic conditions such as droughts and floods, scarcity of a willing labor force, recurrent warfare, African resistance to European intrusion, and absenteeism of the prazero.

The one factor that had the greatest adverse impact on the prazo or landholding system was slave trading within the prazos. From 1806 to 1820, the ownership and exportation of slaves from the prazo increased fourfold — from 5,000 to at least 20,000. The prazeros justified the capture and the selling of Africans by claiming that the Portuguese were naturally superior to them. They further argued that the slaves would lead a better life wherever they were forced to settle. Initially, the prazeros sent their private armies into the interior to capture hundreds of Africans and force them into slavery. As it became more difficult to secure significant numbers of slaves in order to meet the demand, however, the prazeros turned to the *colonos* and prazo settler *achikunda* (slave troops), who generally lived on the prazos, to satisfy the demand of Brazilian slavers, notwithstanding the fact that the law forbade the selling of slaves living on the prazo.

The traffic in human beings led to rampant unrest on the estates. Africans who escaped slavery usually moved away from the prazo to avoid the activities of the slavers, although the lands they were forced to inhabit and cultivate were generally less productive. In their wake, slavers destroyed villages, plundered agricultural fields, and took the most productive members from Mozambican society, thus intensifying the degree of poverty and underdevelopment throughout the area. In return for the hazardous duties assigned to them, the prazo slavers continued to receive ever-declining rewards, at first in the form of gold, and later in such weapons and cheap commodities as liquor, beads, and cloth.

Understandably, with the loss of a good number of reproductive males, the Mozambique societies eventually suffered a shortage of men. Thus, in spite of continuous efforts to revitalize it during the 1880s, the imposed prazo institution had ultimately failed by the end of the century. It is worth noting that, at first, slavery and the slave trade were not part of the prazo institution. During the 19th century, however, both private and official Portuguese citizens were deeply engaged in the capture and the commerce of Africans to the extent that, for the 1820–32 period, no fewer than 50,000 slaves from Mozambique landed on Brazilian plantations. The traffic in humans turned out to be so profitable and entrenched in the colony that Mozambique officials became infamous in the metropolis and elsewhere for resisting the antislavery decrees gradually promulgated by Lisbon. Thus, although, for all practical purposes, the 1836 decree promulgated by Sá da Bandeira eliminated slavery and the slave trade in the Portuguese colonies, Mozambique remained its last bastion, as even high authorities, including governors who received fees from the illegal traffickers, refused to enforce the laws. In fact, as late as 1881, Francisco A. P. Bayão, governor of Tete, complained that the 1836 decree had not been properly promulgated in the colony and that those who knew about it chose to ignore it altogether.

On the political level, the latter part of the 19th century witnessed a reversal in the attitude of the Portuguese toward their colonies, including Mozambique. When they first arrived in the colony, the Portuguese created administrative units mainly to ensure the success of trade and to protect Portuguese citizens in their voyages to India and on their sparse settlements. One can accurately posit that, for centuries, most Portuguese activity remained along the coast because African topography and climate were usually hostile to outsiders; Africans refused to give up their position as middlemen between the interior and the coast (attempts by outsiders into the mainland were met with force); and the nature of the first Portuguese voyages was primarily commercial and religious rather than imperial. Therefore, as long as slaves, gold, ivory, and spices could be obtained along the coast of Guinea, Angola, and Mozambique, the Portuguese navigators and their government in Lisbon remained relatively satisfied.

Imperialism and the Berlin Conference (1884–1885)

Colonial attitudes in the metropolis changed, however, when external factors, such as trade competition with Britain and other powers, the anti-slavery movement, and criticism of Portuguese colonial practices revealed by explorers, such as David Livingstone and others during the 1870s, alerted and worried the Portuguese government. As a result, Lisbon began to show greater interest in the preservation and direct government of its colonies. To that end, it quickly established tighter administrative controls. Portugal's precarious military position in Europe heightened the fear that the colonies could be lost to another power.

Portugal at first welcomed the Berlin Act of 1884–85 but balked at its insistence that the principle of "effective control" of overseas territories be the governing criterium. The Portuguese had a grand design—the so-called rose-colored map—to link Angola and Mozambique so that they could control the hinterland of Central Africa from coast to coast. Unfortunately, Britain strongly opposed the plan through an ultimatum in 1890, after Portugal had occupied the Macololo region. Portugal capitulated, and, in 1891, the two signed an agreement on their disputed territorial borders. Thereafter, political control of the overseas possessions became one of the most important preoccupations of the Lisbon government. The fear of losing the colonies was real. Indeed, despite the fact that the Portuguese had held most of Mozambique for four centuries, their actual occupation was only nominal. Vast areas of the colony continued to be virtually autonomous until the 1890s, and some were not pacified until the 1920s, forcing the Portuguese to wage bloody wars against those local populations who decided to resist encroachment upon their independence and lifestyle. Until 1830, Portuguese control of the colony in the north was limited to the littoral Tungue Bay, including the islands of Cherimba and Moçambique, continental Mossuril and the Cabeceiras (Angoche continued practically independent under powerful sultans with roots in Zanzibar until the 1890s). Elsewhere in the colony, Portuguese control extended only to Quelimane, Luabo, the mouth of the Zambezi River up to Tete, Sofala, Inhambane, and from Lourenço Marques down to Inhaca Island.

Looking more closely at the situation north, south, and center, it appears that until 1890 no Portuguese settlement ever experienced complete peace during the period of "*reconquista*" (1833–1920), except perhaps for the city of Moçambique, the first capital of the province. Even then, Lourenço Marques, Quelimane, Tete, Inhambane, and Cabo Delgado, the major towns and cities, remained insecure places, often suffering periodic African raids which spread terror and forced the Portuguese to constantly deplete the meager military resources. In particular, the Portuguese had to contend with the newly arrived Nguni in the south, the stubborn sultanates of Angoche near Mozambique city, and the Zambezi Valley uprisings personified by arrogant rulers at Massangano, whose hostility "cost the Portuguese more men than all their combined campaigns" prior to the 1914–18 period. Governor of Quelimane Joaquim Pinto de Magalhães wrote to Lisbon that up to the 1850s, the towns of Tete and Sena, for example, continued to suffer from African revolts.

As expected, a major problem was the difficulty of recruiting Africans to strengthen the colonial army. Invariably, the authorities complained that Africans avoided joining the colonial militia, frequently escaped during combat, refused to take active part when fighting against their own, and, when they received their uniform and weapons, vanished into the bush. Under such circumstances, the army contingent was small and the loyalty of the African soldiers to the Portuguese authorities always doubtful, a situation that made conquest and pacification extremely difficult and painful. No wonder Governor Augusto Coelho complained in 1833 that "the garrison of this province consists of soldiers recruited from India belonging to different castes of different customs and religious beliefs, of contingents from Angola, made up of the worst that exists in Africa, of Africans from different parts of this province, of a few old incorrigible European soldiers and *degredados*."

The task of pacification was compounded by the fact that this was also the period when the Portuguese were attempting to radically alter the economy of the colony through the abolition of the slave trade, the imposition of "sound" practices and policies on the prazo system, and the introduction of a capitalist mode of production through monopolistic companies. To pacify and simultaneously chart a new economic course from a distance proved to be extremely difficult for the Portuguese. What made conquest even harder, apart from the African resistance to subjugation, was the abundance of guns and gunpowder among the Mozambican people in both the north and the south.

Furthermore, the use of force in the collection of taxes, which were designed to increase government revenues and assert Portuguese sovereignty over the colony, made pacification a formidable task. Abuses by authorities led to revolts and to further wars. Quite often, the Portuguese attempted to sign treaties, always promising one or another chief protection against his enemies, while attempting to exact from him exorbitant concessions in the form of tribute (taxes); free passage through his land; unhindered trade for Portuguese citizens; construction of schools ("centers of civilization"), posts, or forts in his territory; and a pledge not to wage war against his enemies without Portuguese consent. In Islamic societies, the *sheikh* (or sultan) was forced to swear on the Qur'an his allegiance to Portugal. These terms, which clearly favored Portuguese objectives, became sources of contention and disagreement, as was the case with the 1886 treaty the Portuguese signed with Gungunhana.

Added to these obstacles was the fact that the Portuguese quite often bestowed military titles upon many of the chiefs, a practice that forced conscientious officials to show deference to even recalcitrant chiefs and view them as legitimate military officers. (The honors bestowed on Gungunhana following his imprisonment and the military ceremonies held at Bonga's graveside illustrate the Portuguese dilemma.) Governor-General Fernando Magalhães e Meneses, citing cases in Zavala and Magaia, complained in 1894 that military titles constituted the worst aspect of Portuguese colonial policy as it left the authorities at the whims of tyrants. He also criticized the practice of using gifts to pacify the African authorities.

These conditions were serious threats to the Portuguese presence in the colony and compelled the officials to use whatever military force they could muster, sometimes accompanied by "terrorist" tactics such as executions, destruction of property, house burning, starvation of populations in revolt, and the distribution of weapons to trusted friends. The toll in lives for both Portuguese and Africans was high, especially in areas such as Massangano, Inhambane, Angoche, and Macua country, particularly among the Namarrais.

Yet, until the 1930s, the Portuguese army in the colonies continued to be in a precarious situation, plagued with indiscipline and runaways. To improve the situation, a decree of November 14, 1901, created several infantry divisions (made up of Europeans only); two squadrons of dragoons (also made up of Europeans only); one battery of artillery and a garrison; and two mixed companies of European artillery and African infantry. The African troops were divided into companies under Portuguese officers and served for three years, after which time they remained on active reserve from five to eight years. On June 16, 1926, the statutes further reorganizing the colonial army stressed the absolute necessity of effectively enlisting African recruits in larger numbers. Experience, therefore, had taught the Portuguese that without eliciting the cooperation of the Africans, military victories in the colony would be difficult to achieve. Ultimately, however, racial discrimination (notwithstanding the official colonial policy of assimilation) and the rigors of an army designed to be used against fellow Africans made the Mozambicans unreliable soldiers.

To cushion their difficult military victories in Mozambique during the 1890s and prevent other Europeans from claiming that they were unfit to develop their colonies, the Portuguese began inviting foreign concessionaire companies, of which the best known were the Companhia de Moçambique, the Companhia da Zambézia, and the Companhia do Niassa. These companies controlled thousands of acres, were almost totally sovereign in their concessions, and enacted laws to govern the Africans living under their jurisdiction, who also became subject to heavy taxation and served as sources of cheap forced labor.

The establishment of the companies contributed to improved agricultural productivity, although not at the rate the Portuguese government had expected. Between 1910 and 1930, farm production of major export crops either doubled or tripled. For example, the almost nonexistent banana production reached 7,830 metric tons in 1930, while that of sesame stood at 4,000 tons. In 1933, sugar extraction was estimated at 95,000 metric tons, of which 83,000 tons were exported. Tobacco rose from 119 tons in 1919 to 178 tons in 1920 and to 340 in 1930 (declining, however, to 215 tons in 1933). Rubber extraction was accelerated during the 1910s and 1920s but declined rapidly prior to and after the Great Depression. Cotton proved to be a successful crop even though companies and individual Portuguese *senhores* had to force Africans to grow it. Overall, however, the economic record of the three major companies was not impressive, considering that by 1900 together they occupied two-thirds of Mozambique.

The Colonial Policy of Assimilation

Once the Portuguese had finally pacified the colony (in some areas such as Barue they did not achieve this until the 1920s), they began implementing policies to ensure that Mozambique would be beneficial to the mother country. In the opinion of Portuguese intellectuals and statesmen, such as Marcello Caetano, Lisbon attempted to follow the four political and administrative principles summarized here.

The first principle was political unity. The official policy claimed that "Portugal is a unitary state with only one territory, only one population and only one government . . . hence comes the doctrine, repeatedly emphasized, of the inalienability of any part of the territory." In other words, Mozambique was supposed to be an integral part of continental Portugal. In the spirit of this principle, the designation of colony for Mozambique was struck from official documents in 1930 and replaced by the term province. The Colonial Act of 1930 under António Salazar's regime sanctioned the change. As one expert put it, "The fundamental theory behind all this, with the later modifications of 1951, is that the empire is a whole, that it is a family, that the purpose is to assimilate, within the pattern of common Portuguese nationhood and ways of life, these diverse peoples." Salazar once defended the theory of political unity when he noted: "Contrary to all machinations, we will not sell, cede, lease, or share our colonies. . . . Our constitutional laws do not allow us." In the light of this principle, Mozambique was as much an integral part of Portugal as Algarve or any other province of Portugal proper.

The second principle has been called spiritual assimilation. The Portuguese contended that, "although respecting the *modus vivendi* of the Africans, [the Portuguese] . . . always endeavored to impart their faith, their culture and their civilization in them, thus calling them into the Lusitanian community." Colonial theoreticians have claimed that the Portuguese never tried to impose their system on the Africans but attempted to assimilate them through "education and living together," so that those who were assimilated would always find themselves at ease even in continental Portugal. Outright spiritual assimilation was tried during the age of liberalism and immediately thereafter (1820–1910) but was abandoned because its application proved to be costly and was resented by Portuguese settlers. Instead, gradual assimilation was adopted as more realistic.

The third principle established an administrative differentiation between the metropolis and the colonies in view of the "peculiar circumstances" that were particular to the territory, such as social status and economic development, defending the proposition that, although the empire was politically one, the colonies needed specific laws of administration. These laws, expressed in the Colonial Act of 1930, ultimately aimed at defending and protecting not only the Portuguese settlers but also the Africans themselves. Thus, from 1820 to 1910, as a reflection of the liberal revolution in Portugal, exactly the same administrative statutes of province and districts were imposed both on the metropolis and on the colonies. (The 1910 Republic discontinued the practice since it created more problems than solutions, as the following discussion will show.)

The fourth principle, economic solidarity, stemmed from political unity and established a division of labor across metropolitan and colonial lines. Devising a policy of internal protectionism, the principle compelled Portugal to buy colonial goods even when their prices were higher than those of similar goods coming from abroad. In industry, economic solidarity guaranteed that industrialists from the metropolis would receive similar concessions from the colonies. One fact remained clear, however: Industries in the metropolis were nourished by the raw materials from the colonies. Portugal allowed foreign companies overseas as long as these were not a threat to Portuguese sovereignty.

International criticism of Portuguese policies and resistance in the colonies forced Portugal to adopt international labor laws in 1960. Labor Law Ordinance No. 17771 and Decree No. 43637 set minimum wages and introduced the principle of freedom of contract, regulated safety in the workplace, specified acceptable health standards, and called for factory inspection in all colonies. Unfortunately, these laws remained alive only on paper. Eventually, Portuguese labor policies led to a rise in nationalism and guerrilla warfare in Mozambique.

Nationalism and the Liberation Movements

The history of Mozambique is replete with violence and bloodshed from the time the Portuguese arrived to the 20th century. The difference between the early and the modern resistance lies mainly in scope: While the former was local and regional, the latter comprised the whole territory; while the former was often a revolt against administrators and individual intruders, the latter was a total revolt against the Portuguese government. Thus, the strategy and tactics used by the modern independence movements differed from those of early days. Between 1930 and 1948, Mozambicans did not fight with guns against the Portuguese government, as they had done during the 19th century. Instead, workers illegally went on strike at the docks of the capital, protesting harsh working conditions, thus signaling the covert and overt dissatisfaction prevalent in the colony. During the first half of the 20th century, the failure, contradictions, and impracticability of the four principles of Portuguese colonialism only fueled the awakening spirit of nationalism in the colony. The eventual guerrilla war waged by Africans against the Portuguese in Mozambique directly defied not only the imperfect and inconsistent application of the aforesaid principles but also their very legitimacy. The causes that contributed to the liberation movements such as FRELIMO in Mozambique during the late 1950s and early 1960s can be classified as political, social, economic, religious, and cultural.

Politically, Portugal attempted to destroy the several traditional kingdoms and city-states in Mozambique and replace them with an alien division of the colony into provinces under Portuguese governors-general, districts under lieutenant-governors, *circumscrições* under Portuguese administrators, and administrative posts under lower Portuguese officials. The process completely excluded Africans from political participation, while leaving the government in the hands of a white minority. Political gatherings were not allowed, and criticism of discriminatory practices was considered to be a crime against the nation. Following the outbreak of revolution in 1964, the mere utterance of the term *independence* was an act of rebellion. Meanwhile, thousands of political prisoners filled the jails and suffered all types of torture.

The Portuguese presence in the colony also created new social problems. The division of the population into two polarized groups—the assimilated and the indigenous, the so-called civilized and uncivilized—was a colonial scheme to better control the population. The Portuguese defined a civilized population as follows: "A civilized population is made up of white, yellow, and mixed individuals as well as those members of the black race that satisfy the following conditions: speak Portuguese; do not practice ways and customs specific to the natives; and have a profession, are engaged in commerce and industry, or possess property for their maintenance. Those who do not satisfy these conditions are considered uncivilized."

In theory, the civilized African was a Portuguese citizen. He was entitled to earn the same wages as a Portuguese; to work no more than eight hours a day; to enter any hotel, restaurant, or movie theater; and to travel first class on buses and trains. In practice, however, he was treated differently. He had to carry a pass—the *bilhete de identidade*—and was discriminated against almost as much as the indigenous who carried another kind of pass—the *caderneta indígena*. In reality, therefore, the assimilated always remained a second-class citizen. In short, Portugal attempted to bestow nationality on its subjects without conferring the privilege of true citizenship upon them. As a result of this contradiction, education was so neglected in the colony that only 15 percent of the population could read and write at the time the Portuguese left Mozambique, while health care for Africans received the lowest priority.

Working conditions for Africans were extremely harsh and backward. All males were forced to work at least six to nine months each year either for the government or for a private Portuguese citizen. Although this kind of work was called contract (*contrato*), no consultation existed between the two parties, and the worker was recruited by force. Also, since 1909, thousands of Africans were forced to migrate to South Africa to work in the mines, thus undermining the well being of the Mozambican family. The contracted laborer (*contratado*) worked as many hours as his boss (*patrão*) wished. The government rarely intervened on behalf of the African, who received his pay only at the end of his contract and was expected to pay his taxes immediately and then find his way home. Consequently, by the time he arrived home, perhaps only one-fourth of his salary was left. Often, he was immediately recalled to work for the government without pay—building bridges, opening roads, or clearing new farms. The practice of forcing Africans to grow crops and cash crops such as cotton, sisal, and sugarcane on large plantations officially ended in 1966, although it actually continued in the countryside until independence. Under the pretext of teaching Africans how to use the soil, the authorities forced them to grow certain crops, which were sold as cheaply as possible to the government or its companies. These practices violated international labor laws that Portugal had pledged to enforce in its colonies.

The Catholic Church proved to be the government's best ally. Since most of the primary schools were under the Portuguese Catholic Church, Portuguese priests taught the Africans to think as Portuguese citizens, to obey authority without question, and to humble themselves before their white superiors. The Portuguese authorities despised both African religion and culture, and missionaries, by fostering assimilation, attempted to eliminate the African heritage as inferior and savage.

Liberation Movements

The emergence of liberation movements during the 1960s radically changed the outlook of the colonial state. Anti-Portuguese fronts such as the

União Democrática Nacional de Moçambique (UDENAMO), União Nacional Africana de Moçambique (MANU), and União Nacional de Moçambique Independente (UNAMI) vowed to fight for independence rather than equality. However, as one analyst put it, "Small in numbers, detached from internal bases of support, lacking a coherent strategy, and periodically engaging in divisive exile politics," the three nationalist organizations were almost powerless against the stronger Portuguese army. Realizing that, divided, the nationalist movements were doomed to fail, President Julius Nyerere of Tanzania invited the heads of the three organizations to meet in Dar-es-Salaam, settle their differences, and begin a period of mutual cooperation. President Kwame Nkrumah of Ghana had also urged them to unite. Though UNAMI was not disposed to listen to the appeal, it eventually agreed to merge with the other two movements, out of which the Frente de Libertação de Moçambique (FRELIMO) was born under the leadership of Eduardo C. Mondlane, who was not a member of any of the three liberation movements. After working briefly at the United Nations and at Syracuse University, Mondlane returned to Africa at the invitation of FRELIMO. When the first FRELIMO Congress met in September 1962, its first order was to identify the enemy: "The enemy was not the Portuguese people, nor the Portuguese settlers in Mozambique, but the colonial system."

FRELIMO knew that fighting the stubborn Portuguese government would take time and that the war could not all be won on the battlefield. Thus, the Front combined its military campaigns with an education program that emphasized the basics and the liberation of the mind. Whenever FRELIMO forces liberated an area, they also opened primary schools so that Mozambicans would have the educational opportunities the Portuguese had denied them. In Dar-es-Salaam, the headquarters of the Front, the revolutionary leaders opened the Mozambique Institute, which helped prepare Mozambican students for college. Before they were allowed to continue their studies, however, the college-bound students had to go into the interior first and assist with the education of the people. This educational program was so successful that by 1972 the Front claimed that it had created 160 primary schools in the Mozambique countryside, with an enrollment of 20,000 students taught by 250 teachers.

Another major concern of FRELIMO was the health of the people in the areas under its control. Consequently, trained militants opened several clinics in the interior and a hospital, as well as many first aid stations in the liberated areas. The Front's greatest achievement in health care, however, was the building of the Dr. Américo Boavida Hospital in Tanzania. It was here that the most seriously ill Mozambicans or wounded guerrilla fighters were treated. All other less serious cases were treated at first aid centers staffed by 515 professionals.

Of all the programs, however, it was the guerilla war waged against the Portuguese that determined Mozambique's fate. On September 25, 1964, in a northern section of Mozambique, Cabo Delgado, 250 FRELIMO militants attacked Chai, a Portuguese administrative post. Though the attack killed only one police officer and wounded only a few among the colonial personnel, the Portuguese considered it an act of intolerable treason and took swift action against the insurrectionists. But the secret police and Portuguese soldiers failed to locate the FRELIMO soldiers and had to settle for the sympathizers. The arrests, beatings, and *palmatórias* (hand hitting devices) that followed did not satisfy the threatened colonialist state. Thus, in further retaliation for the attack, Portuguese soldiers went to the village of Micalo, where they murdered many innocent people. They herded the villagers into their homes and then set the houses afire; as the villagers tried to escape the burning structures, they ran into the bullets of the Portuguese soldiers waiting nearby.

The Portuguese response to FRELIMO was a desperate one: In total, the Portuguese brought into Mozambique some 60,000 troops. The presence of the army, unfortunately, contributed to an increase in the level of colonial oppression. Ultimately, the well-organized Portuguese propaganda machine could no longer deny, as it had tried, that there was a serious war in the colonial territories. Although the Portuguese had insisted that Mozambique was an integral part of Portugal, it was a proposition they could not defend convincingly. Portugal also claimed that it had historic rights in Africa and had held Mozambique under the "internationally accepted" principle of *terra nullius* (no man's land), an argument that ignored the fact that Africans had legitimate and stronger rights to their land. At the same time, Portuguese propaganda also strove to convince the world that the resistance was illegitimate because outsiders staged it. However, the overriding reason for Portuguese resistance to African independence during the 1960s seems to have been economic. Portugal was the poorest country in Europe; its economy depended heavily on the colonies. Unwilling to leave behind unlimited prospects of improving the economy of their own country by using many of Mozambique's untapped resources, the Portuguese were determined to stay in Africa forever.

Generally, world opinion was on the side of the colonies fighting for their independence. Since 1961, the UN had passed many resolutions supporting the struggle for independence and urging Portugal to withdraw from Africa. Almost every year, the UN General Assembly reaffirmed "the inalienable right of the people of the territories under Portuguese domination to achieve freedom and independence and the legitimacy of their struggle to achieve this right." In 1970, the General Assembly went a step further and endorsed the liberation movements by affirming the legitimacy of using "all appropriate means" at the disposal of the African nationalists.

Unfortunately, since no binding force accompanied such resolutions, Portugal continued to reject them on the grounds that they interfered in the internal affairs of a sovereign nation. It even barred attempts by the UN Committee on Decolonization to inspect conditions in the colonies. But the moral impact of the resolutions constituted a heavy burden on the Portuguese, as did the widespread publicity about colonial massacres. Another international body that vehemently condemned Portuguese colonialism was the Organization of African Unity (OAU). Regrettably, as with the UN, the OAU could only lend moral support and minimal financial assistance to Mozambican nationalists.

In a Catholic country such as Portugal, the position of the church was a significant factor in the success or failure of a liberation movement. The Vatican took a position of sorts only in 1970, when Pope Paul VI received the three major leaders of the liberation movements of Mozambique, Angola, and Guinea-Bissau. Disappointingly, however, the Holy See never condemned outright the Portuguese government for its wars in Africa. The pope and the Vatican newspaper *Osservatore Romano* vaguely alluded to the massacres in 1973 only as a news item. The Portuguese ecclesiastical hierarchy in the colony was almost entirely behind the government. Moreover, Portugal had powerful supporters and allies in the developed Western world. At the UN, France and Great Britain usually abstained from voting or vetoed resolutions against Portugal. While France continued to sell to Portugal Alouette helicopters to ensure its missile-tracking station at Azores, the British government provided moral and economic support to the Portuguese government.

However, since 1970, the Labour Party in Britain had held a series of meetings on the Portuguese colonies, and many of its members condemned Portuguese colonialism. In 1971 and subsequently, some of the members even sent financial aid to the liberation movements in the Portuguese colonies. To demonstrate to the outside world their support, British Labourites and Liberals joined together and organized a mass protest against the visit of Premier Marcello Caetano to London during the 1970s.

The U.S. government was opposed to the liberation movements, although private American citizens provided moral and financial support to the Africans. Except briefly during the Kennedy administration, United States official policy was crafted in such a way as to favor Portugal. The U.S. position was not difficult to explain: Portugal was (and still is) a member of the North Atlantic Treaty Organization (NATO). Under this pretext, Washington decided to support colonialism, notwithstanding Lisbon's violation of internationally recognized principles. Portugal bought weapons and aircraft from America at will, a fact well proven by guerrillas who often captured or destroyed Portuguese war matériel. Furthermore, America needed to keep its air bases on the Portuguese held Azores islands. The attitude of American business leaders toward the liberation movements was also clear: They supported the white minority regimes in Southern Africa.

The Portuguese reprisals and Western indifference neither deterred the militants nor helped the Portuguese cause. With growing support from the Mozambican people and assisted by sophisticated weapons from the Soviet Union and the People's Republic of China, FRELIMO rapidly expanded its liberated zones from the north into the southern portion of the country. By the end of 1973, FRELIMO had advanced farther south, coming within 400 miles of the Portuguese capital of Lourenço Marques. The advance and continuous FRELIMO victories alarmed Caetano, Salazar's successor as prime minister. To the surprise of the world, on April 25, 1974, several young army officers, questioning Portuguese policy and tired of fighting the colonial wars, overthrew the Lisbon government. The Movimento das Forças Armadas (MFA)/Armed Forces Movement, as the young officers called themselves, supported by the peasants and the working class in Portugal, eventually pledged to end the war in Mozambique and return civil liberties to the people at home and overseas. Within a few weeks, the new Portuguese government began negotiating with FRELIMO and other liberation movements determined to find a permanent solution to Portugal's colonial wars.

On September 7, 1974, FRELIMO and the Portuguese Movimento das Forças Armadas (MFA) reached an agreement in Lusaka creating a transitional government to lead the colony to independence. A new wave of violence, however, greeted the independence euphoria. One day after the Lusaka agreement, a white anti-FRELIMO group, Frente Independente para a Continuidade do Oeste (FICO) (Independent Front for the Continuity of the West), emerged with the support of some military commandos and attempted a coup. FICO captured the national newspaper headquarters and the Mozambique radio station in Lourenço Marques and destroyed a weapons arsenal and a fuel storage area on the outskirts of the city. However, the reactionary movement failed three days later when a combined force of FRELIMO and Portuguese troops intervened to maintain peace. Thus, on September 20, 1974, Joaquim Chissano became prime minister of the transitional government. Nine months later, on June 25, 1975, Samora Moisés Machel assumed the double role of president of FRELIMO and president of the new People's Republic of Mozambique.

Independent Mozambique

Alas, the unrest continued. Reactionary Portuguese citizens joined by Mozambicans who disliked FRELIMO's Marxist policies and dislocated guerrilla fighters who had expected to play a major role in the new government mobilized against the new regime. With logistical, military, and financial assistance from white southern Rhodesia and South Africa, the forces opposing FRELIMO formed the Resistência National Moçambicana (RENAMO) (Mozambique National Resistance) in 1977. Adopting the same guerrilla tactics FRELIMO had used against the Portuguese, the counterrevolutionaries vowed to remove the Marxist government and institute "true democracy" in the country. In the decade and a half that followed, both FRELIMO and RENAMO sought external assistance, although FRELIMO had the upper hand in the process. Meanwhile, the country suffered considerably. People were displaced and their livelihood destroyed, while each side accused the other of massacres of innocent victims.

Yet, progress was made. One of FRELIMO's most successful programs during the recent past has been the accelerated elimination of illiteracy. In contrast with the colonial state, FRELIMO was able to reduce illiteracy from 95 percent in 1975 to 75 percent by 1988. The gigantic effort made by FRELIMO can be seen in the following figures: In 1973, for example, 666,600 children were enrolled in primary school, while 33,000 attended secondary school establishments. By 1983, however, both numbers had doubled or tripled to 1,402,541 students in primary schools and 106,975 in secondary schools. On the university level, 540 students attended the University of Lourenço Marques (now Eduardo Mondlane University) in 1966; that number rose to 1,852 in 1983. On the other hand, the number of secondary school students rose from 20,000 in 1974 to 135,000 by the early 1980s. More recently, in 1997, the number stood at 51,155 in secondary school, with 1,899,531 in primary school. The 1977–92 civil war had a devastating impact on FRELIMO's avowed policy to provide education to as many Mozambicans as possible, children as well as adult. As in most Africa, education is free for all Mozambicans, although admission to secondary school and to university has remained extremely competitive, and fewer than 40 percent of the students pass the qualifying exams.

In health care services, FRELIMO's efforts have had mixed results. When the Portuguese left Mozambique in 1975, only 87 doctors were available in the country, even though they had reached the number of 500 prior to 1974. The intensity of the war forced many of them to leave the colony. FRELIMO was able to recruit many more doctors, the number reaching 500 in 1977. Unfortunately, the number of major hospitals remained at 10, just as they were prior to independence, while the war contributed to a deterioration of most of them. Beds increased from 11,200 in the 1960s to only 13,180 in 1980, and the number of nurses from 1,258 in the 1960s to 2,134 in 1980. There are over 3,000 nurses today. Furthermore, Maputo City continued to enjoy a privileged position in terms of facilities and number of doctors. For example, while the rest of the country had a ratio of one doctor per 257,500 people during the early 1980s, Maputo's ratio was one doctor per 4,450 people. Whereas all Mozambique cities combined then had 128 doctors only (50 doctors in rural areas), Maputo city had a total of 157 (of whom 111 served Maputo Central Hospital alone), despite the fact that only about 5.9 percent of the population of Mozambique lived in the capital. Today, there are about 575 doctors in the country for a ratio of about one doctor per 33,040 people for the estimated 19 million inhabitants.

Notwithstanding the war's nefarious impact, the government was highly commended by the World Health Organization for its successful vaccination campaign against smallpox (altogether eliminated during the late 1970s), measles, and tetanus. By 1980, the campaign had contributed to a 20 percent reduction in the country's infant mortality rate. It is fair to say that, regarding the welfare of the Africans, what the Portuguese had reluctantly accomplished in centuries, FRELIMO proved it could achieve in less than 10 years. However, FRELIMO's accomplishments should not totally obscure its handicaps and failures. As a result of the 1977–92 war waged by RENAMO against FRELIMO, much of the education and health infrastructure was destroyed.

POLITICAL DEVELOPMENT

No one could have predicted that the Mozambican political structure would ever resemble closely that of the West. During the colonial period, Africans in Mozambique had virtually no voice in the decision-making process and were not allowed to form political parties. What existed was a structure that allowed voting to the several interest groups, which were always white, even when an all-out assimilation policy was extended to the African population in 1961–1964. The elected candidates, known as *vereadores*, would represent the colony in the Cortes and later the National Assembly of the metropolis.

In the colonial hierarchy, the governor-general was assisted by lieutenant-governors and by a Legislative Council that never included Africans. However, even then, major political decisions were made by the Colonial Ministry. To ensure that the colonial system would endure unhindered, political oppression and repression were the norm; the judiciary system was applied without regard to African interests; citizen's freedoms were ignored, at least insofar as the African were concerned; and customary law was allowed solely among the *indígenas* in the countryside and only in cases where they did not contradict Portuguese laws. As the liberation movements began to disturb the centuries-old colonial political order, the Portuguese attempted to reverse the situation by appointing Africans to major administrative posts and began a process of extending further educational opportunities to Africans, but still within the unchanging core of the colonial political structure implemented after the overthrow of the republic in 1926. Besides, time was running out: the liberation war had started in 1964, and by 1974, the colonial order had been overturned.

FRELIMO's ascent to power in 1975 signaled an end to Portuguese political structures as well as to any hopes that the new leaders would emulate the political traditions of the West. The new state declared itself socialist after the Marxist-Leninist model and announced the end of private property, including politics. The new People's Republic of Mozambique would pursue "centralized democracy" and follow the policy of a single-party state, where only members could vote and run for office, including the presidency and the People's Assembly. A constitution ratified in 1975 guaranteed on paper the citizens' universal liberties, although these did not include religious freedom or freedom of movement even within the country. In practice, the distinction between party and state did not exist in the country. The party Congress became the highest organ representing the state as well as the nation followed by the Central Committee, the Politburo, the People's Courts, and the local cells. Any citizen who did not join FRELIMO would be marginalized or sent to reeducation camps in an attempt to transform him or her into, in Samora Machel's words, the "new man" and the "new woman" of the new postcolonial state. Collective farms were instituted and private property expropriated, forcing many skilled Portuguese to leave the country. A deliberate policy of humiliation and confiscation of property of the assimilated and the petty middle class or bour-geoisie the party labeled "exploiters of the masses" was followed in favor of the "workers" and the "peasants."

The hastily and unwise application of such policies that had no root or tradition in the country and lack of expected sustained assistance from the socialist bloc countries resulted in widespread discontent that culminated with the emergency of RENAMO in 1977 and Mozambique's inevitable rapprochement with the West during the mid-1980s. Under pressure from the West and from within the country to change the political system, FRE-LIMO leaders caved in, giving way to completely new political structures that began to emerge around the time the peace negotiations were being held, namely, 1989–1992. The General Peace Accord of October 4, 1992, saw the implementation of the following: A new constitution that guaran-teed on paper and in practice the political freedom of Mozambican citizens; legalization of political parties; separation between party and state; univer-sal suffrage through secret ballot for the presidency and the new "Assem-bly of the Republic"; a Western-style judiciary system, even though the president still retained much power in the appointment of the Supreme Court judges; and higher accountability on the part of the police, the armed forces, and government officials.

The new political system has allowed the holding of two multiparty dem-ocratic elections in 1994 and 1999, even though both resulted in the victory of the ruling party. Certainly, the new system has many imperfections, and political abuses have occurred here and there within the country. Yet, over-all, Mozambicans are truly enjoying their newly proclaimed freedoms and may speak out without fear of retribution from the political establishment. Considering where the country was politically 20 years ago, what is hap-pening in Mozambique today is almost inconceivable. It appears that, un-like many other African countries that have recently embraced democratic reforms, Mozambique is inexorably on the road to true democracy and has not just embraced, like many others, the trappings of democracy, which one could call "democratism."

ECONOMIC DEVELOPMENT

Mozambique inherited a colonial economic system that was implemented during various phases. Until the 17th century, Lisbon had no structured economic policy for its overseas territories, including Mozambique. The presence of traders, capitães-mores (captains-general), governors, and adventurers guaranteed, to the extent possible, the pursuit of commerce, mainly in the commodities of spices, slaves, precious metals, skins, guns, and gunpowder. From the 17th to the 19th centuries, the Portuguese introduced a system of agriculture called *prazos da coroa*, which granted lands to Portuguese settlers for at least three generations. Problems associated with slavery and landlord absenteeism forced the abandonment of the experiment, which had been transplanted from Portugal.

This failed economic experiment was followed by the introduction into Mozambique of the concessionaire monopolistic companies. The new companies would develop their domain as if they were "sovereign." The policy was intended to guarantee the preservation of the Portuguese African empire being threatened then by the machinations of Portugal's competitors evidenced by the 1884–85 Berlin Conference's principle of "effective control." Following the enforcement of the Colonial Act of 1930, the concessionaire system was abolished, and Portugal viewed the colonies now mainly as sources of raw materials for the metropolis.

The labor policies of the post-1930 António de Oliveira Salazar era contained the enforcement of a brutally forced labor for the Africans and a focus on an agricultural economy that depended on the forced cultivation of certain cash crops intended for export to the metropolis and abroad, such as South Africa and southern Rhodesia. These included cotton, coconut, sugarcane, peanuts, sisal, and cashew nuts. Corn, millet, cassava, and sweet potatoes abundant in the region, were also encouraged but less so than the export cash crops. *Grémios*, or special purchasing and transport companies, were created to allow goods to be exported by road and rail through the various well-developed ports of the colony. Exploited as sources of cheap labor, Africans remained impoverished in a subsistence economy that developed no heavy industries in the colony. There were, of course, some processing plants, mines, and factories for such goods as cement, cashew nut, shoes, coal, and food items (mainly in the capital city and surrounding areas). Yet, the bulk of the most important raw materials was processed abroad.

Mozambicans had, indeed, entered the age of capitalism without ever enjoying its benefits. Much of the Mozambique labor force, as many as 100,000 a year, was exported to the mines of the Union of South Africa stemming from a convention signed first in 1909 and renewed thereafter. After Portugal, South Africa remained Mozambique's major trading partner throughout the remainder of the colonial period. As the war of national liberation raged during the 1960s, the Portuguese attempted to accelerate the colony's economic development to stamp out the appeal of the nationalists and international criticism by paving many of the major roads, building new bridges, creating new schools, and emphasizing the need for local industrial plants. However, time had run out. By 1975, socialist FRELIMO had wrested power from Portugal.

FRELIMO's avowed policy was to end the capitalist economic structure in Mozambique, as it had embraced the Marxist-Leninist socialist model. This implied nationalization of all means of production and natural resources, the abolition of private enterprise in every sphere, including education, health, law, agriculture, and industry. The state confiscated and expropriated farms and church properties, and it either returned the land to the people or maintained the large farms as state-owned enterprises. People were encouraged and often forced to live in collective villages, work in collective farms, share and sell their products as co-ops, and create what were called peoples' shops. Idle citizens, the homeless, and the unemployed were forcibly removed from the cities and told to resettle in the countryside and engage in agricultural pursuits. Although deemed important, industry was primarily designed to complement and not surpass or compete with agricultural output. Thus, there was no major change in the types of industry left by the Portuguese. In fact, many processing plants deteriorated, as skilled labor migrated to other parts of Southern Africa or to Portugal.

The collapse of state farms and peasant resistance to collectivization signaled the failure of the socialist experiment in Mozambique. The financial impact of the closure of Mozambique's frontier with southern Rhodesia, RENAMO's destruction of the infrastructure and the great loss in lives, the preemptive retaliatory military assaults by the two neighboring white regimes, the collapse of the Soviet Union, and pressure from the West, forced Mozambique to change its economic course and embrace the tenets of market economy. As a result, the country halted its nationalization policy, slowly returned (and continues to return) church property, and encouraged private investment by providing strong tax incentives to foreign corporations that wished to do business in the country. Mozambique has continued to accept loans from the International Monetary Fund (IMF) and the World Bank, along with all the structural adjustments, including devaluation of the currency, downsizing government employment, and scaling down social service subsidies.

If it were not for the floods of 2000 and 2001, experts predict that the Mozambique economy would be growing at the rate of 5 percent per year, while its industrial sector, now being expanded considerably, would yield at least 10 percent of its gross domestic product (GDP) per annum. Indeed, the coal mining industry is being rehabilitated, and natural gas and other natural resources are being processed by international conglomerates. Beer breweries, Coca-Cola, aluminum and cement plants, shoe factories, fisheries, construction, a car assembly plant, new banks, and paved road infrastructure initiatives indicate that the country has embarked on a major financial and economic course that is bound to make a difference in the long run.

All this activity notwithstanding, the external debt is still huge, and people in the villages have not seen their lives improve dramatically over the past 23 years. Goods are very expensive, agricultural methods have not been modernized for the most part, and the lack of expanded educational opportunities and adequate health services make life miserable. What has visibly changed in Mozambique over the past few years is the political atmosphere—people can now speak freely without fear of retaliation, and speak they do—including a cry to put an end to national corruption. Overall, however, it has been remarkable how FRELIMO, headed by a wise president, has been able to adjust its policies both in economics and politics to the realities of today's changing world. This is certainly one major reason why the opposition in the country has been unable to assume government leadership.

THE DICTIONARY

– A –

ACORDO GERAL DA PAZ (GENERAL PEACE ACCORD). Peace accord signed by President **Joaquim Chissano** of Mozambique and **Afonso Dhlakama**, leader of **RENAMO**, on October 4, 1992, in Rome and approved by the Assembly of the Republic on October 15, 1992. Overall, the accord contains the following provisions:

1. A cease-fire agreement to be implemented as soon as the peace accord was ratified by the National Assembly;
2. Withdrawal of both rival forces to assembly points within seven days of ratification;
3. Establishment of new armed forces, entailing 15,000 troops drawn from **FRELIMO** ranks and 15,000 from RENAMO's, for a total of a 30,000-man force;
4. Creation of a Cease-Fire Commission representing the Mozambique government, **RENAMO**, and the United Nations (UN);
5. Withdrawal of foreign troops (Zimbabwean and Malawian) from Mozambique;
6. Presidential and legislative elections to be held one year after the signing of the peace accord; and
7. Return and reintegration of the two million refugees scattered throughout Mozambique's six neighboring countries as well as that of the internally displaced persons.

Problems notwithstanding, within two years, all terms of the General Peace Accord, with close assistance and supervision from the UN, had been successfully implemented. *See also* ELECTIONS; PARTIES (POLITICAL).

ACTO COLONIAL (COLONIAL ACT). A series of colonial policies prepared by Premier **António de Oliveira Salazar** in 1930. In 1933, they

1

became part of the Portuguese constitution. In the document, Salazar imposes a system of centralization designed to subordinate all colonial matters to the Overseas Ministry in Lisbon, abolishes high commissioners in favor of less powerful governors-general, and reaffirms the *indigenato* and the policy of limited assimilation of Africans. On the financial side, the Acto Colonial viewed the colonies as primary providers of raw materials to **Portugal** and the Africans as nothing more than forced laborers. The act also reasserted the "civilizing mission" of the church and its alliance with the state and envisioned an empire of "one state, one race, one faith, and one civilization."

ADMINISTRATION. Mozambique underwent numerous metamorphoses in administrative structure and government throughout the centuries. From 1505 to 1609, colonial authority was vested in a captain or a captain-general residing in **Sofala**. From 1609 to 1750, this authority was passed on to governors of "Mozambique, Sofala and Cunene and Monomotapa **(Zambezi) Rivers**." Thereafter, it was returned to captains-general in order to underscore the need to rely on military-minded individuals who would know how to defend the colony in time of emergency. Assisted by the clergy, the army, and prominent citizens, the captains collected state revenue and made military and civilian appointments. In 1822, the precarious military situation dictated the appointment of military governors for the colony (which 10 years later was divided into prefectures on the French model, the prefects replacing the military governors).

A pattern of administrative structure for Mozambique began to emerge thereafter. In 1836, Mozambique was divided into districts, these into *concelhos*, with ultimate authority over the colony (or province, as it became known in the liberal constitutions of the 19th century) vested in the navy and Overseas Ministry. Although the law had established the position of governor-general in 1833, only in 1836 was a governor appointed. He was assisted by a *conselho do governo* (governing council).

As a result of changes in colonial perceptions in the metropolis, which viewed the colonies as an extension of continental Portugal, a decree of 1842–43 made Mozambique a simple department of Portugal, under the tight control of the Lisbon government. Later, in 1869, in compliance with the Rebelo da Silva Reforms, Mozambique became a province of Portugal, divided into districts and concelhos, with eight governors-general assisted by the Junta da Fazenda, which oversaw the finances; a secretary-general; a procurator; and a *conselho governativo* (governing council) made up of the Prelate of Mozambique, the highest military officer in the Mozambique district, and the secretary-general. The governor-general's term of office was fixed at five years.

To thwart British attempts as well as those of other European governments who coveted the Portuguese empire, Lisbon made Mozambique its East Indian State in 1891 and, in 1893, divided it into two provinces with three districts, namely, **Mozambique, Zambézia**, and Lourenço Marques, the districts being under *governadores subalternos* (lieutenant-governors). In the same year (1891), in the wake of the humiliating **British Ultimatum**, the governor-general was replaced by a high commissioner with broad powers to deal effectively with internal and external threats. However, the new high commissioners, particularly **Joaquim Mouzinho de Albuquerque** (1896–98), proved to be such a threat to Lisbon's authority over the colony that the position was abolished in 1898 (although it was restored on and off during the 1910–1926 period).

The administrative structure of Mozambique continued to be revised, however. The 1907 decrees divided the colony into five districts— Lourenço Marques, **Quelimane, Tete**, Mozambique, and **Inhambane**— each with its own districts and *concelhos, circumscrições civis* (civil municipalities), and *capitanias-mores* (captaincies), depending on whether the local situation dictated civilian or military authority. During that year, the term of office for the governor-general was reduced to three years due to Lisbon's fear that the governor's power might entrench itself in the colony. The government also restricted jurisdiction over indigenous affairs and entrusted it to the district governor. The 1930 Colonial Act changed the governor's term of office to four years. Theoretically, he exercised power over finances and civil service. In practice, however, the governor consulted the Colonial Ministry. Under the new system, the governor-general was assisted by a secretary-general who oversaw the secretariat for civil and political administration (including the police and civil servants) and by five other secretaries, each overseeing one of the following administrative divisions: Public Works and Communications; Education; Housing, Economy, Land and Settlement; and Health, Labor, and Welfare.

A legislative council was established in 1956 to assist the governor but not to approve laws—a function reserved to the governor and the Colonial Ministry. The council was made up of 29 members, 18 chosen by corporate interests (including the *régulos*) and selected individuals who paid taxes in the amount of at least 15,000 *escudos*, and nine chosen by the registered voters from each district. A permanent economic and social council also assisted the governor-general in financial, economic, and social matters.

From the 1890s to the early 1940s, the territories under the monopolistic concessionaires fell under the laws of the companies, which also appointed their own governors-general and district governors. During the 1960s, Mozambique was divided into nine districts, these into municipalities (*concelhos*), towns (*circumscrições*), and administrative posts (*postos administrativos*). Lourenço Marques was under the governor-general, whereas the remaining districts fell under the district governors' authority. In 1964, Mozambique had 61 municipalities and 33 *circumscrições* (townships). Both were under administrators, while the administrative posts fell under the authority of *chefes do posto*. Presently, Mozambique is divided into 11 provinces (Maputo City counting as the 11th). A governor appointed directly by the president of the republic heads each province. *See also* PROVINCES.

AFRICANO, (1909–1918). First black-owned weekly newspaper (replaced by *O Brado Africano* in 1918), established by the Albasini brothers. Just as the *O Brado Africano* a few years later, *O Brado Africano* was published in Portuguese and Rhonga.

AGRICULTURE. Mozambique's population is predominantly agrarian with cultivable land totaling 36,000,000 hectares, showing an increase since 1994 when only 3,600,000 hectares were cultivated. About 87 percent of the people produce their own food and live in nonurban areas. FRELIMO has encouraged and sometimes forced the people to live on collective farms (each containing approximately 50 to 1,500 people) and participate in cooperatives (co-ops)—about 229 in 1982, up from 180 in 1977 but down from 375 in 1981. The number of co-ops reached the 1,352 mark in 1982 with a total of 1.5 million people, covering up to 30,000 acres of land. Co-op productivity fell by half during the 1979–81 period and the state projection of having five million people on co-ops and collective farms by 1990 proved to be unrealistic. Each family living on the collective farm was also allowed to work on a small plot of land for individual food needs. Overall, the government has acknowledged that low productivity stemmed from mismanagement, lack of sufficiently trained technicians and the lack of individual incentives, and inadequate state assistance.

Major crops grown on the collective farms and co-ops were cotton, cashew nuts, sugar cane, corn, millet, sisal, peanuts, tea, and sorghum. The activities of the MNR and government countermeasures against the suspected MNR sympathizers destroyed many of the farms, and people had to flee to the towns and the neighboring countries to seek refuge. In 1944, the 791,000 cotton growers produced 64,000 metric tons of cotton. The production declined to 34,939 tons in 1957 (when some 529,000 Africans were engaged in its production), and to 32,400 tons in 1964. Although the production of cotton dramatically rose to 80,000 tons in 1977 (at a time when 500,000 Africans were still growing the crop), it declined to 19,600 tons in 1981. By 1984, production had plummeted to 5,300. In 1997, cotton production was 18,000 metric tons. Cashew nut production stood at 1.24 million metric tons in 1964 but declined to 18,000 tons in 1981 and 3,800 in 1984. In 1997, cashew nut production rose to 60,000 metric tons. The same trend affected sugar production: 83.3 thousand metric tons in 1964, 165,042 tons in 1965, 227,823 in 1975, 177,200 in 1982, and down to 39,000 tons in 1984. In 1997, sugarcane production was 300,000 metric tons. Copra production rose steadily over the years to attain 74,000 metric tons in 1997. It was 50,000 tons in 1965, 45,507 tons in 1967, 43,507 tons in 1972, but rising to 60,000 in 1980 and to a mere 65,000 by 1985. Tea production figures have not been encouraging either: 9,000 tons (exported) in 1963, 10,746 in 1964, and 18,795 in 1973. Production rose to 22,000 tons in 1981 but declined to 12,800 in 1984 and declined even more in 1997 to 3,000 metric tons.

Insofar as sisal is concerned, the figures have fluctuated as follows: 31,600 tons in 1964; 30,972 in 1965; 22,000 in 1974; down to a mere 2,000 tons in 1985. Rice: 22,000 tons in 1953; 45,000 in 1982; down to 19,100 tons in 1984. By 1997, rice production significantly increased to 180,000 metric tons. After declining from 89,600 tons during 1981–1982 to 82,600 in 1983–1984, corn production rose significantly to attain 1,042, 000 metric tons in 1997.

Since 1986, the government has gradually abandoned its policy of state-centered administration of agriculture. Producer prices have risen, and there are greater incentives to production, especially of export crops. The government encourages foreign investors. Agriculture is the most important sector in determining GDP but is vulnerable to the vagaries of nature. For instance, following the droughts of 1991–92 and 1994–95, in 1996 and 1997, heavy rains brought floods and damaged crops. Nonetheless, grain production was 1.1 metric tons in 1995, and the country is almost self-sufficient in grain. Mozambique was once the world's leading producer of cashew nut; production is recovering and reached an estimated 65,000 tons in 1996. Other crops are sugarcane (313,200 tons marketed in 1995), raw cotton (approximately 50,000 tons annually during the 1990s), copra, sisal, and tea. Maize is an important domestic crop, reaching 173,000 tons in 1995. *See also* ECONOMY.

AIDS (HIV/AIDS). Only during the past five years have Mozambique authorities taken serious steps to study the incidence and prevalence of HIV/AIDS in the country. On May 31, 2001, the XXVI session of the Ministry of Health National Coordinating Council released its most recent estimate of HIV/AIDS prevalence. Major clusters are said to be found in the central and southern provinces (Tete and Maputo registering the highest rates), whereas prevalence in the northern provinces seems to hover between 4 and 5 percent. The government claimed that about 9 percent of the population was affected, but UN estimates for the end of 1999 revealed that HIV/AIDS infections in Mozambique represented 13.22 percent of the population altogether.

The origin and spread of AIDS in Mozambique is still debated today. Writing in 1995, Laurie Garrett claimed that the AIDS epidemic seems to have "radiated outward" from the Lake Victoria area, reaching Mozambique after 1980. She also speculated that Portuguese and African soldiers fighting in the liberation wars (1960s–1970s) may have been the conduits for early HIV cases, especially for the less virulent strain, HIV-2, which, in East Africa, has been found only in Mozambique, but predominates in the former Portuguese West African colonies of Angola, Guinea-Bissau, and São Tomé e Príncipe. It is possible, she noted, that Portuguese soldiers carried it to Mozambique from the metropolis or were infected in one of the colonies and then carried it to the other colonies.

The Mozambican situation has certainly been aggravated by the prolonged **civil war**, which ended in 1992, and the steady movement of refugees and returnees across the borders of the six neighboring countries (Zimbabwe, Zambia, Malawi, **South Africa**, Swaziland, and Tanzania), known to have high HIV/AIDS prevalence rates. Traditional practices and cross-border labor migratory movements, especially to the South African mines, have tended to further favor the rapid spread of HIV/AIDS and other sexually transmitted infections (STIs). The United Nations June 2001 statistics rank Mozambique among the highest infected countries in Africa, with an HIV infection prevalence rate of 13.2 percent, only below Botswana (35.8 percent), Swaziland (25.3 percent), Zimbabwe (25.1 percent), South Africa (19.9 percent), Zambia (19.9 percent), Namibia (19.5 percent), Malawi (16.0 percent), Kenya (13.9 percent), and Central African Republic (13.9 percent). It is also estimated that, as a result of the HIV/AIDS impact, Mozambique will lose about 9.0 percent of its labor force by the year 2005 and 24.9 percent by 2020, while some other Southern African states will lose even higher numbers: Botswana, 17.2 percent (in 2005) and 30.8 percent (in 2020); and Namibia, 12.8 percent and 35.1 percent, respectively. South Africa is expected to lose as much of its labor force as Mozambique. Regrettably, the government spends only 4 to 5 percent of the budget on health, and only U.S.$2 on drugs per capita.

As a consequence of the HIV/AIDS pandemic tragedy, either the patients cannot afford to buy any drugs, or the effective drugs are not available in the drugstores. Throughout the country, the hospitals remain overwhelmed, and government officials cite alarming rates of infection among the youngsters, especially high school students, where the rate is said to be as high as 30 percent or more. A physician in Maputo once said that doctors in the capital city are so inundated with patients apparently afflicted with HIV/AIDS that, quite often, for lack of time and means of treatment, they do not examine them. The situation gets worse if the patient starts coughing in front of the doctor or nurses and reveals that he or she worked in South Africa. As a result, doctors tend to simply prescribe a placebo and send the patient away to die at home. *See* HEALTH.

AIR TRANSPORT. Three of Mozambique's 16 airports are international. Air transportation is provided by two airlines: the state airline, Linhas Aéreas de Moçambique (LAM), and the Empresa Nacional de Transporte e Trabalho Aéreo (TTA), which was privatized in May 1997. LAM flies international routes and links **Maputo** to six other provincial capitals, while TTA provides scheduled and chartered light plane and helicopter services. The civil aviation sector has expanded since 1991. By mid-1992, 17 companies were operating small airplanes in Mozambique. In 1996, the number of aircraft departures was 4,000 and the number of the passengers carried was 163,000.

AJAUA. *See* YAO.

AJI, SULIMANE BONA (OR SULIMAN BWANA HAJI). Aji succeeded Sheikh Janfar Salim in Quitangonha (1817–50). He briefly befriended Governor-General Sebastião Xavier Botelho (1825–29) but ran into trouble with the Portuguese authorities due to his activities as a slave trader. With assistance from Zanzibar and Quiloa and several Portuguese slave traders, Aji successfully attacked Mossuril in 1831 and then sued for peace, without, however, interrupting his slaving activities. At times, he would hoist the Portuguese flag and at other times he would raise the flag of Zanzibar on his territory, while he continued to receive his annual pension from the Portuguese. He was replaced by Sheikh Auly Ben Hery (1850–1873). Yet, Quitangonha, for all practical purposes, continued to be independent from the Portuguese authorities.

ALBASINI, JOÃO (1890–1925). João Albasini and his brother José Albasini were owners and editors of the first black press in Mozambique— *O Brado Africano* (African Call)—established in 1918, based at Lourenço Marques with relatively wide circulation at Beira. The assimilated Albasini father was of Portuguese and African descent. The Albasinis published the review in Portuguese and Rhonga. João was also a novelist and published his historical novel *Livro da Dor* in 1925.

ALBUQUERQUE, JOAQUIM AUGUSTO MOUZINHO DE (1855–1902). Portuguese statesman, cavalry officer, and mathematician. Mouzinho served in India in 1886 and, in 1890–1902, became governor of the military district of Lourenço Marques. Having distinguished himself as commander of a squadron of the first cavalry against **Gungunhana** in 1895, Mouzinho was appointed governor of the military district of Gaza by **António Enes**, the royal commissioner. On December 28, 1895, Mouzinho entered Chaimite, Gungunhana's headquarters, and imprisoned the Nguni king, apparently without firing a single shot. In 1896, Mouzinho pacified the Maputo area and was appointed governor-general of Mozambique on May 21, 1896, to be soon elevated, in November of the same year, to the office of royal commissioner. He led military campaigns against the Namarrais in Mozambique District, where he was wounded. In 1897, he resumed his campaigns against the Nguni (*Vátuas*) under **Maguiguana**, Gungunhana's successor, whom he finally defeated and killed at Mapulanguene.

Mouzinho briefly returned to **Portugal** to receive military honors but came back to Mozambique in 1898 to put an end to the remaining resistance. However, dissatisfied with his autocratic rule of Mozambique, the government limited severely his powers as royal commissioner, which prompted him to resign in protest. He subsequently returned to Portugal and served at the royal palace as confidant and mentor of Prince Dom Luís Filipe.

Accused of attempting to overthrow the monarchy in favor of a military dictatorship, bored with life, and disgusted with the way he had been treated (no longer as a hero), Mouzinho committed suicide at the entrance of the Jardim das Laranjeiras in Lisbon on January 8, 1902. Cruel and often impulsive, Mouzinho despised the Africans, whom he called lazy and savages, favored foreign companies, and was totally opposed to the policy of assimilation. Like António Enes, his mentor, Mouzinho left a series of administrative and political decrees governing the Province of Mozambique.

ALDEAMENTOS (PROTECTED VILLAGE SETTLEMENTS). *Aldeamentos* were villages or hamlets created by the Portuguese government to control and protect the population and ensure peaceful colonization. The aldeamentos were intended to be "strategic" centers in the Portuguese colonies, particularly during the liberation war.

ALEJO, ALDO. Former Italian parliamentarian and United Nations Development Program (UNDP) official, who coordinated the activities of the Organização das Nações Unidas em Moçambique (ONUMOZ) (United Nations Organization in Mozambique) following the October 4, 1992, Peace Accord signed by **FRELIMO** and **RENAMO**. Alejo is credited with ensuring that the two parties to the cease-fire would continue their dialogue even at times when the agreement seemed to unravel. His impartiality became reassuring in the midst of the problems the mission encountered almost daily until its successful completion in 1995. Alejo's strength stemmed not only from his **UN** position but also from the support he enjoyed from the Italian government, which, more than any other government, had backed the peace negotiations since their inception and underwrote many of the financial needs that enabled the negotiations to succeed.

ANGUNI (NGUNI). An ethnic group in southern Mozambique, the Nguni inhabit **Gaza** and around **Maputo**. Known as "Zulu" (or "*Vátuas*" by the Portuguese), the Nguni, who number more than a million, migrated from Natal during the 19th century as a result of ethnic rivalries and disputes over land, cattle, women, and grazing. They observe a strict hierarchy of age groups, are warriors, and, under such famous leaders as **Mazula**, **Gungunhana**, and **Maguiguana** (not a Nguni), fought the Portuguese from 1832 to 1895. The Swazi are considered to be a clan of the Nguni and live in Namaacha, near Swaziland.

ANJOS, PAULO MARIANO DOS. Paulo Mariano dos Anjos was a Goan merchant and colonel in the Portuguese army who settled in the northern section of the Lower Zambezi, between the **Zambezi** and **Quelimane** Rivers, during the 1820s. He acquired several *prazos* in Massingire. He and his son, Paulo Mariano II, known as Matequenha I, became very powerful among the Maganja and Sena people and prospered from the slave trade along the Chire and the Zambezi Rivers, in Tete and Sena towns, during the 1850s. Eventually, Matequenha I established his *aringa* (headquarters) at Chamo, a small island on the Chire. In 1857, Matequenha I was arrested by the Portuguese authorities in Quelimane for slave trading and anti-Portuguese activities.

His brother, Matequenha II (also known as Bonga, not related to the Bonga of the Cruz family in Massangano), organized the Massingire people and raised an army that marched against Quelimane that year. Government troops from Quelimane attempted to take the Chamo aringa but failed to take the prazo, which was defended by *achikunda* (slave soldiers). On September 8, 1858, Governor Custódio José da Silva overran the aringa and erected Fort Mzaro in Massingire. Matequenha II, however, escaped capture.

Meanwhile, in 1860, Matequenha I was tried at **Moçambique** Island, released, and allowed to return to his prazo. Subsequently, he built a new aringa on Mount Morrumbala and resumed his slaving activities. He died in 1861, after moving his aringa farther north, and was succeeded by his son, Paulo Mariano III (also known as Mariano Pequeno). In July 1881, Mariano III was handed over to the Portuguese by the Macololo because of his cruelty and was assassinated on his way to Quelimane in December 1881. By 1882, the Massingire prazo had surrendered to Portuguese rule, although the Macololo themselves would not be conquered (and only temporarily) by the Portuguese until 1889.

ARMAZENS DO POVO. *See* PEOPLE'S SHOPS.

ARMED FORCES. At the height of the war in 1981–83, Mozambique had an army of 22,800 troops, a navy of 700 marines, and an air force of 500 men. The war, however, forced the officials to beef up the country's defense forces. Consequently, according to the *Statesman's Year Book* (1988), in 1987 the Mozambican army consisted of 28,000 men and 9,500 border guards and militias of various kinds, divided into one tank brigade, seven infantry brigades, and two independent mechanized and seven antiaircraft artillery battalions. Some T-34/-55 main battle tanks were also part of the army's arsenal. The navy was composed of 800 officers and men, while its equipment consisted of 10 Indian-built patrol craft, two ex-Soviet antisubmarine vessels, six former Portuguese coastal patrol boats, 10 inshore patrol boats, one ex-Portuguese landing craft for transport, six ex-Soviet gunboats, four ex-Dutch patrol craft, and two ex-Portuguese minor landing craft. The air force personnel numbered 1,000, while its equipment consisted of 20 MiG-17 and 30 MiG-21 fighters, manned by Cubans; one 26 turboprop transport; and some C-47 piston-engine transports, 10 Mi-24 armed helicopters, eight Mi-8 transport helicopters, a few 1-39 jet trainers, Zlin 326 primary trainers, and some ex–Portuguese Air Force Alouette helicopters.

As a result of the 1992 peace accord, the united Mozambique Armed Forces were supposed to number 30,000, evenly split between **FRE-LIMO** and **RENAMO** military cadres. By 2001, the process had not yet been completed, and RENAMO complained that its former military were not being enlisted as agreed and that the officers were predominantly FRELIMO's. Besides the projected 30,000-man force, Mozambique now has 750 men in the navy and 4,000 in the air force. In 1999, the defense expenditure amounted to 1.2 billion *meticais*, approximately U.S.$73 million, representing about 5 percent of the GDP, down from 9.9 percent (in reality likely much higher) in 1990.

AROUCA, DOMINGOS. One of the first Mozambican lawyers, educated in **Portugal** during the 1950s and early 1960s and married to a Portuguese. Arouca returned to Mozambique but could not practice law as the secret police kept him under surveillance and eventually arrested him. Just prior to the establishment of the transitional government in Mozambique in 1974, Arouca, a business owner himself, disagreed with **Samora Machel's** Marxist policies and became a spokesman of **RENAMO**. With the support of a few Portuguese citizens, he founded his own political party known as the **Frente Unida de Moçambique** (FUMO) (Mozambique United Front). Presently, FUMO has no political impact in Mozambique or abroad.

ARRIAGA, BRIGADIER-GENERAL KAULZA DE. Professor at the Instituto de Altos Estudos Militares in Lisbon (1966) and commander of the Portuguese forces in Mozambique (1970–73). Arriaga was determined to end once and for all **FRELIMO** activities in the colony. He led several land and air offensives as part of **Operation Gordian Knot** (Nó Górdio) he launched against FRELIMO, particularly in the **Maconde** Plateau. To win over FRELIMO guerrillas, it is reported that Arriaga gave preference of treatment to wounded guerrillas over his Portuguese army. The guerrillas were also received in the same hospital wards as the Portuguese troops.

Believing that, in the long-run, economic development was essential to winning the war of *assimilação*, Arriaga launched his Operation Frontier (Operação Fronteira) on the banks of the Rovuma River. He literally attempted to build a "human wall," a type of human *cordon sanitaire* made up of dozens of concrete houses, schools, a post office, a market, and a technical college, and planned to provide the new settlement with paved roads to facilitate access and communication. He invited 2,500 Maconde to live in the new town, known as Nangade Village, 75 miles inland from the Indian Ocean. He concentrated his attention on the Rovuma frontier, hoping to block guerrilla infiltration from Tanzania.

To improve his military tactics against the guerrillas, as soon as he was appointed to his post in Mozambique, Arriaga visited General William C. Westmoreland in Washington, D.C., to learn valuable lessons from the American experience in Vietnam. For a while, his military and civilian projects caused some concern among liberation movement circles both in Mozambique and Angola. In a matter of months, however, assisted by the rains, FRELIMO had paralyzed the grand design, and in August 1973, General Tomás Basto Machado replaced Arriaga.

The April 25, 1974, military coup in Portugal proved how unsuccessful Arriaga's military campaign had been in Mozambique. Military experts estimate that between 1961 and 1974, some 110,000 Portuguese engaged in the colonial wars were unaccounted for, most of whom perished in combat. During the 1961–1971 period, some 1,300 Portuguese soldiers were killed in Mozambique alone; and between 1971 and 1974, the death toll on the Portuguese side was 18 soldiers a month.

ASSIMILAÇÃO (ASSIMILATION). The term *assimilation* referred to the Portuguese colonial policy that attempted to transform the Africans into Portuguese citizens once they could speak Portuguese, read and write, and sustain themselves through employment or business. Africans were also expected to abandon their own culture. By law, once assimilated, the African was to enjoy the same rights and accept the same responsibilities as a Portuguese citizen. The assimilated African, therefore, was entitled to enjoy freedom of movement within the colony and the empire, participate in elections, and not be subject to discrimination in public facilities. The roots of the policy are still unclear but might be traced back to the practices of the newly founded kingdom of **Portugal**, which was made up of Moorish populations in the interior, the southern provinces, and villages around Lisbon. A large number of Jewish business communities in the major urban and commercial centers of the kingdom also existed.

The great disparity in religious beliefs among the various heterogeneous communities led the kings of Portugal to force all to convert to the **religion** of the kingdom, Roman Catholicism. This was done not for religious uniformity but for the obvious, more important, reason of national security. After unification during the 1270s, Portugal remained open to Muslim attacks from North Africa in its southern flank. As to the Jews, they were disliked and suspected by the emerging commercial classes in the port cities of Lisbon, Oporto, and others. The integration of these communities into a national entity followed the time-honored assimilationist tendencies of the Roman tradition in the Iberian peninsula, the Arab invasions since 711 A.D., the reverse movement of the *reconquista*, the ideas of the Enlightenment, and the impact of the French Revolution. The Portuguese bestowed assimilation rights on their Indian subjects in Brazil and on other subjects of the interior as long as they had been baptized Roman Catholic. Thus, since the early days, Catholicism was a major qualifying factor for the acquisition of the privileges of citizenship in the Portuguese empire (*see* CATHOLIC CHURCH).

In time, after the independence of **Brazil** in 1822, which all of a sudden made Africa once again a serious national survival option for Portugal, contemporary liberal constitutions simply emphasized being born in the national territories of Africa and Asia, declared parts of Portugal, as a sufficient condition for citizenship. However, historians find no specific laws or decrees issued by the Portuguese state in its history to achieve the goal of assimilation, at least not earlier than its overseas expansion to India, Brazil, and Africa. In these few areas, the Portuguese felt the need to increase locally their numbers or supporters of their cause through new relationships, such as marriages performed according to Portuguese laws. The first recorded attempt at assimilation through marriage was enacted by Afonso de Albuquerque in India, during the very early years of the overseas conquests, and was widely used thereafter in the East.

In parts of West and East Africa, the Portuguese followed a selective policy of marrying Portuguese girls orphaned after their fathers' death in service of the king. In Mozambique, along the **Zambezi** Valley, in particular, the Portuguese assured this policy through the institution called the *prazos da coroa*, which among other things, ensured that the Portuguese cause would have its defenders well into the 19th century, giving Portugal the right to claim those lands. Prior to the Pombaline decrees of 1761–62 and the 1820s liberal revolution in Portugal, while the assimilation of the Moors from Africa in Portugal went almost unnoticed, the same did not happen to the melting of the Jews into the national society. Therefore, during the period of overseas expansion, the assimilation of Asians and Africans were isolated actions implemented by a few Portuguese governors in the areas of their administration in response to specific needs related to commerce, defense, or the expansion of religion by missionaries. The case of Brazil became more conspicuous through its association with the royal decrees during the reign of Dom José I. The decrees so explicitly extended the policy that some historians have called it *assimilação uniformizadora* (uniformalizing assimilation). This policy attempted to completely change all Africans by bestowing on them the rights and privileges of the Portuguese citizens living in the metropolis. The republican legislators of the late 1910s and early 1920s expanded the list of assimilation requirements to include literacy and ability to sustain oneself economically. The Africans who were not covered by these requirements, and, therefore, not assimilated, were referred to as *indígenas*, even though it was not until 1917 and 1920 that specific statutes officially introduced the discriminatory concept of indígenas and assimilados. The Regime do Indigenato (Diploma no. 36, November 12, 1917, and Decree no. 7:15, November 19, 1920) defined the indígena as an African who chose to continue to live under African traditions.

As such, while Africans under this category would be forced to work and be regulated by special laws, the assimilados were free to pursue careers of their choice. Children of assimilated Africans, as well as those resulting from miscegenation when fathered by a nonindígena, would automatically be considered Portuguese citizens. As a result, parents had the obligation to simply register them officially. Whereas the indígenas had to carry a detailed identification pass known as the *caderneta indígena*, the assimilado carried a less complicated pass, called the *bilhete de identidade*. When the law was changed in 1961 making all Africans citizens of Portugal, the former indígenas still continued to carry the caderneta indígena, and in practice, their nonprivileged status did not change.

The uniformalizing assimilationist policy came under heavy attack from **António Enes** and the men who followed his footsteps as governors-general of Mozambique in the aftermath of the **British Ultimatum** of 1890. António Enes had been commissioned by Lisbon to carry out a feasibility study for the colonization of Mozambique following the **ultimatum**. In his report, entitled *Moçambique* and published in 1893, Enes recommended the investment of foreign capital in the colony, the abolition of the prazos along the Zambezi Valley, the utilization of African labor, and the introduction of "hut taxation" or *"imposto de pal-*

hota" as a way of developing the colony to prevent its outright abandonment by the authorities in favor of Angola, which had more natural resources. António Enes is quoted as having once said, "*Basta de complacências liberais com o africano. Deve ser conquistado, produzir e calar-se*" (No more liberal complacency with the African. He must be conquered, produce, and be silent).

Mousinho de Albuquerque followed António Enes as governor of Mozambique. In 1899, Albuquerque had published his own report also entitled *Moçambique*. However, he, as well as Aires de Ornelas, Freire de Andrade, Eduardo Ferreira da Costa, and Pedro Francisco de Amorim, the men associated with the so-called School of António Enes, fiercely opposed the assimilation policy. They argued that, given the state of "savagery" of the African, it was unrealistic to expect to make him a citizen.

Enes was writing on the eve of the establishment of the republican regime in Portugal in 1910. In 1930, **António Salazar**'s **Colonial Act** closely reflected António Enes's view of the colonies as sources of cheap labor for the metropolis, stressing, in the process, cultural differences and discouraging the assimilation of the Africans. Abuses associated with forced labor, heavily criticized by the international community during the 1960s, and the rise of African nationalism in the Portuguese colonies, compelled Lisbon, as noted earlier, to declare all Africans Portuguese citizens in 1961. By then, however, fewer than 5,000 Mozambicans had achieved the status of assimilados.

Various factors contributed to the failure of the assimilation policy, which, in fact, was a form of direct rule. First, although the Crown tended to defend the policy, no consensus about it existed in Portugal itself. Second, assimilation was lukewarmly received by colonial governors, and was therefore never seriously implemented. Third, the assimilado African always remained a cultural hybrid who, never totally accepted by the colonizer, could no longer fit among his own people. This situation discouraged many prospective candidates from applying for citizenship. Finally, the government realized that militants and nationalists tended to come from the ranks of the assimilated who demanded the right to self-determination. In addition, assimilation was intrinsically doomed to failure because, while it advocated equality, it forced the African alone to assimilate to Portuguese culture, clearly implying the inferiority of his culture.

One may conclude by noting that assimilation was never meant to be an equalizer. In its conception, and throughout Portuguese history in the metropolis or, later, in Asia, Africa, or Brazil, assimilation was designed to be a *cordon* of security for the metropolitan territory, a "fifth column," or a front line for the defense and justification of the Portuguese presence overseas. However, in the overseas territories, the premise of racial and cultural superiority of the white colonizer carried the seeds of discredit of the policy in the wake of the ideologies of national liberation. Thus, in the context of modern colonial history, the assimilado was intended simply to be the agent of the Portuguese cause in Mozambique and other Portuguese territories. *See also* COLONIAL POLICY OF ASSIMILATION.

ASSIMILATION. *See ASSIMILAÇÃO.*

ASSOCIAÇÃO DE MOÇAMBIQUE. An association created in Lourenço Marques during the 1920s. Catering at first to the needs of the Portuguese born in Mozambique, the association widened its membership during the 1950s and admitted any Mozambican interested in seeking an end to racial discrimination.

– B –

BANCO AUSTRAL. One of the most prominent banks in Mozambique founded in 1977 but privatized in 1997. Reportedly, it is primarily owned by several high government officials and has assets in the neighborhood of $U.S.1.9 billion. The **International Monetary Fund** (IMF) and the World Bank have had funds in this institution. The bank, which has several subsidiaries in the country, has been featured in the news lately as a result of the banking irregularities that seem to have plagued it, causing many investors and depositors to lose either money or confidence in it. Many borrowers have also been defaulting in debt payments. The names of several debtors and debt amounts were leaked to the press in 2001 and thus publicly discussed in Maputo. The string of adverse reports culminated in the mysterious murder (some claim it was a suicide) of 34-year-old interim bank manager António Siba-Siba Macuacua on August 11, 2001. The government immediately launched an investigation, enlisting the support of the South African police. Yet, little progress had been made in the search for the motives that led to the death of the Banco Austral's official and the individual(s) who perpetrated the crime.

***BANDIDOS ARMADOS* (ARMED BANDITS).** Expression used by the
Mozambique government and its allies to refer to **RENAMO** followers
during the **civil war.** Used similarly in many conflicts in Africa and elsewhere in the world, the expression was designed to delegitimize the struggle waged by RENAMO, weaken the perception of its effectiveness in battle, and create the impression that it had no plans or specific goals for the
country. The history and success of the movement, however, proved that
RENAMO adherents were not simply "bandits" but determined fighters
with a goal in mind, namely, to change the structure of power in Mozambique, to end **FRELIMO**'s socialist policies, and to force Western-type
democratic reforms in the country. Even William Finnegan, a staff writer
for the *New Yorker* and a frelimophile, wrote, "The government and many
Mozambicans called RENAMO *bandidos armados* 'armed bandits,' but
any suggestion that Renamo's operations were uncoordinated banditry
would have been misplaced." (See Finnegan, *A Complicated War*, 1992.)

BANEANES. Hindu merchants who settled in or did long-distance trading with Mozambique, beginning in 1686 and welcomed by the viceroy
of India. At first, administrators encouraged the Baneanes to set up
businesses in Mozambique. As time elapsed and the Baneanes became
successful, however, the **Portuguese** settlers as well as administrators
resented their business methods, accusing them of cheating, usury,
greed, and disrespect for the Portuguese authorities. Their Hindu practices also brought contempt for them from the Portuguese. However,
trading from the interior to the coast of Mozambique and to India, and
enjoying the friendship of the Jesuits and some powerful administrators, the Baneanes continued their activities even up to the 20th century. **Mouzinho de Albuquerque** accused them of taking advantage of
the Africans and curbed their activities in Gaza and in the southern interior. The major contention was that, while their business practices impoverished the colony, the Baneanes enriched themselves and their
families.

BARUE. The Barue people live in the Barue region along the **Manica**
Plateau, with its center at Vila Catandica. They have been classified as a
Shona subgroup. Barue clans seem to include the Choko, Tembo, Makate,
Chiware, Mucatu, Chilendje, and Nyanguru. From the 17th to the 20th cen-
turies, the Abarue were governed by powerful kings known as **Macombe**
(Makombe), who fiercely resisted both **Nguni** and **Portuguese** subjugation.

BEIRA. Port city and provincial capital of **Sofala Province**, located at the mouths of the Pungue and Buzi Rivers on the Mozambique Channel. Founded in 1891 by the **Companhia de Moçambique** as its capital, Beira was taken by the colonial state in 1941. Due to its railway and **roads** that link it to **South Africa**, Zimbabwe, Zambia, Malawi, and even Zaire, as well as its port facilities used by the surrounding countries, Beira used to be a bustling city. Commercial activities in the city were virtually paralyzed during the 1980s as a result of **RENAMO** operations. Beira exports several goods such as tobacco, foodstuffs, wheat, textiles, beverages, and equipment and provides meat and fish refrigeration facilities. The latest estimates put the population of the city at 300,000 people. The people of Beira complain bitterly that their city has been neglected by the government, as proven by the state of road disrepair, abandoned trash in the streets, and the virtual lack of new construction in the city.

BEIRA CORRIDOR. Railway and **road** linking Zimbabwe and Mozambique borders, from **Manica**, Zimbabwe, to the port of Beira, Mozambique. The corridor is a major outlet to the sea for landlocked Zimbabwe. One of the reasons Zimbabwe decided to join the war in Mozambique in 1981 was to safeguard this vital economic corridor. Indeed, in 1982, Zimbabwe dispatched 1,000 troops (upgraded to 3,000 by 1984) to the area, as well as to the **Tete** corridor, since both had become targets of **RENAMO** incursions, especially after it had blown up several petrol tanks and depots in the outskirts of Beira. The strategic Beira corridor consists of a railway, a highway, and an **oil** pipeline that link several countries—Mozambique, Zambia, Malawi, and Zimbabwe—allowing the landlocked countries to avoid both apartheid **South Africa** that was pursuing its racist policies then and the long distance to the Indian Ocean. *See also* RAILROAD; TRANSPORT.

BELO, JOÃO. As a prominent **Portuguese** settler who lived more than 30 years in Mozambique, Belo became the last colonial minister during the republican regime. He was not in favor of the newly approved colonial financial and economic autonomy under the High Commissioner statute, even though he resented the strangling power of the Banco Nacional Ultramarino. As a settler, Belo had opposed the 1909 **Mozambique-Transvaal Convention,** as he realized that it was draining the labor force from the south, thus preventing major economic development schemes here. Instead, he wished to quickly develop the coal mines of Moatize, **Tete**, build more **railroads**, and return the schools from the hands of the lay "civilizing" brigades of the republic to the missionaries in the colonies, especially in Mozambique. Belo is also credited with initiating a revision of the labor code in 1928, just before his premature death that January. Prior to his death, however, Belo had been able to exert pressure on Mozambique high commissioner Vítor Hugo Azevedo Coutinho to approve a Sugar Project at Umbeluzi Valley whose workers would be recruited through the same methods and from the same areas as those contained in the 1909 Mozambique-Transvaal Convention, namely, the **Witwatersrand Native Labour Association** (WNLA, WENELA). On these issues, opinion in the upper echelons of government was highly divided both in Lisbon and Lourenço Marques. The dispute led to the intervention of José Cabral, Mozambique high commissioner (1926–38), who ordered cancellation of the Hornung contract, approved the Umbeluzi Valley Project, and even provided a government grant toward its inception. The move turned into a personal humiliation for Cabral who was forced to cancel the Umbeluzi Valley Industry Project and resign as high commissioner. The 1928 Mozambique Convention, even though it silenced **South Africa** from its intentions of controlling the Mozambique-Transvaal Railway and the **Delagoa Bay Harbor**, returned the status quo to Mozambique. Indeed, while WNLA was given the same labor recruiting rights, Mozambique was unable to rid itself of foreign capital and influence.

BETTENCOURT, JOSÉ TRISTÃO DE. Governor-general of Mozambique (1940–47), who introduced quotas on cotton production to villages forced to grow this cash crop. Bettencourt was the first to appoint *capatazes* (overseers) to ensure that growers would produce the necessary quantity. Peasants forced to grow cotton were provided with free seeds and subject to frequent visits by the *chefe do posto* and his *cipaios* or African policemen. Because of his harsh forced labor and cotton cultivation policies as well as the compulsory military conscription he enforced, Bettencourt did not leave a reputation of a great governor of Mozambique, then officially known as an overseas province of **Portugal**.

BILHETE DE IDENTIDADE. An identification card introduced during the 1920s and required of Portuguese citizens and the assimilated Africans. *See also ASSIMILAÇÃO.*

BOLETIM DA SOCIEDADE DE GEOGRAFIA DE MOÇAMBIQUE (1881–1883). Founded at the capital, the *Boletim* was canceled after only three years of existence due to pressures from the Sociedade de Geografia de Lisboa, which opposed its existence as a competing journal.

BOLETIM DO GOVERNO DA PROVÍNCIA DE MOÇAMBIQUE (May 13, 1854–June 1975). First official organ of the colony of Mozambique, replaced by the *Boletim da República* in 1975.

BRADO AFRICANO, O (BA). A newspaper of protest created by the Associação Africana at Lourenço Marques in 1918 owned and run by the famous Albasini brothers. It survived until 1936, when the Antonio Salazar regime abolished it. *See also* ALBASINI, JOÃO.

BRAGANÇA, AQUINO DE (1918–1986). An Indian by origin, Aquino de Bragança was one of President **Samora Machel**'s most trusted advisers and died with him in an airplane crash on October 19, 1986. A skillful diplomat, Aquino was involved in the peace negotiations that led to the independence of the Portuguese colonies. He was the director of the African Studies Center at Eduardo Mondlane University.

BRAZIL. One of the countries that is exerting considerable influence in Mozambique is Brazil. As a more developed Lusophone country and a part of the world that received on its soil and assimilated so many thousands of slaves from Mozambique, Brazil has much more to offer to Mozambique than many others, including perhaps **Portugal** itself. Apart from its assistance to Mozambique in the areas of economic development, education, and health, Brazil's influence in the country is more pronounced in the sector of culture, television programs, news, the arts (music, dance, and theater), entertainment, books, and magazines, prominently visible in households libraries, airport stands, and university bookstores. As a result, many Mozambicans express the fear that, in the near future, Brazil may replace Portugal as a colonizer. In the area of culture, it appears that the fear is well founded.

BRITISH SENA SUGAR ESTATES. Authorized in 1925, the company concentrated its efforts on sugarcane plantations, mainly in the old Sena *prazos*.

BRITISH ULTIMATUM. Ultimatum delivered to the **Portuguese** government in Lisbon on January 11, 1890. Drafted by Lord Salisbury, the Conservative Party British foreign secretary, it demanded that the Portuguese authorities telegraph the governor-general of Mozambique immediately and order him to withdraw all Portuguese forces from the Macololo area entailing Mashonaland and the Shire River, which Serpa

Pinto had annexed in 1889. The British vessel *Enchantress*, waiting on the Tagus River, was ready to bring aboard the whole British diplomatic corps, should the Portuguese not comply with the ultimatum that afternoon. The ultimatum also contained the threat of the use of force by British troops in the area against the Portuguese occupation. Meanwhile, to reinforce the ultimatum, Britain had dispatched a warship to the Indian Ocean. **Portugal**, a weaker nation, capitulated, and assured the British that the troops would be withdrawn immediately. As a result of this national humiliation, the government of Luciano de Castro (president of the Ministerial Council) resigned on January 13, 1890.

On August 20, 1890, the two contenders signed a preliminary treaty, which the Cortes ratified on June 11, 1891. The terms of the treaty made **Manica** plateau part of Rhodesia and allowed Portugal to keep the Zumbo *prazos*. However, the ultimatum caused an uproar in Lisbon and Mozambique, where foreigners, particularly the British, were harassed. Portuguese historians have long considered the ultimatum to be the greatest humiliation their country has ever suffered since the Spanish occupation of the Portuguese throne in 1580.

– C –

CABO DELGADO. Until 1975, district administrative center and now the northeastern province of Mozambique, with a surface area of 30,260 square miles, inhabited by 1,284,000 people (1997 estimate), most of whom are **Maconde**. Pemba, formerly Porto Amélia, is its capital city and port. Bordering Tanzania through the Rovuma River in the north, **Niassa** Province in the west, the Lúrio River in the south, and the Indian Ocean in the northeast, Cabo Delgado is known for its rivers (particularly Lugenda and Messalo) and its agricultural crops, which include rice, sisal, cashew nuts, cotton, manioc, and sorghum. Its town of Mueda, where the **Portuguese** massacred 500 Africans who were protesting colonial policies on June 16, 1960, has been heralded as the birthplace of the modern revolutionary struggle in Mozambique.

CAETANO, DR. MARCELLO JOSÉ NEVES ALVES (1906–1980). Professor of law and one of the main architects of the **Portuguese** constitution, colonial minister of colonies (1944–49), deputy prime minister (1955–1959), rector of the University of Lisbon (1959–78), and premier of Portugal (September 1978–April 25, 1974). Although he helped revise the Portuguese constitution in 1951 and collaborated with **António Salazar** in changing some of the colonial statutes, Caetano's philosophy did not differ much from Salazar's. His idea of autonomy for the overseas territories would have still relegated the Africans to a colonial status within the Portuguese empire and denied independence to the colonies. His government was overthrown by the **Movimento das Forças Armadas** (MFA) (Armed Forces Movement) on April 25, 1974, which exiled him to Rio de Janeiro, where he died in 1980.

CAHORA (CABORA) BASSA. Portugal's most enduring physical and economic structure, the Cahora Bassa Dam construction started in 1969 and was completed in 1974. The 2,075-MW dam can contain 57 million cubic meters of water, is equipped with 408 MW generators, and is 137 meters high. It has the capacity to generate 18,000 kilowatts of electricity per hour (7,000 more than the Aswan Dam and 9,000 more than Kariba). It was built by a consortium of **Portuguese**, German, British, and South African companies, and it can supply electricity to Mozambique, **South Africa**, Zambia, and Zimbabwe. The South African government is estimated to have contributed about 20 percent to the total construction cost of $517.7 million.

Managed by the Portuguese Companhia Hidro-Eléctrica de Cahora Bassa (CHCH), the dam also irrigates some 140,000 square kilometers (54,687 square miles) of land along the **Zambezi River**. Through a 1,400-kilometer (840-mile) power line, Cabora Bassa provides over 80 percent of South Africa's electricity needs. A 1974 agreement regulating the operation of the dam was amended in May 1984, two months after the signing of the Nkomati Accord, with South Africa pledging to double the rate of its overall payment: 1,450 MW at a total cost of R90 million (about $71.9 million a year), of which between $5 million and $10 million would go to Mozambique and the remainder to the consortium.

During the liberation war, **FRELIMO** had vowed to destroy the dam because it stood for the ongoing Portuguese occupation of the colony and dramatized South Africa's economic stranglehold on Mozambique. Following independence, however, FRELIMO realized the potential benefits from the dam and, therefore, did all it could to protect it against **RENAMO**, which on several occasions succeeded in blowing up its pylons. In fact, in 1984, South Africa and Mozambique, in the spirit of the Nkomati Accord, agreed to establish a joint force to protect the dam and patrol the area. In April 1988, further talks were held to find more effective ways to implement the agreement.

Following the 1992 peace accord, the dam has provided electricity to Mozambique, Zimbabwe, and South Africa. Electricity consumption has increased tremendously in Mozambique from 118 MW in 1977 to 235 MW in 1998, the consumer number rising from 62,000 individuals to 186,000 the same year. Unfortunately, much of the Cahora Bassa energy will go to benefit the neighboring countries. In April 1992, Mozambique and Zimbabwe signed a power line construction contract, at a cost of $45 million, which was completed in January 1998, providing 500 MW of electricity to Mozambique's western neighbor. In 1994, Malawi and Swaziland also signed an agreement for Mozambique to share its electricity with them. Zambia, on the other hand, benefits from the dam's 250-kilometer- (150-mile-) long lake that irrigates 1.5 million hectares of its land.

Several other dams either have been completed or are in the process of being built, including two on the Revue River west of Beira at Chicamba Real and Mavuzi, and two on the Limpopo River, namely, Massingi and Corumana. In 2001, the Zambezi dam flooded the areas along the Zambezi Valley, especially in **Tete** Province, as technicians tried to release the pressure from the rains, which could have burst the dam itself.

CAMACHO, MANUEL DE BRITO. First Mozambique high commissioner (1921–23). The creation of a high commissioner by the **Portuguese** republican regime was intended to elevate the colonial status of the overseas territories to autonomy, allowing each colony to have its own legislative council, control its finances, implement its own inheritance statutes, and liquidate its debts. The newly created high commissioner would be a member of the cabinet in the metropolitan government and empowered, at least on paper, to make political, administrative, and economic decisions in the colony.

Unfortunately, in Mozambique, Camacho would encounter almost insuperable obstacles: a relatively huge debt, a situation that was aggravated by control of the economy by foreign concessionaire companies and the crippling labor recruitment impact of the 1909 Mozambique-Transvaal Convention. Camacho's financial and economic plan envisaged freeing Mozambique from its debt and from the control of the Banco Nacional Ultramarino (BNU), which, with a monopolistic iron hand, issued bank notes for the colonies. He further wished to spur the economy with increased production, while depending less on imports. His task was made the more difficult by the interference of British citizens' interests in Mozambique, who had the ability to block his efforts to secure international loans, and by the efforts of Jan Smuts of Transvaal, who insisted on gaining control of the Lourenço Marques **railroad** and the **Delagoa Bay** Harbor in Mozambique. Thus, in his attempt to reinvigorate the local economy, Camacho granted J. P. Hornung the Sena Sugar Company contract in 1921 and pledged to annually provide the company with 3,000 workers, who would be recruited in Mozambique District. Subsequently, he offered Hornung more hectares of land in Luabo, **Zambézia**. However, both the Portuguese settlers and the international community, including members of the League of Nations, opposed the contract and the forced labor recruitment agreement. As a result, Camacho's policy caused such an uproar that he had to resign after serving only 20 months as high commissioner. Ironically, Hornung was paying his laborers a salary three times higher than that paid by other companies in the neighboring colonies. Economic conditions in the colony deteriorated during Camacho's tenure. Indeed, the only legacy Camacho left was his resistance to **South Africa**'s attempt to control the Lourenço Marques railway, a move that paid off when the 1928 Convention replaced the 1909 agreement, which had expired in 1923. *See also* BELO, JOÃO.

CÂMARAS MUNICIPAIS. Municipal councils created during the 1960s to function in district capitals and townships with at least 500 electors. They were headed by a president, comparable to a mayor in the **United States**.

CANARIN. Indians of Goan descent who were so designated during the early period of **Portuguese** presence in Mozambique. The word is not frequently used today in Mozambique. Early Canarins, usually Catholic, occupied several important positions in Mozambique (e.g., as priests, administrators, soldiers, teachers, clerks, and merchants). Because of their skills, the Portuguese favored their immigration to Mozambique, entrusting them with responsibilities befitting only a Portuguese citizen (and not an African). Thus, taking Portuguese names, many Canarins fought alongside the Portuguese in the wars against the Africans and helped colonize sections of the **Zambezi** Valley during the time of the *prazos*. Their privileged position in Mozambique could be compared only to that of their contemporary *Baneanes* or Indians, most of whom professed Hinduism rather than Catholicism.

CAPECEIROS. Equivalent to a police force operating in and around **RENAMO**'s military bases in northern Mozambique. Many of the capeceiros had served as *cipaios*, police officers, security men, or spies during the colonial period or had been **FRELIMO** lower-level members or sympathizers who became disenchanted with the party. Serving also as intermediaries between the base and the population, the capeceiros were not directly involved in fighting the war, but they protected the combatants and often collected taxes for RENAMO. They were not directly paid either, even though some were often rewarded in kind and at times, with women, especially following a strenuous operation. Some capeceiros did exert influence with the soldiers they protected and advised the base captains whether, for example, someone's life should be spared or terminated.

CARDOSO, CARLOS (1951–2000). Prominent journalist gunned down by hired men in **Maputo** as he left his office on November 22, 2000. Cardoso was born in **Beira** in 1951 and, after completing secondary school, he enrolled at the Witwatersrand University in **South Africa**. Just at the time of Mozambique independence and before completing his studies, the South African authorities expelled Cardoso allegedly because of his political activities. In Maputo, he became founder, owner, and editor of the newspaper *Metical,* which was very critical of government corruption and its financial institutions, such as the Banco de Moçambique and the **Banco Austral**. He condemned organized crime and those who were attempting to derail the movement toward the creation of true democratic institutions in Mozambique. His death caused an uproar not only in Mozambique but also abroad. As in most cases that defy explanation, allegations of conspiracy were widespread throughout the city of Maputo. The government promised to complete its investigation, prosecute, and punish the culprits. Prime Minister **Pascoal Mocumbi** pledged to do just that in his briefing to the press on the occasion of Freedom of the Press World Day, May 3, 2001. In February 2003, the men involved were finally sentenced to prison following a long, unprecedented televised trial of the murderers.

CARTÃO DE IDENTIDADE. An identification card required of the educated Africans prior to obtaining the *caderneta de identidade* as proof of assimilation. *See also ASSIMILAÇÃO.*

CASA DOS ESTUDANTES DO IMPÉRIO (CEI). A student center established in Lisbon by and for assimilated and educated Africans during the 1920s and banned for its political activities in 1961. Prominent members included **Marcelino dos Santos** (Mozambique), Amílcar Cabral (Guinea-Bissau), and Mário Andrade (Angola).

CATHOLIC CHURCH. The role of the Catholic Church remained crucial to the **Portuguese** state since the beginning of the Portuguese voyages across the oceans. All major sea enterprises made provisions to carry a handful of missionaries or priests not only to take care of the spiritual needs of the navigators themselves but also to spread the gospel among the newly "discovered" people. Insofar as the colonies were concerned, the Portuguese monarchs always held the belief that the church would be the best instrument for the advancement of the objectives of the mother country. They saw the church as essentially playing a double role, namely, that of converting and civilizing, of spreading news about **Portugal** and evangelizing the "pagans." In fact, the relations between church and state, the secular and the spiritual, became so entrenched that no African, unless baptized a Roman Catholic, could be granted the rights and privileges of assimilation.

Decrees and pronouncements dating as far back as the origins of Portuguese expansion to the missionary Accords (*Acordos*) and Statutes (*Estatutos*) of the 1940s, had stressed the church's dual role. The 1930 **Colonial Act,** for example, noted that "The overseas religious missions, instruments of civilization, of national influence, and the establishments of training for its service and the *Padroado*, will have juridical personality and be protected by the state as institutions of education." The church itself accepted with eagerness and pride its dual mission, which was well imbedded in the Missionary Statutes, agreed with the Holy See in 1940 and 1941. Therefore, the evangelization of the Africans and their secular education had been entrusted to missionaries for centuries. The hope was that the church would impart in the Africans the fear of God, the virtues of Christianity, appreciation for the value of work, and love for Portugal.

The work of the Catholic Church in Mozambique goes back to the 16th century when the first missionaries arrived, dramatized by the visit to Mozambique Island in 1542 of Jesuit Francis Xavier, who, on his way to India, was forced to stay a few months in the colony. Significant also was the arrival in **Sofala** in 1560 of Father Gonçalo da Silveira, who was brutally assassinated in the following year by agents of the **Mwenemutapa** king whom he had converted to Roman Catholicism. Having run out of steam after the death of Gonçalo da Silveira, the Jesuits abandoned the Mwenemutapa mission soon thereafter, in 1572. Meanwhile, in 1568, Dominican Father João dos Santos landed in Sofala; by 1589, he reportedly had baptized 17,000 people. By 1604, the Dominicans had penetrated as far into the hinterland as Mwenemutapa, where they built churches and baptized not only the common people but also several members of the royal families and their entourage. The Dominicans began their work in Sena and crossed the colony into Zimbabwe. By 1720, Dominican Father Pedro da Trindade was at Zumbo, far into the interior, along the Zambezi River, outside of the *prazo* system of the Lower Zambezi. While the Brothers of São João de Deus had been on Mozambique Island since 1681, where they built a hospital and a convent around 1707, the secular priests had been ministering the Macombe palace in Barue since 1695, and the Capuchins had built churches and evangelized the Africans in the area, along with the Jesuits who, by 1610, had made it back. Until their expulsion by the Marquis of Pombal in 1759, the Jesuits, for the most part, except for Cabeceira in the north, Luabo, Sena, Caia, Chemba, and **Tete**, as well as along the **Zambezi**, opposite to Mozambique island, had established missions at **Quelimane** Valley, and once more in the lands of Mwenemutapa. However, Pombal tried to fill the empty spaces left by the Jesuits by ordering in 1761 the foundation of a seminary, on the model of the Goan seminaries, for the education of white, *mestiço*, and black clergy, to be built on **Mozambique Island**, where the Jesuit College had stood before. The project came to nothing due to a lack of funds.

These setbacks notwithstanding, the pope decided that the prelates for the Catholic Church of Mozambique ought to be consecrated bishops. The first in this line of the hierarchy was Dominican Frei Amaro José de São Thomás, who was appointed autonomous bishop of Mozambique in 1783. Previously, in 1612, Pope Paul V had created the Mozambique Prelacy, dismembering Mozambique from the hierarchical control of Goa. Yet, its occupants did not have to be consecrated bishops. Until 1783, several were simple prelate administrators of the various missions in the colony, and were then elevated to the bishopric. The expulsion of the Jesuits in 1759 was followed by the anticlerical wave of the 1830s that swept Portugal and brought the church in Mozambique to its knees. When all religious orders were expelled from Portuguese territory in 1834, the colonial church experienced a crisis from which it never recovered completely. As a result, by 1887, only eight priests remained in the colony.

Unfortunately, since the 17th century, a religious cancer had been growing slowly within the colonial clergy. Many priests had simply put aside their vows, particularly those of poverty and chastity. Ignorance was rampant to the extent that some priests had to be sent back to Portugal or Goa because they were neither adequately trained nor committed to properly evangelize the people. In fact, the clergy was in such disarray that Goan Bishop Henrique, prelate of Mozambique, resigned his post in 1886, convinced that there was no hope for Christianity in the colony. During the 1890s, Bishop Francisco Ferreira da Silva complained about the moral decay he found among the missionaries. This situation was complicated by the fact that, although the monarchy relied on the church, the government did not provide it with adequate financial support. Some priests were so poor, says military historian and Governor-General Xavier Botelho, that they had to steal the shoes they wore.

Until the late 1880s, almost no missionaries arrived from Portugal, since the government had closed the Seminary of Cernache do Bomjardim, a source of missionaries, in 1834. The Seminary of Cernache do Bomjardim in Portugal had been designed as a stop gap institute in 1791 for the education of Portuguese secular clergy for the colonies replacing the Jesuits after 1759. The Cernache priests had worked all over the empire, mostly in Africa and in Timor. Regrettably, for two reasons, the seminary was closed in 1834. One was the fact that its teachers were Lazarists, considered to be a religious order, and the other being that unwanted Jesuits were known to have previously taught there.

The rocky relations between church and state from the 1830s to the 1880s had improved considerably just prior to the Republic, which was inaugurated in Lisbon in 1910. Yet, immediately thereafter, until 1922, relations soured again, to a point where, in 1913, the government attempted to replace the missionaries in the school system altogether by sending the so-called Missões Civilizadoras Laicas (or the lay civilizing brigades) to Mozambique. The experiment failed miserably, and, in 1922, and again in 1926, although declaring separation between church and state, the government decreed that the Catholic Church would be supported by the state and its priests be considered, for subsistence purposes, as functionaries of the state.

Ironically, at this critical junction, it was the priests of Cernache do Bomjardim, for a long time also known as the Missionaries of Cucujães, who once again stepped in to save the missionary situation in the colonies. After being abolished, along with the religious orders in 1834, as noted earlier, the Seminary of Cernache do Bomjardim was reinstituted in 1844 at the request of Bishop Veríssimo Vaz Serra, who had worked as a missionary in China. Thus, Cernache missionaries were once again sent to serve in Angola, Mozambique, and Timor. They worked side by side with their lay counterparts, the Missões Civilizadoras.

Conditions began to improve during the 1880s. The Jesuit Order was allowed to return in 1881, when its missionaries began founding new mission stations along the Zambezi Valley, in **Quelimane**, Chupanga, Caia, **Sena**, Boroma, Zumbo, and Nhamussua in **Inhambane**. They also reoccupied the parish church of Tete, left vacant in 1838 by the death of the last Dominican priest, Fr. António Nunes da Graça. In 1908, the Jesuits opened the Angónia mission in the upper Tete Province, their last station before the republican decrees of 1910. Meanwhile, the Franciscans joined the Jesuits in the field at **Beira** City in 1898. As a result, by 1891, some 21 priests had resumed missionary work in Mozambique, and church buildings began to rise again.

Yet, the Jesuits saw themselves being expelled once again from Mozambique. They did not return except to their missions in Boroma and Angónia in 1941. In the meantime, the Holy See, Germany, and Austria-Hungary, and, to a certain extent, France had succeeded in convincing Portugal to let the Missionaries of the Divine Word replace the Jesuits in their vacated missions along the **Zambezi** Valley. However, given the fact that the missionaries of the Divine Word were, for the most part, German and Austrian, their stay in Mozambique lasted only until 1916, when Portugal entered World War I against Germany.

The missionary impetus of the 1880s continued although at a very slow pace, so that, in 1933 the church erected 27 new churches in Mozambique, served by about 60 priests. The number of Catholics in the colony also began to increase steadily, from fewer than 1,000 in the 1870s to 3,500 in 1905, 40,000 in 1936, 85,333 in 1940, and 900,000 in 1967. During the 1960s and 1970s, more than 600 priests toiled in the colony, administering more than 230 churches in eight dioceses. At that time, the religious orders included Franciscans; Capuchins; Lazarists; Priests of the Blessed Sacrament; White Fathers or Missionaries of Africa; Marist Brothers; Montfortins; Priests of the Consolata, Priests of the Heart of Jesus, and Priests of the Sacred Heart of Mary; Overseas Catholic Mission Fathers, the new name the old Missionaries of Cucujães adopted after the 1975 revolution in Portugal; the Priests of Burgos; and the Jesuits, along with several secular priests in the town parishes and episcopal sees.

The secular, educational task in Mozambique started as early as the 18th century, especially at Mozambique Island, the seat of the prelate, where schools for African and European children, particularly the poor, had just been established. In 1875, Prelate José Caetano Gonçalves tried to re-create the century-old idea of the Marquis de Pombal by founding a seminary on Mozambique Island. The seminary enrolled 12 African seminarians but was abandoned two years later due to an insufficient number of candidates. In 1910, Catholics administered several educational institutes: Dona Amélia at Lourenço Marques, Santa Catarina de Sena at Messano, São José de Lhanguene, Pio X at Beira, Santa Joana at Quelimane, and Leão XIII at Cabeceira Grande. Eventually, all rudimentary schools (called Escolas de Adaptação) were entrusted to the missions.

The fastest growth of the Catholic schools occurred during the 1960s, as a result of an unprecedented increase in the number of priests and Catholic missions. In 1964, for example, the Catholic missions had 2,233 rudimentary schools and 268 other types of institutions, which provided instruction to more than 400,000 students. The idea of an African indigenous clergy finally came to fruition when the dioceses, established in the aftermath of the Missionary Accords of 1940 and Statutes of 1941, established seminaries in the colony for the training of Africans to the priesthood. Initially, there were three such institutions. While the Seminary of Santa Teresinha do Menino Jesus of Magude served the dioceses of the south, the Seminary of São João de Brito, at Zobue, Tete Province, received candidates from the central areas of Mozambique. The Seminary of Unango served the only diocese of the north at the time, **Nampula**. Some missionary congregations, such as the Jesuits back in their own missions, sent their most hopeful priesthood candidates to their own seminaries in Portugal.

As independence approached, the Catholic hierarchy, symbolized by the archbishop of Lourenço Marques, **Dom Teodósio Clemente de Gouveia** and **Custódio Alvim Pereira**, sided with the Portuguese state, denouncing nationalists and even allowing the secret police to harass vocal priests, especially if they happened to be foreign. Exceptions to this attitude could be found, however, as was the case of the bishop of Beira. **Dom Sebastião Soares de Resende** was convinced that independence for the colonies was inevitable (although he envisaged the closest ties between the mother country and its former colonies). Eventually, there was a split between the Portuguese clergy and the majority of the foreign missionaries: The latter tended to favor the nationalist aspirations of the Africans. Thus, in 1971, the White Fathers, Brothers, and Nuns, numbering more that 50, refused to be tools of Portuguese colonialism and left the colony, a rare occurrence in recent missionary history, not only in Mozambique but also in Africa as a whole.

The centuries-old alliance between church and state explains why FRELIMO viewed with suspicion the Catholic clergy, including the African priests, numbering only about 20, in 1974. Churches were confiscated and their properties expropriated by the government, forcing many of the priests to celebrate mass under trees or in secular places. The Catholic bishops spoke out against the government's overt anticlericalism and reminded the authorities that the Mozambique constitution upheld religious freedom. Yet, the situation began to improve only during 1980s, especially after **Joaquim Chissano** assumed the presidency of Mozambique. In 2001, the Catholic Church boasted some six million faithful and had 11 dioceses, Maputo, Beira, Inhambane, **Xai-Xai, Chimoio**, Tete, Quelimane, Nampula, **Pemba, Nacala**, and Gurue.

CAVALO MARINHO. Along with the *palmatória*, the *cavalo marinho*, a whip made out of hippopotamus skin, was an infamous device used by the **Portuguese** to punish school children and grown up Africans accused of crimes and misdemeanors. The Portuguese teachers, prison wards, and workers' overseers, all used the cavalo marinho. In the fields, on plantations and **road** construction projects, the whip was intended to punish those considered to be lazy and insubordinate. With time, Africans who assumed the position of the Portuguese in schools and elsewhere, such as the *cipais* (or *cipaios*), also availed themselves of the device to punish recalcitrant fellow Africans.

CENTRAL COMMITTEE (FRELIMO). FRELIMO's executive, elected by the Congress, and responsible for the day-to-day activities of the party. It meets once a year at the request of the Politburo. The Central Committee elects the Congress members and has a secretariat. The number of Central Committee members has varied, but it had 130 members in 2001.

CHAIMITE. Gungunhana's headquarters in the **Gaza** empire on the Save River, where **Mouzinho de Albuquerque** arrested the **Nguni** leader on December 28, 1895.

CHAPA-CEM. Designation of small size public transportation vehicles that crisscross the Mozambique **roads** and highways. Fast and overloaded with twice as many passengers as they are supposed to carry, Chapa-Cems cause hundreds of deaths in the country every year. They stop virtually anywhere on the road and do not leave their station until they are full to capacity. The designation comes from the Portuguese words *chapa,* which means "patch," and *cem,* meaning "100." This name means that the vehicles are usually in bad shape, and, when they started to operate after independence, they were very cheap to ride, the fare being as low as one hundred *meticais* (less than U.S.$0.10) at that time. A Chapa-Cem is comparable to the Matatu in Kenya.

***CHARLES ET GEORGES* AFFAIR.** An incident that occurred in 1857, when the **Portuguese** authorities in Mozambique intercepted the French vessel *Charles et Georges*, loaded with 110 Mozambique slaves on their way to the French islands on the Indian Ocean. The behavior of the French contravened the 1836 law abolishing the slave trade in the Portuguese colonies. *See also* SLAVERY.

CHIBALO, NTALATO. African vernacular words used for the forced labor to which the Africans were subjected. According to the law, a contract had to be put in written form, and an employer could not mistreat his employee or cheat the laborer out of his due salary. However, in practice, an African usually worked from six to nine months a year on forced labor for a company, a private **Portuguese** citizen (including the *assimilado*), or the government, almost always away from his home, and was paid only at the end of his contract, at which time he also had to pay taxes. Meanwhile, he had to leave his family unattended at home. His wages were so low that they would not allow him to provide for them. Chibalo or ntalato, depending on the area of the country, contributed to rebellion in the colony, which culminated in the liberation movement. *See also* ASSIMILAÇÃO.

CHICUNDA. The Chicunda, about 1,200,000, were originally warrior slaves who, from the mid–16th century to their demise in the wake of the Zulu invasions in the early and mid-19th centuries, served mainly as the military arm on the *prazos* or crown estates along the **Zambezi** Valley. In time, they developed their own ethnic identity. The Chicunda descendants, who acknowledge themselves as such, are found in pockets scattered throughout the geographic reaches formerly encapsulated within the prazo system in Zambia, Malawi, and the upper and lower Zambezi Valley in Mozambique.

CHIMOIO. Formerly Vila Pery, now a city of 171,000 people, Chimoio used to thrive on the Beira-Mutare **railroad** and its rail link with the port of **Beira**. During the 1960s, it was a significant commercial center, enriched by a cotton factory run by the Sociedade Algodoeira de Fomento Colonial (Colonial Cotton Development Company), which employed some 3,000 workers. Beside the cotton industry, Chimoio had sawmills and steel and other minor industrial plants. The town's surrounding areas produce tobacco, corn, castor beans, kenaf, peanuts, and millet. The Revue River generates hydroelectric power for the town. Trucks loaded with cash crops (mainly cotton and corn) from far away places such as Vila Gouveia (now Vila Catandica) constantly arrived in this town which housed a significant European population. Today, Chimoio is a bustling city and is known throughout Mozambique for its cleanliness. Lack of adequate water supply is, however, the city's most crippling problem.

CHIMWENJE. A little-known Zimbabwe dissident group operating mainly in Mozambique **Manica** Province in 1995. Its aim was to overthrow Robert Mugabe's government in Zimbabwe. **RENAMO** was accused of collaborating with the movement, but the two movements' leaders always denied the charges. In early 1996, several violent confrontations occurred between the Mozambique armed forces and Chimwenje rebels who frequently crossed the borders, disturbing the peace on both sides. Security forces from Mozambique and Zimbabwe mounted several combined assaults on the dissidents who were eventually eliminated or disbanded in late 1996.

CHINESE. Fewer than 5,000 Chinese business people have made Mozambique their permanent home.

CHINGONDO. Word pejoratively used by southerners to refer to the northerners in Mozambique. The etymology of the word is disputed, but the term itself seems to come from the African word *N'gondo* (war), which can be translated as "one who wages war."

CHISSANO, JOAQUIM ALBERTO (1939–). Appointed by the **FRE-LIMO Central Committee** president of Mozambique following the death of **Samora Machel** in 1986, Chissano was born in southern Mozambique and, after completing his secondary schooling in the colony, went to **Portugal** on a scholarship to study law. However, before completing his degree, inspired by nationalist motives and harassed by the **Portuguese** secret police, Chissano sought refuge in France, where he remained active as a nationalist. He became a member of **FRELIMO** in 1962 and, in 1963, he was elected to the Central Committee. He occupied the position of secretary to the presidency from 1966 to 1969. Between 1969 and 1974, he was the chief representative of FRELIMO in Dar-es-Salaam. He also served as chief of security during the war period. As a rising star on the Central Committee and a committed Marxist-Leninist, Chissano enjoyed the trust of Samora Machel. He served as prime minister of the **transitional government** in Mozambique in 1974–75 and was named foreign minister in independent Mozambique in 1975, a post he held until assuming the presidency of Mozambique in 1986. Chissano is reputed to be intelligent, educated, and a shrewd politician and statesman. Despite his commitment to Marxism, Chissano is thought to be much more pragmatic than Machel, notwithstanding his previous utterances that Mozambique would never abandon its close ties to the **Soviet Union** or his pledge to fight **RENAMO** until military victory was achieved. In fact, one of his first acts as president was a visit to the **United States** in 1987 to meet President Ronald Reagan and solicit assistance for his war-torn and drought-stricken country. In New York, he called and held a formal meeting with former Mozambican students and invited them to come home either to visit or to stay and contribute to national development. In 1987, he requested and received assistance from the **International Monetary Fund**, whose terms resulted in a drastic devaluation of the *metical*. Chissano is married and has three children.

Chissano was elected president in 1994 (by a vote of 53.3 percent to 33.73 for **Afonso Dhlakama**) and reelected in 1999 (52.29 percent Chissano and 47.71 percent Dhlakama) under Mozambique's new multiparty system. The 1999 election was angrily disputed and denounced by RENAMO, which called it fraudulent, as the first reports from the country had claimed victory for the opposition. The country's Supreme Court pronounced the election valid. In 2001, Chissano, whom people had for long considered an atheist, married his former wife in the **Catholic Church**, stunning everyone in the country.

CHOPE (SHOPE). Considered to be among the earliest inhabitants of Mozambique, the Chope (Chopi) are a small group and live in **Inhambane** and **Gaza** Provinces. The early Chope nucleus is believed to have come from two clans: the Nkumbe and the Vilankulu. According to oral tradition, Nkumbe, the founder, was related to the people of Inhambane and migrated from the north. Vilankulu, on the contrary, originated from the southwest and was related to the **Thonga**. The Vilankulu were the masters of the art of weaving and of the African piano, the *mbila*, a legacy they transmitted to the Chope. The Valenge and the Bitonga are Chope subgroups. The Chope and Bitonga combined entail about 600,000 people.

CHUABO. The patrilineal Chuabo encompass the Boror, the Maganja, and the Mahindo and live in **Zambezia** Province. Many of them live in **Maputo**, however, and hold prominent positions in government.

CIPAIO (SIPAIO, CIPAI, SIPAI). An African police officer usually assigned to a lower-level administrator or to the (African) *régulo* (chief) in colonial Mozambique. When attached to the régulo, the cipaio's function was to help recruit workers, arrest and beat individuals suspected of crimes or disobedience, and carry messages. Often, the ire of the Africans was directed against the cipaio, although in most cases he simply followed orders from his superiors.

CIRCUMSCRIÇÃO (TOWNSHIP). *See* ADMINSTRATION.

CIVIL WAR (1977–1992). Only two years into its independence, Mozambique was faced with a major political conflict that culminated in a full-blown civil war between **FRELIMO** and **RENAMO.** In 1977, a group of disgruntled party members and lower-level officers, including **Andre Matsangaissa,** from **Sofala** Province, were sent to reeducation camps by the new government on charges of corruption and embezzlement. However, these factors were only the tip of the iceberg, as discontent in the country had set in beginning the very day of the declaration of independence, June 25, 1975. For one, FRELIMO was selected by the **Portuguese** to be the inheritor of the colonial state without a referendum or an election, as many Mozambicans had expected. Therefore, many non-FRELIMO nationalists, would-be politicians, citizens, and the Portuguese settlers in the country resented the nonconsultative nature of the transfer of power to FRELIMO. FRELIMO Marxist nationalization policies and the announcement that it would be a vanguard party with strict membership requirements added to the already built-in pent-up frustrations. Mozambique's assistance to the **Zimbabwe African National Union (ZANU)** through the closure of the border with Southern Rhodesia to comply with **UN** sanctions prompted Ian Smith, leader of that strayed British territory, to assist logistically and militarily the first nucleus of the African resistance movement against the FRELIMO government.

When Zimbabwe became independent in 1980, **South Africa** took RENAMO under its wing, thus further infusing life to the movement, which by then was causing irreparable damage to Mozambique's infrastructure, **roads,** schools, health centers, and agricultural and industrial projects. To its dismay, RENAMO was accused of torture and the indiscriminate killing of civilians and of receiving aid from apartheid South Africa. While FRELIMO was intent on simply wiping out RENAMO fighters, which it called "armed bandits," the rebels' goal was to topple the socialist regime and implant what they termed a "democratic" government and a market-oriented economy.

An agreement between Presidents **Samora Machel** of Mozambique and Pieter Botha of South Africa making the two pledge not to support the **ANC** and RENAMO, respectively, collapsed the very day it was signed in March 1984. The demise of the **Soviet Union**, an ally of Mozambique, economic problems, and increased RENAMO's support in the country, convinced the government that a military solution was undesirable and perhaps impossible. This realization led to the **Acordo Geral da Paz** signed in Rome on October 4, 1992. The accord ended all hostilities in the country, introduced a market-oriented economy, legalized political parties, and, through UN auspices, facilitated the return of the nearly two million **refugees** scattered throughout Southern Africa.

After years of refusal to negotiate with RENAMO on account of its being "a gang of armed bandits," FRELIMO's change of heart surfaced when **Joaquim Chissano** authorized the **Catholic Church** and the Conselho Cristão de Mocambique of 17 denominations to initiate exploratory contacts with RENAMO representatives in Nairobi, Kenya, in August 1988. These contacts proved disappointing until February 1989 when the archbishop of Maputo, Cardinal Alexander dos Santos, Beira archbishop **Jaime Gonçalves**, and Maputo Anglican bishop Denis **Sengulane** met RENAMO's Army General Chief of Staff Raul Domingos and Secretary of Information Vicente Ululu. Through the clergy, both FRELIMO and RENAMO expressed the desire to establish official contacts and initiate negotiations that might end the armed conflict. Subsequently, the **United States** and South Africa declared their support of the effort.

On July 24–31, 1989, the Fifth FRELIMO **Congress** in Maputo endorsed a 12-point "statement of principles," letting RENAMO know that the government was willing to initiate negotiations through the mediation of President Daniel arap Moi of Kenya and President Robert Mugabe of Zimbabwe. In the document, however, FRELIMO asked RENAMO to renounce the use of violence, accept the Mozambique constitution, and abandon its "operation of destabilization, which should not be equated to a struggle between two parties." It called on Dhlakama to end "all acts of terrorism and banditry." This "Declaration of Principles" was presented by the three bishops to **Afonso Dhlakama** and his council in Nairobi in August 1989.

RENAMO was irked by the tone of the principles, which still viewed the adherents of the movement as *bandidos armados*. It was also dissatisfied with the statement on the inviolability of Mozambique's present constitution. In its formal reply, contained in a 16-point statement, REN-

AMO urged the withdrawal of Zimbabwe troops from Mozambique, while insisting on the recognition of RENAMO by FRELIMO as "an active political force" in Mozambique. While RENAMO leaders saw the "Declaration of Principles" as nothing more than a clever way of forcing RENAMO's capitulation, FRELIMO considered RENAMO's response unacceptable, as advocating the overthrow of the government by force and was unwilling to renounce all it had stood for during the past 15 years regarding a multiparty state, the complete rewriting of the constitution, and the establishment of a market-oriented economy. Thus, hopes of a quick solution were dashed, and RENAMO stepped up its activities, particularly in the provinces of **Zambézia, Manica,** Sofala, **Gaza,** and **Maputo,** cutting off electricity to the capital city on certain occasions, and capturing the town of Luabo on the Zambezi River on August 19, 1989.

In early December 1989, however, contacts between the two parties were reestablished, and Joaquim Chissano, in an address to a meeting of Lusophone African presidents at the city of Praia, Cape Verde, announced that presidential and general elections in Mozambique would be held in 1991 and that FRELIMO was willing to resume negotiations with RENAMO. Dhlakama's initial response was positive, although further clarification of positions on both sides was expected to follow. The two sides had finally agreed, therefore, that a military solution was unrealistic and that both had to swallow their pride and compromise to save the country and the people from continued destruction, famine, and death.

COLONATO. **Portuguese** system of colonization. *See COLONO.*

COLONO. A **Portuguese** term meaning "settler." As early as the 17th century, the Portuguese government unsuccessfully attempted to ensure the colonization of Mozambique by systematically sending settlers to the colony. During the mid–19th century, Sá da Bandeira tried to rationalize and expedite the process of colonization by selecting, whenever possible, educated individuals and those who demonstrated skills in industry, agriculture, and craft to occupy the lands of Mozambique and render them productive. Within the *prazos*, the term *colono* was also used to designate the Africans who lived on the premises with their landlords (*senhores*). The term *colonato* is a derivative, meaning settlement (mostly by Europeans), particularly along the **Zambezi** and Limpopo Valleys. Organized settlements proved to be such a failure that in **Zambézia**, for example, only 300 whites had settled in 1722, declining to 113 in 1735 and to 63 in 1782. For the colony as a whole, there were 2,141 white colonos in 1800,

18,842 in 1930, and 27,000 in 1940. The number rose to more than 48,000 in 1950 and reached 200,000 during the years prior to independence.

COMISSÃO NACIONAL ELEITORAL (CNE) (NATIONAL ELECTION COMMISSION). Established on January 21, 1994, the CNE was to prepare the country for the first multiparty democratic elections scheduled for October 27–28 that year. **Brazão Mazula,** a former Catholic priest and a civil servant in the Ministry of Education, was appointed chairman. The commission was composed of 10 members selected by the government, seven by **RENAMO,** and three by the remaining parties. On February 15, 1994, the commission announced its election timetable: June 1–August 15, voter registration; September 10–October 24, electoral campaign; and October 27–28, presidential and national assembly elections. The national assembly, called the Assembly of the Republic, would have 250 seats to be contested by the parties officially registered. Provincial and district elections were to follow. Financial assistance, totaling $64.5 million, coming mainly from the **United Nations** Development Program (UNDP), was designed to monitor the process and prepare the parties for the elections. Foreseeing problems, **Chissano** and **Dhlakama** agreed in November on a five-member Electoral Tribunal consisting of two Mozambican and three international judges, as proposed by the United Nations, whose responsibility was to hear electoral complaints and serve as an appeals court against the CNE. The members and alternate judges were sworn in on June 8, 1994. The electoral process itself was undoubtedly a major undertaking, requiring the training of 2,600 electoral officials at every national level, 8,000 census agents, 1,600 civic education agents, and 52,000 polling officers, joining a 12-person UNDP advisory team working with the CNE, and three to five United Nations volunteers, assigned to each of the 11 electoral constituencies. As expected, the CNE received much criticism as well as praise from both the Mozambican nationals and the international community. Ultimately, however, the CNE was credited with the relatively peaceful conduct of the electoral process, causing the international community to declare the elections free and fair. As a result of **Mazula**'s performance before the international community, President **Joaquim Alberto Chissano** appointed him rector of Eduardo Mondlane University in Maputo.

COMISSÕES MUNICIPAIS. Municipal (advisory) commissions in small towns and *circumscrições* with at least 300 electors, created during the mid-1960s.

COMITÉ NATIONAL INDEPENDENTE DE MOÇAMBIQUE (CON-IMO) (MOZAMBIQUE NATIONAL INDEPENDENT COMMIT-TEE).

A group of dissidents who disagreed with **RENAMO**'s alliance with **South Africa** but who could not support **FRELIMO** totally either, formed CONIMO in West Germany in 1985 and coalesced with the Democratic Party for the Liberation of Mozambique (PADELIMO), formed in Kenya in 1986. Following amalgamation, the new group called itself **Comité para a União Independente de Moçambique** (CUNIMO) (Committee for Mozambican Union), or what became known as the "Cologne Group." Both FRELIMO and RENAMO attempted to attract CUNIMO to its side, sensing how the German government was beginning to listen to the dissidents. While FRELIMO even took the pain of flying some prominent CU-NIMO members into selected provinces of Mozambique, RENAMO held important meetings in West Germany in an attempt to bring CUNIMO into its fold. Eventually, the Cologne Group strove to position itself as an intermediary between the two rivals but its projected role was taken over by the **Catholic Church**, the Italian (rather than the West German) government, and by such African countries as Kenya, Botswana, and Zimbabwe. During its existence, CUNIMO held only three meetings in Nairobi, Cologne, and Philadelphia during the 1986–87 period, before it faded into oblivion.

COMITÉ PARA A UNIÃO INDEPENDENTE DE MOÇAMBIQUE (CUNIMO) (MOZAMBIQUE NATIONAL UNION INDEPENDENT COMMITTEE).

Organization established during the mid-1980s, headquartered in Sacavem, **Portugal**, whose aim was to bridge the differences between **FRELIMO** and **RENAMO**. It disagreed with both: it detested FRELIMO for its Marxist-Leninist philosophy and abhorred RE-NAMO for its ties with **South Africa** and its "terrorist" tactics. Its leader was Carlos Alexandre. A few intellectuals, including António Disse Zengazenga, who resided in Germany, and **José Chicuarra**, once student in the **United States**, supported CUNIMO. Chicuarra was a former FRE-LIMO member who escaped Mozambique to reside in Portugal during the early 1980s, after spending considerable time in jail for allegedly being a Central Intelligence Agency (CIA) agent. Artur Vilanculo, former FRE-LIMO member and, briefly, representative of RENAMO in the United States, was also originally a member of CUNIMO but decided in the late 1980s to found his own organization called **Friends of Mozambique**. CUNIMO leaders allegedly expelled him from their organization on January 7, 1987. The organization had absolutely no power and thus no impact on the war in Mozambique, which it wished to mediate.

COMITÉ REVOLUCIONÁRIO DE MOÇAMBIQUE (COREMO) (MOZAMBIQUE REVOLUTIONARY COMMITTEE).

Revolutionary movement created by Mozambicans living in Lusaka, Zambia, in 1965, headed by Adelino Gwambe. Successor to the little-known movement called the Mozambique Revolutionary Council (MORECO), established in 1964, COREMO consisted of splinter nationalist groups in the aftermath of the establishment of FRELIMO. President Kenneth Kaunda urged COREMO to unite with FRELIMO at a meeting attended by **Eduardo Mondlane** in Lusaka in 1965. When COREMO representatives refused to join FRELIMO, Mondlane walked out of the meeting. During its early stages, when it launched an attack on **Tete** District in 1965, COREMO promised to be a strong rival to FRELIMO. However, the **Portuguese** retaliated severely against the attack and killed suspected COREMO sympathizers, forcing 6,000 people to seek refuge in Zambia. This was COREMO's last meaningful activity. The front survived only until 1969, although it maintained its branches in Lusaka and Cairo. The Lusaka-based COREMO eventually split into two factions, one of which named itself the **União Nacional Africana da Rombézia** (UNAR) (Rombezia African National Union), with headquarters in Blantyre, Malawi. From its inception, COREMO was plagued with internal bickering that led to executive members firing each other. The demise of the short-lived revolutionary movement guaranteed FRELIMO's supremacy over the war against the Portuguese colonial state in Mozambique.

COMPANHIA DA ZAMBÉZIA (ZAMBEZIA COMPANY). This corporation received its 150,000-square-kilometer (58,593-square-mile) concession in **Tete** and **Quelimane** districts in the lower **Zambezi** Valley, essentially composed of the area's former *prazos*, on May 20, 1892. Its initial **South African**, German, British, French, and **Portuguese** capital was estimated at 30,601 *contos*. The company invested heavily in livestock as well as in agriculture and palm tree plantations in Coalane, Mavilembo, Rafael, Idigo, Namerrumo, Tonge, Maguival, Marrongane, São Domingo, and Timbue prazos. By 1930, the company had planted and owned some 541,354 palm trees valued at more than 500,00$05 *reis*. In 1906, it owned some 4,299 head of cattle, valued at 28$386 a head. In 1902, it paid some 60,655$856 to the government in taxes collected by force from workers, and 74,819$729 in 1906. The corporation's margin of profit was $593,922.9 (*escudos*) in 1930. Its term expired in 1932.

COMPANHIA DE MOÇAMBIQUE (MOZAMBIQUE COMPANY). With an initial British and French capital of £5 million, the Mozambique

Company received its charter on November 21, 1890, comprising a 50-year land concession over an area of 140,000 square kilometers (54,687 square miles) between the **Zambezi** and the Luenha Rivers and the 22nd parallel. It established its capital at **Beira** and engaged in the production of rice, cotton, rubber, and sugarcane; extracted gold, diamonds, and salt; managed several factories; and developed commercial and industrial plants, and raised cattle. It built or improved towns such as Beira, Buzi, Cheringoma, **Chimoio**, Gorongoza, Mexameje, Morebane, Neves Ferreira, **Sofala**, Vila Gouveia, Chiloane, Guveiro, Macequece, Mossurize, **Sena**, Lacerdonia, Sone, Chemba, Tambara, and Sanca. It recruited thousands of Africans by force every year and collected taxes from them. In 1928, for example, it collected some 247,806$95 (*escudos*) in household taxes and 112,142$43 in head taxes (or *mutsonkho*) from the Africans under its jurisdiction. The company functioned relatively well until 1923–24. In 1924 and thereafter, an economic crisis befell Mozambique, culminating in the Great Depression of 1929. While the value of the company's export was estimated at 8,700,000$00 in 1922 and 2,600,000$00 in 1927, it plummeted to a mere 700,000$00 in 1933. The monopolistic company was finally abolished during the **António Salazar** regime in 1941.

COMPANHIA DO AÇÚCAR DE MOÇAMBIQUE (MOZAMBIQUE SENA SUGAR COMPANY). Approved in 1890, the Mozambique Sugar Company was predominantly British and had a concession in the **Tete**, **Barue**, and **Quelimane** areas for 15 years only. In 1894, it produced some 717,714 kilograms of sugar in its **Barue**, Mazaro, Mopeia, and Sena *prazos*.

COMPANHIA DO BOROR (BOROR COMPANY). A subconcession of the Companhia da Zambézia, the Companhia do Boror was authorized in November 1899, and had its seat at Macuze, Mozambique District. It had an initial capital of 270 *contos*, equivalent to some £60,000. Abolished in 1930, the company left an impressive record in three plantations (cocoa and sisal: 1,287,842 and 3,596,101 trees, respectively, in 1920) and in sugar production (4,245 metric tons of sugar in the 1908–18 period). It operated mainly in the former *prazos* of Boror, Tivie, Macuze, Licungo as well as in Maganja, Baixo Molocue, Ligonha, Bulubuda, Vila Ribeiro, Colocote, Meluli, Larde, and Nhamareda.

COMPANHIA DO BÚZI (BUZI COMPANY). Approved by the government on April 1, 1898, to engage in any commercial and industrial activity, explore every forest, and exercise exclusive hunting privileges, the Companhia do Búzi was actually a subconcession of the **Companhia de**

Moçambique, controlling some 135,000 hectares of land in Buzi. It lasted until 1940. Its major activity, however, was sugar-cane plantation and sugar extraction, producing as many as 12,000 metric tons of sugar every year.

COMPANHIA DO MADAL (MADAL COMPANY). French owned and controlled, with an initial capital of 68,000$000 *réis*, the Madal Company was authorized to do business in **Quelimane** in 1904. It was engaged mainly in sugar extraction.

COMPANHIA DO NIASSA (NYASA COMPANY). This company received its concession of about 200,000 square kilometers (78,125 square miles) (to last 35 years) in the regions located between the Rovuma and Lurio Rivers and Lake Nyasa, on September 26, 1891. Its predominantly British capital was estimated at 4,500,000$000 (*réis*). Liquidated by statute in 1932, the Companhia do Niassa's performance was not impressive. It did not build a single railway or an acceptable number of **roads** within its own area. Although its concession included about one-fourth of the colony, its export volume was one-fourth less than that of its counterpart, the **Companhia de Moçambique**. It thrived on the collection of taxes and the forced labor of its African inhabitants. Its profit margin was 44,586$888 in 1895 and only 11,153$00 (*escudos*) in 1930.

CONCELHO. Municipality. *See* ADMINISTRATION.

CONFERENCIA DAS ORGANIZAÇÕES NACIONALISTAS DAS COLÓNIAS PORTUGUESAS (CONCP) (CONFERENCE OF THE NATIONALIST ORGANIZATIONS OF THE PORTUGUESE COLONIES). Established in Casablanca in 1961 at the insistence of such African leaders as Kwame Nkrumah and Julius Nyerere, CONCP sought cooperation and the exchange of information among the nationalists from the **Portuguese** colonies and the advancement of the idea of independence. It served as a forum for nationalist movements from Angola, Mozambique, Guinea-Bissau, Cape Verde Islands, and São Tomé e Príncipe.

CONGRESS (FRELIMO). Supreme organ of **FRELIMO**, made up of representatives from all walks of life, that gives the leadership and the **Central Committee** its fiat. The congress meets every five years and elects the Central Committee, which carries out its resolutions and mandate. In a complicated process, the localities—the cells—elect district councils and these, in turn, elect provincial delegates to the **Congress**.

Internal criticism is allowed both at the congress and the Central Committee level. In the past, criticism outside these parameters could cause ouster from the party, censorship, or internship in reeducation camps. *See also* EIGHTH CONGRESS; FIFTH CONGRESS; SIXTH CONGRESS.

CONSELHO CRISTÃO DE MOÇAMBIQUE (CCM) (MOZAMBIQUE CHRISTIAN COUNCIL). The official organization of the Protestant churches in Mozambique, representing 17 denominations and religious groups, founded during the 1920s to counter **Portuguese** antagonism. Reverend **Denis Singulane**, Anglican bishop of Libombos, is the highest-ranking and most influential member of the organization. During the period when the government was making a concerted effort to weaken the influence of Christianity in Mozambique, especially the **Catholic Church**, the CCM gained strength and eventually became involved in the peace negotiations between **RENAMO** and **FRELIMO**. The Protestant churches like to think that they were the first to press the view that a dialogue between RENAMO and FRELIMO be initiated. However, the Catholic Church claims that, when the Protestants were silent during the trying times of the 1970s and early 1980s, only its clergy was vocal and had stated its position regarding the **civil war** clearly. Indeed, whatever initiatives the CCM suggested to the government in 1984, it favored a "low-key and confidential" dialogue, whereas the Catholic Church, through the various pastorals published by the Mozambique Episcopal Conference and read at Masses to all faithful on Sundays, had a clear position on the situation in Mozambique: Only a dialogue and not military means could save the country.

CONSELHOS. The Overseas Organic Law of 1963 created advisory boards in the colonies, known as *conselhos*. The registered citizens elected half of the councilmen (*vereadores*) to the boards on the administrative post, township, and district levels. The other half was selected by several interest or cultural groups. Rarely were any Africans elected to the **councils**, however. The advisory boards were designed to assist the governor in policy and administrative matters. In consultation with the highest local administrator, the governor-general appointed the council's chairman.

CONSELHOS DE PRODUÇÃO **(PRODUCTION COUNCILS).** Created in 1979 but eliminated during the 1980s and replaced by labor unions, production councils could be compared to executive committees of labor unions. Elected by industry and factory workers, they were designed to speak for the workers, enhance morale and productivity, and instill in the workers a sense of social responsibility. Council members met with party representatives, presented grievances, and learned of government objectives and goals. **FRELIMO** wished to ensure that workers would feel that they occupied a special place in the nation and wanted them to realize that socialism does not necessarily mean the abolition of work incentives and rewards.

CONSTITUTION. Mozambique has ratified two constitutions since achieving its independence in 1975. The first, approved in 1975, declared the Mozambican state socialist and guaranteed citizens' freedoms but made no distinction between party and state. It declared **FRELIMO** the only legal party in the country, prescribing that only party members could run for office or vote. An interesting clause, however, was the non-adoption of the death penalty. Although the document was not very different from others in Africa at that time, enforcement of the clauses on freedom of the press, freedom of religion, and freedom of movement was contrary to the law, leading Amnesty International to accuse the government of violating the human rights of Mozambique citizens.

The second constitution, resulting from **RENAMO** pressures on the battlefield and international arm twisting on the issue of democratic reforms, often linked to financial assistance, was ratified in 1990. The new constitution reaffirms all freedoms, guarantees multipartism in the country, and makes a clear distinction between party and state. The president and the Assembly of the Republic, previously known as the Popular Assembly, are to be elected by universal suffrage and by secret ballot. While the president may be elected and reelected only once for five-year terms, members of the assembly may run for many five-year terms. The constitution also upholds the principle of a free market economy and private property and changes the designation of the country from the People's Republic of Mozambique to the Republic of Mozambique. *See also* ACORDO GERAL DA PAZ; CONSTITUTIONAL REFORMS; ELECTIONS.

CONSTITUTIONAL REFORMS (1990). Foreseeing the changes that would inevitably follow as a result of the ongoing negotiations with **RE-NAMO, FRELIMO** enacted its own constitutional reforms as a pre-emptive move in April–June 1990, approving a new constitution (the first was ratified in 1975), which contained the following new clauses:

1. separation of party and state;
2. legalization of multipartyism in Mozambique;

3. universal suffrage in the election of president and the "Assembly of the Republic";
4. reaffirmation of public "freedoms" and the independence of the judiciary;
5. affirmation of religious freedom;
6. the renaming of the People's Republic of Mozambique as the "Republic of Mozambique."

Along with these changes, the country would hold a competition for the creation of a new national anthem to replace the one introduced in 1975, which had specific references to **FRELIMO**. The competition was still going on in 2001. Approved by the People's Assembly, the new constitution became binding on November 30, 1990.

CONTRATADO. In the colonial context, the *contratado* was an African forced by the **Portuguese** government to work for a certain period of time, up to nine months, usually far from home to prevent his escape. According to law, the workers were under contract (*contrato*) from the government, a private Portuguese citizen (white or assimilated), or a company. Known by the Africans as ***chibalo*** or ***ntalato***, this labor policy was hated in the colony, and it came increasingly under attack by the international community and private citizens in Europe and the **United States**. Thus, it was officially ended in the early 1960s. Early Mozambique governors, including High Commissioners **António Enes** and **Joaquim Mouzinho de Albuquerque**, had argued that forced labor was the only way to civilize the African and free him from his lazy nature. Although several provisions were made between 1914 and 1927 to protect the Mozambique worker from abuses, most often they were simply ignored by the authorities and private employers. *See also* ASSIMILATION.

COOLELA. Township in the **Gaza** empire where **Joaquim Mouzinho de Albuquerque**'s troops and **Gungunhana**'s forces met on November 7, 1895, resulting in the temporary defeat of Gungunhana.

COOPERANTES. Ex-patriate FRELIMO sympathizers, usually socialists and Communists, who came to Mozambique as volunteers in the various sectors of development following independence. Many of them replaced in city, town, and countryside the skilled *Portuguese* who left Mozambique in the wake of the implementation of **FRELIMO**'s socialist policies. As a result of the collapse of the communist world and the change of policy on the part of the Mozambique government from socialism to capitalism, most of the expatriates became disenchanted and returned home. Few of them are in the country today. The word *cooperante* is rarely used in postsocialist Mozambique.

COUNCILS. See *CONSELHOS*.

COUTINHO, JOÃO DE AZEVEDO (1865–1944). Portuguese statesman, military officer, and writer, Azevedo Coutinho participated with **Serpa Pinto** and **Mouzinho de Albuquerque** in the campaigns against the Macololo and the Namarrais in Mozambique in the 1890s. In 1902, he led the Barue campaign (which he described vividly in his *Relatório da campanha do Bárue*, 1902). In 1904, Coutinho served as governorgeneral of Mozambique and was appointed minister of the navy in 1909.

CRAVEIRINHA, JOSÉ (also known as José Gr. Vetrinha) (1922–). A native of Maputo (Lourenço Marques), Craveirinha is one of the bestknown Mozambican poets, short story writers, and journalists. He worked for the newspapers *OBrado Africano, Notícias*, and *Tribunal*. He published his poem *Chigobo* in 1964 and has other writings featured in *Modern Poetry from Africa*. Like many other Mozambican writers, Craveirinha was jailed several times by the **Portuguese** authorities.

CRUZ (FAMILY). The Cruzes were one of the dynasties that controlled the **Massagano** and Tipue *prazos* in **Tete** District. The founder of the dynasty was Nicolau Pascoal da Cruz, a Sino-Thai who, after serving in the **Portuguese** army, settled in Mozambique in 1767. Through marriage alliances with African chiefs, he was able to carve out for himself and his family considerable territory between the Luenha River and the Lupata Valley. One of his sons, António José da Cruz (1777–1813), married a daughter of the king of Mwenemutapa but was arrested and hanged by the Portuguese, accused of conspiracy with the king in the murder of Lieutenant General António Roberto de Barbosa Vilas Boas de Truão in 1807. His other son, Joaquim José da Cruz, also known as the Nhaude (the Spider), inherited his father's estate (1805–55) and built an *aringa* (fortified headquarters) at Massangano. He maintained such good relations with the Portuguese that the later bestowed on him the rank of *capitão-mor*.

However, the peaceful coexistence was completely disrupted in the 1850s. In 1850, the governor sent one Lieutenant Raposo to arrest and bring Nhaude to Tete as a prisoner for illegally blocking river traffic.

Nhaude tricked the officer when he secretly convened his men and fired upon the visitor, wounding him. Arrogantly, Nhaude told Raposo to go back to Tete and report to his administrator. Consequently, in 1854, the Portuguese made a major attempt to invade the aringa and capture Nhaude. They sent an expedition, first under António Cândido de Pedroso Gamito and, subsequently, under Tito Augusto de Araújo Sicard, to the aringa. The expedition was unsuccessful, however, and lost many of its soldiers.

Nhaude died in 1855 and was succeeded by the most famous of the Cruzes, his oldest son, António Vicente da Cruz (1825–79), commonly known as Bonga (the Fox). Surrounded by some 15,000 soldiers (*achikunda*), Bonga at first declared himself a friend of the Portuguese. However, his insolence, demonstrated by his refusal to pay the *mutsonkho* (taxes) and his unchallenged control of the river trade, angered the Portuguese, who (between 1867 and 1869) sent several expeditions to destroy his aringa and capture him. All expeditions, however, resulted in heavy casualties for the Portuguese. At the beginning of the hostilities, in 1867, the governor of **Tete** himself, Miguel Augusto de Gouveia, surrounded the aringa to arrest Bonga in person. Using guerrilla tactics, however, Bonga overpowered the governor, captured him, cut his ears off, and then sent him back to Tete. His victories forced the Portuguese to sign a treaty with him on June 19, 1875.

Bonga was succeeded by his son, Luís Vicente da Cruz, also known as Muchenga or Muirima. Luís made peace with the Portuguese. A skilled diplomat, Muirima was able to convince the governor of Tete to send a priest and soldiers to bless the tomb of his father, claiming that they owed this honor to him because he was an officer of the Portuguese army. Yet, when the Portuguese insisted on recovering the remains of three officers killed by Bonga in the aringa, Vicente da Cruz refused to comply and instead demanded a ransom. Powerless, the Portuguese authorities paid the ransom and recovered the three skulls, which were sent to Moçambique, the capital, for honorable state burial. Vicente's rule was brief, and his brother Vitorino da Cruz succeeded him in 1880.

Vitorinos' reign was equally short. In 1885, António Vicente da Cruz (Chatara), as arrogant as his predecessors, assumed power. To punish him, the Portuguese, in collaboration with the Gouveia family, prepared an expedition that converged on Massangano from four directions—namely, Sena, **Manica**, **Barue**, and Tete—in 1887. Sensing imminent defeat, Chatara abandoned the aringa, which the Portuguese subsequently burnt to the ground. Chatara and his family sought refuge in the

Makaranga kingdom of the Pereiras, but his own brother, João Santana da Cruz, handed him over to the Portuguese authorities, who exiled him to the Cape Verde islands. João Santana da Cruz (Mutontora), however, succeeded in rebuilding the aringa and refused to pay taxes to the Portuguese authorities in 1888. Consequently, the Portuguese invaded the aringa and defeated the *prazero*. Mutontora and his whole family were taken prisoner to the capital city, Moçambique. In 1894, his threatened brother Inácio Vieira da Cruz (Garde), who had assumed the leadership, escaped into British territory but was also captured. Gande was the last of the Cruzes. Sporadic fighting continued around Massangano and Tipue until 1917.

Overall, the Cruzes succeeded in defeating the Portuguese authorities for more than 80 years and caused more deaths than any rebel family or political coalition during the course of Portuguese military history in Mozambique, including even the expeditions against **Gungunhana** and the Namarrais. In fact, in their struggle against the Cruz family, the Portuguese lost no fewer than three ranking officers and three governors, more than 750 white soldiers, and thousands of Africans.

CURANDEIRO. Portuguese word for "traditional healer." Even during the colonial era, the curandeiro remained a respected and often powerful individual in the village setting. Combining his deep knowledge of natural plants and herbs with magic, the curandeiro (invariably a male, except in matrilineal societies where a woman may be a *curandeira*) treated his patients physically and spiritually by claiming to have invisible powers that could divine, predict, and prescribe treatment that would cure the whole person. His services were not free but were more affordable than those provided by biomedicine, considered foreign and inefficient against certain ailments, such as mental illnesses. Due to the impact of Western influence, especially Christianity, many educated Mozambicans prefer Western treatment but avail themselves of the traditional healer as an insurance against noncurable diseases.

In its attempt to weaken the power of the traditional authorities or *régulos* and eliminate religious and spiritual beliefs, **FRELIMO** attempted to curb the power of the curandeiros said to be based on superstition and an anachronic political power structure. During the **civil war**, however, the government began courting the traditional healer when it realized that **RENAMO** was gaining ground in the countryside as a result of its open support for the chiefly authorities and healers. Today, the knowledge, power, and prestige of the curandeiros have been reasserted and the government is attempting to rehabilitate the tradition by providing the curandeiros with elementary Western training in medicine and allowing them to maintain their own association, known as the Associação Nacional de Curandeiros de Moçambique.

– D –

DEGREDADO. Exiled criminal from **Portugal** or India (Goa, Damão e Diu) sent to the **Portuguese** colonies to serve as a soldier, settler, or even as a civil servant. Often accompanied by female prostitutes, orphans, widows, or women of dubious reputation and criminals, the degredados flocked into the colony of Mozambique and occupied prominent positions, particularly during the 19th century. Although Mozambique governors and army officers generally opposed this policy, the Lisbon authorities continued to send unwanted criminals to Mozambique. Most degredados were undisciplined and ignorant, and led shameful lives in the colony to the embarrassment of decent Portuguese citizens. Most did not survive the rigors of their new life and the hostile climate. In 1860, Governor-General João Tavares de Almeida wrote, "Among the *degredados* sent to this Province, many are sick and incapable of doing any service, either because of their advanced age or due to previous illnesses contracted in jail or during the voyage. When they arrive in the Province, they almost all die during the first rains and the flu season. While their transportation has been enormously costly, those who survive lead miserably sick lives and are incapable of earning a living and serving in the army—their only means of sustenance once they are caught up in the country's fever." Instances of violence among the degredados themselves were also common.

DELAGOA BAY (BAÍA DA LAGOA). Inlet of the Indian Ocean into the coast of Mozambique where the port of **Maputo** (former Lourenço Marques) is located. It is also the name originally associated with the Delagoa Bay Railway built by Edward McMurdo between the Bay and Pretoria (1887–95). Seaman António do Campo, captain of one of the 20 ships accompanying **Vasco da Gama** during his second voyage to India in 1502, "discovered" the bay and named it Baía da Lagoa. In 1544, Lourenço Marques explored the bay and opened it to **Portuguese** vessels trafficking in ivory and slaves. Until the 19th century, practically all European powers disputed Portuguese claims over the bay. (The dispute with Britain was finally submitted for arbitration to French president Edme Patrice

MacMahon in 1872. The British lost the claim in 1875.) The Delagoa Bay, now called the Baía de **Maputo**, is 26 miles long and 22 miles wide, land-locked on three sides and surrounded by Inhaca Peninsula on the east, Inhaca Island north of the peninsula, and open on its northern side. The following rivers flow into the Bay: Nkomati, Maputo, and the Rio do Espírito Santo estuary, made up of Rivers Matola, Tembe, and Umbeluzi.

DEMA. Little is known about the Dema people, the Atande, the Gova, and the Pembe who live in Capoche and Mucanha.

DESLOCADO **(DISPLACED INDIVIDUAL).** Term used to refer to Mozambicans who were displaced during the civil war. Many of the deslocados ended up as **refugees** in the surrounding countries. By 1992, about two million Mozambicans had sought asylum abroad.

DHLAKAMA, AFONSO (1953–). Second president of **RENAMO.** Born at Mangunde, Chibabava, **Sofala** Province, on January 1, 1953, Dhlakama attended a Catholic school and a commercial school at Beira, where he graduated in 1969. He worked as a clerk in Beira until 1973, when he joined **FRELIMO.** Dhlakama was made the logistics provincial commander of Sofala Province and was responsible for military supplies. Like **Andre Matsangaisa**, RENAMO's first president, Dhlakama was purged during the 1974–75 anticorruption campaign. Sent to a reeducation camp, Dhlakama escaped and joined the **Resistência Nacional Moçambicana** (RENAMO) at Chimanimani in 1977.

Following Matzangaisa's death in 1979, and after defeating two factions within the resistance movement in mid-1980 and enjoying the support of Orlando Christina, one of RENAMO's founders, Dhlakama was declared president of RENAMO. In August 1985, he escaped a concerted assault on his Gorongaza headquarters by FRELIMO and Zimbabwe parachutists. Since then, through a very sophisticated radio communication network, he eluded some of the best organized FRELIMO ambushes in the Gorongoza area, and, in 1988, assured of himself, he began traveling abroad.

As a man of war, Dhlakama is said to be a determined leader who knew exactly how to elude and demoralize FRELIMO's soldiers; although he did not fight in the liberation war, Dhlakama behaved as a master of guerrilla tactics and enjoyed the unquestionable loyalty of his followers. One of his problems has been the inability to attract some of the best-educated minds that can provide intellectual coherence to his philosophy and articulate it abroad and thus bring credibility to his movement. In the past, some who claimed to represent him abroad were actually doing him more harm than good as they continued to vie for control of the movement's external affairs in **Portugal**, West Germany, Canada, and the **United States**, at the expense of unity.

Dhlakama ran for president in 1994 but lost, with 53.30 percent of the vote going to Chissano and 33.73 percent to him. In the 1999 elections, he won only 47.71 percent of the vote, 52.9 having gone to Chissano. At first, Dhlakama refused to accept the election results. In 2000–01, he and Chissano held several meetings to resolve the impasse and respond to other grievances RENAMO has voiced, but nothing concrete has come out of the talks, which were broken off in May 2001. Within RENAMO, Dhlakama has experienced several problems, including ideological and political differences. Resulting from RENAMO's First Congress in peacetime in 2001, Dhlakama assumed the position of secretary-general of the party, which had been occupied by Joaquim Vaz.

DIÁRIO DE LOURENÇO MARQUES (1952–1975). The *Diário de Lourenço Marques*, formerly *The Guardian of Lourenço Marques*, was purchased by the archbishop of Lourenço Marques, **Dom Teodósio Clemente de Gouveia**, in 1952. It ceased its publication at the time of independence.

DIÁRIO DE MOÇAMBIQUE (1951–1971). *O Diário de Moçambique* was the first Catholic newspaper in the colony, founded by the bishop of **Beira**, Dom **Sebastião Soares de Resende**. Because of its critical attitude toward **Portuguese** colonialism, *O Diário* was suspended for 30 days in 1968 and soon thereafter was sold to Portuguese engineer Jorge Pereira Jardim. It discontinued circulation in 1971 but resumed in 1981.

DIAS, JOÃO (1926–1949). Son of Estácio Dias, one of the editors of the *Brado Africano*, Dias was born in Mozambique and died in **Portugal**. He studied at the Universities of Coimbra and Lisbon. He was a storywriter whose writings include *Godido e outros* contos, published posthumously in 1965, and *Poetas e contistas africanos de expressão portuguesa*, published in 1963.

DIVISÃO DE EXPLORACÃO DE TRANSPORTES AÉREOS (DETA). The Mozambique airline and air transport authority known as DETA was established in 1936. By 1950, DETA linked some 20 Mozambique cities. Along with the Transportes Aéreos Porugueses (TAP), Central African Airways (CAA), and South African Airways (SAA), DETA provided national and international flights during the colonial period. In 1984, Mozambique's three international airports provided service to 399,300 air passengers and handled 9,800 metric tons of freight. DETA was replaced by Linha de Transportes Aéreos (LTA), which was international, and by Transporte e Trabalho Aéreo (TTA) for domestic flights. Linhas Aéreas de Moçambique (LAM) is now the official Mozambique airline. *See also* AIR TRANSPORT.

– E –

ECONOMY. Mozambique's economy is recovering after almost two decades of war, destruction, neglect, and underdevelopment. The government's reconstruction and reform program has won approval from the international financial institutions and from donors. Growth from the mid-1990s has been strong, and new confidence in the economy is beginning to attract investment. This growth begins from a very low base: Mozambique is still one of the world's poorest countries, and two-thirds of the population live in poverty as a result of drought and chronic underdevelopment that dates from **Portuguese** colonization and most importantly from 15 years of war. The country is heavily dependent on foreign aid.

The government's first economic rehabilitation program (PRE) adopted in 1987 aimed at undercutting the unofficial economy, give real value to the currency, and remove administrative hindrances to productive enterprises. State enterprises that operated deficits saw their subsidies progressively reduced. Food subsidies in urban areas were removed in 1988. For the first three years of the PRE, gross domestic product (GDP) growth was positive. The program emphasized recovery and rehabilitation rather than major new projects. However, continued lawlessness, worldwide recession, and drought shrank GDP growth in 1992. Peace and good rains in 1993 brought a surge. In 1989, the government began focusing on reducing poverty, improving living standards, and strengthening the country's institutional capacities. The government's 1995–96 economic and social plan included building schools and health clinics. An ambitious privatization program is being implemented, and almost 1,000 firms have been privatized since 1989, and efficiency has risen, especially among foreign-owned firms less affected by the high national interest rates. The following table illustrates the economic conditions in Mozambique, especially in reference to the last few years.

Average Annual Growth Rates in Mozambique (Percentage)

	1977–1987	1988–1998	1997	1998
Agriculture	—	3.1	7.6	7.0
Industry	—	5.3	23.9	22.9
Manufacturing	—	—	29.8	7.5
Service		5.7	7.1	9.7
Private consumption	-5.0	2.4	8.3	11.8
General government consumption	-4.8	-5.7	9.9	32.2
Gross domestic investment	0.5	7.4	17.1	29.4
Imports of goods and services	-6.7	0.1	0.7	24.2
Gross national product (GNP)	-4.8	4.8	12.2	11.8

Source: World Bank, *Country Data,* "Mozambique at a Glance," www.worldbank.org/data/countrydata/aag/moz_aag.pdf, 1999.

Mozambique is a country struggling to overcome the legacies of decades of colonialism following the arrival of the Portuguese in 1498. After settling in Mozambique, the Portuguese established protective forts and *feiras* (trading centers), which extended up to present day Zimbabwe. However, this territorial and economic expansion was not without opposition. Facing stiff opposition from Arabs and Africans, the Portuguese often resorted to the use of force. By the 19th century, they had lost most of the east coast and were left with Mozambique alone, only effectively controlling the coastal towns of Sofala, Angoche (temporarily), Quelimane, and Lourenço Marques, and the Zambezi Valley.

To guarantee sovereignty in the areas occupied and to promote economic development, particularly agriculture, during the mid–17th century, the government transplanted the European institution of the *prazo* into the colony. This action allowed Portuguese citizens to lease land for a period of three generations, where according to law, inheritance would be bestowed upon the female offspring who married a Portuguese. In practice, the prazeros relied on slave labor yet invested little to develop the land. The prazero institution relied heavily on raising armies of Africans to defy both the Portuguese government and the African traditional authorities. Some prazeros owned acreage larger than Portugal itself and grew only a subsistent amount of crops such as rice, corn, millet, sorghum, cotton, and cassava. The European prazero institution was so disastrous for the economy that during the mid–19th century, the government attempted to abolish it or at the very least radically reform it. The reform measures did not work, and in 1888–89 a formal inquiry pronounced the institution corrupt, violent, and unsuccessful. Although some advocates of the prazero system fought to save the broken institution, it was abolished in 1930.

In 1928, cotton cultivation became mandatory for the Africans. During harvest periods, they were forced to sell their crop at the low prices dictated by the multinational corporations. This policy of controlled economy had a tremendous effect on the financial stability of the colony's African population. In 1961, the forced cotton cultivation was made illegal and the system was abolished in 1966.

In the 1960s, the country's industry was gaining importance and showing the beginning of expansion in undertargeted areas such as food processing and mineral extraction (particularly coal). Cement, textiles, and soft drinks also became important industrial items in this expansion. It was against this backdrop that FRELIMO (once it had inherited the colony from the Portuguese in 1975) decided to radically change the economic direction of the colony. This was the beginning of a new era, the reversal of the colonial capitalism and the beginning of the Marxist-Leninist economic philosophy. Marxism-Leninism became the official economic philosophy of the new republic, based on the premise that **FRELIMO**, as a vanguard party, had to bring together the peasants and the workers as allies—the peasants being the "principal force," while the workers would be the "leading force"—that would eliminate bourgeois aspirations and exploitation of the masses. In socialist terminology, agriculture was to become the basis of the economy, and industry would be the "dynamizing force." In 1978, the Marxist-Leninist-based government nationalized all land, farms, businesses, banks, the housing industry, schools, hospitals, and legal and medical practices. Peasant cooperatives (co-ops) and communal villages of at least 50 to 2,000 people were instituted in 1975–1976 (there were 180 such collective farms in 1977), and factory workers were organized into *conselhos de produção* (production councils) to manage their own affairs under the party's guidance.

However, as the socialist experiment began to encounter serious setbacks internally and abroad, President **Samora Machel** toned down his Marxist rhetoric, traveled abroad to garner political and financial support, and opened up the country to moderate private enterprise. This attempt by the president to open up the market did not lure a significant number of businessmen and investors from abroad. Instead, the government was compelled to sell its "people's shops" and as an incentive allow individual profit in economic ventures. Subsequently, attacks by the Mozambique National Resistance Movement and military, economic pressures from **South Africa**, and drought paralyzed the country. From

1978 to 1984, South Africa's refusal to sell Mozambique's gold at a lower price cost Mozambique approximately \$2.6 billion in foreign exchange potential earnings, which would not only have assisted the nation in payment of its debts but also would have provided a cushion to its huge deficits.

Mozambique's problems with South Africa were further exacerbated in 1976, when Mozambique showed its solidarity with the Zimbabwean nationalists and complied with the **United Nations**'s sanctions imposed on the government of Ian Smith. The government also closed its transit routes to Rhodesian goods, a move that cost the country some \$550 million between 1976 and 1980. To compound Mozambique's financial problems, South Africa reduced the number of Mozambique miners to fewer than 50,000 during the 1980s. In 1986, South Africa refused not only to accept new recruits from Mozambique to work in the mines but also to renew the contracts of those already working there (about 65,665 workers), alleging that FRELIMO was still assisting the African National Congress (ANC). However, in January 1988, Mozambican workers would be welcomed once again to work in the South African mines. Meanwhile, the country was in a deep economic crisis in every sector: agriculture, industry, trade and tourism. Undoubtedly, the flight of Portuguese business owners, hotel managers, technicians, and others in critical developmental positions aggravated the economic situation. On the other hand, the state farms, which encompassed 350 acres in 1981, had become so expensive and unproductive (they yielded only a half a ton of corn per acre) that the plan to expand them to cover 2.5 million new acres was abandoned by the Fourth **FRELIMO** Congress in 1984. As a result of serious financial and economic failures and sustained pressure from the West, Mozambique had fully embraced the market economy by 1992. *See also* INDUSTRY; INDUSTRY AND MANUFACTURING; INFLATION; TRADE.

EDUCATION. There is no doubt that Mozambique has come a long way in its effort to provide education to all its citizens. Unfortunately, even today, statistics on education are hard to come by.

Archival sources mention that priests at the Convent of São Domingos on the Mozambique Island built the first primary school in Mozambique in 1799. They also show that the colonial government completely neglected education elsewhere in Mozambique for both African and European children until April 11, 1845, when a decree authorized the creation of the first public schools in the colony and specified that students should be taught "history, writing, Christianity, principles of geography, sacred history, Portuguese grammar, linear drawing, business writing, Latin, and French." Thus, by 1849, nine primary schools had been built in the major towns, staffed by 11 poorly paid teachers.

In 1857, a "principal" (secondary) school was created on the Mozambique Island. It enrolled 63 students in 1858 and, to prove that the government was seriously committed to education, provided for the creation of *conselhos inspectores de instrução pública* (inspecting councils) to supervise the educational effort. Not much was noticeable in terms of progress, however, as, by 1874, there were only 332 students in the whole colony, of whom only 125 were black. In 1900, the number of students rose to 1,195; a decade later, the number of primary schools had risen to 48. Yet, no secondary schools were available. In 1913, the anticlerical republic attempted to replace the **Catholic Church** as far as teaching was concerned and sent the so-called Missões Laicas Civilizadoras (lay civilizing brigades) throughout the colony to take over primary education. The experiment ended in failure and was, therefore, discontinued.

In 1918, Mozambique had its second secondary school—the Licéu Nacional Sidónio Pais, later known as the Licéu Nacional 5 de Outubro, at Lourenço Marques. Enrollment figures continued to grow throughout the colony but at a very slow pace. In 1929, the 258 schools had an enrollment of 30,613 students, although most of them attended missionary school. With the signing of the 1941 Missionary Statutes (*Estatutos*), the Catholic Church's involvement in education increased tremendously. Thus, government-sponsored schools numbered only 63 in the 1950–51 school year, taught by 164 teachers, with a student population of 5,055; private schools enrolled 931 students only.

By 1956, however, the total number of students in primary schools had risen to 253,000. In the following year, approximately 296,000 out of 900,000 school-age children attended school. However, of the 2,040 rudimentary schools, only 40 were government run. In 1960, the number of government schools totaled 191, Catholic missions ran 3,162 schools, while the Protestants operated 61: a total of 3,414 schools, registering an increase of 153 percent over 1967. In the 1963–64 school year, 34,000 more students enrolled in 3,920 schools taught by 7,921 teachers. During the 1964–65 school year, however, the total numbers remained: 426,904 primary schools; 19,761 secondary schools; and a first university, the University of General Studies, inaugurated that year.

According to **United Nations** statistics, 635,000 students attended school in Mozambique in 1971–72—595,000 in primary school and

40,000 in secondary and technical schools. When the Portuguese left Mozambique in 1975, 600,000 students were enrolled in school, out of a population of 9 million, still registering an illiteracy rate of 95 percent. Whereas the colonial government spent less than 3 percent of its budget on education, the **FRELIMO** government apportioned more than 15 percent for that purpose (4.071 million *meticais* out of 22.07 million meticais in 1984). Due to FRELIMO's expansion of educational opportunities, the number of secondary school students increased from 20,000 in 1974 to 135,900 in 1981, while the number of children enrolled in primary schools rose from 700,000 in 1974 to 1.376 million by 1981. The numbers continued to increase thereafter, to the extent that FRELIMO was able to decrease illiteracy in the country from 95 percent to 75 percent by 1988. While the primary schools registered 1,376,865 students taught by 18,751 teachers in 1981, the secondary schools enrolled 135,956 students taught by 3,784 teachers; and the number of preuniversity and university students stood at 3,886 with a faculty numbering 157.

During the colonial period, the educational system had been plagued by a lack of funds; teachers had no incentives, as their salary could be compared to that of forced workers and the government-run schools discriminated against Africans in favor of white and *mestiço* children. In 1953–54, the racial ratio in primary schools was 5,177 Africans to 4,412 whites, almost a 1:1 ratio, notwithstanding the fact that the Portuguese population was not higher than 200,000. On the secondary level, 800 white students enrolled in the licéus, compared to only 5 Africans. Moreover, 803 white students were registered in commercial institutions, contrasted to only 73 Africans. In 1966, the number of university students stood at 540, but only one was a Mozambican African. Furthermore, in 1970, of the 627,319 students, 550,701 were black, 59,941 white, 6,850 Indian, 7,795 *mistos*, and 2,034 "yellow."

As a way of fostering patriotism, students were forbidden to speak their mother tongue, and, since 1920, classes were taught in Portuguese. To facilitate the assimilation process, the Portuguese created a few schools for the training of teachers in the colony: the normal schools at Boroma (the oldest, founded in the 1890s) and Alvor at Manhiça (1926), which registered a total of 73 students in 1928. In general, the educational system in the Portuguese colonies was thus organized: the *ensino de adaptação* (two to three years); the *ensino primário comum* (three to four years); *licéus and colégios*, or secondary schools (7 years); *escolas normais* (teacher training schools); *escolas de artes e ofícios* (trade and business schools); *escolas de agricultura* (agricultural schools); and *seminários*

Católicos (Catholic seminaries), which provided an equivalent to both the ensino primário comum and the licéu. The constant indoctrination that went on in the schools on the virtues of assimilation succeeded in creating assimilated individuals who sometimes despised their own culture and attempted to behave as whites.

This partly explains why the Portuguese colonies were slow in achieving their independence. The teaching methods were antiquated, as memorization was emphasized. Textbooks were hardly available. The *palmatória* and the *cavalo marinho* were both used extensively in the schools. The buildings where education took place were miserable: Most often they consisted of a wood-and-mud structure with logs as desks for students. The only schools that looked decent were those run by the state, although many of the missionaries did their best with the meager financial resources allocated for education, which amounted to less than 1 percent of the colony's budget.

Overall, under the Portuguese, the educational conditions remained precarious in the colony. In this respect, FRELIMO made gigantic inroads against illiteracy and toward the improvement of educational opportunities for all Mozambicans, regardless of race. During the 1980s, however, FRELIMO's efforts were thwarted by **RENAMO** activities, which reportedly destroyed or forced the closing of more than 200 schools and halted the education of some 113,000 students. The educational conditions improved after the **Accord Geral da Paz (General Peace Accord)** in 1992. Thus, by 1994, the **United Nations** and other international organizations had built or rehabilitated 167 schools: 25 in **Maputo**, 14 in **Gaza**, 36 in **Manica**, 14 in **Sofala**, 56 in **Tete**, and 22 in **Zambézia**. More teachers were being trained, and only 4.7 percent of the schools were nonfunctional. This was the case of those facilities located in areas of "double administration" by FRELIMO and RENAMO. However, overwhelmed by the return of refugee children, in many parts of the country students attended school in shifts. In 1995, Mozambique ran 6,025 elementary or primary schools, 75 secondary schools, and six government and private institutions of higher learning.

How many children attended schools at the end of the 20th century? Unfortunately, the most recent official government figures available before 2001 refer only to the year 1997 period, the year the government published its statistics on education. In 1995, about 40 percent of school age children (45 percent males and 35 percent females) attended primary schools, reaching 1,899,531 children by 1997. Yet, only 6 percent of those finishing primary school attended secondary school, about

51,544 for the whole country. Of these, 75 percent were male and 25 percent female. Due to the scarcity of resources, Mozambique schools are packed, and students continue to attend classes in shifts, which makes the classsroom students per teacher ratio acceptable. Thus, in the primary school, the ratio between teacher and student is 1:60 in the first two years and 1:39 in the second two years. In high school, the ratio is 1:35 in the first two years and 1:24 during the second two years. In the elementary and basic technical schools, the ratios are 1:11 and 1:22, respectively. There were 12,000 students in the 25 technical schools in the country in 1997.

At the tertiary level, some 7,156 students were enrolled at the three government institutions of higher learning, namely, Eduardo Mondlane University, Universidade Pedagógica, and Instituto Superior de Relações Internacionais, all located in Maputo. The Catholic University of Mozambique, with branches in **Beira**, **Nampula**, and Maputo, which has registered at least 500 students, and two other private colleges in Maputo and Nampula, will certainly increase the opportunities for Mozambican secondary school graduates to attend college. It appears, however, that the government will have to spend much more than the 4 percent or less it spends of its GDP. Yet, 4 percent is not bad compared to countries such as Chad and Niger that spend much less (*see* the accompanying tables on education).

According to *Africa: South of the Sahara* (2001), education expenditures from all sources (government, donor, and private) amounted to $72,264 million *meticais,* which represents about 12 percent of government expenditures, although the World Bank believes that the figure has actually been in the neighborhood of 5 percent (contrasted with 5.4 percent for the military in 1995, down from 9.9 percent in 1980). However, the problem is that much of the budget depends on private and donor financial assistance. The dilemma for Mozambique is that almost half of its population is between the ages of 10 and 24 years. As a result, in 2000, overall literacy in Mozambique was estimated at 40 percent, which, for anyone familiar with the situation, is an overestimation—65 percent appears more realistic. Adult illiteracy, ages 15 and over, stands at 43 percent for males and 75 percent for females, an overall rate of 64 percent for the country. Females are, therefore, the most disadvantaged. Of the 1,415,428 students attending primary school in 1995, only 43 percent were female, the percentage becoming smaller as school level advances. The situation will remain the same for many more years to come, unless the effort to enroll more women is redoubled.

EGIDIO (SAINT) (SANT'EGIDIO). A 10,000-member Catholic charity lay organization based in Rome where it was founded on February 7, 1968. It has maintained strong ties with the church hierarchy, including Pope John Paul II. Saint Egidio's mission has been to help the poor and the sick, resolve disputes through dialogue, pray for peace, and strengthen the ecumenical movement. The Vatican used this lay community to initiate and advance peace talks in Mozambique. **Archbishop Jaime Gonçalves** of Beira became a close friend of Saint Egidio while a young priest in Rome in 1976. As the influential members of Saint Egidio realized, through Dom Jaime Gonçalves, that the problems the **Catholic Church** was experiencing in Mozambique were partly caused by the conflict between **FRELIMO** and **RENAMO,** so they initiated direct communication with members of the Italian government. The Italian government too showed interest in helping resolve the **civil war** in this former **Portuguese** colony. Once these ties had been established, the archbishop, chosen by his bishop colleagues to represent them at the peace negotiations that began in 1988, worked closely with Saint Egidio, thus bringing to fruition in 1992 their own ideas and the influence of the Italian government and the Vatican. This led to the October 4, 1992, **Acordo Geral da Paz.** *See also* GONÇALVES, JAIME.

EIGHTH CONGRESS (FRELIMO). FRELIMO'S Eighth Congress took place in June 2002. Discussions centered on how to consolidate and capitalize the gains on the past, stressed a willingness to move the country forward politically and economically, and debated ways to devise a strategy to outsmart the opposition. The most important outcome of the congress was **Joaquim Chissano**'s decision not to run for the presidency and the selection of **Armando Guebuza,** the new party secretary-general, as the party's standard bearer in the 2004 presidential elections.

ELECTIONS. Upon assuming power in 1975, **FRELIMO**'s electoral process called for cells to elect local assemblies; these elected district assemblies, which in turn elected municipal assemblies. The latter elected provincial assemblies. The Popular Assembly, which was the highest legislative body in the country (with more than 220 members in 1977), was appointed by the **Central Committee** (a body of 130 members in 1987) and was not popularly elected. The majority of the members of the Popular Assembly were peasants. Workers, men and women, and representatives from the armed forces, the masses, and the country's "significant" organizations made up part of the assembly. This system has, of course, been abolished and replaced by a multiparty system that has brought wider popular participation in the electoral process. Since the first multiparty elections in 1994, the Assembly of the Republic has numbered 250 members. In 1992, FRELIMO held 129 of the 250 seats; **RENAMO;** 112; the União Democrática, 9. Eighty percent of the 6.1 million electorate participated in the elections. In the presidential elections, **Joaquim Chissano** won by 53.30 percent to Dhlakama's 33.73 percent. In 1999, some 4,934,352 people went to the polls, with 4,471,988 votes declared valid. Chissano garnered 52.29 percent of the vote, and **Afonso Dhlakama** 47.71 percent. For the National Assembly, out of 250 seats, FRELIMO took 133 and RENAMO 117. The parties that ran for the Assembly of the Republic were as follows: Frente de Libertação de Moçambique (FRELIMO), Resistência Nacional Moçambicana-UNIÃO Eleitoral (RENAMO-UE), Partido Trabalhista (PT), Partido Social-Liberal e Democrático (SOL), União Democrática (UD), União Moçambicana de Oposição (UMO), Partido Nacional dos Operários e Camponeses (PANAOC), Partido Independente de Moçambique (PIMO), Partido Democrático e Liberal de Moçambique (PADELIMO), Partido de Progresso Liberal de Moçambique (PPLM), Partido de Ampliação Social de Moçambique (PASOMO), and Partido Liberal e Democrático de Moçambique (PALMO). Interesting was the fact that, out of 11 provinces, FRELIMO won five. RENAMO won **Manica, Sofala, Tete, Nampula, Niassa,** and **Zambezia**, clearly indicating the areas where FRELIMO has had problems in the past and the country's regional division. RENAMO and its coalition disputed the results of the elections, took its complaint to the Supreme Tribunal on Elections, but lost. Thus, even as recently as early 2001, **Dhlakama** was still refusing to officially recognize **Chissano** as president.

ELEITOR **(ELECTOR).** According to a 1963 law, males over 21 years of age who could write and read Portuguese were eligible to vote in colonial as well as Portuguese national elections. Illiterate males and females over 21 could vote if they were heads of family. Females were allowed to vote if they had an education equivalent to the first three years of high school or were taxpayers.

ENES, ANTÓNIO (1848–1901). Portuguese writer, politician, librarian, and statesman, Enes became keenly interested in colonial matters after his appointment as minister of the navy during the government of João Crisóstomo, in the aftermath of the **British Ultimatum.** In 1891, Enes was sent to Mozambique to enforce the terms of the June 11 treaty signed that year with Britain, stemming from the 1890 ultimatum. In 1895, Enes assumed the office of royal commissioner of Mozambique, with the specific mission of terminating **Gungunhana's** threat in **Gaza** and in Lourenço Marques

District. His mission accomplished, Enes promulgated several laws to force Mozambicans to work, and reorganized the colony's administration. No friend of Africans, Enes scorned their assimilation as citizens and strongly advocated the use of concessionaire companies to develop the colony. His most celebrated written work, *Moçambique*, was published in 1893.

ESTADO NOVO. The period of Portuguese history inaugurated by the assumption of power by Dr. **António de Oliveira Salazar** in 1926, following the overthrow of the republic by the army. The Estado Novo was characterized by a strong anticommunistic current, a tilt toward corporate fascism, and an alliance with the **Catholic Church** (Salazar was a former seminarian). Salazar viewed the colonies primarily as sources of manpower and raw materials for the benefit of the mother country. During his tenure as prime minister (1933–1968), forced labor was intensified, a sharper distinction was made between *indígenas* and *não-indígenas* (nonindigenous or assimilated, a status that became much more difficult to achieve), and the systematic repression of freedoms was instituted with the creation of the **Polícia Internacional de Defesa do Estado** (PIDE) in 1957.

To ensure national control of resources, Salazar abolished the early monopolistic companies and accelerated colonization through the settlement of **Portuguese** *colonos*, who arrived in unprecedented large numbers from the metropolis. As was his ruling style in the metropolis, Salazar governed the colonies with an iron fist. The colonial policies, which he drafted when he was colonial minister for a brief period, were embodied in the 1930 **Acto Colonial (Colonial Act)** and became part of the 1933 Portuguese **constitution**. However, resistance from the colonized Africans, who eventually waged against **Portugal** a successful liberation war that ended in April 1974, met Salazar's repressive colonial policies and the denial of independence to the colonies.

ETHNIC GROUPS. Mozambique is inhabited by at least 10 major ethnic groups and dozens of subgroups. The major groups include the **Ajao, Chope, Chicunda, Chuabo, Maconde, Macua-Lomwe, Maravi, Nguni, Nyngwe, Shona**, and **Tonga**. The numerical composition is as follows: **Macua-Lomwe**, 47 percent; **Tonga**, 24 percent; **Maravi**, 12 percent; Shona, 12 percent; Ajao (Yao), 3 percent; **Swahili**, 7 percent; **Maconde**, 0.5 percent; Portuguese, 0.2 percent; and others, 0.6 percent.

EXTERNAL DEBT. Mozambique is a highly indebted poor country (HIPC) with a greater than 80 percent debt burden. Total external debt was U.S.$4.653 billion in 1990, U.S.$5.781 billion in 1995, and U.S.$5.991 billion in 1997, representing 135 percent of GNP. In 2000, the external debt was estimated to be $1.4 billion. At that point, foreign development assistance represented 29.6 percent of GNP, about $58 per capita, considerably down from 45.6 percent in 1990, or about $76 per capita. External debt is now over 427 percent of the GDP, an improvement over the 1992 figure of 495 percent. Hence, despite growth in the export sector, Mozambique will continue to have a serious debt problem and will need more debt rescheduling and debt relief.

In November 1996, the Paris Club decided under the Naples Agreement to write off two-thirds of the debt incurred from 1975 to 1984. The remaining U.S.$200 million is to be repaid over the next 20 years. Between 1987 and 1995, the international donor community provided more than U.S.$8 billion in grants, credits, and debt relief. The main bilateral donors are Germany, Italy, Sweden, the **United States,** and Norway. The World Bank and the **International Monetary Fund** (IMF) have shown confidence in Mozambique's future. This has encouraged other donors to further assist Mozambique. Thus, in 1995, the Paris Club of creditor countries pledged U.S.$119 million under the enhanced structural adjustment facility in support of the government's reform program for the 1996–1998 period. More aid from Canada, Sweden, and the European Union (EU) was pledged in early 1997.

– F –

FEIRA **(FAIR, MARKET).** An economic institution promoted by the **Portuguese** during the early years of the discoveries. The Portuguese established *feiras* in every major settlement along the coast, such as **Sofala,** Luanda (Angola), Bissau (Guinea), **Quelimane,** Lourenço Marques, Mombasa, Malindi, and Zimbabwe, although, with time, the term was used more often for markets opened up in the hinterland of the colonies.

FEITORIAS. Another term for trading sites the **Portuguese** established early along the coast and interior of their colonial possessions, usually identifiable through physical establishments such as warehouses, fortresses, and colonial dwellings.

FIFTH CONGRESS (FRELIMO). FRELIMO's Fifth Congress, which took place on July 24–31, 1989. At this **congress,** the Frente de Libertação de Moçambique (FRELIMO) renounced Marxism, even though scientific socialism remained theoretically the party's philosophy. The congress retained FRELIMO as the single, centralized party in Mozambique, while allowing private initiative, including ownership of information media (e.g., newspapers), even though the radio and television remained in the hands of the state as prescribed by the **constitution**. Political indoctrination of the armed forces, which would no longer be subject to the party, was prohibited. On the incipient negotiations with **RENAMO**, the congress remained moot. This was interpreted as giving President **Joaquim Chissano** and the 12-member Politbureau a free hand in pursuing either a negotiated settlement or a military solution to the **civil war** in Mozambique.

FIRST CONGRESS (RENAMO). The **Resistência Nacional Moçambicana** (RENAMO) held its first congress inside Mozambique on June 5–9, 1989. Some hold the view that its first congress was actually held near **Chimoio, Manica** Province, in May 1982. RENAMO denies this claim, saying, instead, that a meeting, and not a congress, had then taken place in **South Africa** only to attract Mozambicans into RENAMO's "leadership." The 1989 congress was attended by several journalists and foreign observers. It focused on several practical issues that resulted in seven general resolutions on National Unity; National Policy; International Policy; the Frontline States; **Southern African Development Coordinating Conference** (SADCC), now **Southern African Development Community** (SADC); African Unity; and Peace and Reconciliation in Mozambique. According to Alex Vines, "RENAMO appears to have reaffirmed its 1981 programme with commitment to building a market economy, protection of private property, restoration of religious freedom, and respect of traditions, and a confirmation of its post-1986 condemnation of apartheid in South Africa, almost all of it contained in RENAMO's 1981 *Manifest and Program*."

FIRST, RUTH. African National Congress (ANC) ideologue killed on August 17, 1982, by a bomb explosion at her office at the Eduardo Mondlane University. She was a white South African, an antiapartheid activist, and a political writer.

FISHING AND FORESTRY. Because of its long coast and its many rivers and its vast woodlands, Mozambique could develop a strong fishing and forestry industry. Following the **civil war**, Mozambique fishery has improved considerably. From 26,900,000 metric tons in 1995, it jumped to 36,600,000 tons in 1997. The last figures on forestry reveal a slight growth from 18,467,000 metric tons in 1995 to 18,529,000 metric tons in 1997. The booming construction industry and the return of the **refugees** have put vegetation and its trees at risk. In fact, the World Bank reports that, between 1990 and 1995, some 1,162 square km (453.906 square miles) of land were deforested, representing about 0.7 percent of the available trees in the country.

FLAG. The Mozambique flag has four wedge-shaped diagonal stripes in green, black, and yellow, linked by white bands. A book, topped by a gun and a hoe, is enclosed in a white cogwheel.

FLECHA(S). Airborne commando-trained units established in 1973 by the **Portuguese** secret police **Polícia International de Defesa do Estado** (PIDE) and later the Direcção Geral de Segurança (DGS) on the Rhodesian frontier to combat nationalist insurgency. The units consisted of no more than 12 men, predominantly African, who had a military and intelligence gathering mission, and operated independently from the police and the army. Southern Rhodesia eventually supported these units against **FRELIMO**.

FLOODS (2000 and 2001). In February 2000, intense flooding, especially out of the swollen **Limpopo**, **Zambezi**, and Pungue Rivers, devastated Mozambique's southern and central provinces. The country experienced its heaviest rains since the 1850s, affecting two million people. Reportedly, 500,000 were displaced. The floods killed 640 people and 20,000 head of cattle, contributing to outbreaks of cholera and dysentery, while destroying much of the infrastructure. An appeal to the international community netted close to U.S.$500 million, the amount of assistance the government was seeking. The World Bank estimated that the floods had cost Mozambique between $270 million and $430 million. Unfortunately, flooding reoccurred during the same period in 2001. However, the rains affected mostly the central provinces, namely, **Manica, Sofala**, **Tete**, and **Zambézia**.

FREIRE, ALBUQUERQUE (1935–). Mozambican poet, author of many poems, including *O livro dos sonetos* and *Canção negra e outros poemas*, both published in 1960.

FRELIMO. *See* **FRENTE DE LIBERTAÇÃO DE MOÇAMBIQUE**.

FRENTE DE LIBERTAÇÃO DE MOÇAMBIQUE (FRELIMO) (MOZAMBIQUE LIBERATION FRONT). A liberation front organized in June 1962 by Mozambican nationalists against **Portuguese** colonialism.

Initially, FRELIMO was a combination of three revolutionary movements formed by Mozambicans working and living abroad, namely: the **União Democrática Nacional de Moçambique** (UDENAMO) (Mozambique National Democratic Union), established in Salisbury in 1960; **União Nacional de Moçambique Independente** (UNAMI) (African National Union of Independent Mozambique), created in Blantyre by **Tete** exiles in 1961; and **União Nacional Africana de Moçambique** (MANU) (Mozambique African National Union), based in Mombasa, Kenya, in 1961.

At first, the diverse and dispersed nationalist movements viewed each other with suspicion and refused to form a united front that would pose a real threat to **Portugal**. In 1961, however, a Conference of the Nationalist Organizations of the Portuguese Territories was held in Casablanca, and UDENAMO participated in it. The conference called for unity. Both Presidents Kwame Nkrumah of Ghana and Julius Nyerere of Tanzania urged the movements to unite. The three liberation movements heeded the call and finally met in Dar-es-Salaam. On June 25, 1962, FRELIMO emerged out of the delicate negotiations. As a compromise, to ensure that none of the former leaders would assume the front's leadership and thus create potential rivalries, **Eduardo Chivambo Mondlane**, a professor at Syracuse University, was invited to become the president of the new front. Educated and enjoying notoriety in the **United States**, Mondlane, who had refused to join any of the movements but had urged them to unite instead, proved to be an effective leader. On September 25, 1964, FRELIMO launched its first armed attack against the Portuguese government in northern Mozambique.

FRELIMO began its incursions out of bases in Tanzania from **Cabo Delgado** and **Niassa**, and, by 1974, its guerrillas had reached Tete, infiltrating, as it claimed, more than one-fifth of the colonial territory. From a handful of 250 fighting men in 1964, FRELIMO had successfully enlisted some 8,000 guerrilla fighters by 1967, while the Portuguese mustered a force of at least 60,000 troops. Fighting simultaneously in three colonies against determined Africans who were assisted by the **Soviet Union**, the then–East European countries, and the People's Republic of China (and backed by international opinion), as well as detached from the mother country thousands of miles away in Europe and unaccustomed to the rugged colonial terrain, the Portuguese troops were unable to stop the tide of the revolution led by FRELIMO in Mozambique. While casualties mounted on the Portuguese side, communications were constantly disrupted between the major cities, and the population was no longer trustworthy because many Mozambicans sympathized with FRELIMO.

In Portugal, despite efforts to silence criticism of the conduct of the war, the army was demoralized and the people horrified not only by the casualties but also by the cost of the war. Unexpectedly, on April 25, 1974, the army toppled Premier **Marcello Caetano**'s government in Lisbon and began negotiations with the revolutionary movements in the colonies. In September 1974, the **Lusaka Agreement** was signed in Zambia, allowing a transitional government in Mozambique consisting of FRELIMO and Portuguese representatives. **Joaquim Chissano**, a prominent member of FRELIMO's **Central Committee** and the movement's chief representative in Dar-es-Salaam, assumed the position of premier of the **transitional government**.

FRELIMO's initial emphasis on territorial liberation as the highest priority obscured its long-range plans for the future government of Mozambique. FRELIMO officials expected that independence would be won only after many years of war and therefore were as surprised as anyone else when the fighting ended abruptly in April 1974. Until the death of Eduardo Mondlane in 1969 and the expulsion from the party of **Urias Simango**, the former vice president of FRELIMO who dared to criticize the Central Committee and claimed that the adoption of "scientific socialism" had created divisiveness within the party, FRELIMO did not have a clear and concrete plan to lead the future nation, one that would be plagued with insurmountable economic and social ills. In fact, no one was clear as to whether the new nation would be a democratic, Western-style republic, an oligarchy of the Central Committee on the Eastern bloc model, or simply an authoritarian regime under a Marxist-Leninist dictator. With the ascent of **Samora Machel** to the presidency of the movement in 1970, however, and the growing influence of **Marcelino dos Santos**, secretary for external affairs at one point, and Mariano Matsinha, deputy for administration, it became apparent that the Marxist-Leninist hard-liners would triumph and chart a socialist course for future Mozambique.

As a way of maximizing its military victories, the Front set up health centers, schools, and cooperatives in the liberated areas, thus gaining the hearts and the minds of the people and beginning to implement its as yet undeveloped policies. Interestingly enough, FRELIMO never declared itself, as the MPLA did in Angola, a government in exile. As its goals and objectives began to be refined, however, FRELIMO solidly stood for the nationalization of the means of production, limitations to private property, the collectivization of farms under peasants alongside state farms, and the expropriation of foreign-owned businesses and property. It also advocated the primacy of the party over the state, the discouragement or abolition of religion, the rapid elimination of illiteracy, the nominal delegation of minimal authority to people's assemblies, the emancipation of women, the support of liberation movements in Zimbabwe and Namibia, and the elimination of racism in **South Africa.** These principles and goals were eventually introduced in independent Mozambique, especially during the 1975–78 period. However, their implementation was so hastily done that, instead of helping to rebuild the war-torn country, they contributed to economic chaos and further social dislocation that bred discontent, especially among the peasants who were often forcibly removed from their lands to work in collective farms. The policy created favorable ground for the **Resistência Nacional Moçambicana** (RENAMO), which had begun its operations in southern Rhodesia almost as soon as FRELIMO assumed power.

Internal political crises, exacerbated by the debilitating economic conditions, and the psychological impact of RENAMO's attacks, forced the Central Committee of FRELIMO to relax its nationalization policy and encourage the return of those Portuguese businessmen and technicians who, intimidated by the new policies, had left the country. Foreign investors were invited in, the Marxist rhetoric toned down, and exiles invited back. Machel traveled to the West, including Portugal, to temper the radical image of his state, solicit financial assistance, and garner military support. Confronted with the stranglehold posed by apartheid on the subcontinent and wishing to see South Africans free, Mozambique had openly supported the African National Congress (ANC), as it had successfully done with Robert Mugabe's **Zimbabwe African National Union** (ZANU). South Africa retaliated militarily and economically and stepped up its assistance to the Mozambique National Resistance Movement. The internal and international pressures became so unbearable that Machel accepted a formal treaty with South Africa, which bound the two sides not to interfere in each other's internal affairs. Essentially, Mozambique pledged to deny military bases to the ANC, while South Africa would stop assisting RENAMO. While Mozambique adhered to its part of the bargain, South Africa did not. Worsening the situation was the sudden death of the president in an airplane crash in South African territory on October 19, 1986. Mozambique foreign minister **Joaquim Chissano** assumed the presidency in November 1986, but the prospects for the country's stability remained grim, notwithstanding the fact that the new president was reputed to be a shrewder statesman than his predecessor.

FRELIMO had and continues to have a complex political structure. In the past, the People's Assembly was the highest political body and the "supreme organ of the state," made up of members of a large Central Committee, the Executive Committee, provincial governors, the Ministerial Council, two provincial representatives, and elected citizens representing all walks of life. Prior to the first multiparty elections in 1994, the People's Assembly elected members of the Central Committee, which met every two years. It decided on the make-up of the executive. A Permanent Commission of the People's Assembly (initially consisting of a dozen members) oversaw the functioning of the party and the nation between sessions. In 1994, the Assembly of the Republic made up of elected members from the ruling party and the opposition replaced the People's Assembly. As expected, the president is now popularly elected. Although at present the party is assessing its relation with the state, the president of FRELIMO is still the president of the Republic of Mozambique and the commander in chief of the Mozambique (Armed) Defense Forces (FADM). He appoints a large Ministerial Council, presided over by the prime minister. The president also appoints and dismisses at will provincial governors, although this may change in the future, if the opposition has its way.

The Mozambique **constitution**, ratified for the first time on June 25, 1975, and amended in 1990, guarantees individual freedoms, including religious freedom, and upholds universal suffrage for those at least 18 years of age. Despite these written guarantees, however, international organizations have in the past accused Mozambique of violating human rights in the so-called reeducation camps and jails. Summary in-chamber and public executions of opponents, particularly of **RENAMO** suspects, are said to have occurred in the country. On December 17, 1987, FRELIMO adopted a six-month amnesty for all RENAMO collaborators. By November 1988, the government claimed that 2,000 sympathizers or guerrillas had turned themselves in.

Fortunately, the shrewd new president encouraged a government dialogue with the country's Christian and Muslim leaders, slowly improving church and state relations turned sour during the first five years of FRELIMO's rule. The **Catholic Church** presented a special problem, as it was accused of having collaborated with the colonial state and was suspected of favoring RENAMO's activities. However, the pope's visit to Mozambique in September 1988 further contributed to a better atmosphere between the Catholic Church and the secular state.

As a result, FRELIMO and RENAMO held their first direct negotiations in Rome in the summer of 1990. Unfortunately, the talks brought no cease-fire and collapsed immediately thereafter. Events in South Africa, the belief that RENAMO had become weaker, and the potential impact of internal changes on international opinion, contributed to the hardening of FRELIMO's negotiating position.

The most interesting development in 1989 and 1990 was FRE-LIMO's volte face on several fronts: continued revision of the constitution on political participation; acceptance in principle of a multiparty state; apparent abandonment of the commitment to an extreme Marxist-Leninist philosophy; enforcement of religious freedom; reliance on private peasant agricultural output from privately owned plots of land; voluntarism for cooperatives; reinstitution of private, state, corporate, and peasant property; and introduction of a free market-oriented economy endorsed, as it were, by international financial institutions such as the **International Monetary Fund**. The party would no longer be restricted to workers and peasants but would be open to all members of Mozambique society, including those regarded earlier as enemies of the state, such as property owners, religious citizens, and businessmen. To ensure support for Chissano's programs and expand popular representation, FRELIMO's **Fifth Congress** raised the number of the **Political Bureau** (Politburo) members from 10 to 12 and those of the Central Committee from 130 to 160.

Evidently, observers were waiting to see whether these changes would actually be implemented as promised. Eventually, they were, and Mozambique held its first multiparty elections in 1994 and then in 1999, the ruling party claiming victory in both elections. Despite its victories, FRELIMO has faced serious challenges over the years. Even though the party remains cohesive, there is a divide between the old generation FRELIMO leaders who have not totally abandoned Marxism and the new generation that is much less ideological. People continue to question the government's sincerity on democratic reforms, accuse government officials of rampant corruption cynically called *cabritismo* (goatism), criticize the inefficient bureaucracy, dislike the policy of bringing white South Africans and Zimbabweans to occupy vast tracts of land for agricultural development, and would like to see a more equitable sharing of resources between South, Center, and North. In fact, many think that Mozambique does not suffer from the problem of chronic ethnicity but from regionalism, which, since the colonial period, has favored the South over the rest of the country. The next few years will be very crucial to the party, given that President Joaquim Chissano has repeatedly announced that he will not be seeking reelection. The favorite following FRELIMO's Eighth Congress in June 2002, is Armando Guebuza, who was selected as the party's secretary-general.

FRENTE DE SALVAÇÃO DE MOÇAMBIQUE (FRESAMO) (MOZAMBIQUE SALVATION FRONT). Reportedly a **RENAMO**

splinter group, following **André Matsangaissa**'s death in 1979, FRE-SAMO was led by Zeca Caliate in 1981. The leaders disagreed with RE-NAMO's policy of accepting military assistance from **South Africa**. Lacking popular support, the group soon disbanded.

FRIENDS OF MOZAMBIQUE. A nonprofit humanitarian organization created in the early 1980s by Artur Vilanculo, former **FRELIMO** member and briefly **RENAMO** representative in the **United States**. Vilanculo says that his organization was nonpartisan and aimed at providing scholarships to Mozambican students and humanitarian aid to the people of Mozambique. Vilanculo founded the organization following disagreement with the leaders of **CUNIMO** and his ouster by Dr. Luís B. Serapião from his position as representative of RENAMO in the United States in 1986.

– G –

GAMA, VASCO DA (1469–1524). Renowned **Portuguese** navigator chosen by Dom Manuel I to lead the expedition to find a sea route to India in 1497. Vasco da Gama departed from Belém, Lisbon, to India on July 8, 1497, sailed past the Cape of Good Hope, reached 10 years earlier by Bartolomeu Dias; spent Christmas at Natal (present **South Africa**); and disembarked at **Inhambane** on the Mozambique coast on March 1, 1498. Calling Inhambane the land of *boa gente* (good people), he proceeded to **Quelimane** and Mozambique Island, and claimed both as Portuguese territories. He sailed up to Mombasa and Malindi (where he planted a Portuguese *padrão* or landmark) and reached India in May 1498. Named the admiral of the Indies by the Portuguese monarch, Vasco da Gama made another voyage to India (1502–03), stopping along the coast of Mozambique. Appointed viceroy of India in 1524, Vasco da Gama died in the same year at Cochin.

GAZA. Mozambique southern province, along the Indian Ocean, bordering **Manica** Province in the north, **Inhambane** in the east, **Maputo** Province in the south, and Zimbabwe and **South Africa** in the west. It is 32,022 square miles large and has a population of 1,034,700 (1997 estimate). Such rivers as the **Limpopo**, Rio dos Elefantes, Changane, and Save flow toward the Indian Ocean, allowing extensive irrigation and the cultivation of crops such as rice, corn, wheat, cashew nuts, cassava, sorghum, and fruit trees (orange and lemon), along with animal husbandry. Some of the agricultural products are processed locally and exported. Gaza has an important port at **Xai-Xai** (formerly João Belo), which is also the provincial capital.

GONÇALVES, JAIME PEDRO (1936–). Born in Nova **Sofala, Beira**, Gonçalves attended the Zobue Minor Seminary during the 1950s and the Namaacha and Malhangalene major seminaries during the 1960s. He was ordained diocesan priest on December 17, 1967, and served at the St. John the Baptist Matacuane Parish for 20 months. Thereafter, he attended universities in Canada and Rome, having received degrees in leadership, education, social sciences, and theology. Selected bishop, he was consecrated on March 28, 1976, amid much pomp and pageantry. On June 29, 1984, he was elevated to the rank of first archbishop of Beira by Pope John Paul II, in Rome, returning to his archdiocese of Beira to start the most difficult period of his clerical career.

A dynamic and fearless bishop, Gonçalves became a popular name when he was selected by the Mozambican Episcopal Conference (of which he served as president for over a decade) to facilitate the peace negotiations between **FRELIMO** and **RENAMO** during the 1988–92 period. Without his tireless effort, which led him even to RENAMO's headquarters in Gorongoza under extremely dangerous conditions, the **Acordo Geral da Paz** might not have been signed in 1992. Yet, being a Ndau himself as Afonso Dhlakama, he was put in a delicate position not to give any indication that he favored one side over the other.

Since becoming bishop and archbishop, Gonçalves has been an outspoken clergyman and has defied many attempts by government officials to curb religious freedom, to such an extent that the late president Machel had singled him out for public humiliation among his bishop colleagues. As a result, quite often he was confronted by the authorities and was actually detained and arrested at least twice, as he attempted to fulfill his responsibilities as a bishop of a large and active diocese. At Beira city, made up mostly of **Sena** and **Ndau** populations, the archbishop became controversial when, in accordance with the ordinances of church councils and papal encyclicals that prescribe the use of the language of the original people of an area during ritual, he ordered that Sunday masses be said in the language of the majority (Ndau) and the original population. His religious and political opponents accused him of "ethnic discrimination" favoring the Ndau over the Sena population. Dom Jaime Gonçalves himself says he was maliciously and deliberately misunderstood and that several government officials fomented ethnic dissent in order to undermine his authority. He believes, as many others do, that the Ndau preceded the Sena in settling Beira. However, others dispute the claim, pointing out that the Sena were descendants of the Karanga who left the plateau of **Mwenemutapa** centuries before the Ndau inhabited the area. Fortunately, by 2001, animosities had subsided considerably, and Archbishop Dom Gonçalves, as always, has been able to ride the waves and come out stronger. Admired for his intellect, eloquence, and honesty, Dom Gonçalves remains one of the most respected bishops in the country.

GOUVEIA, (DOM) TEODÓSIO CLEMENTE DE (1890–1961). Archbishop of Lourenço Marques and first cardinal of Mozambique. Before his appointment, Dom Clemente de Gouveia had played a crucial role in the successful negotiations with the Holy See, which led to the now famous Acordo Missionário of May 20, 1940, and the Estatuto Missionário (Missionary Statute) of 1941. Politically, however, he was opposed to the independence of the **Portuguese** colonies and believed that patriotism and Portuguese Roman Catholicism were only different sides of the same coin. He vehemently warned the African seminarians (being trained at Namaacha by the priests of the Holy Sacrament, who were accused of encouraging Mozambican nationalism among the students) to stay out of politics.

GOVERNMENT. See ADMINISTRATION; FRELIMO.

GOVERNO, BERNARDO FILIPE (1939–). Bishop of the diocese of **Quelimane** since October 10, 1976, Dom Governo was born in Macuse, Quelimane, and attended the Zobue Minor Seminary and the Namaacha and Malhangalene Major Seminaries in Mozambique. He was ordained a Capuchin priest in 1969. Full of wit, Dom Bernardo is a no-nonsense clergyman. Simple and affable, he may be called the people's "missionary" bishop. Responsible for a large diocese, Bishop Bernardo walks, uses the bicycle, and drives his own car to visit every corner of his diocesan territory. He has had numerous brushes with the authorities, recalcitrant foreign missionaries, and insubordinate catechists of the old Portuguese order. But nothing has dampened his enthusiasm and determination. He has created his own minor seminary and a convent for the religious education of diocesan priests and nuns, and his diocese runs a flour mill and a cocoa plantation to supplement the diocese's meager resources. Bishop Bernardo is a polyglot who speaks Portuguese, French, Italian, and three African languages fluently and is a world traveler, but always with an eye toward the welfare of his diocese.

Despite the fact that he was very reluctant to accept the nomination to the bishopric of the vacant diocese of Quelimane, Bishop Bernardo has restored the respect of the **Catholic Church** before the authorities whom he faces without fear. In the process, he has become one of the best administrator bishops in the country. His ability to communicate the church message easily and effectively has contributed to the many responsibilities he has assumed within the Mozambique Episcopal Conference, including the position of spokesperson and Social Communication Overseer.

GOVERNORS (*GOVERNADORES*, GOVERNORS-GENERAL). *See* APPENDIXES.

GRÉMIO. Provided by the **Acto Colonial** of 1930, *grémios* (six were functioning in 1964) were business and labor representative bodies (the Chamber of Commerce of Lourenço Marques, the Mozambique Industrial and Economic Association, the Cereal Growers Guild, and the Development Association of Zambézia). Each had three representatives in the colonial Legislative Council and two on the Economic and Social Council, "the highest advisory body of the governor-general." The grémios defended the interests of their members but collaborated hand-in-hand with the government and its policies. The only meaningful power they had was the appointment of labor judges who interpreted disputed labor laws.

GRÉMIO AFRICANO. An association of educated, assimilated, and mulatto Mozambicans created in Lourenço Marques during the 1920s, whose major demands were equality for all and an end to forced labor. Eventually, it changed its name and became the Associação Africana. As the association began to be perceived as too moderate in its demands, some of the members, mostly Mozambican blacks, broke away and formed the **Instituto Negrófilo**. As a result, its membership became predominantly mulatto. The Instituto Negrófilo later took the name of Centro Associativo dos Negros de Moçambique.

GRÉMIO NEGRÓFILO AFRICANO DE MANICA E SOFALA. Cultural Association created in Manica and Sofala by **Kamba Simango** in 1935.

GRUPOS DINAMIZADORES. The *grupos dinamizadores* (dynamizing groups) served as mass mobilizers in committees of 12 **FRELIMO** members or sympathizers, elected by the people locally, whose major function was to raise "the political consciousness" of the masses. They conducted "schools of democracy," taught people how to participate in the electoral process, and often acted as vigilantes. Local grupos dinamizadores were abolished in the countryside and the small towns in 1978 and allowed only in urban areas. They were replaced by the *grupos de vigilância popular* (groups of popular vigilance) who were tightly controlled by the National Service of the People's Security, the party, and the political police. Following the 1992 **Acordo Geral da Paz**, the groups were disbanded.

GUEBUZA, ARMANDO EMÍLIO (1943–). Armando Emílio Guebuza was born on October 20, 1943. Educated in the primary and secondary schools of then Lourenço Marques (**Maputo**), Guebuza was active in the **Núcleo dos Estudantes Africanos Secundários de Moçambique** (NESAM), a cradle of nationalist ideas of a small group of assimilado African youths of Lourenço Marques, of which **Eduardo Chivambo Mondlane** was a member and cofounder during the 1940s. Guebuza was eventually arrested by the **Portuguese** secret police, **Polícia International de Defesa do Estado** (PIDE). In 1963, he joined **FRELIMO** in Dar-es-Salaam. He taught in FRELIMO schools in Tanzania and in the liberated areas of Mozambique. At FRELIMO's **Second Congress** in 1968, Armando Guebuza was elected to the **Central Committee** and later to the Executive and Politico-Military Committees, becoming in 1971 the party's national political commissar. Portuguese high commissioner Rear Admiral Vítor Crespo made Armando Guebuza minister of internal administration of the **transitional government** of Mozambique after the **Lusaka Agreement** of September 1974.

After independence in June 1975, President **Samora Machel** named Armando Guebuza minister of the interior. Guebuza later introduced the so-called **Operação Produção** (Operation Production). In 1977, Guebuza relinquished the portfolio of the Interior Ministry to become deputy minister of defense and political commissar for the Armed and Security Forces. He served as minister in Cabo Delgado in 1979 and was appointed one of the three lieutenant-generals when military ranks were introduced in the Mozambican army in 1980. In 1983, Armando Guebuza returned to his post at the Ministry of the Interior and was named minister of transport and communication by President **Joaquim Alberto Chissano** in 1987. At FRELIMO's **Eighth Congress** in June 2002, Guebuza was selected to be the party's presidential candidate during the 2004 presidential elections, since Chissano has taken his name off the list. Currently, Guebuza is the chief of the "Bancada Parlamentar" (majority leader) of FRELIMO in the Assembleia da República, or the Mozambican National Assembly. Since June 2002, he has become the party's secretary-general.

GUNGUNHANA (1850–1906). Last king of the **Nguni** (Vátua) of the **Gaza** empire. He ascended to the throne in 1885, one year after the death of his father, Mzila, through a palace coup with the support of the **Portuguese**, who had also assisted his father in 1861. Gungunhana's first task was to thwart the Portuguese threat. Consequently, he sent envoys to Lisbon in October 1895, a diplomatic move that resulted in a treaty of November 1895. While **Portugal** guaranteed Gungunhana sovereignty over the lands of his father acknowledged by a treaty of 1861, he pledged not to declare war even on his enemies without Portuguese permission and agreed to allow free commerce and transit in his territory, particularly to Portuguese citizens and subjects.

Ultimately, Gungunhana was unable to abide by the treaty, as he faced constant rebellion in Gaza, **Manica**, and **Inhambane**. Furthermore, he harbored chiefs who were inimical to the Portuguese such as Maazila, Magude chief, and Matibejane, chief of the Zixaxa. Gungunhana often showed obvious contempt for the Portuguese and played them against the British, whom he led to believe were his allies. On more than one occasion, he met British officials or envoys of Cecil Rhodes's British South African Company who were seeking mineral concessions. The flirtation with the British ended in 1891, however, following the **British Ultimatum**, which recognized Gazaland as falling under the Portuguese sphere of influence.

António Enes, Mozambique royal commissioner, entrusted **Joaquim Augusto Mouzinho de Albuquerque** with the task of eliminating forever the power of the Nguni kings. Thus, on December 28, 1895, following a series of battles, Mouzinho arrested Gungunhana at Chaimite. The arrest signaled the demise of the vast Nguni empire. Gungunhana's lieutenant, Maguiguane, continued the tradition of resistance against the Portuguese, but Mouzinho pursued him and finally had him killed by troops he commanded in August 1897. Along with his son Godide and his companions, including Matibejane, Gungunhana was taken to Lisbon, where he became a great spectacle for the Portuguese. He was subsequently baptized and exiled to Azores where, after enjoying limited freedom, he died in 1906.

Gungunhana's ultimate defeat can be attributed to the constant revolt of the subjects he attempted to control, Portuguese intrigue and military tenacity, and the inconsistency of his generals who led the several *mangas* (battalions) of his army. The vastness of the empire, the unending pillage of cattle, the capture of women and young men in reprisal against revolt, and the exacting of heavy annual tributes presaged the eventual fall of Nguni hegemony in southern Mozambique. Simultaneously, *prazeros,* such as Manuel de Sousa Gouveia, defied Nguni power in

Manica, forcing Gungunhana to shift his headquarters from there to the mouth of the **Limpopo** River.

During his prime, the Portuguese authorities feared Gungunhana, who was often, in their eyes, insolent toward the governors or their representatives. When the king, accompanied by 60,000 people moved his headquarters in 1890, the governor issued orders not to obstruct his transit, even if that meant massive cattle loss due to looting by his entourage. Unfortunately, his final days as king ended in tragedy, as Mouzinho, apparently accompanied by only some 49 white soldiers, arrested Gungunhana without resistance at **Chaimite**. Interestingly enough, however, even at the last minute, Gungunhana showed his royal pride and dignity. When Mouzinho attempted to humiliate him by ordering him to sit down, Gungunhana refused to do so, claiming that the ground was dirty. This led Mouzinho to force the African king to sit, declaring thereafter that he was no longer the king of the Vátua.

– H –

HARBORS. *See* PORTS.

HEALTH. Due to its tropical climatic conditions and the lack of adequate health facilities, Mozambique suffers from many infectious and chronic diseases, as its low life expectancy and high infant mortality rates indicate. Its birthrate, however, is among the highest in the world. In 1988, Mozambique's vital statistics were as follows: birthrate estimated at 45.1 per thousand (29.0 world average); death rate, 19.7 per thousand (11.0 world average); and life expectancy at birth, 44.4 years for males and 46.2 years for females. As the table on Mozambique health indicators shows, these estimates did not change much by 1996. The Mozambique population is extremely young at present.

The first protohospital in Mozambique was built only in 1704 by Frei Francisco de São Tomás and run by the Brothers of São João de Deus on the Mozambique Island. The second hospital was erected in Lourenço Marques only in 1877 (by 1912 it became known as Hospital Central Miguel Bombarda), followed by the construction of the Hospital Militar e Civil in the same city in 1917. Other major towns had either a hospital or an infirmary, such as the Enfermaria Regimental e Civil de **Tete**, built in 1877. All of these facilities, however, had very limited capacity. The

Tete infirmary, for example, could accommodate only 20 patients in 1907. During the early 1900s, the **Portuguese** set up two schools for the training of African nurses at Lourenço Marques and **Inhambane**. The two merged into one training center at Lourenço Marques in 1920. Ten poorly equipped hospitals existed in Mozambique during the 1907–1950 period: at Lourenço Marques, Mozambique Island, Tete, **Quelimane, Inhambane**, Chinde, Angoche, Memba, Chibuto, and Mossuril. The number of patients visiting the hospitals increased as the health facilities began to expand slowly. Thus, in 1825, some 2,685 patients used the health facilities; in 1925, 8,517; in 1929, the number rose to 10,938. During the 1950s, the number had more than doubled as a consequence of the decrees implemented in 1922 that created eight hospitals, which became known as Delegacias de Saúde. Each Delegacia de Saúde oversaw surrounding health care centers, classified into first- and second-class centers, depending on the availability of medicines, the number of doctors' visits, and whether or not there was a nurse in residence. Each Delegacia was asked to create as many health posts as possible, targeting its efforts primarily toward the creation of first-class centers.

The number of doctors grew slowly during the colonial period. In 1883, for example, the colony had only 11 doctors. In 1907, the number had risen to 24, 60 in 1925, and 75 in 1930, when the ratio between doctors and the population was estimated at one per 533,000. During the 1940s, some asylums for the mentally disabled were created, several leper houses established, and centers for the study and eradication of tropical diseases set up in Lourenço Marques.

Throughout the centuries, however, the government did not provide sufficient funds to build new facilities; doctors complained about the awful facilities they had to work in and with, such as the lack of windows for ventilation, mortuaries situated too close to kitchens, leaking roofs, lack of private rooms, and so on. Furthermore, hospital facilities were segregated during the colonial period, and doctors attended the white and assimilated patients first. The *indígenas*, if unable to pay, were supposed to have free consultation and medication. However, since most Africans did not live in towns, the majority of Mozambicans died without ever going to a hospital when they fell seriously ill.

During the 1920s, the government issued decrees compelling employers with more than 100 African laborers to build health facilities and provide free medical assistance to them and their families. But employers often ignored these regulations. As expected, the Portuguese sent their serious patients to Lisbon, to a special hospital catering to the colonial personnel. During this time, medical education in the colony was out of reach for the Africans. When the University of Lourenço Marques was established in 1964, it offered no medical training. Only Lisbon could provide such training and almost always to white Portuguese only, so that, when independence came, there were no more than five Mozambican doctors, who invariably practiced medicine in **Portugal** and not in the colony. It was against such a background in the health care service that **FRELIMO** had to operate when it assumed power in 1975.

Lack of satisfactory and reliable data makes it impossible to ascertain accurately the state of health care services in Mozambique. During the 1980s, there were at least 10 good hospitals located in the major towns, the best being the Hospital Miguel de Bombarda in Maputo. Just prior to independence, 550 medical doctors were working in the country (most being Portuguese). The number represented an increase of 139 from 1963, when the ratio was about one doctor per 1,680 persons. By 1973, however, the number had dropped to 87 as a result of the war of independence. In 1977, FRELIMO was able to recruit 500 foreign doctors. Overall, FRELIMO was commended by the World Health Organization for its successful vaccination campaign against smallpox, measles, and tetanus, a campaign that reached 90 percent of the population in 1979. Maternities have more than doubled from the few that existed in the 1960s, and the same has been true of the 1,258 nurses and the 11,200 beds that were available in the entire colony in 1964.

However, the major diseases that existed a hundred years ago continue to afflict the population. Epidemics of meningitis, cholera, influenza, and widespread cases of schistosomiasis, sleeping sickness, malaria, yellow fever, yaws, and tuberculosis are very common in the country; cure is not easy to attain due to an inadequate number of both medical centers and doctors, particularly for people living far away from the major cities and towns. Since the 1980s, **AIDS** (Acquired Immune Deficiency Syndrome) has become a major catastrophe for Mozambique. Understandably, the precarious health conditions in the country are partly a legacy of the colonial past, when the Portuguese made very little effort to provide for the medical needs of the African population.

Unfortunately, the adverse impact of **RENAMO** has also been felt in the health care sector. The government claims that, from 1977 to 1992, RENAMO destroyed 822 health care centers. Presently, popular participation to build the centers has decreased, and the government has been forced to charge people for the medicine dispensed. Also, maternities are not used to their full capacity as many women, still haunted by the ghost of the past war, remain hesitant to deliver at the centers and the hospitals. A major hospital in **Quelimane** has been putting two people in the same bed due to bed shortage. While all hospitals feel the impact of the AIDS epidemic through the large numbers of patients with opportunistic ailments, such as tuberculosis and other pulmonary diseases, others, especially those in the small towns, have become simply overwhelmed by the sheer numbers of new patients and the lack of electricity and running water. The government and the international organizations mounted a concerted effort after 1992 to build, repair, or rehabilitate the infrastructure, including hospitals and health care centers throughout the country. As a result, according to the **United Nations** High Commissioner for Refugees (UNHCR), by 1994, 103 new or rehabilitated health care posts were functioning, 19 in Maputo, 13 in Gaza, 25 in **Manica**, 6 in **Sofala**, 24 in Tete, 12 in Zambézia, 2 in Niassa, and 2 in **Cabo Delgado**, for a total of 1,142 health centers in 2001. In addition, doctors began to return after the war, although their exact number was unclear at the beginning of the new century. Official estimates claim the ratio of one doctor per 131,991 people in the country at the time and one bed per 1,133–1,146 persons.

Present vital statistics data reveal the following: infant mortality, 130/1,000 (down from 135 in 1997 and 145 in 1980); life expectancy at birth, 45 for males and 50 for females; crude birthrate, 44/1,000; crude death rate, 18/1,000, with an annual population increase of 2.5 percent (down from 3.4 percent in 1980–1990 and 2.6 percent in 1996–1998); and maternal mortality rate per 1,000 live births, 110 during the 1990–1997 period. Prevalence of child malnutrition, age 5, stands at 26 percent of the children. In 1982, only 10 percent of the population in the country had access to sanitation and 23 percent in 1995. Access to safe water increased only from 10 percent in 1982 to 24 percent in 1995. In the cities, sewage is a major problem not only in terms of quantity but also of its management. The latest figures available refer to 1993, when only 23 percent of the urban population had sanitation facilities in the homes, 37 percent had regular waste collection, and 73 percent had potable water. Of course, things are improving, as Mozambique comes out of its war constraints.

Mozambique is experiencing a surge in cholera cases, most likely as a result of the war ravages, hunger and malnutrition, and the most recent **floods**. From August 1997 to February 9, 1998, for instance, there was a cholera outbreak that affected the center and the south of the country, Beira, Manica, Maputo City, **Gaza**, and parts of Maputo Province. Some

14,679 cases were diagnosed, with an intervening death rate of 3.2 percent, resulting in 477 fatalities. In late January 1998, 1,657 more cases of cholera were reported, with an accompanying death rate of 4.1 percent, especially in the city of Beira. Doctors reported that the impact was so swift that, within a period of 48 hours, out of 800 cases, 80 deaths were registered, mostly among children, as expected. The virulence of the epidemic was made clearer in Beira where, between January and February 9, 1998, out of 2,000 cases, 109 deaths occurred.

Adding to the problem of cholera are the recurrent cerebrospinal meningitis cases in the country, especially in the north, where in July 1996, 18 cases with four deaths were detected in **Montepuez** and Belanua Districts. Since the time the refugees began returning from abroad, especially Malawi, the bubonic plague has also been recurrent in Tete Province, particularly in Tete City and Mutarara District. Thus, in late 1994, 216 cases were diagnosed in Mutara alone. Between August 8 and November 1997, 335 new cases afflicted the population of Tete, especially Mutarara, but fortunately with no registered deaths. Of course, these epidemics worsen the impact of endemic malaria, yellow fever, bilharziasis, and typhoid, all of which are aggravated by the floods, a favorable breeding ground for the deadly mosquito vectors.

The government and the private sector claim they are doing their best under the circumstances. There is no doubt that funding, accounting for about 3 percent (down from 4.6 percent in 1990–97) of GDP (most of which goes to salaries and administration), is inadequate, and primary health care and family planning, the benchmark for major improvements in health, are paid only lip service, especially in the rural areas. The Associação Moçambicana para o Desenvolvimento da Família (AMODEFA) (Mozambican Association for the Development of the Family) is working in tandem with the government, donor agencies, and nongovernmental organizations (NGOs) to raise health consciousness, assist the sick, provide family planning advice and resources, and promote health education.

Presented here is a summary of major health indicators in Mozambique. In view of these conditions, what are the vital statistics for Mozambique? Even though figures from different sources are often contradictory or nonexistent, the following are Mozambique's health indicators published by the World Bank. Once the data are contrasted against one another, the real figures most likely lie in between.

Fertility is high in Mozambique, about 5.6 children for women ages 15–49 in 2000, compared to 6.5 in 1980 and 5.3 in 1997; and among youngsters between 15 and 19, about 17 percent of them having one live

Mozambique Health Indicators (1990–1996)

	Year	Mozambique	Africa
Total health expenditures (government, donor, and private) as percentage of GDP	1990	6	4
Real per capita in U.S. dollars		$6	$24
Public health expenditures per capita as percentage of GDP	1990	4.5%	1.7%
Public sector health expenditures per capita in U.S. dollars	1990–1996	$5.08	$10.83
Crude birthrate/1,000	1995	44	42
Crude death rate/1,000	1995	18	19
Infant mortality rate/1,000 live births	1996	130	92
Under-five mortality rate/1,000 live births	1995	212	151
Maternity mortality ratio/1,000	1995	431 males 339 females	448 males 376 females
Access to sanitation (1990–1995) as % of population	1990–1995	21	36
Access to clean water (1990–1995) as % of population	1990–1995	32	44
Life expectancy at birth	1995	45 males 48 females	50 males 54 females
Inpatient hospital beds/1,000	1990–1995	3.1	1.2
HIV percentage prevalence	1995	0.1	4.3
Per capita GNP in U.S. dollars	1990–1996	$90	$496
Population growth (%)	1990–1996	2.5	2.7
Population growth in millions	1990	14.18	511.5
	1995	16.58	599.0
Female literacy rate as percentage of population	1995	77%	53%
Immunization coverage (1990–1996) as percentage of population	1990–1996	70 (BCG)	65 (BCG)
		52 (DPT3)	52 (DPT3)
		62 (measles)	53 (measles)
		27 (TT2)	35 (TT2)
Physician/1,000 population	1995	.86	.11

Source: Adapted from *Health Expenditures, Services, and Outcomes in Africa: Cross-National Comparisons, 1990–1996* (Washington, D.C.: World Bank, 1999), pp. 39–52.

birth each year. They contribute to a 2.2 to 2.7 percent annual population growth in the country. It is also known that, due to poverty, male resistance, and cultural traditions, only 5 percent of Mozambican women use modern contraceptives. With few resources, Mozambique sees its population grow but is unable to provide adequate health services. In 2001, it was projected that in 2002, only 39 percent would have access to health services and that one health post would serve 20,000 people, while one health center would serve as many as 60,000 Mozambicans on the average, with one doctor for each 33,040 people.

HIJA, TWAKALY. Cheikh of Quitangonha District in Mozambique Province who successfully challenged **Portuguese** garrisons in the area during the 1775–1804 period. In spite of his continuous rebellion, Hija continued to receive an annual pension from the Portuguese government.

HOMOÍNE MASSACRE. The massacre of 424 people, including patients and nurses at the town hospital, in late July 1987, shocked the world. **FRELIMO** revealed the massacre to the world and blamed **RENAMO** for the horrendous act. RENAMO denied responsibility and claimed, instead, that government troops had perpetrated the massacre following a brawl within the ranks of the army, which was protecting the hospital and its vicinity. An American *cooperante*, purporting to be a witness who survived by hiding under a shade, blamed RENAMO for the massacre. The U.S. State Department report of April 1988, based on interviews with refugees and displaced people in Mozambique and Zimbabwe, also put the blame on the resistance movement. Subsequently, however, these claims were seriously challenged by several statesmen and scholars (see, e.g., Cabrita's *Mozambique: A Tortuous Road to Democracy*, 2000).

HONWANA, LUÍS BERNARDO (also known as AUGUSTO MANUEL) (1942–). Honwana is a short story writer and journalist, the son of an interpreter. He grew up in the outskirts of **Maputo**, formerly Lourenço Marques. To pay for the completion of his secondary school education, Honwana worked as a cartographer and a newspaper article writer. His writings, which include "Nós matámos o cão-tinhoso" (1964) and "Dina" (1967), both short stories, landed him in jail, as the **Portuguese** considered his portrayal of social conditions, particularly those related to forced labor in Mozambique, to be politically inflammatory. In 1988, he was appointed minister of culture after serving as director of the

President's Office. He later became the secretary of the Permanent Commission of the People's Assembly, a position he no longer holds.

HOTEL POLANA. One of the most enduring and popular establishments in Mozambique. Located in **Maputo**, the Polana Hotel was built by architect Walter Reid on behalf of the Delagoa Bay Company in 1922. Totally renovated in 1992, the Polana remains one of the most memorable monuments of colonial Mozambique, attracting wealthy Mozambicans, government officials, expatriates, international agencies, and diplomats.

– I –

IMPOSTO DE CAPITAÇÁO (HEAD TAX). See *MUTSONKHO.*

IMPOSTO DE PALHOTA (HUT TAX). See *MUTSONKHO.*

INDIAN, PAKISTANI. Mozambique is also the home of some 20,000 Indians from India (particularly from former Goa, Damão e Diu), Pakistani, and immigrants from Bangladesh. Indians tend to be merchants and petty traders and live in the big cities with stores scattered throughout the country's towns.

INDUSTRY AND MANUFACTURING. Mozambique's industrial base is small. Light industries still functioning include food processing, textiles, brewing, cement, and soap production. Industrial output declined in the 1990s due to such problems as lack of raw materials, inability to compete with imported products, the destruction of factories and equipment, and a lack of skilled labor and managerial experience. Among a number of projects designed to stimulate manufacturing industry, the government has set up production corridors along transport routes linking Mozambique's ports with neighboring countries. Output grew by 13.7 percent in 1996.

Cement output has been as follows: 200,000 metric tons in 1956; 610,000 tons in 1973; down to 260,000 tons in 1982; further down to 110,000 tons at the end of 1984. Cement production began gradually recovering in the 1990s, from 146,000 metric tons in 1995 to 179,000 metric tons in 1997. While industrial production stood at 35,000 tons in 1982 and 15,000 tons in 1984, cooking oil stood at 21,900 tons in 1982 and at only 7,600 tons by 1984. Wood production, on the other hand, declined from 38,839 tons in 1982 to 3,178 tons by 1984. The construction industry, however, has done relatively well. In 1964, Mozambique built 638 new units; between 1977 and 1981, construction rose by 25 percent and by a further 4.4 percent in 1982. A reasonable rate of productivity was also sustained in the fishing industry, which produced 42,100 metric tons in 1981; 39,700 tons in 1982; and 42,400 tons in 1983. In 1984, it contributed by 29 percent to Mozambique export earnings. Also, 1984 was the year when South Africa began providing a R2 million package assistance to Mozambique for the expansion of its fishing industry. Overall, 1981 proved to be the best year.

Overall, the various industries are doing better than they were some years ago. Between 1994 and 1996, raw sugar production rose from 21,000 tons to 38,000 tons during the same period; beer brewing increased from 118,000,000 kl to 374,000 kl; and electric energy rose from 490 kilowatt hours in 1994 to 560 kilowatt hours in 1996. While cigarette production fell from 343 million to 250 million cigarettes (it appears that people are smoking less), wheat flour fell from 40,000 tons to 38,000 tons during the same period, reflecting the country's lack of wheat production or sufficient flour import. As a result of this renewed activity, notwithstanding the setbacks in the production of coal (whose mines are now being rehabilitated), bauxite, and unrefined salt, the Mozambique industrial sector grew annually at an average of 8 percent of the GDP between 1990 and 1998, up from 4.5 percent in 1980–90. Should Mozambique not suffer further calamities, such as floods and war, the future of industry and manufacturing may not be as gloomy. However, improvement will be sustained only if Mozambique does not depend too much on foreign assistance and curbs rampant corruption. *See also* ECONOMY.

INFLATION. Although the Mozambican government has tried to stabilize the economy, especially prices, inflation has remained a source of macroeconomic instability. In 1993, the rate of inflation was 44 percent. Consumer price inflation, which averaged 50 percent a year in the early 1990s, fell to under 17 percent in 1996 and to 9 percent in 1999, but rose to 16.8 percent in 2000, as a result of the March **floods**, which displaced 200,000 people, mainly in the south. However, the **International Monetary Fund** gives a mixed overall picture on consumer goods inflation during the last 10 years: 1983–1992, 48.1 percent; 1993, 42.3 percent; 1994, 63.1 percent; 1995, 54.4 percent; 1996, 44.4 percent; 1997, 6.4 percent; 1998, 0.6 percent; 1999, 2.9; and 2000, 12.7 percent. The new banking laws approved in December 1991 led to the split of the national bank into the Banco Commercial de Moçambique and a central bank. The strengthening of the central bank should provide more monetary and inflation control.

INHAMBANE. Mozambique southeastern province, 26,492 square miles large with a population of 1,112,000 (1997 estimate). It is bordered by **Sofala** and **Manica** Provinces in the north through the Save River, in the east and south by the Indian Ocean, and Gaza Province in the west. Its capital is the city of the same name, located on the Indian Ocean. Cattle raising has saved this province, while the population grows rice, cashew nuts, copra, beans, corn, and mafura trees. Inhambane is a major industrial city whose activity centers on the processing of agricultural products, particularly cashew nuts. **Vasco da Gama** stopped at Inhambane on his way to India in 1498 and called it "the land of good people" (*terra de boa gente*).

INSTITUTO PARA A PAZ E DESENVOLVIMENTO (IPADE). Organization created by Raul Domingos, deputy in the Assembly of the Republic, and former prominent member, **RENAMO**'s general chief of staff. Expelled from the party on September 22, 2000, Domingos organized IPADE in mid-2001. The mission and function of the new institute are still vague, although they appear to be nonpartisan.

INTERFAITH MEMBERSHIP OF THE BISHOPS OF SOUTHERN AFRCA (IMBISA). An interfaith organization of southern African bishops, who meet at least once a year to discuss and find solutions to the religious and social problems facing the people of this part of the continent. IMBISA conference appoints its president. Even though relations among the bishops have generally been harmonious, the issue of the language to be used at the conference has at times caused friction, as bishops from Anglophone countries have tried to ignore the importance of other languages, especially **Portuguese**, which is spoken by over 15 prelates who come from Mozambique and Angola.

INTERNATIONAL MONETARY FUND (IMF). From 1987 on, Mozambique has undergone several **structural adjustment** programs (SAPs) under the International Monetary Fund (IMF) with the assistance of a structural adjustment facility (SAF). This included two major devaluations of the metical in 1987, from MT40 to the U.S. dollar to MT200 in January and then to MT300 in June. In 1988, further devaluations occurred bringing the

Mozambique Industry and Manufacturing Indicators

	1980	1986	1987	1988	1989	1990	1991	1992	1993	1995	1997	1998	1999
Tea exports (1000s metric tons)	30	2	1	1	0	1	1	0	0				
Cotton exports (1000s metric tons)	6	1	4	4	5	6	5	13	10				
Sisal (1000s metric tons)	7	0	0	1	1	0	0	0	0				
Sugar (1000s metric tons)	64	20	10	12	13	18	25	11	5				
Rice yields (Thousands of hectograms/hectare)	8.3	9.3	8.6	8.9	8.6	8.7	5.3	3.0	6.3				
Corn													
Cement output													
Industrial production													
Cooking oil													
Wood production													
Construction industry													
Fishing industry													
Agricultural production Index (1986 = 100)	110	101	100	99	103	108	102	85	98				

(continued)

Mozambique Industry and Manufacturing Indicators (continued)

	1980	1986	1987	1988	1989	1990	1991	1992	1993	1995	1997	1998	1999
Total external debt (Millions of U.S.$)0	3,491	4,125	4,163	4,362	4,649	4,718	5,130	5,211	7,458	7,637	8,314	6,958	
Debt-GDP ratio Concessional	—	66	175	198	188	185	189	262	247	311	217	212	175
Long term loans (including IMF) (Millions of U.S.$)	0	3,205	3,794	3,789	3,871	4,230	4,353	4,718	4,858	6,977	7,128	7,742	6,371
GNP per capita (U.S.$)	166	107	117	128	132	135	138	121	130	139	162	177	185
Trade balance (Millions of U.S.$)	-439	-409	-480	-559	-662	-663	-646	-630	-727	-536	-454	-491	
Overall production Deficit (% of GDP)	-22.3	-15.8	-16.5	-13.9	-18.3	-9.3	-12.3	-12					

Source: World Bank, *African Development Indicators 1996,* (Washington, D.C.: World Bank, 2001); *World Development Indicators on CD-ROM 2001 data* (Washington, D.C.: International Bank for Reconstruction and Development/World Bank, 2002).

Critical Economic Indicators

	1977–1987	1988–1998	1997	1998
Agriculture	—	3.1	7.6	7.0
Industry	—	5.3	23.9	22.9
Manufacturing	—	—	29.8	7.5
Service	5.7	7.1	9.7	
Private consumption	–5.0	2.4	8.3	11.8
General government consumption	–4.8	–5.7	9.9	32.2
Gross domestic investment	0.5	7.4	17.1	29.4
Imports of goods and services	–6.7	0.1	0.7	24.2
Gross national product (GNP)	–4.8	4.8	12.2	11.8

value down to MT620 to the U.S. dollar in October. With the devaluation came an 18 percent increase in industrial production. By 1989, as much as 70 percent of the population was living in poverty. In 1990, the country adopted new strategies under the enhanced structural adjustment facility (ESAF). On June 23, 1999, the IMF approved a third ESAF. This included incentives toward privatization, investment, and rehabilitation, which lured many white South African and Zimbabwean farmers to the country. However, this has in itself created problems. Meanwhile, although poor, the Mozambicans are striving to rebuild the **economy**, and the international community remains optimistic about Mozambique's future.

INVESTMENT. Foreign investment has mainly been directed toward mining, energy, tourism, privatization of transport infrastructure, and farming. A number of guarantees and incentives—including tax holidays—are offered to foreign investors, and joint ventures are encouraged. The government is attempting to reduce the complexity of its investment laws. Three industrial tax-free zones are being developed.

Foreign investment in Mozambique improved dramatically in the 1990s vis-à-vis the 1980s, when it remained below $10m. But it was not until 1995 that significant foreign investments began pouring into the country. Between 1995 and 1999, foreign direct investment increased eightfold from a mere $45m in 1995 to $384m in 1999. These investments have been in the area of aluminum and steel production, natural gas, electricity generation, agriculture, fishing, timber, and transportation services.

ISLAM. It is estimated that there are some two million Muslims in Mozambique scattered throughout the north of the country, the northeastern coast and the hinterland, especially among the **Yao** and the Macua.

Central and Southern Mozambique have fewer Islamic pockets due in part to the fact that, from the 16th century onward, these regions were easily accessible to colonialists and **Portuguese** missionaries. It was the Arab traders along the East African coast who introduced Islam to Mozambique during the seventh century. The new religion took firm roots in northern Mozambique, where it became a bastion of resistance to Portuguese penetration, especially during the latter part of the 19th century, in the wake of the 1884–85 Berlin Conference. Angoche, Sancul, Sangage, Moma, Quitangonha, and others were the latest sultanates to convert to Islam. These political entities, led by sultans, traded in slaves and ivory with the coastal Islamic towns and made it difficult for the Portuguese to establish their presence here. The resulting show of force involved such Portuguese war captains and colonial wizards—the so-called generation of pro-consuls—as Augusto de Castilho, **António Enes, João de Azevedo Coutinho, Joaquim Mousinho de Albuquerque**, Freire de Andrade, Eduardo Costa, Aires de Ornelas, Neutel de Abreu, Massano de Amorim, and countless others, not only in the conquest of the Islamic north but also in the pacification effort from the lands of **Gungunhana** in the south to the remnants of the *prazo* lords in the center. Therefore, as a religion, Islam has a long history of ups and downs in its encounters with the Portuguese in Mozambique.

Historically, Islam has been Portugal's traditional enemy, openly targeted by the Portuguese during the centuries of their overseas expansion. Indeed, Portuguese poet Luís de Camões left several negative comments about Islam in his *Lusíadas*. He once called the young Portuguese king Dom Sebastião *"terror da moura lança"* (terror of the Islamic armies) not only in North Africa but wherever the Portuguese would encounter the Muslims, as was the case in Mozambique coastal towns and **Quelimane** at the mouth of the **Zambezi,** on their way to India. Thus, while on Mozambique Island in 1497, **Vasco da Gama** fired for the first time his weapons in east African waters as a statement of power against what he perceived to be the ambivalence of the local Islamic sultan, Sacoeja. Da Gama feared Sacoeja might betray his *armada* to the Islamic city-states farther north. As a result, da Gama avoided Kilwa on his first voyage to India. Confrontation became more open as the Portuguese tried, often successfully, to dislodge one by one the Muslim merchants from their commercial strongholds along the east coast and in the interior, and from the merchant towns along the Zambezi—**Quelimane, Sena,** and **Tete**. In 1505, Castillian seaman Pero de Anaya began building a fortress at Sofala. Both the Portuguese and the Muslim merchant community saw this move as the beginning of the end of the Islamic commerce of that port town with the hinterland **Mwenemutapa** Kingdom. Mozambique Island was next to follow the fate of Sofala, when the Portuguese established themselves there permanently in 1507. Soon thereafter, in 1511, António de Saldanha ravaged the coast opposite Mozambique Island, causing havoc on the Muslim community that traded at Angoche. The Muslims had fled similar Portuguese chastisements at Kilwa. As an important city-state, Kilwa was plagued with constant dynastic wars of succession at the critical moment when the Muslims needed a united front against the Europeans. However, a more ominous future was to befall them. In 1531, Vicente Pegado opened up the **Zambezi** Valley to Portuguese commerce and vowed to oust all Muslim merchants from their traditional commercial strongholds at Sena and Tete river towns. Elsewhere, by 1540, the Portuguese had finally established themselves permanently in such places as Quelimane.

However, the mutual mistrust continued. In 1561, the Muslims started retaliating, killing Jesuit priest Gonçalo da Silveira at the court of Mwenemutapa, suspected to be a Portuguese spy. Led by Francisco Barreto, the then governor of India, and Jesuit priest Francisco de Monclaro, the Portuguese responded by sending a large expedition from India in 1570. Many Muslims (whom the Portuguese also called Moors) and Swahili merchants from the coast north of Quelimane were put to death at Sena in 1571 "based on strange lies, some being impaled alive," as Francisco Monclaro narrates the events in his *Relação da Viagem*. Thus, 1571 became a landmark in Portuguese-Islamic relations not only in the Zambezi Valley but also throughout the coastal area, from Tete to Quelimane, Angoche, and Mozambique.

A relative pause in the hostilities was followed by what one may call the "missionary phase," which heightened the conflict. Now, not only Portuguese merchants but also missionaries—Jesuits, Dominicans, and Augustinians—became involved in a protracted confrontation with Islam everywhere in the area, from Mwenemutapa to Mombassa and the Querimba islands off Mozambique Island, where the Dominican missionaries had begun their work during the 1580s. For the time being, the missionaries seemed to have their way. Dominican Father João dos Santos tells the story of the baptism he administrated to a nephew of the king of Zanzibar who had fled to the Querimbas when he learned about the new religion. João dos Santos named the Zanzibar prince André da Cunha, after his Portuguese godfather, who was then the "lord of the island."

The chess match of commercial and religious competition continued with lesser intensity, however, during the years in which the Portuguese had to commit most of their energies to the defense of their empire in the East, namely, **Brazil**, against those they called the "enemies from Europe"—the Dutch and the British—during the Philippine occupation of **Portugal**. As a result of the distraction, the coastal sheikhs and sultans, including those at Angoche, consolidated their old positions. The Muslim merchants were able to create new commercial centers, while strengthening the old ones, Sancul, Sancage, Quintagona, north of Angoche, and Moma in the south. For the Islamic merchant communities, this meant the opening of a new front of competition with the Portuguese, not only for the gold trade channeled through the commercial stations on the Zambezi Valley but also through Muslim merchant involvement in the ivory and slave trade from the Yao and the **Macua** interior to the coast.

In Mozambique, the Zambezi Valley or the old *prazo* holding areas and the coastal sultanates had become points of major concern for Portugal in its effort to effectively control the colony, as mandated by the Berlin Conference, and avoid being ousted by the other European competitors, Britain and Germany nearby, and even France off the coast, on the islands of Madagascar and Mauritius. A struggle with the sultanates ensued as a result. Insofar as the Islamized areas were concerned, Portuguese ire was first aimed at Angoche, led by its legendary leader, Moussa Quanto. Quanto offered stiff resistance to Portuguese occupation. Similar resistance from the sultanates of Sangage, Sancul, and Quintagonha followed. The Portuguese had also to contend with the resurgence of the Swahili merchant communities in the coastal areas, as well as with the interior Yao, who had been branching out from the north-center since the 1840s to the coastal plateau of Lake Nyasa, opposite Zanzibar. Here, Muslim traders had become the main carriers and agents of Islamic culture into the interior, north of the Zambezi and Shire.

The battle for Mozambique in the coastal sultanates and in the Islamized interior was not over yet when World War I broke out and Portugal joined the Allies against Germany, whose ambitions on northern Mozambique were already well known. During the course of the war, the German general, Lettow-Vorbeck, and his captains were able to enlist the support of the Yao in the heartland, where the Macua and the Maconde chiefs joined what they thought to be their moment of liberation. Likewise, Angoche and the northern sultanates greeted the German newcomers as partners in the struggle against their longtime Portuguese enemies.

The Germans waged their war against the Portuguese as far as Namacurra, Quelimane's vicinity, before returning north to their colony of Tanganyika and the Great Lakes. However, the Portuguese, suffered a major defeat: they lost their precious war resources, including some of their best fighting men, among whom stood "military genius" João Teixeira Pinto, hero of the campaigns of pacification in Guinea-Bissau. As the chronicler noted, Pinto was "*abatido a tiro pelos alemães*" (he was cut down by German fire) at Negomano, on the border banks of the Rovuma, in 1917.

It was certainly the old memories of World War I that made the Portuguese particularly uneasy in 1964. The Portuguese had no reason to trust anybody there, certainly not the Maconde, the Macua, or the Yao Machinga, and, least of all, the coastal sheiks, even though the latter were operating with reduced power and fewer resources. Yet, as far as the Portuguese were concerned, the Muslims were still unpredictable. Obviously, things had changed at the time **FRELIMO** began its liberation war. In the past, the Portuguese had showered these sheiks with honors to win them over. At one time, the sheik of Angoche was also known by his Portuguese title of "*capitão-mor de Angoche*." As in the past, the Portuguese used the same title to calm down several of the *prazo* lords on the Zambezi Valley who, as with the oriental princes, were awarded the prestigious medal of the Order of Christ. Women, too, were used for this purpose. Unfortunately, this time, it appears that the Portuguese did not seem to know how to take firm control over the recalcitrant Muslim leadership.

With Islam entrenched in the north, however, creating similar conditions was virtually impossible. All the Portuguese knew about Islam was that it had its power brokers in the north, perhaps in Zanzibar, Mombasa, Comoros, Saudi Arabia, Egypt, even in the Far East. **António Enes**, the Portuguese royal high commissioner to Mozambique in 1890, voiced his own frustration regarding the Islamic situation, when he commented that Islam was too strong in the north. He recommended that the best policy was to deal with it locally, taking each Islamic sect or leader one by one, using what he called "strong psycho-social diversion" (*acção psico-social*). The plan included Portuguese officials attending Islamic services, picture taking with sheikhs and their subordinates, translating portions of the Qur'an into Portuguese, and creating incentives for the use of the Portuguese language in Islamic schools. As a consequence of the implementation of the policy, the Portuguese thought during the 1960s that they had created a force against the nationalist movement in northern Mozambique. Indeed, they had co-opted the Islamic leaders through a mutual understanding that was severed only by the April 1974 coup in Lisbon.

Recapitulating, as a form of religious culture, Islam undoubtedly came to Mozambique earlier than either of the two branches of Christianity, Catholicism and **Protestantism**. While Western Christianity came first through the European caravels during the 15th century, Islam was a part and parcel of Mozambique early links with some of the oldest of Indian Ocean traders who sailed from the East. Consequently, insofar as Mozambique is concerned, Islam has been a phenomenon associated with trading centers along the coast and the waterways. In this context, Mozambique and the Querimba Islands of Angoche, Saancul, Sangage, and Quitangonha have historically been the most known centers, which, with time, developed into Islamic sultanates from **Cabo Delgado** in the north to Quelimane and Sofala in the south. In the interior, Islam followed the Zambezi River. Sena and Tete, after Quelimane, became their earliest trading centers, their caravans penetrating as far as Mwenemutapa. South of Sofala, Islam seems to have entered through the commercial triangle of the islands of Bazaruto, Sofala, and Chiloane toward Chibuene, the known terminus of the Muslim coastal trade with the lands of Mwenemutapa, south of the Zambezi River. Eventually, the trading network extended to **Inhambane** and beyond, toward the **Limpopo** Valley. By the first half of the 18th century, Inhambane saw an unusual commercial upsurge form the activities of one Indian merchant by the name of Calcanagi Velabo. Velabo also operated from Angoche and the other northern commercial emporia.

When Livingstone appeared in the Shire Highlands, north of the Zambezi, during the 1860s, he found the Yao Machinga, who were active in the Central Shire Highlands around Mwembe, land of chief Mataka. Subsequently, Catholic missionaries, beginning with the White Fathers of Cardinal Lavigèrie, founded their first mission station at Mponda. The Montfortin missionaries followed the White Fathers and established their station at Nankhunda, later at Nsanje, the future Port Herald. These missionaries witnessed firsthand Yao slaving activities in these areas, which were still under Portuguese jurisdiction before the **British Ultimatum** of 1890. In fact, in the Zambezi and Shire Valleys, memories still linger among the Sena, **Nyungwe**, and Manyanja about the slaving raids of the "Amachinga," the Yao slave traders from further afield in the northern highlands. This was, in a sense, the religious battle line Portugal faced during the 19th century both on the coast and in the northern interior, where Augusto de Castilho, Eduardo da Costa, **Azevedo Coutinho**, Massano de Amorim, and Neutel de Abreu, to name just a few of the Portuguese war captains, made name for themselves in the process of pacification, occupation, and consolidation of Portuguese rule in Mozambique. From this general picture, one may assume that Islam has therefore been the dominant religion in Mozambique. While from a historical perspective Islam can be considered to be the older of the two imported religions, in fact, Islam is dominant only in the northern provinces of Mozambique, north of the Zambezi and Shire Rivers. The expansion of Islam into the northern interior was mostly a 19th-century phenomenon promoted, for the most part, by the Yao and Makua agents who were trading with the coast in slaves and ivory. As for the rest of Mozambique, the presence of Islam has continued to be as spotty as it has been for centuries. Islam has found it difficult to penetrate the Zambezi Valley barrier, traditionally the stronghold of syncretic Christianity of the *prazo* lords, since the Barreto expedition and the heavy punishment inflicted by the Portuguese on the chiefs of the Islamic merchant community at Sena in 1571, as retaliation against the murder of Father Gonçalo da Silveira.

Yet, along the old coastal trading centers from Quelimane to Safala, the neighboring Bazaruto and Chiloane islands, and the surrounding areas of the Sabi River, which had been, in the past, the Islamic thoroughfares into the lands of Mwenemutapa south of the Zambezi and Inhambane, Islam continued to hold its own as a cultural reference among certain layers of the population. However, in most cases, it has not been a matter of believing and practicing orthodox Islam with its five pillars, namely, one God (Shahada), daily prayers (Salat), alms to the poor (Zakat), fasting (Sawn) once a year during the month of Ramadan, and pilgrimage to Mecca (Hajj). Most Muslims in Mozambique consider themselves to be so on account of the family name they have adopted, along with a few external Islamic symbols and practices, such as circumcision, traditions related to diet, or avoidance of certain foods considered unclean—pork, for example, or the killing of consumable animals through their own hands. Thus, in some districts, as is the case along the Zambezi and Shire Valleys, certain skills related to iron technology, including smelting, the manufacturing and trading of such domestic items as iron hoes, are considered taboos to every Muslim and are therefore reserved to those who claim to be *a-sendzi* (tendji) or *a-muenhi* (**monhés**), or second-class Muslims. Traditionally, these pursuits have been the purview of the a-sendzi, or pagans, the lowest stage of Islamic acculturation in Mozambique. The practices suggest, therefore, that it is the Yao syncretic version of Islam rather than the orthodox Islam that exists on the coast.

The hard Islamic stance known as fundamentalism, which considers the secular state an enemy and speaks of spreading Islam and fighting the infidels by all available means, does not exist in Mozambique presently. Islam is a religion integrated into the Mozambican national ethos, just like the other religions, such as Catholicism. In Mozambique, there have been no conflicts between the hard line the Mozambican government has adopted against international terrorism associated with some brands of Islam and the position of the Islamic community in the country. Mozambican Muslims have participated actively in the mansifestations against fundamentalist terrorism across the globe. In fact, Muslims have one of their own in government, scholar and devout Muslim, Dr. Jose Ibrahimo Abudo, who is the minister of justice. In addition, Muslims have their own institutions of higher learning in the north of the country, most notably, the Islamic University in Nampula, just as the **Catholic Church** has the Catholic University of Mozambique.

The **constitution** does not discriminate on the basis of religion for one's own political participation at any level. As a result, Muslims are represented in the Assembleia da República (National Assembly) through their own officials elected by Islamic parties based mostly in the north of the country where for centuries Islam has been strong. At the national and international levels, therefore, Islam in Mozambique could be presently classified as belonging to the more liberal or moderate brand of Islam. It has, by and large, maintained friendly relations with the government and the other religious faiths in the country.

– J –

JEHOVAH'S WITNESSES. As a result of **FRELIMO**'s hostility to religion, which its leaders considered to be superstition and a consequence of brainwashing, the Witnesses' avoidance of participation in the electoral process, and their refusal to pay "allegiance" to the party, the government of Mozambique waged a sustained campaign to discredit and eliminate their presence in the country, especially during the late 1970s. Many of the 22,000 Jehovah's Witnesses were either sent to reeducation camps or forced to go into exile in the surrounding countries where they have also been persecuted. Those who remained in the country were eventually forced into the District of Milange in **Zambézia**. The persecution was not relaxed until the late 1980s. Presently, however, Jehovah's Witnesses are only tolerated in the country, but their numbers are increasing, as one can surmise from the many Kingdom Halls that are emerging even in the capital city.

JUDICIARY. Several changes, including the functioning of the court system in Mozambique, were enacted by the revised **constitution** of 1990. Six court categories are now in operation in Mozambique. At the top is the Supreme Court, whose professional judges are appointed by the president and the Assembly of the Republic. The court serves many functions: as a trial court of "primary jurisdiction," an appellate court, and a court of final instance. While cases related to civil administration and public funds expenditure are the domain of the Administrative Court, military cases are the purview of Courts-Martial. Maritime Courts, Labor (dispute) Courts, and Customs Courts (in the countryside) are also part of the new complex judicial system. *See also* PEOPLE'S COURTS.

JUNTA DE EXPORTAÇÃO DO ALGODÃO. A government corporation established in 1938 in Lisbon to regulate and coordinate the production and the exportation of cotton in the colonies. Under the terms of the junta, concessionaire companies were to sell their cotton to **Portuguese** manufacturers once they had bought it from the African producers, most of whom were forcibly engaged in the activity. The junta was disbanded during the early 1960s following the abolition of the forced cultivation of cotton. In 1944, some 267,000 hectares, mostly in northern Mozambique, sustained cotton cultivation, involving close to 791,000 peasants. According to Malyn Newyt, by 1950, Mozambique was exporting 25,900 tones of raw cotton, mostly to **Portugal**. *See also* ECONOMY.

JUNTAS DISTRITAIS. Created in 1965, the district juntas were advisory bodies to the district governors during the colonial period.

JUNTAS LOCAIS. Advisory bodies in *circumscrições* (major post areas) with at least 20 electors, established during the 1960s.

– K –

KAVANDAME, LÁZARO. Organizer of **Makonde** peasants in the province of **Cabo Delgado** in the early 1960s, prominent member of **FRELIMO**'s first **Central Committee**, and provincial secretary. Kavandame ran into trouble within the Central Committee when he espoused a hard line against the appointment of whites to FRELIMO administrative positions. On this, he was joined by Father Mateus Pinho Gwengere, and both were viewed as reactionaries. Furthermore, along with Vice President **Urias Simango**, he disagreed with the Marxist-Leninist philosophy of the Front. Subsequently implicated (without proof) in the death of **Dr. Eduardo Chivambo Mondlane** and accused of corruption and of favoring a "tribalist" independence for Cabo Delgado, Kavandame was censored by the Central Committee. In 1969, he defected to the enemy side and joined the **Portuguese** propaganda machine against FRELIMO.

KAZEMBE. Military leader of one of the 12 districts into which the Maganja Confederation was divided. The Maganja rebelled against the Portuguese from the 1870s through the 1890s and were subdued only in 1909.

– L –

LAND MINES. The **civil war** in Mozambique left thousands of miles of **roads** and **railroad** tracks laced with land mines (some say as many as three million), causing deaths and severe injuries, mainly to women and children, in the countryside, particularly in the central Mozambique provinces of **Tete** and **Zambézia**, where the war was fought more intensely. In 1992, the **United Nations** took the initiative of enlisting the assistance of Italy, Sweden, and the Netherlands to demine 2,000 kilometers (1,200 miles) of Mozambique road. This effort was later joined by Norway, Britain, and the **United States**, which signed bilateral agreements to help Mozambique. In May–July 1994, a demining accelerated plan was put in place and the UN assumed responsibility for the land mine clearance program, with its center at Tete. As a result, 400 Mozambicans were trained for the demining program, which was managed by various supervisor, surveyor, and instructor teams. Further demining financial assistance has come from such countries as Germany, Australia, Bangladesh, **South Africa**, China, and New Zealand. It is expected that mine clearing, even if accelerated, will take at least 10 more years, even though skeptics say 100 years is the most realistic time frame.

LEMOS, VIRGÍLIO (also known as DUARTE GALVÃO). Born on November 29, 1929, in **Maputo** (formerly Lourenço Marques), Lemos worked for *O Brado Africano, Notícias, Tribuna,* and *Itinerário* and was arrested in 1960 as a sympathizer of the emerging nationalist movements. He was eventually forced to leave Mozambique and seek asylum in France. His best-known work, published both in Portuguese and French, is *Angola et Mozambique: Esclavage et révolution* (1966).

LIGA AFRICANA (LA) (AFRICAN LEAGUE). Association of a few dozen intellectuals, mainly assimilated and *mestiços* from the **Portuguese** colonies, established in Lisbon in 1920. The LA functioned until 1926. Its objective was not the achievement of independence but the elimination of colonial abuses associated with forced labor, taxation, and discrimination. The association also sought to foster solidarity among the subjects of the Portuguese empire as well as with the rest of the African world. Thus, in 1923, it hosted the second session of the Third Pan-African Congress organized in London by W. E. B. DuBois. However, Portuguese censorship, the insignificant impact of its membership, and the physical and social environment far removed from the motherland prevented the league from exerting any enduring influence in colonial matters.

LIGA DE DEFESA E PROPAGANDA DE MOÇAMBIQUE. A right-wing organization that surfaced at Lourenço Marques during the 1930s, whose aim was to promote more autonomy for Mozambique at the expense of the Africans and the Portuguese not born in the colony, using **South Africa** as a model. In 1933, the governor-general, supported by the attorney-general, the director of the newspaper *Notícias*, and the military commander, passed a decree stipulating that only those Portuguese born in the colony could hold government jobs. Aware of the potential for separatism (*bairrismo*), as the opponents called the purpose of the Liga, Lisbon opposed the decree. The Liga did not survive the totalitarian and centralizing policies of **Antonio Salazar's** *Estado Novo* (New State).

LIMPOPO RIVER. The Limpopo, 1,000 miles long, rises from the highlands of the Transvaal, serves as a frontier between **South Africa** and Botswana and between South Africa and Zimbabwe, runs through southern Mozambique, and empties into the Indian Ocean. During the rainy season, the river usually **floods** and causes severe damage.

LITERATURE. An expert on African literature, Russell G. Hamilton, writes in the *Encyclopedia of Africa: South of the Sahara* (1997) that modern Lusophone African literature is still in its "formative stage," a comment that is certainly applicable to Mozambique. Noteworthy written literature, in the form of both fiction and poetry, did not emerge in the colony until the

1930s and 1940s, respectively. In fact, much of it flourished in **Portugal** among the Mozambican students who lived at the Casa dos Império in Lisbon, which was founded during the 1940s to house students from the Portuguese colonies. The hostel was closed in 1965 due to the militancy prevailing among the students.

Until now, the best-known fiction writer has been Ronga Luís Bernardo Onwana mainly because of his work titled *Nós matámos o cão-tinhoso* (1964), later translated, along with others of his stories, into English and published by Heinemann. Mozambique's most-known poetry collection emerged only during the 1950s and 1960s through the published poems of **José Craveirinha**, also known as José G. Vetrinha. Craveirinha called his first collection *Chigubo*, which was published in 1964. The still-unpublished works of **Noémia de Sousa**, the first "significant female writer of color," followed. Themes of Mozambique writers have focused on racism, revolt against the colonial system, exploitation, racial pride, and racial identity. Names that have been cited often in Mozambique literature include **Marcelino dos Santos**, who lived at the Casa do Império, poet; **João Albasini**, novelist; **João Dias**, novelist and story writer; **Virgílio Lemos**, untrained history writer; **Rui Nogar**, poet; **Rui de Noronha**, poet; and **Malangatana Gwenha Valente,** poet and painter.

This brief summary of modern written literature is not intended to ignore or minimize Mozambique's wealth of oral traditions manifested in fiction, poetic narratives, songs, proverbs, riddles, epics, prayers, animal stories, and daily and ceremonial rhetoric. It is clear, however, that very little study has been devoted to this aspect of Mozambique's patrimony by Mozambique institutions of higher learning. In contrast to parts of West Africa, it appears that the griot tradition, both in music and literature, was never entrenched in East Africa, with the exception perhaps of Uganda.

LIVINGSTONE, DAVID (1813–1873). Scottish missionary of the London Missionary Society, explorer, humanitarian, and physician. Dr. Livingstone made two expeditions through Portuguese territories, including Angola and Mozambique. In Mozambique, he explored the **Zambezi River** valley in January 1856, and in December 1857, he visited Zumbo and **Tete.** His biting remarks about Mozambique not only publicized this Portuguese East African colony abroad but also exposed the colonial abuses in the territory. Livingstone deplored the human conditions in the colony and accused the colonial administration of being directly involved in **slavery** and the slave trade as a means of supplementing the little financial support officials received from the metropolitan government.

Yet, in spite of his harsh criticism, his advocacy of the expansion of a British empire in Central Africa, which would have encroached upon the Portuguese domain, and his push for free navigation on the Zambezi River, the Mozambique colonial authorities received him politely, afraid that the British government might retaliate diplomatically should they treat him otherwise. In May 1858, Livingstone returned to Mozambique accompanied by eight British citizens. He had been appointed British consul at **Quelimane**, which forced the Portuguese to deal with him directly. Rather than engage in a quarrel with Livingstone, the Portuguese government sought the work of a famous Portuguese scholar, Dr. José de Lacerda, to write a rebuttal to his disparaging remarks about the situation in the Portuguese East African colony.

LUSAKA AGREEMENT. A September 8, 1974, agreement between **Portugal** and **FRELIMO** establishing a transitional government to facilitate the colony's road to independence. Its several clauses can be summarized as follows: (1) Mozambique's right to independence under FRELIMO; (2) independence date set for June 25, 1975; (3) appointment by Portugal of a high commissioner who would set up a transitional government and, in consultation with FRELIMO, create a joint military commission; (4) preservation of Mozambique's territorial integrity and accelerated decolonization ensured by the high commissioner, who represented the president of the Portuguese republic; (5) establishment of a transitional government with executive and legislative power; (6) appointment of a FRELIMO prime minister for the transitional government; (7) appointment of six FRELIMO and three Portuguese ministers; (8) enforcement of a cease-fire; (9) law and order guaranteed by the prime minister and the high commissioner; (10) authorization for a new police force to be created by the transitional government; (11) coordination of military activities by FRELIMO and Portugal in case of threat against the colony; (12) maintenance of cooperation and friendship between Portugal and Mozambique; (13) agreement by FRELIMO to honor financial obligations signed by the previous government as long as they were in the interest of the colony; (14) a pledge by FRELIMO to follow a policy of nondiscrimination based on race; (15) creation of a Central Bank in Mozambique and the transfer of all assets from the Banco Ultramarino; (16) request for aid from external sources allowed to the transitional government; (17) following independence, Mozambique to act freely as a sovereign state; and (18) a pledge by both parties to maintain a fraternal and harmonious relationship.

LUSOTROPICALISMO. Theory advanced by Gilberto Freyre, a Brazilian sociologist, which claims that the **Portuguese**, more so than any other Europeans, were apt to live in the tropics and mingle socially with the Africans to the point of favoring miscegenation and dispensing the rights and privileges of a Portuguese citizen through the colonial policy of assimilation (*assimilação*). Arguing that the Portuguese held a benign attitude toward their slaves in **Brazil** and the colonies, Freyre has attempted to prove that the Portuguese were less racially conscious and more humane than their Anglo-Saxon counterparts. Portuguese colonial apologists have used the theory to advance the claim that the Portuguese were not racist. Although some Africanists, including those who have been critical of **Portugal**, such as Charles Boxer, admit that the Portuguese were more liberal in their relations with their African subjects and Indians from Damão, Goa, and Diu, most do not view them as color-blind, particularly in regard to their African colonies.

LUTA CONTINUA, A. Translated from Portuguese as "the struggle continues," "*A Luta Continua*" was **FRELIMO**'s slogan during the liberation war against the Portuguese. Ironically, this same slogan was adopted by the **Resistência Nacional Moçambicana (RENAMO)** to convey the message that the war against oppression was not over with FRELIMO's victory—that it would end only if FRELIMO were removed from power. RENAMO also sponsored a magazine called *A Luta Continua*, the official organ of the movement, which was edited and printed in Portugal.

– M –

MACHEL, GRAÇA SIMBINE (1945–). Graça Machel was born Graça Simbine on November 17, 1945, in a village north of Lourenço Marques (**Maputo**), then capital of Mozambique. Her father, a Methodist preacher and a labor migrant to the gold mines of **South Africa**, died 20 days before the birth of his daughter. In 1968, Graça Simbine became active along with other African students of the **Casa dos Estudantes do Império,** made up of students from Angola, Mozambique, Guinea-Bissau, Cape Verde, and São Tomé e Príncipe, in Lisbon. She returned to Mozambique in 1973, at the height of the war of independence. She made her way to Dar-es-Salaam, Tanzania, where she joined **FRELIMO,** the movement that led Mozambique to independence in 1975, where she also met **Samora Moisés Machel,** her future husband and the first president of Mozambique. In the new government of independent Mozambique, Graça Machel was appointed minister of education and culture. She married Samora Machel in 1975. They had two children. In 1986, her husband was killed in a plane crash widely suspected as related to the civil war in the country between FRELIMO and **RENAMO**. Graça Machel resigned then as minister of education.

In 1988, Machel was appointed by the **United States** UNESCO delegate to a UNICEF Conference in Harare, Zimbabwe, and later became president of the National Commission of UNESCO in Mozambique. In 1992, with the help of the American MacArthur Foundation, Graça Machel established a Community Development Foundation (FDC) in Mozambique for the support of projects developed by members of poor communities, designed to improve their own living standards. In 1996, Graça Machel made international headlines when she and then–South African president Nelson Mandela announced that they were romantically involved and planned to get married. To some people's surprise, they were actually married on Mandela's 80th birthday in July 1998. Mandela flies constantly to Mozambique to Graça Machel's sumptuous palace in **Maputo**.

MACHEL, SAMORA MOISÉS (1933–1986). Born in Xilembene, **Gaza** Province, on September 29, 1933, Samora Machel was the son of a pastor and claimed to be a descendent of peasants and military leaders of the Gaza empire. He attended a Catholic mission school where he completed his elementary education and took courses leading to a career in nursing in **Xai-Xai** and Lourenço Marques (**Maputo**). In 1963, he left Mozambique for Dar-es-Salaam and joined **FRELIMO**. FRELIMO immediately sent him to Algeria to be trained in guerrilla warfare along with other young Mozambicans who had joined the revolutionary movement. Upon his return, the young Samora joined the army and became the commander of the revolutionary forces in **Niassa** Province in 1965. In the aftermath of the assassination of Filipe Magaia in 1966, Machel was appointed secretary of defense, thus becoming a member of the **Central Committee**.

Machel also became a member of the Triumvirate (along with **Marcelino dos Santos** and **Urias Simango**), which shared top executive leadership after the assassination of **Eduardo Chivambo Mondlane**, president of FRELIMO, in 1969. In May 1970, following a bitter power struggle within the Central Committee, Machel emerged as the president of FRELIMO while at the same time retaining the supreme leadership of the revolutionary forces. After a protracted 10-year war against the colonial government in

Mozambique—a war that ended abruptly in 1974—FRELIMO's Central Committee selected Machel to be president of Mozambique on June 25, 1975. At FRELIMO's **Fourth Congress** in 1983, Machel was reelected president of Mozambique, while retaining his earlier position of commander in chief of the armed forces of Mozambique.

Upon assuming the presidency of the new nation, Machel was confronted with almost insurmountable political, social, and economic problems resulting from five centuries of Portuguese colonialism. A committed Marxist-Leninist, Machel opted for socialism as the remedy for the nation's ills. Immediately, however, discontented Mozambicans, allied with former **Portuguese** nationals supported by Ian Smith's regime in what used to be Southern Rhodesia, began mounting an armed campaign against his regime, causing much havoc throughout the country. At the same time, in his attempt to follow a revolutionary path in southern Africa, Machel faced the economic and military wrath of **South Africa**, as he allowed the African National Congress (ANC) to establish guerrilla bases in Mozambique.

The **Soviet Union**, the principal backer of the socialist state, proved to be an unreliable ally particularly in the delivery of economic assistance. Also, the massive socialist nationalization policies, hastily adopted with little or no understanding by those who were put in charge of their implementation, the flight of Portuguese technicians and businessmen, and the crippling activities of the **Resistência Nacional Moçambicana** (RENAMO) aggravated the political and economic situation. As a result, Machel, in an attempt to solve the economic crisis, ordered a slowdown of the nationalization process, welcomed foreign public and private investment in the country, and began courting the West for economic and military assistance.

Pressured by RENAMO, as well as by economic and military retaliation from South Africa due to the presence of the ANC, Machel saw himself signing an unpopular and humiliating military pact, the Nkomati Accord, with South Africa on March 16, 1984. The heart of the pact dictated that, while Mozambique would stop its support for the ANC, South Africa would cease arming and providing logistical assistance to the RENAMO insurgents. However, notwithstanding the fact that Machel kept his part of the bargain, South Africa did not. A real crisis ensued as the guerrilla activities intensified and, by 1986, threatened Maputo itself. Paradoxically, Machel's new pragmatic approach toward the West was beginning to pay some dividends as **Portugal**, Britain, France, and West Germany pledged to provide military and accelerated economic assistance to the endangered socialist state.

While attempting to slow down the tide of an impending catastrophe on all fronts (except his own popularity, which never wavered in many parts of the country), Machel died in an airplane crash on October 19, 1986, as he was returning from a strategic minisummit on southern Africa in Zambia. His Tupelov TV-134 jet, manned by a Soviet crew, crashed into the Libombo Mountains, three miles from Namaacha, inside South African territory. The international investigation that followed absolved South Africa from involvement in the crash and laid the blame on the Soviet crew. Mozambique rejected this verdict and accused South Africa of having caused the crash through radar manipulation. Within a fortnight, the Central Committee had selected **Joaquim Chissano**, the foreign minister, as president of Mozambique.

Skillfully able to maintain his popularity within Mozambique and abroad, Machel was a strong supporter of sanctions against South Africa. However, he tempered his rhetoric with pragmatism, aware of the stranglehold South Africa had on the Mozambique economy, including trade, tourism, technical assistance, harbors and railways, and **Cahora Bassa**. He was a cofounder of the **South African Development Coordination Conference (SADCC)**, now the **Southern African Development Community (SADC)**, in 1980 and played a prominent role among the Frontline Heads of State. In 1976, in spite of the foreseen economic price, Machel ordered the frontier between Mozambique and Southern Rhodesia closed in compliance with **United Nations** sanctions against the white minority regime and backed the **Zimbabwe African National Union** (ZANU) and the **Zimbabwe African People's Union** (ZAPU) unconditionally. His death is still a topic of discussion today in Mozambique, some definitely maintaining that there was a conspiracy headed by apartheid South Africa.

MACHILA. A device made out of two long pieces of wood or bent bamboo linked and interwoven with ropes and a net, built and used by Africans to carry a European in the colony. Four porters (two on each side) would rest the ends of the poles on their shoulders and carry a white Portuguese, who meanwhile would be reading, writing, giving orders, eating, or even whipping the porters and telling them to stop bouncing the machila sideways.

MACOMBE (MAKOMBE). Title of the rulers of **Barue**, in central Mozambique. The Macombe kingdom was an offshoot of the Monomotapa or **Muenemutapa** kingdom in present-day Zimbabwe (formerly

Southern Rhodesia). Macombe I, son of Matope of Muenemutapa, engineered the split during the late 15th century. The Macombe held various headquarters, including Macossa (the main seat) and Mungari. The dynasty always experienced problems of succession, and quite often the contenders to the throne fought against each other. However, when one of them was crowned, all rivals recognized him as the new king and pledged their unconditional obedience.

The Macombes refused to be considered subjects of the Portuguese government, the *prazeros*, such as Manuel António de Sousa Gouveia, or the Mozambique Company, which inherited the area from the **Portuguese** government in the 1890s. Curiously, beginning during the 17th century, a Portuguese representative of **Companhia de Moçambique** was present at every coronation. This envoy always brought with him the blessed water of the **Catholic Church** and anointed the new king with it. However, the ceremony never symbolized Barue acceptance of Portuguese sovereignty over the realm.

During the 1840s, the Macombes repulsed the Nguni who had been exacting tribute from them. Several factors accounted for their power: they controlled the trading activities of the area, received in-kind tribute from subjugated ethnic groups, and manufactured their own guns and gunpowder, contrary to Portuguese directives and decrees. In defiance, the Macombes also refused to pay taxes to anyone, including the Companhia de Moçambique. Consequently, when company agents attempted to collect taxes in 1890, the Barue people revolted and defeated the intruders, even though the latter were assisted by prazero Gouveia and his lieutenants as well as by Captain Lieutenant **João de Azevedo Coutinho** (who gathered a force of some 720 men, of whom 240 were white), an infantry division, several marines, and artillery men assisted by some 20,000 company troops. The same episode was repeated in 1902, when Portuguese troops converged on Barue from three directions, this time subduing the revolt. They captured Chipitura, the famous rebel leader.

In March 1917, the Macombes Nongwe-Nongwe and Makossa, two rival relatives, united against the Portuguese and forged an unprecedented alliance with the **Tonga**, the Tawara, the Nyungwe, the Sena, the Gorongaza, and the Atsenga. The Portuguese led a major offensive in early 1918, using troops from different ethnic groups but particularly from the feared Angoni warriors, who eventually numbered between 10,000 and 15,000 men. Sensing imminent defeat in October 1918, both Nongwe-Nongwe and Makossa escaped to Southern Rhodesia. Barue tradition holds that 35 Macombes ruled the region. Unfortunately, the history of the kings is obscured by the dynastic rivalries and becomes quite unreliable prior to the mid–19th century. A partial list of the Macombes includes the following kings who ruled between 1811 and 1918: Chimbata, Capanga, Sazua, Bingo, Inhamaguada, Chibutu, Chipapata, Nongwe-Nongwe, and Makossa.

MACONDE (MAKONDE). The matrilineal Maconde live on the plateau of **Cabo Delgado** Province and numbered 300,000 in 1997. The Muerea, a group closely related to the Maconde, live on the Muerea or Rondo Plateau, while the Mavia, a subgroup of the Maconde, live south of the Rovuma River on the Mavia Plateau. Arabs and the **Nguni** devastated these areas and plateaus in search of slaves during the 19th century. The Maconde are farmers, hunters, fishermen, and warriors.

MACUA-LOMWE. Little is known about the origins of the Macua and the Lomwe. Numbering, according to some sources, more than a million, the matrilineal Macua-Lomwe inhabit lower **Zambézia**, the **Niassa** and **Cabo Delgado** Provinces, and parts of the northeast coast and are the largest ethic group in Mozambique. In the distant past, they were organized into separate political entities under a chief who exercised almost unlimited powers.

MAMBO. A widely used term for paramount chief, *régulo*, lord. The word gained prominence in northern Mozambique (**Niassa, Nampula**, and **Cabo Delgado** Provinces) during **RENAMO**'s incursions and successes among the Macua, beginning in 1984. All chiefs supporting RENAMO, many of whom lived close to the movement's military bases, assisted in information gathering, organizing the people against the government, collecting food and special taxes, and providing manpower. RENAMO called them *Mambo*. It is widely believed that, without the assistance of the Mambo, RENAMO would have found it much more difficult to wage the war in the north.

MANDLATE, PAULO (1934–). Born in Macupalane-Manjacaze, diocese of **Xai-Xai**, ordained first Mozambican bishop of **Tete** on October 26, 1976. Dom Paulo was educated in the Minor Catholic Seminary of Zobue and trained at the Major Namaacha Seminary near **Maputo**. When Archbishop **Custódio Alvim Pereira** closed the Namaacha Seminary in 1964, charging that the docent body, the Sacramentin Order, was not preparing priests but disguised politicians, the future priest and bishop joined the Order of the Holy Sacrament and completed his studies in Holland. He was ordained priest on June 6, 1968.

Tete is one of the provinces whose infrastructure was almost completely destroyed by the 1977–92 civil war. It remains one of the poorest dioceses in the country, where much distrust still exists between the **Catholic Church** and the government. As a result, Dom Paulo's immediate task was to repair the relations between the Catholic Church and the government (a task that was facilitated by his southern Mozambican origins), rehabilitate the destroyed churches and schools, and restore the morale of the Catholic population, while redoubling, at the same time, the evangelization effort. In the past, Bishop Paulo served as president of the Mozambican Episcopal Conference and is personally involved in charitable work in Tete, especially in the areas affected by the drought and the **floods**. He has run the branch of Caritas very effectively, bringing much-needed assistance to returning **refugees** and displaced Mozambicans. He is a man of great interpersonal skills and leadership qualities, which were apparent, even in the Minor Seminary where he once was the dean of the student body.

MANGA. African term associated with the Zulu military structure in **Gungunhana**'s army in southern Mozambique, meaning a battalion. Troops were assigned to the mangas according to age.

MANICA. Since independence, west central province of Mozambique. Manica was dismembered from the western part of the former district of Manica e Sofala. Manica's gold and ivory attracted the first **Portuguese** adventurers, and a decree of June 14, 1884, made it a district. The province has an area of 23,807 square miles and a population of 975,000 (1997 estimate), bordering **Tete** Province in the north, **Sofala** Province in the east and north, **Inhambane** and **Gaza** Provinces in the south, and Zimbabwe in the West. Manica is dominated on the Zimbabwean border by the Mashonaland (Manica) Plateau, which harbors Mount Binga (7,992 feet), the highest peak in Mozambique. The Pungue, the Save, and the Buzi Rivers provide water, hydroelectric power, and irrigation to the province. The **Beira** railway that crosses the province from west to east and a relatively extensive road system have enabled Manica to become one of the most developed provinces in the country. Its soil contains gold, iron, asbestos, copper, and bauxite. The province also produces the major agricultural crops of Mozambique: cotton, cashew nuts, sugarcane, corn, copra, and sisal. Its capital city is **Chimoio**, formerly known as Vila Pery, which is also an important textile center. Manica Province became a major target of the Mozambique National Resistance, which disrupted several of its communication networks and industrial projects.

MANJACAZE. Once **Gungunhana**'s headquarters in the **Gaza** empire. It was burnt and occupied by **Mouzinho de Albuquerque** on November 11, 1895.

MAPUTO. Mozambique's southern province since 1975; 6,324 square miles in area with a population estimated at 809,000 in 1997 (excluding that of Maputo City, former Lourenço Marques). Maputo is also the name of the provincial capital and the capital of Mozambique, with a population of 1,000,000 people (from a population of 888 in 1858, 26,079 in 1912, 68,223 in 1940, 178,546 in 1960, and 378,348 in 1970). Maputo Province borders Swaziland in the west, Gaza Province in the north, and **South Africa** in the northwest and the south. Most of the country's light industries, such as Mozambique's sole oil refinery, are located in this province, particularly in and around Maputo City. The province, especially the capital, is linked by a network of railroads heavily used by such neighboring countries as Malawi, Zimbabwe, South Africa, Swaziland, and Zambia.

Since its early beginnings, Lourenço Marques (Maputo) has always been a relatively busy port. For example, 40 ships entered its harbor in 1882, 46 in 1883, 82 in 1884, and 55 in 1885, representing diverse nationalities, namely, British (162), French (18), Portuguese (17), Dutch (6), and German (3). The province is known for crops such as rice, cotton, sugarcane, and corn, and it is suited for cattle raising. Maputo is also the largest city in Mozambique, with a surface area of 232 square miles located on the northern bank of Espírito Santo estuary on **Delagoa Bay**.

One of the earliest **Portuguese** seamen, Lourenço Marques, disembarked in 1544 at Delagoa Bay, where a fort was erected in 1787. The settlement became a town in 1887 and the official capital of the colony in 1907. It thrived as the commercial, intellectual, and administrative center of the colony. Maputo City was a commercial center for shipbuilding activities, breweries, fish canning, food-processing and cement plants, and textiles, and it produces quality furniture for domestic and foreign consumption. Maputo is the second largest port in Africa. Once the seat of the governors-general, today it is the administrative center of **FRELIMO**. It has the best schools in the country and houses the country's major national university. It also has the best infrastructure in the whole country. Although **RENAMO** did threaten the city during the last years of the **civil war**, Maputo does not show signs of war or deterioration like the rest of the cities in the country.

MAPUTO DEVELOPMENT CORRIDOR (MDC). Established in May 1996, the MDC is a project entrusted to a consortium composed of the

government of Mozambique and **South Africa**, with the goal of rehabilitating the Maputo-Ressano Garcia railway and completing construction of a toll road between **Maputo** and Witbank, South Africa.

MARAVI. A Mozambique ethnic group, the Maravi live mainly in the
north, near Lake Nyassa, and in the east, along the Luanga River. They
are subdivided into the Nyanja of Lake Nyassa, the Chire, the Mutarara,
the Chewa (in Capoche and Angonia), the Chipeta, the Zimba, the
Makanga, and the Tsenga (of **Tete** district). Numbering about 412,000,
the Maravi are said to have migrated from the Congo Confederacy in the
year 1500, following a succession dispute within the Undi dynasty. They
followed Karonga, the king's nephew, who entered Mozambique and settled in the area which is now known as Vila Gamito in Tete Province.
They are divided into small political units, each with its own chief.

MASSANGANO. Headquarters of the *prazero* **Cruz** family. A fortified
aringa, Massangano became the capital of the Cruz dynasty during the
tenure of Joaquim da Cruz, also known as the Nhaude, sometime during
his reign (1805–55). Several times, particularly during the 19th century,
the **Portuguese** attempted unsuccessfully to destroy the Massangano fort.
Finally, in 1887, they burned the aringa after António Vicente da Cruz,
chased by the Portuguese who had allied themselves with the Pereira
prazero family, had decided to abandon it. However, João Santana da Cruz
rebuilt the aringa in 1888, and once again he fortified Massangano. Eventually, however, the Portuguese subdued the Cruz family and occupied
Massangano in 1894.

MASSINGA, JOSÉ CHICUARRA (1930–). José Massinga was born in
Massinga, **Inhambane**, on January 30, 1930. He attended the Catholic
Namaacha Major Seminary for the priesthood and left for the **United
States** during the early 1960s. There, he studied international relations
in which he eventually received a Ph.D. from the University of Lausanne, Switzerland, before returning to Mozambique, where he served
as the director of the Department of Research, Planning, and Vocational
Training in the Ministry of Foreign Affairs from 1975 to 1981. Falsely
accused of being a CIA agent, he was put in jail and later released allegedly at a request by the United States. During the period leading to
the first presidential elections, he founded his own party called the Partido Nacional Democrático (PANADE), legalized in 1993, and formed
a coalition called União Democrática (UD), comprising his party and
the Partido Nacional de Moçambique (PANAMO) for the 1994 legisla-

tive elections, in which he was elected a representative. His party did not win any seats in the 1999 elections—it received only 1.48 percent of the vote.

MATEQUENHA I and II. *See* ANJOS, PAULO MARIANO DOS.

MATSANGA. Word used during the **civil war** to designate a **RENAMO** follower. The term is derived from the name of RENAMO's first president, **André Matsangaissa.** However, the word also means "bush, bushy" in some of the central Mozambican languages and is therefore used pejoratively to designate a RENAMO member as a "person of the bush," a follower of Matsangaissa.

MATSANGAISSA, ANDRÉ MATADI (1950?–1979). Born in Gorongoza, Matsangaissa was the first president of **RENAMO.** A former **FRELIMO** platoon commander in Gorongoza, Matsangaissa had joined the Front in 1972. During the 1974–75 corruption purges, Matsangaissa was accused of embezzling a Mercedes Benz and was sent to a reeducation camp. He escaped from the camp and sought refuge in Southern Rhodesia, where he joined RENAMO, later becoming its leader. He subsequently invaded the reeducation camp where he had been detained, freeing many of the detainees who later turned out to be his best guerrillas. Once he had organized his followers, Matsangaissa used Gorongoza as the headquarters from which to launch his assaults on FRELIMO. Wounded following an assault on RENAMO bases in October 1979, Matsangaissa allegedly died aboard the helicopter that was carrying him back to Rhodesia for treatment. Both FRELIMO and many of his followers thought they had witnessed RENAMO's end.

MAZULA, BRAZÃO (1944–). Rector of Eduardo Mondlane University in **Maputo.** Born in Messumba, **Niassa,** Mazula completed his Catholic priesthood studies at the Major Seminary of Malhangalene in 1971 and was ordained diocesan priest in 1972. He was appointed rector of the Seminary of Cuamba in 1973–77, subsequently joining the Ministry of Culture and Education as a civil servant (1977–88). He pursued doctorate studies in **Brazil,** leaving the priesthood and marrying thereafter. He was appointed director of the National Elections Commission in 1994. Following the successful completion of the first multinational elections in the country, he was appointed rector of the national university in 1995–1996 and then reappointed.

His task as a rector has not been easy, as he tries to expand and update the curriculum, providing equal opportunities to students from every province, strengthen the standards, hire qualified faculty, and break the subservience to **Portuguese** institutions, including severing links with the University of Coimbra. In the process, he has met with criticism from faculty, especially the colonial leftovers, and alienated those who were hired prior to the **Acordo Geral da Paz**, when sound hiring principles were not always followed. During 1996–97 and in 2001, student demonstrations took place at the university, some in favor and some against his leadership. Despite the unrest, Mazula continued to plough along and has survived the crisis.

MEDIAFAX. A daily newssheet put out in **Maputo** by independent Mozambique journalists who have recently created an association called **MEDIACOOP** based in **Beira**. It stopped operating in early 2002, pending trial of family members who have been accused of involvement in the assassination of Carlos Cardoso, the founder of the newspaper. Just like the *METICAL*, *MEDIAFAX* could only be obtained by subscription via fax.

MENDONÇA, STELLA PIEDADE (1970–). First and only Mozambique opera singer from **Beira** District, **Sofala** Province. Born in **Nampula**, District of Membra, on August 10, 1970, her father, José Ferramenta Mendonça, is a retired schoolteacher and a government census registrar. Mendonça completed her high school in Beira, Mozambique, and **Portugal**, before attending the Conservatoire Supérieur in Lyon, France, on a full scholarship from the French government. She continued her vocal studies in Paris and Bern, Switzerland. She holds a B.A. and a master's degree in fine arts. Since 1993, Mendonça has lived in Switzerland and studied Belcanto technique with the late Dennis Hall of the Gracia y Lamperti School. The rising star also attended Oratorio Master Classes in Zurich with Ernst Haefliger and studied Italian Belcanto and Verismo repertoire in Barcelona with noted soprano Magda Oliveira. Her Lieder teachers include Verena Schwermer of Germany and Peter Berne of Austria.

Singing mostly in Europe and southern Africa, Mendonça made her first professional appearances in several oratories: Pergolesi's *Stabat mater*, Rossini's *Messe Solennelle*, and Faure's *Requiem*. She has performed Haydn's *Creation*, Bach's *St. John Passion*, and Mozart's *Requiem* and *Mass in C Minor* in France and Switzerland, proceeding to perform in Germany and Belgium. In her first stage performance, she appeared in the title role of Franz Lehar's *La Veuve Joyeuse* in Villefranche, France. Other roles she has played include "Bess" in Gershwin's *Porgy and Bess* and "Mimi" in Puccini's *La Bohème*, presented in the Opera Studio of Fribourg—Centre Le Phinx, Switzerland.

At the end of 2001, Mendonça and her American colleague; opera singer, Mark Jackson, with whom she has appeared on several occasions, began the process of Africanizing and adapting *Carmen* to African audiences, which, in spite of skepticism on the part of several prominent individuals, she performed successfully in Maputo and Beira (the first opera concert the city of Beira had ever hosted). In this endeavor, she collaborated with the University of Pretoria's Music Department. Mendonça has also officially represented the Eduardo Mondlane University abroad, where she has tried to establish and strengthen ties with overseas universities. Not forgetting the plight of her own people in Mozambique, Mendonça has held several concerts for **flood** victims and other causes in Mozambique and abroad and is now working toward renovating and rehabilitating the Eduardo Mondlane University's Cultural Center.

MERCADO MUNICIPAL (CITY MARKET). The largest popular market in Mozambique located in downtown **Maputo**. Founded in 1903, the market attracts people from all walks of life and sells varied merchandise at prices that are often more competitive than those in the shops, most often owned by Indians or **Portuguese** nationals.

MESTIÇO (MISTO, MULATTO). Synonym with *mestizo* and *misto*: someone of mixed parentage. In Mozambique, those of mixed origin as well as the assimilated were treated better than the rest of the population by the **Portuguese**. In most cases, the mistos received free education, grew up in free boarding schools, and were more easily allowed to mingle with the Portuguese. As a result of this colonial policy, the rest of the population resented them, even though many joined the liberation movements and have occupied prominent positions in independent Mozambique. Despite the policies of nondiscrimination announced by **FRELIMO**, however, many of their compatriots looked at the mestiços with suspicion regarding their loyalty to the state and the nation. At the time of independence, only about 0.5 percent of the population consisted of mistos.

METICAL. Currency unit in independent Mozambique, which replaced the Portuguese *escudo*. A metical has 100 centavos (cents). Its value has fluctuated between 97.9 meticais to a U.S. dollar in 1984 to 202.2 meticais to a dollar in 1988 (MT405 on the black market), to 22,700 meticais to a dollar in 2001 and 23,600 in 2003. The term *metical* was borrowed from a 17th-century exchange currency in western and central Mozambique, particularly **Tete**.

METICAL. A daily newssheet founded in **Maputo** in 2000 by **Carlos Cardoso**, also its late editor, who was assassinated in Maputo in front of his office in 2000. This controversial information organ, whose news items subscribers get by fax, has tended to be critical of the government in its editorials, perhaps the reason why, in spite of its unappealing appearance, it has attracted many readers and subscribers.

MINING. In 1993, minerals accounted for 3 percent of overall exports. This potentially valuable sector has been handicapped by insecurity, obsolete equipment, and transport problems. Limited quantities of coal, limestone, and salt are produced. The most significant minerals are pegmatite deposits in **Zambézia** and tantalite (used in electronics industry and for special steels). Also mined are copper, marble, garnet, kaolin, asbestos, bentonite, limestone, gold, titanium, graphite, and iron ore. There are large reserves of nepheline syenite, which could be used to produce aluminum, and deposits of bauxite, apatite, and tin. Sea salt production has increased and the salt is now exported to neighboring countries.

M'JIBA. Macua term applied to **RENAMO**'s scouts or young soldiers, at times selected by the **Mambo** or by RENAMO authorities, usually living near a military base. The m'jiba were designed to protect the soldiers by scouting the new areas where the combatants had to initiate operations, carried weapons and supplies, prepared camping zones, contacted the local populations on behalf of RENAMO, pillaged the farms and the villages when supplies were needed, transported fuel, guarded the hostages, and informed the guerrillas about the enemy's movement and whereabouts. M'jiba members were usually fed by the population until replaced by another contingent of m'jiba, following performance of a one week's task with or ahead of the army. ·

Armed with machetes and other crude weapons rather than guns, these youngsters, usually eager to take up arms, were extremely brutal in their first weeks of service, committing, as a result, untold atrocities along the way. Occasionally, they were directly engaged in combat. In the words of anthropologist Christian Geffray, m'jiba scouts became, at times, the true "armed bandits," who, after combat, went back to their homes disarmed. Despised by the soldiers, the m'jiba lacked military training and remained scared, using at times marijuana (*suruma*) and alcohol, notes Geffray, to maintain their courage.

MOÇAMBIQUE. Port and city in **Nampula** Province on Mozambique Island, originally known as Saint Sebastian City, former capital of the colony until 1897 (transfer to Lourenço Marques occurred only in 1907). **Vasco da Gama** set foot on the island in March 1498, but the first **Portuguese** settlement here dates back to 1506 with the erection of Fort Saint Sebastian. Moçambique was the seat of the governor-general and, as Mozambique's Electoral Circle Number One (also known as the North Circle), it used to send a deputy to Lisbon during the 19th century. The city has a poor climate, lacks sufficient potable water, and is infested with mosquitoes. These factors were responsible for its abandonment as the capital of the colony. Even though it has good facilities, since 1951, the time when the port of **Nacala** was opened, Mozambique port has been declining slowly. Recently, beginning in 2001, the government has attempted to rehabilitate the town mainly because of its historic significance.

MOCUMBI, PASCOAL (1941–). Born in former Lourenço Marques **(Maputo)** on April 10, 1941, Mocumbi is the son of Manuel Mocumbi Malume and Leta Alson Cuhle and has been prime minister of Mozambique since December 1994. A Presbyterian by faith, Mocumbi completed his primary education at the Mocumbi Mission in **Inhambane's** Nharrime District, in 1952, having completed his secondary education at the Licéu Salazar in Maputo in 1960. In 1973, he received a medical degree from the University of Lausanne, Switzerland, with a specialty in internal medicine (surgery, obstetrics, and pediatrics). He was also trained and worked as a nurse at the Canton University Hospital at Lausanne. Subsequently, he obtained a diploma in health planning, in Dakar, Senegal, in 1975. Prior to becoming prime minister, Mocumbi held several posts including that of a medical intern at the St. Loup Hospital in Switzerland (1973–75); obstetrician-gynecologist in Maputo Central Hospital (1975–76), while he was director of the José Macamo Hospital; obstetrician-gynecologist at **Beira** Central Hospital (1976–80), while serving as chief provincial medical officer and provincial director of health for **Sofala** Province; minister of health (1980–87); and minister of foreign affairs (1987–94).

Mocumbi is a member of the Mozambique Public Health Association, the Mozambique Association for the Defense of the Family (AMOD-EFA), and the Special Working Group of the World Health Organization on Health and Development. He has also coauthored several articles on health, including "Obstetrícia Práctica" (1987) and "Intervenções em Obstetrícia" (1982). A man of much talent and valor, Pascoal Mocumbi is a recipient of several national and international honors, including the

Veteran of the National Liberation Struggle and Socialist Labor Medals, the Grand Cross Order of Bernardo O'Higgins of Chile, and the Grand Order of the Southern Cross of **Brazil**. A founding member of **FRE-LIMO**, Prime Minister Mocumbi has remained a member of the party and the Association of Liberation Struggle Combatants.

In contrast to many who have held similar positions in the country, Mocumbi is able to focus on government affairs, family matters (he is married and has four children), and civic concerns. As one of the most educated and experienced individuals in the country, Mocumbi speaks **Portuguese**, French, English, Cichopi, Cishangana, and Chironga, which makes him comfortable both at home and abroad and keenly aware of the country's problems beyond the issues of health. As the country moves toward the third multiparty presidential elections, speculation abounded as to whether he might run for the presidency because **Joaquim Alberto Chissano** will not run a third term. However, when friends and journalists asked him about this eventuality, he brushed them aside, telling them that he does not have such ambitions. In fact, he has not made himself a candidate for the 2004 elections in the country. He has been an effective prime minister at a very difficult time, during the transition from a single-party to a multiparty state. Mocumbi has spoken against corruption and defended the right of journalists to speak and write freely and unobstructed by the government, as he did on May 3, 2001, against the assassination of **Carlos Cardoso** in 2000.

MONDLANE, EDUARDO CHIVAMBO (1920–1969). Born of peasant parents in the district of **Gaza**, Mondlane attended primary school at a Swiss Protestant mission and left for Transvaal to complete his high school. He enrolled at Jan Hofmeyer School, where he received a certificate in social work. Through his contacts, Mondlane was admitted at Witwatersrand University to pursue studies in social science. According to his biography, Mondlane was deported from **South Africa** to Mozambique as a result of his political activities among the Mozambique students at the university and in the community. Interrogated by the **Portuguese** secret police—the **Polícia Internacional de Defesa do Estado** (PIDE)—and judged not dangerous, Mondlane was released rather than sent to jail. According to other accounts, he became an unwelcome individual at the South African university because, as a black man, he once represented white students at a conference in Cape Town. This gave the authorities a pretext to expel him from the university and to deport him to his country of origin.

Once again, Mondlane's good contacts came to his rescue. An American professor he met at Jan Hofmeyer, Darrell Randall, secured a scholarship from the Phelps Stokes Fund and the Methodist Crusade Scholarship Fund to continue his studies in the **United States**. Unfortunately, the Portuguese authorities sent him instead to Lisbon. Mondlane successfully argued, however, that, since the university there did not offer a degree in sociology and anthropology, he should be allowed to study in the United States. Consequently, the Portuguese government allowed him to leave Lisbon for Ohio, where he enrolled at Oberlin College and finished his B.A. degree in sociology and anthropology in 1953. His contact with anthropologist Melville Herskovits landed him admission to Northwestern University, where he completed his M.A. and Ph.D. degrees in sociology and anthropology in 1957. Thereafter, Mondlane accepted employment as a researcher for the Trusteeship Section of the **United Nations**.

In 1961, Mondlane resigned his post and visited Mozambique under UN protection. In Mozambique, both the Africans and the Portuguese enthusiastically received him. While the Africans saw him as a symbol of their own success, the Portuguese authorities attempted to take credit for his unparalleled high educational status. Upon his return to the United States, Mondlane taught at Syracuse University. Recognized in the United States as a Mozambique nationalist, one of the very few Mozambican students at the time, Mondlane was often on the lecture circuit on behalf of his motherland. He strengthened his contacts with the incipient revolutionary movements in Dar-es-Salaam, Lusaka, Mombasa, Blantyre, and Salisbury, insisting that they should unite before waging a war against the Portuguese.

When the **União Nacional Democrática de Moçambique** (UDEN-AMO), the **União Nacional Africana de Moçambique** (MANU), and the **União Nacional de Moçambique Independente** (UNAMI) decided to unite in Dar-es-Salaam in 1962, Mondlane became the obvious compromise candidate, as he had had no ties with any of the three movements, while possessing international credentials and a high academic status. Mondlane assumed the presidency of the new movement, Frente de Libertação de Moçambique (**FRELIMO**), on June 25, 1962—the official date of the establishment of the new revolutionary movement. On September 25, 1964, Mondlane proclaimed the beginning of the armed struggle to free Mozambique from Portuguese colonialism. As proof of his leadership abilities, he was reelected president of FRELIMO in 1968. Following a period of internal crises within FRELIMO that culminated with the expulsion of white Portuguese instructors at the Mozambique Institute in Dar-es-Salaam, the closing of the institute itself, and mysterious deaths within the revolutionary movement, Mondlane himself was killed on February 3, 1969. A bomb contained in a mail package exploded in his face, tearing him to pieces. A triumvirate consisting of **Marcelino dos Santos**, **Samora Moisés Machel**, and **Urias Timóteo Simango** took over the front's leadership temporarily until the **Central Committee** appointed **Samora Moisés Machel** as president of FRELIMO.

Mondlane was married to a well-educated white American woman from Chicago by the name of Janet Ray. She bore him three children and has remained a faithful and a very active member of FRELIMO in independent Mozambique. Mondlane's contribution to the liberation of Mozambique should not be underestimated. Not only must he be given credit for the initial unification of the various liberation movements, but also he must be credited with the transformation of FRELIMO into a viable force against the Portuguese army and government. Despite the split that subsequently occurred among members of the former liberation movements and the bickering that plagued FRELIMO's Central Committee, Mondlane focused his attention on making sure that the initial stages of the guerrilla war inside Mozambique would be successful. Respected in his native land as well as abroad, Mondlane traveled frequently to the West, particularly the United States, campaigning on behalf of the Mozambican cause and soliciting funds.

Mondlane's untimely death in 1969 did not allow him to elaborate his vision of a future Mozambique, although his philosophy of development leaned toward some form of democratic socialism. In an interview with Helen Kitchen in November 1967, he said, "Our model is the neighboring state of Tanzania." He admired Julius Nyerere's *ujamaa* in Tanzania and would have liked to see something similar instituted in Mozambique to improve the plight of all Mozambicans, particularly the farmers. Although stressing the importance of **education** and advocating fair salaries for the working class, Mondlane rarely spoke of a class struggle in Marxist terms or about the elimination of the "petty bourgeoisie," about which the first generation of FRELIMO leaders would later be obsessed. He was against all types of discrimination based on ethnicity, region, race, sex, or religion.

While Mondlane was president, FRELIMO enjoyed a relatively balanced Central Committee in terms of ethnic and regional representation. Although supporting the separation of church and state, Mondlane believed in genuine religious freedom (as practiced in the United States where he had studied). As a result, his programs received considerable assistance from the American Protestant churches. He held the view that

Portuguese whites should be integrated into the new Mozambican society but without special privileges. Yet, he envisaged limited roles for them in the government of a future Mozambique.

MONHE. A pejorative term used to designate Asiatic **Indians**, particularly merchants, who were disliked by both the Africans and the **Portuguese**. While the Africans saw them as usurers imbued with a superiority complex, the Portuguese considered them to be ruthless competitors on the marketplace, a resentment that began against the so-called **Baneanes** during the 17th century.

MONTEPUEZ. A town in the northern Province of **Cabo Delgado** where, according to official accounts, some 100 prisoners died from asphyxiation and overcrowding in jail on November 9, 2000. The opposition had organized several demonstrations in the town to protest the government handling of local affairs and the result of the 1999 elections. The police arrested and jailed several of the demonstrators. While **RENAMO** blamed the authorities for the tragic incident, **FRELIMO** accused RENAMO of inciting the demonstrators and allowing them to use any means, including violence. This was one of the major topics of the three meetings between **Joaquim Chissano** and **Afonso Dhlakama** held in December 2000 and in January and March 2001.

MOTRACO. Consortium of electric companies from Mozambique, **EDM, South Africa** (ESKOM), and Swaziland (SEB), created in November 1998, to supply 435 megawatts of electricity to the Mozambique Aluminum (**MOZAL**) smelting plant at Beloluane, near **Maputo**. As a result, a 300-kilometer (120-mile) power line from South Africa to Beloluane was inaugurated in early 2000.

MOVIMENTO ANTI-COLONIALISTA (MAC). A political association founded in Lisbon in 1957 by assimilated and educated colonial subjects, the MAC was an offshoot of the **Casa dos Estudantes do Império.** The movement created strong bonds among future revolutionary leaders such as **Marcelino dos Santos**, Amílcar Cabral, Mário Andrade, and Agostinho Neto, and led to the establishment of the Frente Revolucionária Africana para a Independência Nacional das Colónias Portuguesas (FRAIN) (African Revolutionary Front for the National Independence of the Portuguese Colonies) in Tunis in 1960, designed to coordinate the programs and activities of the revolutionary movements against the **Portuguese** government. Unfortunately, FRAIN lasted only a year and was replaced by the **Conferência das Organizações Nacionalistas das Colónias Portuguesas** (CONCP) (Conference of Nationalist Organizations of the Portuguese Colonies), established in Casablanca, Morocco, in April 1961. Marcelino dos Santos was the first director of the conference's permanent secretariat at Rabat. The second meeting of the conference took place in Dar-es-Salaam in 1965.

MOVIMENTO DAS FORÇAS ARMADAS (MFA) (ARMED FORCES MOVEMENT). **Portugal** had been fighting its African wars since 1961. From 1961 to 1974, over a million young **Portuguese** recruits were forced to participated in the effort, with thousands of casualties for the army and the air force, without an end in sight. In Portugal, the middle class, especially businessmen and bankers, who looked now to integration in the European Community rather than rely on Africa, and intellectuals began questioning the army's role in the Portuguese colonies and grew disappointed as the casualties mounted. Within the armed forces themselves, three schools of thought had developed by the early 1970s. Most military officers became convinced that the war was not winnable and believed that the best course of action was to attempt to create and preserve a Lusitanian community of independent republics, just as Charles de Gaulle had tried (unsuccessfully) in Francophone Africa in 1958. General **António Spínola**, who had been governor-general of Guinea-Bissau, led this group of officers. The second faction spoke for the continuation of the war until victory. Younger officers, however, who sustained the brunt of the war, were disappointed at the promotion of noncareer officers to high positions by **Marcello Caetano**. They also sympathized with the socialist leanings of the revolutionary movements, especially in Mozambique, favored an immediate end to the war, and wished to hand over power to those liberation movements that had actually had an impact on the course of the conflict. They called themselves Movimento das Forças Armadas (MFA), or the Armed Forces Movement.

Unfortunately for the government, the young officers had planted military officers of similar philosophy in important positions in the colonies and the metropolis. In Mozambique, for example, this was the case of the Portuguese Air Force commander, Colonel Diogo Neto and of Major Agnas Varela, who was in charge of the Special Intelligence and Intervention Forces. The Portuguese army chief of staff, also a member of MFA, who had visited Mozambique just prior to the overthrow of the regime in Portugal, strengthened the young officer's ranks. Thus, confident that it would prevail, the MFA overthrew Caetano on April 25, 1974, named Spínola president of Portugal, and began secret negotiations (without even the knowledge of the president and the new prime minister, **Mário Soares**) with FRELIMO, with whom many Portuguese soldiers and officers had begun to fraternize.

As a way of exerting further pressure on Portugal, FRELIMO had refused to implement a unilateral cease-fire. The MFA gave orders to its troops to fire only in self-defense. By September 1974, the MAF and FRELIMO had signed the **Lusaka Agreement**, which made provisions for a **transitional government**, put aside the issues of compensation to the Portuguese settlers, the political role of other independence movements, and democratic elections in Mozambique. Early in the process, political prisoners had been freed, the DGS eliminated, and the governor-general dismissed.

In spite of "heroic" efforts by the Portuguese settlers, including Jorge Jardim, the Portuguese millionaire in Mozambique and the political power shaker par excellence, to guarantee a settler takeover in the new country in tune with Caetano's conservative approach or Spínola's Luso-African community, which asked for a referendum on the future of the colonies, the MFA went ahead with its determination to hand over power in the colonies, dismissing Spínola as president on September 30, 1974. After installing the transitional government and quelling with **FRELIMO** a settler rebellion in Maputo, which captured the radio station, the MFA ordered its troops to leave Mozambique and return to Portugal where the people received them as heroes. On June 25, 1975, Mozambique became an independent nation under FRELIMO.

MOVIMENTO NACIONAL DE MOÇAMBIQUE (MONAMO) (MOZAMBIQUE NATIONAL MOVEMENT). A **Portuguese** reactionary movement established and led by Máximo Dias in Mozambique following the April 25, 1974, coup in Lisbon. MONAMO's program was to form a government of only the Portuguese who were born in Mozambique. Because of its narrow roots, it attracted only a few Portuguese, Indians, and *mestiços*. The **transitional government** was able to disband this reactionary group.

MOZAMBIQUE CONVENTION. A series of agreements between the **Portuguese** government and **South Africa** allowing South African companies to recruit mine workers from Mozambique. Since the 19th century, Mozambicans had been migrating to South Africa to work on sugar plantations in Natal and in the Kimberly diamond mines. In 1909 (with revisions in 1928 and 1930), **Portugal** and South Africa signed the so-called Mozambique Convention, which allowed South Africa to recruit up to 100,000 Mozambicans a year to work in the mines of the Transvaal. The **Witwatersrand Native Labour Association** (WNLA or WENELA) enjoyed a monopoly over workers' recruitment until 1966, when three other South African companies, commonly known by the acronyms of ATAS, CAMON, and ALGO, were added to the list of legal recruiters of Mozambican workers, particularly from the southern provinces of **Inhambane, Gaza,** and **Maputo.**

Between 1896 and 1898, even before the convention, Mozambicans constituted about 62 percent of the workforce in the gold mines. During the past century (including the time following independence), the number of Mozambican workers never fell below 20 percent. In June 1974, Mozambican workers numbered 91,000 (about 24 percent of the total workforce). The convention was a cornerstone of Mozambique's relations with her southern neighbor, given that it also regulated the use of Mozambique ports and waterways by South Africa. FRELIMO allowed the continuation of the convention because of the benefits it brought to the country and the employment opportunities it provided to Mozambicans. Before independence, FRELIMO officials had vowed to stop the policy. The financial consequences of such a move were weighed more realistically during the postindependence period, and FRELIMO realized it could not find local employment for so many people.

According to the terms of the convention, after six months of full salaries paid to the miners, 60 percent of the Mozambican miners' wages in South Africa would be remitted to **Portugal** (to Mozambique following independence) in gold bars at the low price of $35 an ounce. The remaining 40 percent were paid to the workers in *escudos* at the end of their contracts. Portugal (and Mozambique until 1978), with South African assistance, would sell the gold bars at the free market price. In 1978, however, South Africa stopped selling Mozambique gold bars at the 1928 convention price. Instead, it sold the gold at the world market price "on behalf of Mozambique." Economists estimate that this cost Mozambique a loss of some R160 million a year in foreign exchange earnings.

The convention assured South Africa of a steady and cheap supply of labor. By using foreign workers, South Africa was also assured that its own African labor force would never become a significant force that could disturb the nature of apartheid. The number of Mozambique mineworkers going to South Africa decreased over the 1980s, from 115,000 in 1971 to 128,000 in 1975, to 45,000 in 1985, and even fewer during the 1990s. The cause of the decline, however, was not FRE-LIMO's revolutionary stance but South Africa's internal policy aimed at providing employment to its own population. (South Africa's unemployment ran at more than 20 percent in the late 1980s and higher in 2000.)

In 1980, Mozambique, Malawi, Zambia, Lesotho, and Swaziland established a Labor Minister's Commission to study the feasibility of stopping export labor to South Africa. However, the commission failed to devise an alternative strategy to counter South African hegemony, and frontline governments have continued to facilitate labor recruitment by South Africa. Of the estimated 470,000 workers employed by the South African Chamber of Mines in the mid-1980s, 42 percent were foreigners (with 42 percent of these recruited from Mozambique and Lesotho). Since contracts are renewable, about one-fourth of the Mozambican miners (ages 18–60) spend two-thirds of their lives in South Africa, often leaving their families unattended. If they do return, they spend an average of seven months in Mozambique before going back to the mines. At present, just a few thousand are allowed to work in the mines. Given South Africa's high unemployment conditions, the forcible return of Mozambican **refugees** after 1992, and the high rate of **HIV/AIDS** infected among mine workers, the future of Mozambican workers going to South Africa is gloomy.

MOZAMBIQUE NATIONAL MOVEMENT (MONAMO) / (INDEPENDENT MOVEMENT FOR NATIONAL RECONSTRUCTION). One of the first but insignificant **RENAMO** splinter groups following **André Matsangaissa's** death in 1979, based in Lisbon, and led by Máximo Dias. The split was caused by RENAMO's acceptance of South African assistance. MONAMO also abhorred Mozambique's multiracial policy. MONAMO never waged war, however, and is said to have supplied only "material" to *Voz da Africa Livre*, following the signing of an agreement with RENAMO in 1979.

MUEDA. A town in the province of **Cabo Delgado** made famous by a massacre perpetrated by the **Portuguese** government when it killed 500 demonstrators on June 16, 1960. Apparently, the governor requested the victims to appear at the administration center and present their grievances formally as they had been protesting against forced labor, low salaries, and the lack of freedom. The governor then proceeded to order the arrest of many who had appeared. People began to protest against the order. The governor called the army he had already alerted and had the populace shot to death. Nationalists consider the incident to be the precursor and catalyst of the armed resistance against the Portuguese government.

MUSEU DA REVOLUÇÃO. Located at 2999 Avenida 24 de Julho, the Museu da Revolução houses **FRELIMO**'s historical documents, including those related to the war of liberation from Portugal.

MUTSONKHO. Infamous head tax (*imposto de capitação*) introduced by the **Portuguese** in the colonies. During the 18th and 19th centuries, the Portuguese had also attempted to introduce the hut tax (*imposto de palhota*) but abandoned it at the turn of the century because of the problems it presented in counting the number of homes and determining the owners and occupants. The Africans resisted both taxes, however, mainly due to the abuses associated with them. In some cases, as in **Barue** in 1902 and 1917, the mutsonkho contributed to armed resistance against the Portuguese and the **Companhia de Moçambique**.

MUZILA (MZILA, UMZILA, NYAMENDE) (1810–1884). King of the **Nguni** of **Gaza**, who succeeded to the throne in 1861–62 with assistance from the **Portuguese**. His brother Mawewe had allied himself with the Swazi and usurped power at the death of their father, Soshangane, in 1858 and had forced Muzila to seek refuge in the Transvaal. Mzila signed a treaty with the Portuguese authorities in December 1861, allowing them free commerce and transit and granting them privileges such as unobstructed elephant hunting and freedom to erect forts in his territory. The Portuguese, in turn, pledged to assist him against his enemies. Although Muzila did not take the treaty seriously and acted at will toward his subjects and those he decided to conquer, the Portuguese were unable to curb his power. He died suddenly in August 1884, but his death was kept a secret until October 1884. His body was not buried until December 1884.

MWENEMUTAPA (MONOMOTAPA). Title of the kings of the Karanga state in the interior of **Sofala** and former Rhodesia. The term was also used to designate the kingdom itself. Dating back to the 15th century, the Mwenemutapa kingdom, with its capital at Great Zimbabwe, attracted the attention of the **Portuguese** mainly because of its allegedly abundant gold and silver, and it was eventually dismantled by the Portuguese and the British. Led by the rebellious king Changamire, the Rozwi people dismembered the kingdom during the latter part of the 15th century. One offshoot of this split was the small kingdom of **Barue**, which fell under the **Macombe** kings in central Mozambique. In 1629, however, Changamire Dombo defeated both the Portuguese and the Mwenemutapa forces. As a result, the kingdom never recovered its unity. The record of the Mwenemutapa dynasty is fragmentary, but the first kings are said to have been Mutota and his son Matope during the 15th century. Some of the Mwenemutapas who ruled the kingdom between 1790 and ca. 1860 were Chiwewe, Chissandu, Kandeya, and Kataruza.

– N –

NACALA TRANSPORT CORRIDOR. Since January 2000, the Nacala Corridor has been entrusted to a consortium of the Empresa Nacional dos Portos e Caminhos de Ferro de Moçambique (CFM) and South African, **Portuguese**, and American companies. The consortium will manage both the port of Nacala in **Nampula** and the Nacala Malawi railway. The Nacala road and railway link Malawi to the Indian Ocean. The corridor was a major target of **RENAMO** incursions during the **civil war**, forcing Malawi at the end of the war to side with the Mozambican government to the point of providing troops to protect the line. In August 1989, **Afonso Dhlakama** had announced an aborted moratorium on the attacks, fueling speculations that Malawi had made a secret deal with RENAMO. *See also* RAILWAYS; TRANSPORT.

NADIA, CYCLONE. A cyclone that devastated **Nampula** and several northern provinces in Mozambique in March 1994, killing 52 people and injuring 312 others. At the time when thousands of **refugees** and internally displaced people were returning home, close to a million Mozambicans lost their homes or experienced crop damage. Much of the infrastructure, such as schools, hospitals, water supplies, roads, electric posts, as well as the indispensable cash crop trees, were razed to the ground, compelling the **United Nations** and other international agencies to once again come to the rescue of a country that was just emerging from a 17-year-old **civil war**.

NAMASHULUA, MARCOS G. (1942–). Marcos Namashulua was born on October 15, 1942, in Njunguntavala village in the district of Muidumbe, Maconde Plateau, in **Cabo Delgado** Province. He attended the Catholic primary school of Nangololo Mission, before enrolling in the Minor Catholic Seminary at Mariri, where he did part of his secondary school studies. He went on to complete it at the Major Seminary at Porto Amelia (the capital of Cabo Delgado Province), now renamed Pemba. For political reasons, he fled the country in 1963 and joined **FRELIMO** in Dar-es-Salaam, Tanzania. While in Tanzania, he worked as information officer in **FRELIMO**'s Information and Propaganda Department.

Namashulua received assistance through the African-American Institute to come to the **United States** to study, and he spent a year and a half at the University of Rochester, New York, to complete his English language training. From Rochester, he transferred to the University of Bridgeport in Connecticut. In 1968, he was elected president of the **União National dos Estudantes de Mocambique** (UNEMO) (National Union of Mozambican Students), USA section. He completed his bachelor's degree in political science at Bridgeport and went on to earn a master's degree in international relations at Fordham University, New York. He subsequently attended Boston University, in Massachusetts, where he pursued studies toward a Ph.D. in comparative politics.

He taught at a high school in Trenton, New Jersey, as a foreign language teacher. For the next seven years (1972–79), Namashulua taught in the black studies and political science departments at various colleges and universities: Trenton State College, Trenton, New Jersey (1972–73); Brandeis University, Waltham, Massachusetts (1973–79); Salem State College, Salem, Massachusetts; and University of Massachusetts, Boston (1977–79).

In an attempt to fulfill long-nurtured career goals, Namashulua did not hesitate to leave academia and join the **United Nations** in 1979, serving as political affairs officer in the Division of the United Nations Council on Namibia, Department of Political Affairs from 1979 to 1989. From 1989 to 1991, Namashulua was on secondment to the United Nations Development Program, where he served at its office in Malabo, Equatorial Guinea, as assistant resident representative. In 1991, he returned to UN headquarters in New York, where he served as a political affairs officer, Division for Regional Cooperation and Self-Determination.

In 1994, notwithstanding the fact that his future was unsure in a new Mozambique, Namashulua decided to return home and offered his services to the government of Mozambique. Prior to his nomination as ambassador to the United States, Canada, and Mexico, in 1995, he served in the Ministry of Foreign Affairs and Cooperation as director of the Division for Asia and Oceania. A rising star in the Mozambique government, he completed his term as ambassador in 2001, waiting for the next assignment, which took him to Kenya as the new Mozambique ambassador in 2002.

NAMPULA. Province since 1975, formerly known as **Mozambique** Province, Nampula has an area of 30,218 square miles and is inhabited by 3,065,000 people (1997 estimate). Nampula is also the name of the capital city of the province. Situated along the Indian Ocean coast, and bordering **Niassa** Province in the northeast, **Cabo Delgado** Province in the north, and **Zambézia** Province in the south, Nampula is served by the Lurio and Ligonha Rivers which irrigate several areas that produce cotton, cashew nuts, sugarcane, sisal, peanuts, and tobacco. Its roads and rail link it with Mozambique's neighboring countries, particularly Malawi, and it has two excellent natural ports: one at Nacala and the other at Moçambique. Nampula is also known for its highlands, including Mount Namuli (3,280 feet), and its several mineral resources such as iron, gold, tantalite, and colombite. Nampula gained notoriety in the mid-1960s, when its capital city was governed by its first African mayor.

NAPARAMAS. A militia movement initiated in 1990 by a certain Makua Manuel António in **Nampula** and **Zambezia** Provinces. Basing his teachings on African traditional beliefs, António claimed to be invulnerable to **RENAMO** bullets. **FRELIMO** is said to have enlisted his assistance against RENAMO in the two provinces. RENAMO forces eventually killed António, a factor that virtually eliminated the Naparamas as a force by late 1991 and allowed RENAMO to once again take control of some of the coastal towns prior to the **Acordo Geral da Paz.** António was also a *curandeiro* or a *naparama (naparma)*, meaning "irresistible force," in the **Makua** language. He claimed to have died from measles at one point and been resurrected after remaining six days in the tomb. He also told his followers that Christ had appeared to him in the mountains and showed him how to make himself and his followers invulnerable to RENAMO. As a result, many of his followers believed him to be Jesus Christ in person. His gift of persuasion as well as his daring resistance to RENAMO helped him resettle some 100,000 of his people in the lands that had been under RENAMO control. In the final analysis, António's genius consisted in his ability to synchronize traditional beliefs related to magic and medicine with Christian eschatological teachings.

NDAU (VANDAU). A **Shona** subgroup, the Ndau are also said to have come from Rodzi country and became militarized by the **Nguni**, who incorporated them into their regiments. The Shanga (Machangana), the Gova, the Danda, the Watombodji, and the Zezuru (of Zimbabwe) may be classified as Ndau clans. They formed the backbone of **RENAMO**.

NGUNI. Cattle raisers historically, the Nguni number more than a million and live in southern Mozambique, in **Gaza** and around **Maputo**. They speak a dialect of Zulu, and the use of the "click" shows their contact with the Khoisan and the Xhosa. The Nguni *nkosi* (lord) used to hold absolute power and was the commander in chief of the army. The Nguni people observed a strict social and military hierarchy based on age.

NIASSA (NYASA). Mozambique's northwestern province, 120,135 square miles in area, with a population of 764,000 (1997 estimate), made up of the predominantly Islamized **Yao** (Jaga, Ajawa), who live between the Rovuma and the Lugenda Rivers. Niassa is the most sparsely populated of the 11 Mozambique provinces. With a rainforest and monsoon climate, Niassa produces cotton, potatoes, tea, beans, and sorghum. Administered by the **Companhia do Niassa** from 1894 to 1929, it was annexed to **Cabo Delgado** during the 1930–1941 period and became a separate district. With its provincial capital at Lichinga, formerly known as Vila Cabral, **Niassa** Province is bordered by Tanzania (through Rovuma River) in the north, Malawi in the west (through Lake Nyasa), **Nampula** Province in the southeast, Cabo Delgado in the east, and **Zambézia** Province in the south.

NOGAR, RUI (also known as RUI MONIZ BARRETO) (1933–). Born in **Maputo** (formerly Lourenço Marques), Nogar was an intellectual associated with literary journals in Mozambique, including *Notícias de Bloqueiro*. His articles appeared in the *New Sum of Poetry from the Negro World* (1966). He was arrested by the PIDE on December 22, 1964, and remained in jail until independence.

NORONHA, RUI DE (1909–1943). Born in **Maputo** (formerly Lourenço Marques), Noronha was the son of an Indian father and African mother, and he is considered to be the "father of modern Mozambican writers." He wrote several poems, one of which, the *Sonetos*, was published posthumously in 1943. Noronha was also an artist.

NOTÍCIAS. The newspaper *Notícias* was founded by Eduardo Saldanha, Paulino dos Santos Gil, José Joaquim de Morais, and Captain Manuel

Vaz Simões as a morning paper in 1926. In 1952, the editors added an afternoon edition under the same name.

NÚCLEO DOS ESTUDANTES SECUNDÁRIOS AFRICANOS DE MOÇAMBIQUE (NESAM) (1949–1964). An association founded in Lourenço Marques by Mozambican secondary school students, some of whom, including **Eduardo Chivambo Mondlane**, were studying in **South Africa**. Its main objective was the improvement of educational opportunities for blacks, the preservation of cultural identity, and the end to colonial abuses. The secret police (PIDE) became suspicious of it, however, particularly after some of the students began joining **FRELIMO** in 1962. Consequently, several members were arrested and, in 1964, the government banned the association. Its official organ was the magazine *Alvor*.

NYUNGWE. The better-known patrilineal Nyungwe inhabit both margins of the **Zambezi** River but are concentrated in the **Tete** district. They seem to be the hybrid of the Maganja and the central **Tonga**. They live from fishing, agriculture, and livestock.

– O –

OIL AND GAS. Since 1948, the Gulf Oil Corporation of the **United States** has been given prospecting rights on oil inland and offshore, and, in 1958, Pan American Oil Company also received similar rights. However, the search has not been rewarding, except for natural gas. Thus, Mozambique imports all of its oil. There is one refinery that can handle up to 800,000 tons of crude oil; its production reached 683,000 tons in 1981, up from 518,716 in 1974. Foreign debt, inflation, and South African reversal on the gold agreement with Mozambique in 1978 have forced the country to reduce drastically its oil imports from 641,000 tons in 1982 to 105,000 tons in 1983, a move that has further aggravated the country's economic problems. Natural gas for steel smelting near **Beira** has attracted multinational corporations from **South Africa**, the United States, Japan, Austria, and Switzerland, to complement one at Pande, whose contract was signed in September 1998.

OPERATION FRONTIER. A project initiated but never completed by Brigadier-General **Kaulza de Arriaga** along the Rovuma River during the period 1970–73. If completed, the project would have created new towns to block infiltration of guerrillas from the north and entice Mozambicans to live peacefully.

OPERATION GORDIAN KNOT. A military strategy adopted by Portuguese Brigadier-General **Kaulza de Arriaga**, particularly in northern Mozambique in the 1970–73 period, stressing the use of aerial bombing and sudden air assaults on insurrectionists' positions and **FRELIMO** hideouts to complement military surface operations. The strategy proved too expensive, and it cost so many Portuguese lives without achieving the intended results that it was abandoned in August 1973.

OPERATION PRODUCTION. Enacted by **FRELIMO** in July–September 1983, Operation Production was intended to clear the cities, especially **Maputo**, of the unemployed (some of whom had lost their mining jobs in **South Africa**), beggars, criminals, and homeless and turn them into productive citizens by forcibly removing them from the urban areas and settling them in the countryside where they would engage in agriculture and other self-sustaining activities. As a result, some 50,000 people were actually removed from the cities, especially Maputo. Unfortunately, the end result was a failure. Understandably, resentment against the authorities heightened and many returned to the cities shortly after being forced to settle often in areas that were unknown to them or in communities that were culturally strange to them. Alex Vines (1991) and other experts on Mozambique hold Operation Production partly responsible for **RENAMO**'s successful recruitment efforts.

ORGANIZAÇÃO DAS NAÇÕES UNIDAS EM MOÇAMBIQUE (ONUMOZ) (UNITED NATIONS ORGANIZATION IN MOZAMBIQUE). Following the 1992 **Acordo Geral da Paz** between **RENAMO** and **FRELIMO**, the mission of the **United Nations** in Mozambique was to verify and monitor its implementation. According to the terms, the UN would "supervise the cease-fire between the two parties, provide security for key transport corridors, monitor a comprehensive disarmament and demobilization program, coordinate and monitor humanitarian assistance operations throughout the country, and provide assistance and verification for national elections." ONUMOZ consisted of an overall Supervisory and Monitoring Commission (CSC) that oversaw three main components: the Cease-Fire Commission (CCF), the Commission for Reintegration (CORE) of refugee returnees, the internally displaced, and demobilized soldiers, and the Joint Commission for the Formation of the Mozambique Armed Defense Forces (CCFSDM).

The gigantic UN mission and operation eventually involved a force of over 6,000 troops: 1,632 from Bangladesh, 1,010 from Italy, 899 from India, 831 from Zambia, 816 from Uruguay, 721 from Botswana, and 280 from **Portugal**; 354 military observers, charged with the task of monitoring assembly points and investigating cease-fire violations; a 1,095-man International Civilian Police, whose mission was to investigate complaints about police conduct, human rights violations, and irregularities in the implementation of the agreed democratic reforms. The International Civilian Police is said to have investigated 511 complaints between its inception, September 1994, and December 9, 1994, date of **Joaquim Chissano**'s presidential inaugural under the new electoral process. This marked the unofficial end of the UN mission in Mozambique, although the last ONUMOZ contingent did not leave until January 1, 1995.

ONUMOZ's task in Mozambique was complicated by various factors, including constant delays caused by logistics and disagreements between **FRELIMO** and **RENAMO**, violations of the cease-fire agreement, refusal of soldiers and their leaders to demobilize, accusations of violations of human rights by both sides, and the unexpected speed and magnitude of the number of returnees that soon overwhelmed the international agencies' resources, as well as hindered access to areas under the control of the two contenders, especially RENAMO. At one point, things were so contentious that UN secretary-general Boutros-Boutros Ghali had to make at least two visits to **Maputo** to reconcile the two parties and move the process forward. All problems notwithstanding, the end result of the ONUMOZ mission was a triumph for all parties involved. Demobilization was eventually achieved, and election results, although contested by the opposition, were accepted, and, in a sense, a free Mozambique was born.

– P –

PALÁCIO DA PONTA VERMELHA. Built by the **Portuguese** in 1880 as a military barrack, this walled establishment, measuring one-fourth of a kilometer along the Indian Ocean, served as the governor-general's mansion beginning with **António Enes** in 1895. It is now the presidential mansion.

PALMATÓRIA. A punishing device that has become infamous in the history of **Portugal** in Africa. It was a wooden device shaped like the palm of a hand with a handle and several holes, which sucked the flesh when applied against the palm of the hand. The palmatória (*mbalamatodiya*, in the African vernacular of central Mozambique) was used to punish schoolchildren and adult Africans accused of crimes as well as prisoners. Both Europeans and Africans in positions of responsibility used the palmatória. Following independence, FRELIMO outlawed the device, although reports hinted that the party had reintroduced it to punish Mozambicans suspected of undermining its stand in the country.

PARDON, AMNESTY LAW. At the end of 1987, at the height of the **civil war**, FRELIMO's People's Assembly passed a law forgiving all those imprisoned for crimes against the state and "people's security." The People's Assembly also approved a law providing amnesty to those in combat or those who were using or had used violence against the people of Mozambique, if they would voluntarily turn themselves in. The generosity notwithstanding, the law was shunned by most guerrillas and resulted only in a few thousand amnesties. Thus, between December 1987 and December 1989, only 3,958 sought and received amnesty in Mozambique, disappointing the government, which had expected much larger numbers.

PARTIDO DE COLIGAÇÃO NACIONAL (PCN). Immediately following the military coup against the fascist Caetano government in Lisbon in April 1974, several nationalist, reactionary, and political parties surfaced in Mozambique, one of which was the PCN. Founded on August 24, 1974, the PCN was actually a loose coalition of urban movements that essentially stood for a peaceful transition to independence, the holding of a referendum on the future of the colony, and opposed FRELIMO's ascent to power. The PCN included Lazaro Kavandame's União Nacional de Independência Popular de Moçambique (UNIPOMO), Father Mateus Pinho Gwenjere's Frente de Independência Nacional (FREINA), Jorge Jardin's Movimento de Convergência Democrática (MCD), Amos Sumane's **Comité Revolucionário de Moçambique** (COREMO), and the obscure Associação Nacional de Moçambique (ANM). However, immediately after the **transitional government** had been installed in Mozambique on September 20, 1974, all parties, except FRELIMO, were banned, and virtually every party leader who did not join FRELIMO was arrested and jailed. While some activists escaped the country, others were never found alive.

PARTIES (POLITICAL). There are at least 35 political parties in Mozambique, most registered prior to the 1994 multiparty elections. They range from truly democratic parties to communist, socialist, peasant, and, chiefly, workers', religious, liberal democratic, confederative, mass, and elite parties, as the following list indicates: União Democrática de Moçambique (UDM), under Pereira Branquinho; Aliança Independente de Moçambique (ALIMO), under General Ernesto Sérgio; Confederação Democrática de Moçambique (CODEMO), led by Domingos Cardoso; Congresso Independente de Moçambique (CONIMO), led by Vítor Marcos Saene; Frente de Libertação de Moçambique (**FRELIMO**), led by **Joaquim Chissano**; Frente Unida de Moçambique–Partido de Convergência Democrática (FUMO-PCD), under the leadership of Domingos António Mascarenhas Arouca; Movimento Nacionalista Moçambicano-Partido Moçambicano da Democracia Social (MONAMO–PMDS), led by Máximo Dias; Partido Agrário de Moçambique (PAM) (no clear leader); Partido Comunista de Moçambique (PACOMO) (no clear leader); Partido do Congresso Democrático (PACODE) (no clear leader); Partido de Convenção Nacional (PCN), under Lutero Chimbirimbiri Simango; Partido Democrático de Libertação de Moçambique (PADEMO), under Joaquim José Nota (based in Kenya); Partido Democrático de Moçambique (PADMO), led by Wehia Monakacho Ripua; Partido Independente de Moçambique (PIMO), led by Magalhães Bramugy; Partido Internacionalista Democrático de Moçambique (PIDEMO), led by João Kamacho; Partido Liberal e Democrático de Moçambique (PALMO), led by Martins Bilai; Partido Patriótico Independente de Moçambique (PPIMO) (no clear leader); Partido Popular de Moçambique (PPPM) (no clear leader); Partido Progressivo e Liberal Federalista das Comunidades Religiosas de Moçambique (PPLFCRM), under Neves Serrano; Partido de Progresso do Povo Moçambicano (PPPM), led by Padimbe Mahose Andrea; Partido Renovador Democrático (PRD), under Maneca Daniel; Partido Revolucionário do Povo Socialista Unido de Moçambique (PREPSUMO) (no clear leader); Partido Social Democrático (PSD), led by Carlos Machel; Partido de Todos os Nativos Moçambicanos (PARTONAMO), led by Mussagy Abdul Remane; Partido do Trabalho (PT), under Miguel Mabote; Partido Social, Liberal e Democrático (SOL), led by Casimiro Miguel Nhamithambo; Partido de Unidade Moçambicana (PUM) (no clear leader); Partido de Unidade Nacional (PUN) (no clear leader); Partido Verde de Moçambique (PVM) (no clear leader); Regedores e Camponeses de Moçambique (RECAMO), led by Arone Sijamo; Resistência Nacional Moçambicana (RENAMO), under Afonso Macacho Marceta Dhlakama; União Democrática (UD), led by José Chicuarra Massinga, coalesced with the Partido Nacional Democrático (PANADE), Partido Nacional de Moçambique (PANAMO), led by Marcos Juma; União

Democrática de Moçambique (UDEMO), led by Gimo Phiri; and União Nacional Moçambicana (UNAM), led by Carlos Alexandre dos Reis.

PEACE ACCORD. *See* ACORDO GERAL DA PAZ.

PEMBA. Formerly known as Porto Amélia, Pemba is a major port and the capital city of **Cabo Delgado** Province, located near Mozambique Channel. Settlements here date back to the mid–19th century (1858). The **Companhia do Niassa** renewed the settlements in the 1890s and made Pemba the capital of its domain. Its surroundings produce cashew nuts, sisal, and copra, and, as a port, it has become, since the 1960s, an important commercial center known for its seafood freezing and processing plant.

PEOPLE'S COURTS. FRELIMO local, district, and provincial tribunals created after independence. Provincial courts dealt with serious cases, while the district courts took cases that required penalties or imprisonment of at least two years. Local courts had jurisdiction over less important cases. At each level, the people, including men and **women**, most of whom were not professional lawyers or judges, elected the judges. The provincial courts had several sections overseen by a trained appointed judge. Citizen judges were elected and performed their duties for two paid months a year while on leave from full-time employment. On a rotation basis, judges sat in every section of the court before their term expired and acquainted themselves with the whole judicial system. The district and local courts also had at least one trained appointed judge. All sessions were open to the public, and, as Allen Isaacman notes, most people could follow the proceedings easily, particularly at the local level because it was common sense that prevailed rather than complicated judicial harangues and principles.

In 1981, the country had at least 300 people's courts. In 1988, the number rose to 803 (11 provincial, 83 district, and 346 local). Prior to 1977, the **grupos dinamizadores** (dynamizing groups) performed the function of lay judges. The people's courts had replaced the **Portuguese** legal system, but the backlog, particularly on the provincial level, impaired justice in many cases. In 1988, Mozambique finally established its first Supreme Court. As a result of the guerrilla movement within the country, in 1979 FRELIMO created a Military Revolutionary Tribunal to try cases concerned with the security of the state. The tribunal rendered sentences that could be appealed, but those condemned to die were quickly executed. The whole judicial system came under review following the **Acordo Geral da Paz.** *See also* JUDICIARY.

PEOPLE'S SHOPS. Warehouses established as part of the economic system introduced by FRELIMO in the liberated areas of Mozambique and expanded after independence. The idea was to encourage people to cultivate crops and exchange them for imported as well as local products such as salt, sugar, soap, paper, shoes, tobacco, bicycles, hoes, and blankets, in order to make them self-sufficient farmers. After independence, hundreds of these stores were established, and, supervised by party officials, they became centers for food rationing and distribution throughout the country. Recently, the government had to sell many of the warehouses to the people because they were becoming unproductive. Party officials believed that the move would promote private initiative in business and offset some of the damage caused by RENAMO. Since the **Acordo Geral da Paz**, the People's Shops have become a thing of the past.

PEREIRA, (DOM) CUSTÓDIO ALVIM. Archbishop of Lourenço Marques (1962–75). Opposed to independence, Dom Custódio Alvim Pereira equated independence with communism, collaborated with the secret police, **Polícia Internacional de Defesa do Estado** (PIDE), against his own priests, and vowed to wage a religious and patriotic war against FRELIMO. For his own safety, the Holy See had to recall him to Rome immediately following independence.

PEREIRA DYNASTY. The Pereiras were a family dynasty that controlled part of the lower **Zambezi** from 1760 to 1902. Gonçalo Caetano Pereira (also known as Dombo Dombo or Terror), a Goan who arrived in Mozambique in 1760 with the desire to enrich himself, founded the dynasty, north of **Tete**. Assisted by one of his sons, Manuel Caetano Pereira, he carved a *prazo* from the Maravi people of Makanga who controlled the ivory and gold trade in the area. His other son, Pedro Caetano Pereira (Choutama), is credited with founding the Makanga prazo kingdom on the lower Zambezi. In 1843, however, Choutama was forced to submit to the **Portuguese** authorities.

He died in 1849 and was succeeded by his son, Cypriano Pedro Pereira (Chissaka). Cypriano refused to recognize Portuguese authority and caused much havoc among the Portuguese *prazeros* south of the Zambezi. Having distinguished himself as the strongest of the Pereiras, Chissaka practically became the sole lord of the trade in ivory, gunpowder, gold, and slaves in Makanga and its surroundings. He died in 1858 and was succeeded by one of his sons also known as Cypriano Caetano Pereira (Kankuni or Sakasaka), who did not assume power until 1874. To ensure his political survival, Cypriano allied himself with the Portuguese authorities and died in 1886.

One of Kankuni's sons or nephews, Chanetta Caetano Pereira, rejected his predecessor's collaboration with the Portuguese government in 1888, and, in alliance with the Massangano Cruz family, waged war against Tete. His major encounter with the Portuguese occurred in October 1888, when he defeated a Portuguese contingent that had attacked his *aringa*. Chanetta succeeded in disbanding the soldiers, some of whom returned naked to Tete after Chanetta killed many others. Two Portuguese officers perished during the skirmish, and one obscure officer committed suicide. Second Lieutenant Joaquim Macieira was killed and his body pinned in a tree fork in front of the aringa.

Chanetta died five years later and, after a period of dynastic rivalry, he was succeeded by Chegaga Pereira, his nephew, who ruled for a few months only. The last of the Pereiras was Chinsinga Pereira (one of Chissaka's sons), who, upon assuming power in 1893, allied himself with the **Companhia da Zambézia**, chartered in the 1890s. In 1898, he and the company conquered the Ngoni kingdom north of Makanga. Eventually, he ended up assuming the position of administrator of the company in 1901. However, accused of embezzlement and his kingdom invaded by the Portuguese for refusing to pay taxes, Chinsinga saw his power rapidly diminish. Led by António Júlio Brito, the company's troops overran Muchena, the Makanga capital, and captured Pereira, who had attempted to escape to Nyasaland. He was executed and his head was taken to Brito.

PINTO, A. A. DA ROCHA DE SERPA (1846–1900). Portuguese army captain who served in Mozambique and was hired by the Sociedade de Geografia de Lisboa to explore west-central Africa in 1877–79. He and Roberto Ivens (a former seaman in Angola) and Hermenegildo Capelo (another adventurous marine) were asked to undertake a transcontinental exploration of central Africa from Angola to Mozambique. However, the three split even before they left for the planned venture because they could not agree on where to start and where to end their mission. Whereas Pinto was more interested in making a transcontinental trip exploring the possibilities of linking Angola and Mozambique (an effort later known as the **rose-colored map** scheme), the other two wished to explore less distant areas, limiting themselves to Angola and perhaps central Africa.

Pinto left from Moçamedes in 1878 and arrived in Durban in 1879 after visiting King Lewanika in Rozi country, in what later became Northern Rhodesia. In 1889, he attempted to subdue the recalcitrant Macololo on the High Shire River through a series of skirmishes. In November 1899, Pinto's army under Lieutenant **João de Azevedo Coutinho** subdued Chief Mlauri. The British, however, considered the Makololo their subjects, and refused to honor Pinto's conquest, an incident which precipitated the humiliating **British Ultimatum** of January 1890. The terms of the ultimatum forced the Portuguese to capitulate and abandon their claims. Serpa Pinto temporarily served as governor-general of Mozambique in 1899.

PODZO. The Podzo live around Marromeu and encompass the following clans: Bande, Botha, Chinde, Chifungo, Chilenje, Malunga, Mbadzo, Nynangombe, Sase, Simboti, Zinjo, and other smaller groups.

POLÍCIA INTERNACIONAL DE DEFESA DO ESTADO (PIDE). A police and surveillance force the **Portuguese** government created in its overseas colonies in 1957 mainly to locate, arrest, interrogate, and imprison individuals suspected of working against the state. Also operating in the international arena, the much-feared PIDE was abolished during the 1960s and replaced by the Direcção Geral de Segurança (DGS), which in practice had the same functions and used the same methods as the PIDE. Although short-lived (1957–68), the PIDE was the most-hated colonial institution.

POLITBURO. FRELIMO's most important and powerful unit. It is selected by the party's Congress and includes the president of the republic (as long as FRELIMO is in power).

PORTS. Mozambique has four main ports: **Maputo, Beira, Nacala,** and **Quelimane**. While Maputo is the second largest seaport in Africa, Nacala is considered the best deepwater port in East Africa. These ports provide vital outlets for Mozambique's land-locked neighbors. In 1997, Mozambican ports handled about 8.2 million tons of total freight. In 1986, the **Southern African Development Coordination Conference** (SADCC), now called the **Southern African Development Community** (SADC), began to rehabilitate the port of Beira and improve transport links to Zimbabwe, Malawi, and Zambia. Capacity at Beira has risen from 1.7 metric tons in 1991 to 7.5 million metric tons in 2000. Malawi trade through Beira tripled in 1993–1994.

The history of the Mozambique harbors has been mixed. For example, they handled some 17 million metric tons of the freight in 1974. During the 1980s, however, due to a boycott by apartheid South Africa, mismanagement, and the activities of **RENAMO**, port freight was reduced considerably. Thus, in 1983, all Mozambique ports handled only 3.6 million tons of cargo. Mainly as a result of South African use, Maputo port alone handled 2,451,863 tons of merchandise in 1975, but the tonnage had plummeted to 3.4 million tons by 1985. The end of the war promised to restore the ports' full capacity. In fact, in 2000 Mozambique had 127 vessels (three more than in 1998), with a total displacement cargo of 37,400 GVT, about 2,000 GVT higher than in 1998. Plans are under way to spend $515 million to upgrade Maputo Harbor, while other ports, such as Ponta Dobela, 42 miles south of Maputo, chosen for development in 1999, are being upgraded or built.

PORTUGAL. The relations between Portugal and its former colony, Mozambique, have had their ups and downs since the end of the war of liberation in 1974. Until then, it appeared as if the two, unable to reconcile their differences, would not develop and maintain cordial relations in the foreseeable future. Yet, as soon as the government of **Marcello Caetano** was overthrown in Lisbon in April 1974, the two immediately solved their differences through the **Lusaka Agreement**, which led to a harmonious **transitional government** in **Maputo** until June 25, 1975, independence day. Unfortunately, their harmony was just a truce in the long war of nerves. The noncompensated nationalization of property, which **FRELIMO** promulgated in 1977 and 1978, forced thousands of angry **Portuguese** settlers to return to Portugal or move to South Africa, irritating the Portuguese government to a great degree.

Given the level of poverty in Portugal, which was exacerbated by the loss of revenues used to fight three wars in Africa simultaneously, and the country's low degree of industrialization, Mozambican leaders were convinced that they had nothing to lose by snubbing Lisbon. Unfortunately, several issues would force the two adversaries to respect each other. These included Mozambique's old and new debt, the dam at **Cahora Bassa**, which is managed mostly by the Portuguese; long-standing educational and scientific ties; the threatening presence and influence of **RENAMO** in Lisbon; Portugal's close ties with the **United States** and its membership in NATO and the European Community; as well as a long history of economic and financial interdependence. Mozambique seems to have been the first to realize the benefits of rapprochement, as it attempted to develop closer ties with the West.

The thaw in relations was facilitated by high-level contacts that culminated in 1981 with Portuguese president Ramalho Eanes's visit to

Maputo, where, in an elaborate ceremony, he bestowed upon **Samora Machel** the sword of a Portuguese general. Eanes's visit to Maputo was reciprocated by Machel's own visit to Lisbon in 1983. To cement the relationship, Portuguese prime minister Pinto Balsemão, accompanied by a group of powerful Portuguese businessmen, visited Mozambique two years later. The expulsion from Lisbon of Mozambique embassy diplomat Rafael Custódio Marques, accused of masterminding the assassination of a RENAMO high official, Evo Fernandes, against which Mozambique retaliated by expelling a Portuguese diplomat from Maputo, did not imperil the postcolonial entente between the two. As a result, presently, the relations between the two countries are quite cordial, and Portugal continues to be Mozambique's biggest trading partner (for 15 percent of its exports). Furthermore, as a leading member of the Lusophone community, Portugal has exerted much influence during the past decade, especially in education, business, technology, television programs, and culture.

The change in relations has also contributed to a yearly return of a large number of former Portuguese settlers and others, who are buying property, building homes, and opening hotels, restaurants, and stores in Mozambique, particularly in the capital city. As with **Brazil**, however, many Mozambicans are asking themselves whether they might now be experiencing the second phase of colonization, namely, neocolonialism disguised in bilateral understanding and cooperation.

PORTUGUESE. The Portuguese population, which in 1974 numbered 200,000, was reduced to fewer than 20,000 as a result of the end of Portuguese rule in 1975 and the economic policies of **FRELIMO**. The activities of **RENAMO** also slowed down the return of other Portuguese citizens who may have had roots in the former colony. Following the **Acordo Geral da Paz** in 1992, hundreds have been returning to Mozambique every year.

POWER (ELECTRICITY). In Mozambique, most of the electricity provided to commercial establishments and residences comes from hydroelectric dams on the Revue, **Limpopo**, and **Zambezi** Rivers. In 1964, there were 668 power-producing stations, which generated about 363,727,000 kilowatt hours. Since then, electricity production has risen to 658 million kilowatt hours in 1975, to 4.94 billion kilowatt hours in 1977, and to 14 billion kilowatt hours by 1980. Construction of a dam at Corumana on the Limpopo River was completed in 1988 and was expected to have the capacity of generating 14.5 megawatts of power. Paradoxically,

Cahora Bassa, the largest electricity-generating dam, provides 98 percent of its electricity not to Mozambique but to **South Africa**. In 1988, it remained almost paralyzed by **RENAMO** but, following the **Acordo Geral da Paz**, it has increased its supply of electricity to Mozambique.

PRAZERO (PRAZEIRO). Owner of a *prazo* (estate) for the duration of three consecutive generations.

PRAZO. Portuguese landholding institution established in Mozambique during the 17th century. This was a Portuguese medieval institution transplanted to Mozambique during the 17th century. Based on the law of Sesmarias promulgated by Dom Dinis during the 13th century to improve agriculture, reinforced later by the Ordenações Afonsinas and the Ordenacões Manuelinas promulgated by Dom Afonso V (1438–81) and Dom Manuel I (1495–1521), respectively, prazos were landholdings or estates granted to private individuals by the Portuguese government. The *prazero* (prazo owner) had to be a female Portuguese citizen who would pass the prazo on to her female offspring married to a white Portuguese. The heiress would in turn pass it on to her female offspring, the whole landholding to last three generations or three consecutive female lives. Thereafter, the estate would revert to the state, with the possibility of renewing the contract.

The prazos in Mozambique were located along the **Zambezi** Valley, on Querimba islands, and in **Sofala**. No prazero could own more than one prazo, although some prazeros illegally acquired two or more estates. During the 19th century, for example, 32 prazeros owned 57 prazos in **Tete**. Although the law prescribed that the prazos were not to exceed 500 leagues, most prazos exceeded this limit and were as long as 3,600 leagues "and therefore had a surface larger than the kingdom of Portugal itself," as a government survey put it. The prazo holder was allowed to employ Africans (*colonos*); raise a private army, often made up of slaves commonly known as *achikunda*; trade in all commodities; and maintain law and order in the prazo, always pledging allegiance to the Portuguese government which, in principle, ultimately owned the land. The prazero was also required to live on the prazo and not sell or quit-rent it to anyone else.

The institution was primarily supposed to guarantee Portuguese sovereignty over the areas conquered, stimulate agricultural production, increase and facilitate European settlement, and be a source of revenues for the state through a fixed rental fee paid by the prazero to the government. By law, the prazero would lose the prazo if the land was left idle. But the prazo institution did not produce the desired results. Rampant absenteeism, violent rivalries among the prazeros, scarcity of Portuguese women, lack of capital, and African resistance, all contributed to the failure of the system. African resistance to the institution itself was probably the most serious challenge to its success. The precepts of three lives, female inheritance, and individual land ownership were all foreign to African tradition. Some Portuguese as well as other historians have unsuccessfully argued that the institution was African, introduced long before the Portuguese arrival by the Arabs to enable the sultans to collect tribute from Africans. They claimed that the Portuguese simply replaced the sultans and that therefore a smooth transfer took place, one that was not challenged by the Africans. Given the non-African nature of the essential elements of the institution, however, others insist that failure had to be expected.

Several decrees (e.g., in 1832 and 1854) attempted either to abolish the institution or to improve it, but to no avail. Many of the prazeros neglected agriculture and spent their time in leisure, causing unprecedented miscegenation and the Africanization of the Portuguese settler. In November 1888, the government created a royal commission chaired by historian Oliveria Marques to study the institution and make recommendations. (**António Enes**, later high commissioner for Mozambique, was one of the commission members.) The *Oliveira Martins Report*, published in 1889, called the prazo institution violent, abusive, and inefficient, one that was kept in an "anarchic state," but it did not recommend its abolition. Instead, the commission stressed private ownership of the prazos, specifying how much of it should be cultivated, guaranteeing unlimited rights to exploration, and providing more authority to the prazero for the administration of justice on the prazo and the maintenance of law and order. António Enes and **Mouzinho de Albuquerque**, high commissioners for Mozambique during the 1890s, argued in favor of the institution and attempted to increase the rental fees. They laid emphasis on the actual cultivation of the land. But the coming of the concessionaire companies, the impact of the **British Ultimatum** of 1890, and the provisions of the **Acto Colonial** of 1930 contributed to the ultimate demise of the institution.

PRETORIA DECLARATION. A statement following aborted negotiations held in Pretoria by **FRELIMO** and **RENAMO** through South African mediation in October 1984. **South Africa** declared that the two sides had agreed on a cease-fire (which was never implemented), while rumors circulated that South African troops would be stationed in Mozambique to supervise the cease-fire. Mozambique negotiators left the South African capital claiming that the *bandidos armados* (armed bandits) had recognized

FRELIMO, while RENAMO representatives announced that they had been willing to accept, in principle, **Samora Machel** as president of Mozambique during an interim period prior to national elections. Their ultimate goal all along, they claimed, was the elimination of FRELIMO's Marxist government and the establishment of a new nationally representative government.

PRIVATE SCHOOLS. Private schools run by missionaries and citizens were abolished in 1975 when **education** was made free for all Mozambicans. Private schools are slowly returning to the country now.

PROTESTANTISM. The history of Protestantism in Mozambique goes as far back as the confrontation between **Portugal**, a Catholic nation, and its Protestant neighbors in Europe, all of whom combined religious and economic interests on the continent. The first attempts to introduce organized Protestantism in Mozambique began in the early 17th century, when the Dutch tried to drive out the Portuguese from their stronghold on Mozambique Island. From the mid–18th to the mid–19th centuries, they made another concerted effort to dislodge the **Portuguese** from the Bay of Lourenço Marques itself, now **Maputo** (Mozambique's capital).

In 1856, Scottish missionary **David Livingstone** reached the coast of Mozambique through the area where the Jesuits and the Dominicans had established their Catholic missions, namely, the Upper **Zambezi** and Shire Highlands. He successfully persuaded the London Missionary Society and the British public to organize a Zambezi Expedition, which arrived in Mozambique in 1858. In 1857, Livingstone had been instrumental in the founding of the University Mission to Central Africa (UMCA). The Mission opened the path to Scottish missionary work among the **Yao** in the Shire Highlands under Bishop Mackenzie, who arrived in the area in 1861. Following the collapse of Bishop Mackenzie's expedition, which resulted from the death of its leaders in 1862, the UMCA relocated to Zanzibar. Yet, in 1875, Mackenzie's missionaries returned to the Shire Highlands and established a mission at Mwembe, Chief Mataka's territory south of Rovuma, and west of Lugenda.

All newly founded missions and expeditions, including those led by Livingstone, were soon considered by the Portuguese to be politically motivated. A December 15, 1858, letter from the then overseas minister, Sá da Bandeira, to the Finance and Overseas Commission in Lisbon, while acknowledging these movements as peripheral to the areas of Portuguese immediate interest in Mozambique, called them dangerous encroachments against which Portugal had to prepare to defend itself.

As usual, the Portuguese responded to Protestant advances by encouraging the opening of Catholic missions not only on the Shire Highlands, where Scottish missionaries were most active, but also in the old Zambezi Valley, where Afro-Portuguese, Jesuits, and Dominicans had earlier opened missions. Thus, the Portuguese surprised their Protestant competitors by opening a mission at Mponda in the Shire Highlands, territory later claimed by the commercial interests of the British African Lakes Company. The mission was founded by the White Fathers or Missionaries of Africa, who were the brainchild of Algerian-based, French cardinal Charles Lavigèrie. Lavigèrie had well prepared his clergy to work in Islamic Africa. However, his initiative was short-lived, because, soon thereafter, the **British Ultimatum** of 1890 forced the Portuguese to abandon the disputed Shire Highlands.

Other Protestant groups, working independently, entered Mozambique as early as the beginning of the competition, but they concentrated their effort on certain areas of the colony. The presence of the Wesleyan Mission in Lourenço Marques goes as far back as 1823. Swiss missionaries began their work along the Inkomati River in 1875. In 1879, the Boston American Board of Commissioners for Foreign Missions started its work in **Gaza**. The Episcopal Church arrived in **Inhambane** in 1890. Encouraged by the 1884–85 Berlin Conference's stipulation that freedom of **religion** in the new colonies in Africa be respected, several more denominations followed suite. Indeed, the Berlin Conference constituted the first phase of missionary expansion in Mozambique for both the Protestant and the official **Catholic Church**'s counteroffensive to gain African converts.

Although severely restricted by the government because of their competition with the official Catholic Church, the Protestant missions used the African languages in their teachings, translated the Bible and other texts into the vernacular, and ran many health care centers. Also, in contrast to the Catholic Church, the Protestant churches, particularly the Episcopal Church, ordained several African ministers as early as the 1920s. These ministers eventually established their own "Ethiopian" congregations, independent from their parent churches. The "Ethiopian" churches were the forerunners of several independence movements in parts of Africa, hence the fear that they instilled not only among the Portuguese colonizers in Mozambique but also among the colonial powers all over the continent. Realizing their precarious situation in Mozambique and the type of covert persecution to which they were subjected by the civilian and religious authorities in the colony, some of these Protestant missions would at times fuse to form new groups, such as the **Conselho Cristão de Moçambique** (CCM) or the Aliança Evangélica (Evangelic Alliance), an amalgam of Methodist and Episcopal Churches, to present a common front against the threat presented by the colonial government and the Catholic Church.

Notwithstanding the problems, by 1936, the German Swiss Mission had ordained 5 priests, trained 134 catechists, converted 3,418 Africans, and operated a hospital and a school system with 3,000 students at 11 stations supervised by eight European missionaries. The Methodist American Mission at Inhambane had two central missions and 75 subsidiary stations, 8 dispensaries, 165 subsidiary posts, 8 primary schools, and several trade training centers. The Wesleyan and Methodist Missions in Lourenço Marques District operated 82 stations, provided as well with several health care centers and schools. In total, by 1964, the Protestant missions registered some 200,000 students in their missions. The Missão Suiça de Lourenço Marques (the Swiss Mission of Lourenço Marques), alma mater of one of the founders and first president of **FRELIMO**, **Eduardo Chivambo Mondlane**, became famous for its work in Mozambique. The atmosphere created by the FRELIMO regime, which formally declared itself Marxist-Leninist in 1975, helped neither Protestant nor Catholic missionary activity in the country.

However, since the Protestant missions were known for their lack of enthusiasm in enforcing Portuguese laws and in instilling Portuguese patriotism in the Africans, FRELIMO was not as critical of their work in the then People's Republic of Mozambique. Thus, while in 1988, there were two dioceses of the Anglican Church, one in Maputo and another in **Niassa** Province, the Baptist Church freely maintained its headquarters at Maputo. Today, Protestantism enjoys no more privileges than the other faiths in Mozambique, including the Anglican Church, which contributed, at least initially, to the signing of the peace accord in the country in 1992. Protestants account for about two and half million people in Mozambique. *See also* JEHOVAH'S WITNESSES.

PROVINCES. After independence, in 1976, FRELIMO created 11 provinces in Mozambique: **Niassa, Cabo Delgado, Nampula, Zambezia, Tete, Manica, Sofala, Inhambane, Gaza, Maputo**, and **Maputo City** (the capital is considered a province). Each province is headed by a governor appointed by the president of the republic.

– Q –

QUELIMANE. Town and provincial capital **of Zambézia** Province, located at the mouth of the Rio dos Bons Sinais, on the Indian Ocean. **Vasco da Gama** disembarked at Quelimane on January 25, 1498. Founded as a settlement in 1544, Quelimane became a town in 1763 and a municipality (*concelho*) in 1763. During the 18th and 19th centuries, Quelimane thrived as a town trading in slaves, exporting between 8,000 and 10,000 slaves a year to **Brazil** and the French islands in the Indian Ocean. More recently, the city has experienced a boom resulting from the agricultural activities of the province, which produces copra, sugarcane, sisal, cotton, tobacco, and coconut plants (four million trees in 1987, occupying some 50,000 acres of land). The population of Quelimane was estimated at 100,000 in 1997.

– R –

RAILROAD. The railroad is the principal means of transportation of goods in Mozambique; its services are invaluable to its domestic and foreign trade. Rail passenger traffic increased significantly from a mere 26 million passenger-kilometers in 1992 to 403 million passenger-kilometers in 1997. Goods transported by road reached 110 millions of ton-kilometers in 1997, while the actual number of passengers carried by rail and road was 163,000 in 1996. Mozambique has seven principal lines: Maputo-Ressano Garcia, Maputo-Goba, **Limpopo** (Maputo-Chicualacuala), **Beira**-Mutare, Trans-**Zambézia**, **Tete**, and Nacala-Malawi. The line linking Beira port to Zimbabwe was completed in 1987. Likewise, a major part of the Nacala line was renovated during the same year. Construction on the Limpopo line, linking Zimbabwe to the port of **Maputo**, was completed in early 1993. Railroad transportation provides vital **trade** links for export cargo.

Mozambique has a relatively extensive railroad system, which links some of the major production centers internally and also provides adequate transport facilities for goods in transit from its landlocked neighbors, including **South Africa**. Major routes include the Maputo-Ressano Garcia-Pretoria line, the Maputo-Goba-Swaziland line, the Maputo-Chicualacuala-Zimbabwe line, the Beira-Mutare line (the so-called Beira Corridor), the Trans-Zambezia-Malawi line, and the Nacala-Malawi and the Moatize-Beira lines (the latter not yet rehabilitated).

Railroad construction in Mozambique began during the 1880s, the first completed line having been the **Delagoa Bay** railway linking Maputo with Pretoria, started by Edward McMurdo in 1887 and completed in 1895. Overall, railroad construction and mileage increased dramatically thereafter, reaching 300 miles in 1910, 600 miles in 1923, and 1,500 in 1933. Railroads carried thousands of passengers and tons of cargo every year, thereby generating much needed revenue for the colony. The Delagoa Bay railway alone, for example, carried 264,610 passengers and 1,203,518 metric tons of cargo in 1925, a load that rose to 318,225 passengers and 1,233,533 tons of cargo in 1928. During the 1940s and 1950s, further rail miles were added so that by 1964, Mozambique could boast having 2,157 railroad miles, representing almost a fourfold increase over 1910. Presently, the Mozambique railway network is 2,177 miles (3,512 kilometers) long. In 1984, the Mozambique railway system carried 5.4 million passengers and some 536.3 million metric tons of freight. The most recent official figures refer to 1999, when transportation passenger-kilometers were 1.4 million, down by 4.1 million and the freight was 721.2 million metric tons, up by almost 200 million from 1984.

South Africa and Zimbabwe are particularly dependent on Mozambique's rail system. For example, in 1977, the use of **Maputo's** rail system and harbor by South Africa generated some U.S.$93 million to the country. During the 1980s, South Africa deliberately decreased its use of Mozambique transport facilities in retaliation against the Maputo regime for its support of the African National Congress. Zimbabwe has attempted, since independence in 1980, to reroute its goods through Mozambique (using the Beira-Mutare line) in order to become less dependent on South Africa. However, **RENAMO** made the line insecure, and Zimbabwe troops had to guard it. Assistance from the Netherlands, the **United States**, and the Scandinavian countries to the tune of $300 million allowed the reopening of the **Beira Corridor** in 1986 and in May 1987, while the European Community pledged some $599 million to maintain the line open and in good condition during the next eight years.

Malawi, Zambia, and Swaziland also use the Mozambique railroad system, and the **Southern African Development Coordination Conference** (SADCC), now called the **Southern African Development Community** (SADC), has made railroad improvement in Mozambique one of its priorities. However, the cost of the infrastructure improvements and the activities of **RENAMO** during the war have made rail transport increasingly more expensive. In March 2000, the government estimated that rehabilitating roads and railroads would cost as much as

U.S.$250m. As calm returns to Mozambique, the use of the rail has become more promising. *See also* NACALA TRANSPORT CORRIDOR.

REFUGEES. During the recent period, most of the refugee exodus from Mozambique has been caused by war. The war of liberation from **Portugal** (1964–74) forced 250,000 Mozambicans to seek refuge in the surrounding countries, especially Tanzania, Zambia, and Malawi. The 1977–92 civil war between **FRELIMO** and **RENAMO** compelled some 2 million Mozambicans to flee to Malawi (1 million), South Africa (300,000–500,000), Zimbabwe (237,000–400,000), Zambia (40,000), Tanzania (72,000), and Swaziland (21,000). While most lived in refugee camps, many remained in settlements and mixed with the local populations, a process that was facilitated by ethnic and language affinity and the short distances between the borders where the refugees lived before seeking asylum. However, by 1995, most of them had returned home. *See also* REPATRIATION.

REGEDORIA. During the colonial period, the lowest administrative unit entrusted to a **Portuguese** citizen or an assimilated African was the *posto administrativo*. The posto was divided into *regedorias*, a number of villages inhabited by at least a thousand people under a traditional African authority called *régulo*. The objective of the regedoria was to allow the continuation of traditional law for the *indígenas* population and ensure the proper distribution of government schools, health posts, and commercial centers.

RÉGULO. Hereditary African authority who, during the colonial period, had to be confirmed or sanctioned by the **Portuguese** to exercise control over a certain number of villages. Assisted by a council of his own choice, the régulo or chief dispensed justice according to traditional law, wore military insignia bestowed on him by the Portuguese government, received a monthly salary, administered a force of African policemen known as *cipaios*, furnished recruits for forced labor and the army, and collected taxes for the administration. Heads of villages were also salaried dignitaries. *See also **REGEDORIA.***

RELIGION. Interreligious relations in Mozambique have always been either cool or tense over the past 50 years. The **Catholic Church** and the colonial government never liked the influence of **Protestantism** or **Islam**. During the 1970s and 1980s, the **FRELIMO** government disliked all of them but attempted to play one against another through selective criticism.

It assaulted the Catholic Church with vehemence and maintained a dialogue of low profile with Islam and the Protestant denominations, except the **Jehovah's Witnesses.** However, the government's ultimate aim was to eliminate all religions, including African **traditional religions**, in the country, as a corollary and requisite of its Marxist-Leninist philosophy. Cooperation among the religious faiths, excluding Islam, in the country occurred during the late 1980s and early 1990s, as the government had accepted the proposition of peaceful negotiations with **RENAMO.**

Recently, Muslims have been more or less on the defensive as a result of the terrorist incidents that have been attributed to Islamic extremists. A Muslim delegate in the Assembly of the Republic complained shortly after the September 11, 2001, incidents in New York and Washington, D.C., that he was being harassed both internally and externally, especially by the **United States.** In 1997, the Muslims had attempted to have one of their holidays declared a national holiday, a move that was supported by the president. However, the Catholic Church as well as the Protestants were adamantly opposed to the bill that had received approval from the Assembly. Thus, Catholics as well as Protestants were jubilant when the Supreme Court pronounced the measure unconstitutional, reaffirming the principle of the separation between church and state.

Following the ratification of the 1990 constitution, which clearly upheld religious freedom, the three major religious have redoubled their effort to gain new adepts. However, Islam seems to be making some inroads in the north and the coast, while the Christian denominations are finding it difficult to attract the generation that grew up during the decades of the 1970s and 1980s when Marxism was enforced in the country.

Overall, one might say accurately that, presently, interfaith relations in the country are cool, to put it mildly. In fact, there is no strong ecumenical movement in Mozambique and no efforts to increase interfaith dialogue. Of the three major religions in the country, however, it appears that traditionalism is the one losing ground, as more youngsters, despite the problems, are embracing Christianity and Islam. Debatably, some estimate that 66.6 percent of Mozambicans are still traditionalists, 25 percent Christians, and only 10 percent Muslims. The major point of contention about these figures has been the number of Muslims in the country, some government figures arguing that Muslims outnumber Christians by perhaps 2:1, which appears to be a calculated move to downplay the role of Christianity in the country.

RENAMO. *See* RESIST NCIA NACIONAL MOÇAMBICANA.

RENAMO-UNIÃO ELEITORAL (RENAMO-UE). In July 1999, 11 Mozambican opposition parties announced they were forming an electoral union with **RENAMO** for the upcoming December elections and presenting a single slate of candidates for the presidential and legislative elections. They chose **Afonso Dhlakama** as their presidential candidate. The elections, which took place on December 3–5, 1999, resulted in the victory of **FRELIMO**'s **Joaquim Chissano**. While Chissano won 52.9 percent of the vote, his party secured 133 of the 250 assembly seats, the remainder having gone to RENAMO-UE. Despite irregularities, and notwithstanding the fact that **FRELIMO** had lost in the most populous provinces of the country, a situation that was aggravated by the slow and allegedly nontransparent way the National Electoral Commission counted or received the votes from the provinces, the international community and the Mozambique Supreme Court declared the elections free and fair.

Defiant, Dhlakama and his coalition refused to accept the final verdict. RENAMO threatened to move its headquarters to **Beira, Sofala** Province, and declare and run a parallel government. However, none of these threats materialized, and a series of meetings between Chissano and Dhlakama took place in late 2000 and early 2001. When Chissano refused to let RENAMO appoint governors in the six provinces it won, Dhlakama broke off the talks in May 2001. Perhaps to silence the opposition, Chissano announced in April and May that he would not stand as a candidate for a third term, although most political observers did not believe him at the time. Skeptics claimed that FRELIMO officials have so much stake in the continuation of the status quo that they would not allow him not to seek another term. Under such circumstances, Chissano could claim that he was drafted. The constitution is ambiguous on a second reelection, as it simply mandates: "The President of the Republic may only be reelected two times consecutively" (Art. 118. 4), which seems to imply that one can run for a third five-year term.

Dhlakama, for his part, was severely criticized for his loss as a single opposing presidential candidate, for not following up his threats, as well as for not convening the overdue, first peacetime RENAMO Congress, which had been scheduled for July 1999. To complicate matters, a split occurred within the party in 2000, and the number one member of the National Assembly, **Raul Domingos**, was expelled from the party on September 22, 2000. Domingos was accused of secretly negotiating with the government, from which, according to President Chissano, he was allegedly asking $500,000 to pay a loan. He apparently held meetings with the former minister of planning and finance, Tomás Salomão, a few months prior to the elections, without RENAMO's knowledge. By mid-2001, several RENAMO and UE members were advancing the concept of a "third front" or "third force" to oust Dhlakama from prominence and prevent him from running for the third time in 2004. Even though Raul Domingos and others were entertaining such an idea, many observers were doubtful that he or any other leader in the opposition could revolutionize the situation and defeat FRELIMO at the poles. Meanwhile, many people still cling to the belief that the election was "stolen," and jokes abound comparing the Mozambican election with the U.S. November 2001 presidential election that brought George W. Bush to the White House. *See also* ELECTIONS; PARTIES.

REPATRIATION. During the 1992–95 period, the **United Nations** organized the largest **refugee** repatriation effort in its history of assistance to refugees. While many Mozambican refugees had begun to return home as early as 1986 (320,000 returned that year), the bulk of the refugees returned home following the October 4, 1992, **Acordo Geral da Paz**. Between then and mid-June 1995, the whole operation had been completed. Some 1,728,002 Mozambicans had returned home, 78 percent spontaneously or without significant assistance from the international organizations, and the remaining 28 percent relying on assistance organized and provided primarily by the United Nations High Commissioner for Refugees (UNHCR).

RESENDE, (DOM) SEBASTIÃO SOARES DE (1906–1967). Portuguese Roman Catholic bishop of the diocese of Beira, Mozambique. Dom Sebastião Soares de Resende was an outspoken critic of the **Portuguese** government's treatment of Africans, advocated justice and equality, and, in principle, supported the self-determination of the colonies, but within the context of a Lusophone community. In his pastoral letters and writings, the bishop criticized forced labor and the compulsory cultivation of cotton and held the Portuguese morally responsible for the education of Africans and the provision of better housing. His views were often printed in the *Diário de Moçambique*, a newspaper his diocese owned and controlled. He was met with the ire of his fellow Portuguese, including most of the higher clergy, such as Dom **Teodósio Clemente de Gouveia**, cardinal of Lourenço Marques, and **Custódio Alvim Pereira**, who became archbishop of Lourenço Marques following the cardinal's death in 1961. He died from cancer in Mozambique in 1967 after refusing to be taken to **Portugal** as he battled against the disease. He chose to be buried in the city of **Beira**.

RESISTANCE AND PACIFICATION. The occupation and pacification of the colony of Mozambique turned out to be an arduous and bloody task for the **Portuguese.** Since the early days of colonization, the Mozambican people had constantly defied Portuguese attempts to control them, to take their land, and to make them submissive subjects of the Crown. The *prazos* failed in part due to the revolt of the African political authorities as well as the *colonos*. Revolts against slavery, forced labor, and taxation were also common throughout the colony. The concessionaire companies experienced the same resistance as the colonial state did. Given that only the late wave of resistance (1820s–1920) had been relatively well documented, the following is just a summary, region by region, of the wars the Portuguese and the Africans waged against each other in Mozambique. (Scholars further interested in the subject may consult, among others, the works of Xavier Botelho and René Pélissier.)

The town and city of Lourenço Marques (now **Maputo**) suffered constant attacks and assaults by the surrounding populations. The **Nguni** posed a major threat to the city and its *praesidium* in 1822, when they succeeded in defeating the garrison and massacred Governor Miguel de Cardinas, whom they considered to be a cruel administrator. Between July 26 and September 12, 1834, the Nguni, allied with chiefs Machacana of Matola, Massacano of Maputo, and Encolene of Moamba, who had refused to pay taxes, waged intermittent assaults on the praesidium and eventually burned it and turned it over to the chief of Matola. Governor Dionísio Ribeiro escaped and took refuge on the island of Xefina but was tracked down and killed in Magaia on October 5, 1834. The most serious threat to the city occurred on January 25, 1872, when Chief Amula of Zixaxa and several other chiefs from Maputo carried out a sudden assault on the Portuguese settlers. The Portuguese, however, were able to repulse them.

Taxation continued to be a major source of revolts. Thus, in 1894, Matibejane, chief of Zixaxa, accompanied by 2,000 warriors, defied the authorities and publicly "spanked" Lieutenant-Colonel M. Inácio Nogueira, the praesidium adminstrator. Assisted by Chief Maazul of Magaia, Matibejane attacked Lourenço Marques on September 24, 1894. Fortunately for the Portuguese, Maazul abandoned the battle on October 14, 1894, thus forcing Matibejane to give up the fight. Both he and Maazul sought refuge from the Portuguese in **Gungunhana**'s territory. However, the revolt spread to Marracuene, and only the intervention of Major José Ribeiro, Caldas Xavier, and **Joaquim Mouzinho de Albuquerque** was able to pacify Matola, Moamba, Mapunga, Maputo, Zixaxa, Marracuene, and Macassene.

Inhambane was not a peaceful place, either, mainly due to the activities of the Nguni who claimed it as their territory. During the 1840s, they terrorized the Portuguese and their African allies in Inhambane District. In 1844, the Nguni even dared to kill the governor of the fort, and, in 1849, they also killed Captain António Manuel Pereira Chaves. The Portuguese, in alliance with friendly chiefs, responded militarily to restore peace in the district, which was pacified only in 1877. That year, the Portuguese defeated a combined force of **Inhambane** chiefs and repulsed the Nguni threat.

In **Gaza**, the Portuguese faced the most organized southern resistance led by the Nguni. The Nguni defied Portuguese authority, raided the territory of their allies, and, as a diplomatic move, showed friendship to the British, which heightened Portuguese annoyance. In 1851, the Nguni attacked **Manica** and **Sofala** and forced the Shona to pay annual tribute. In spite of the treaties they signed with the Portuguese in 1861 and 1886, the Vátua, as the Portuguese called them, continued to pose a major threat, forcing High Commissioner **António Enes** and his hand-picked collaborator Mouzinho de Albuquerque to assemble better trained troops and plan a systematic assault on Gungunhana's forces. The crowning of the Portuguese military effort started on November 7, 1895, when Mouzinho de Albuquerque defeated the **Nguni** at the battle of Coolela, followed by the burning of Manjacase, one of Gungunhana's most important headquarters. On December 28, 1895, Mouzinho captured Gungunhana at **Chaimite**, and between August 8 and 16, 1895, he led a campaign against Maguiguana, Gungunhana's lieutenant, who was finally killed by one of Mouzinho's African soldiers.

The region of Barue is remembered for its revolts in 1890–1891 against the **Companhia de Moçambique**. The ruler of Barue, carrying the title of Macombe, demanded his independence and refused to pay taxes. Company troops and government soldiers led by Captain-Lieutenant **João de Azevedo Coutinho** attempted unsuccessfully to subdue the "rebels." In May 1902, Barue once again revolted against the Portuguese. This time, Coutinho, fueled by his 1891 defeat, devastated Inhangoma, Tambara, Inhacafura, Chiramba, Inhampanga-panga, Missongue, Mungari, Macossa, Zinto, Suncura, and Massin-guire, and declared victory on October 30, 1902. The Abarue would not give up, however. Their last revolt began on March 27, 1917, sparked by the recruitment of soldiers for World War I and workers for road construction. Led by **Macombes** Makosa and Nongwe-Nongwe, the Abarue forged an unprecedented alliance with the **Tonga**, the

Tawara, the **Nyungwe**, the Atsenga, and the people of Gorongaza. The Portuguese response was swift: a force estimated at between 10,000 and 15,000 men, most of whom fearsome Angoni warriors, descended on Barue in April 1918 and, through the use of terror and the indiscriminate burning of houses and crops, succeeded in finally subduing and pacifying Barue.

The region of Angonia was pacified between 1899 and 1900 by the **Companhia da Zambézia**, which used troops led by Lieutenant António Júlio de Brito. Recalcitrant chiefs were killed or deported as prisoners to **Tete**. Although the Portuguese had settled in **Sena** as far back as the 17th century, they still experienced several revolts from the surrounding populations. Encouraged by the defeat and death of prazero Manuel António Sousa de Gouveia, the Sena people refused to pay taxes in 1891 and joined Cambwemba, Gouveia's lieutenant who claimed the *prazos* between the **Zambezi** and the Pungue Rivers. The revolt was not crushed until August 1897, when Captain-Lieutenant João de Azevedo Coutinho and Lieutenant Delfim Monteiro began a sweeping assault on **Sena** and its vicinity, Gwengwe, Goma, Maganja de Alem Chire, Mavira, Chitangue, Zague, Maroa, and Inhatenge in July 1897.

The family **Cruz** at **Massangano** posed the most frustrating and successful resistance against the Portuguese anywhere in the colony. The revolts and resistance began during the 1840s with the ascension to power by prazero Captain Joaquim José da Cruz. The Portuguese responded with several punitive expeditions, which met with disaster. The 1854–55 expedition was defeated, as were the 1867–68, 1868, and 1869 expeditions. On January 19, 1875, the Portuguese found themselves compelled to sign a treaty with Bonga António Vicente da Cruz. As the arrogance of the Bonga continued, the Portuguese prepared another expedition that converged on Massangano from four directions: Sena, Manica, Barue, and Tete. Bonga escaped, and the Portuguese burnt his headquarters (*aringa*). In 1888, João Santana da Cruz (Mutontora) refused to pay taxes to the Portuguese government and, in defiance, rebuilt the aringa. The Portuguese returned in force, took Massangano on November 29, 1888, and captured the Mutontora family, which was taken prisoner to Mozambique, the colonial capital.

The **Yao** of **Niassa** District, under their chiefs titled Mutaka, became intolerable to the Portuguese government during the 1880s and the **Companhia do Niassa** during the 1890s. In 1890, for example, they massacred Lieutenant Eduardo Prieto Valadim and members of his reconnaissance expedition. In mid-August 1899, however, the Portuguese defeated the Mutaka, who escaped capture. Pacification was not achieved here until 1912, when the Mutaka suffered a major defeat and fled to Tanganyika.

During the 1870s, the Macololo of Massinguire under the control of the Anjo prazero family, particularly Paulo Mariano dos Anjos (Matequenha II), began presenting problems to the Portuguese. To complicate matters, the area was in dispute between the Portuguese and the British, as the latter had established several military and missionary posts there. **Serpa Pinto** subdued the Macololo in 1889, but the Portuguese had to relinquish the area as a result of the now famous 1890 **British Ultimatum**.

In Maganja da Costa, where the Silva prazero family reigned in alliance with the Portuguese authorities, the Africans had offered resistance since the 1850s. The period 1858–59 witnessed several skirmishes at Kazembe, Chunga, and Chiramo, which ended with a Portuguese victory. In 1887, the Maganja killed several members of a Portuguese reconnaissance expedition under Lieutenants Macieira and Pereira at the margin of Tujungo River. In 1890, however, the government sent some 600 *cipaios* under Lieutenant Manuel António, who temporarily subdued the "rebels." As the area continued to resist taxation, Lieutenant João de Azevedo Coutinho commanded a force of 6,000 cipaios who marched to the area on April 19, 1898, and imposed a semblance of peace. However, it was not until 1909 that the area was pronounced pacified.

The Pereiras of Macaranga had constituted a problem for the Portuguese since the 1840s. In fact, in October 1888, Chaneta, leader of the Macanga, defeated a Portuguese expedition and killed one of the commanding lieutenants by the name of Macieira (Makaranga). When the Makanga refused to pay taxes in 1902, the **Companhia da Zambézia** dispatched Lieutenant António Júlio Brito, a company administrator, with 3,000 Angoni warriors. They subdued the recalcitrant chiefs on May 15, 1902, and Chissinga, the prazero, was killed as he attempted to flee to Nyasaland.

The **Maconde** of Niassa District revolted in 1912–13 against the Companhia da Zambézia's imposition of the obligation to collect rubber. They defeated a company contingent assisted by troops from Lourenço Marques on September 12, 1913. A revolt against the company's forced labor policies began on June 10, 1916, and lasted until 1917, when company troops finally restored peace.

Since the 1870s, the Namarrais had scorned the Portuguese authorities and raided their neighbors for slaves and the control of trade in **Cabo Delgado**. A Portuguese expedition sent to prevent the raids ended in disaster in 1887. Joaquim Mouzinho led his own expedition in October 1896, but, wounded at Mjoenga, he was forced to retreat. He returned in

February 1897, however, accompanied by his protégés Lieutenants Ayres de Ornella and João Coutinho de Azevedo. Although Mouzinho was recalled to Matibane, the campaign was successful in subduing Mossuril, Muchelia, Mucuto, Monguinguale, Muecate, Infusse, Ibraimo, Mutibane, Natule, Lunga, Mocambo, and Calaputi. The months of January and February 1913 witnessed the last regional skirmishes, which had been caused by abuses in tax collection. Captains José Augusto da Cunha and Neutel de Abreu put an end to all disturbances. Almost absolute sheikhs and sultans had controlled the district of Angoche since the 1830s. Not only did the Islamic authorities defy Portuguese sovereignty but they also profited immensely from their slave trafficking activities. In the 1860s, Sheikh Mussa Quanto successfully assailed Maganja against prazero João Bonifácio Alves da Silva, a Portuguese ally who had threatened his domain. Eventually, Quanto was captured and taken to Fort São Sebastião but escaped to Zanzibar. He returned in 1862 and reassumed power in 1863. Assisted by other slave traders, including some Portuguese, Quanto overran and annexed Sancul and Sangage sheikhdoms. Following years of unsuccessful attempts, the Portuguese left the sheikh alone.

In Quitangonha sheikhdom, on the Matibane Peninsula, the Muslim population had also been in rebellion since 1857. Captain Miguel Vaz Guedes Bacilar's expedition of 1874 finally restored peace there. Angoche itself likewise posed serious difficulties to the Portuguese administration. João de Azevedo Coutinho had failed to ensure peace in 1885, and only in 1897 was a temporary truce achieved. In 1910, Captain Massano de Amorim defeated Fareley, the most important sultan, and his allies, but sporadic incidents of insurrection continued. Finally, in 1918, after securing assistance from **Macua** chiefs, the Portuguese were able to claim total victory over their "disloyal" subjects.

RESISTÊNCIA NACIONAL MOÇAMBICANA (RENAMO) (MOZAMBIQUE NATIONAL RESISTANCE) (MNR) or MOVI-MENTO DE RESISTANCE MOCAMBICANA (MRM) (MOZAMBIQUE NATIONAL RESISTANCE MOVEMENT) (MNRM). The precise origins of RENAMO are yet to be ascertained accurately. Unfortunately, most analysts have based their writings solely on interviews held with the late Ken Flowers, former Rhodesian intelligence officer, who claimed to have founded RENAMO. While some attribute its years of formation (1975–77) to the **Portuguese** intelligence commandos, known as *flechas*, who aimed to track down and neutralize **FRELIMO** activities and sympathizers, others stress its original links to the Rhodesian Special Branch of the army and intelligence, a type of scout's organization made up of both Rhodesian and Mozambican recruits. The armed scouts were sent to Mozambique to serve as intelligence guides and interpreters about the whereabouts and activities of the **Zimbabwe African National Union** (ZANU) in the then People's Republic of Mozambique. However, so far, no study has been able to pinpoint the moment these "insurgents" became RENAMO and turned their attention to the overthrow of the FRELIMO government.

Two points are clear nevertheless: The white Southern Rhodesian regime, particularly after Mozambique closed its borders to comply with **United Nations** sanctions in March 1976 until the Lancaster House Agreement that led Zimbabwe to independence in 1980, provided logistical, military, and financial assistance to the group; and the new guerrilla group was not only intent on neutralizing ZANU's objectives but also planned to destabilize the FRELIMO government, which was totally supportive of Robert Mugabe's nationalist movement. Following Lancaster House, **South Africa** assumed Rhodesia's role not only to obtain information on African National Congress (ANC) activities in southern Mozambique but also to retaliate against the Marxist Mozambique government's support of the ANC and the South West People's Organization (SWAPO) and its active participation in the **Southern African Development Coordination Conference** (SADCC). Established in 1980 by the front-line states, SADCC was diametrically opposed to South Africa's "constellation of states" policy announced in November 1979.

The extremely diverse composition of RENAMO in its formative years sheds some light on its nature and goals. RENAMO emerged as an organization of individuals purged from FRELIMO, particularly after February 1977, when the front was transformed into a Marxist-Leninist vanguard party. Some veteran guerrilla fighters who had been disbanded to allow the creation of a conventional army joined the new opposition. **Portuguese** citizens, such as Orlando Cristina, an ex-PIDE (**Política Internacional de Defesa do Estado**) agent, and millionaire Jorge Jardim, former undersecretary of state to **António Salazar** and landowner in the colony, saw their property and role taken away as a result of the new socialist policies. Former African and Portuguese military and political collaborators within the defeated colonial regime and some intellectuals who disagreed with the Marxist-Leninist approach, such as **Domingos Arouca** and Miguel Murupa, decided not to support but to fight the newly installed **Maputo** government.

As FRELIMO attempted to impose its new policies, which were quite often haphazardly and hurriedly implemented, discontent became a natural phenomenon in the urban areas as well as in the countryside, where collective farms and cooperatives became the new lifestyle and mode of production. While some had legitimate grievances, others simply refused to accept change. Both of these elements became the core components of what turned out to be RENAMO by the end of 1977. Whatever the motives, this amalgam of guerrillas with heterogeneous political backgrounds was led by one unifying goal: the overthrow of the FRELIMO Marxist government at all cost, including assistance from the pariah states of Southern Rhodesia and South Africa, an accommodation that turned out to be the most embarrassing stigma as RENAMO sought national and international recognition as a legitimate guerrilla movement.

RENAMO received radio facilities at Gwelo, Rhodesia, in 1976, and began broadcasting in Portuguese as the *Voice of Free Africa* (*Voz da Africa Livre*). South Africa allowed continuation of the broadcast at Phalaborwa in Transvaal after April 1980. Rhodesia also provided the rebels with a military base at Bindura along the Mozambique border. In 1980, South Africa made Zabostad available to the insurgents. By this time, RENAMO had established two major bases inside Mozambique on the foothills of Gorongaza, one of them located on the very 5,500-foot plateau later known as Casa Banana. The base controlled an 800-meter airstrip. Realizing the scarcity of its resources, RENAMO, which by 1979 counted only a few thousand guerrillas and open supporters, chose to operate in small groups of 200 and 300 men in an effort to split and confuse FRELIMO's conventional forces. Their goal was to paralyze the country through destruction of the communication and transportation infrastructure and elimination or physical punishment of FRELIMO leaders, members, and sympathizers, beginning in the rural areas and slowly moving into the urban centers.

One of RENAMO's first major successful attacks was on the fuel depot at Munhava, on the outskirts of **Beira**, on March 23, 1979, causing fire and extensive damage. However, on October 13 through October 22, 1979, the Forças Populares de Libertação de Moçambique (FPlLM) (Mozambican Liberation Popular Forces) stormed the two Gorongoza bases, capturing much ammunition, killing some 100 guerrillas, and taking 22 prisoners. During the assault, RENAMO's first president, **André Matadi Matsangaissa**, was wounded and died while trying to escape in a helicopter. The assault was so successful that FRELIMO declared RENAMO, "the internal reactionaries" and **bandidos armados** (armed bandits), defunct. RENAMO leaders, including **Afonso Dhlakama**, the next president, feared that the remaining 500 men might not be able to withstand the FRELIMO challenge. Against the odds, however, and in spite of internal leadership strife that followed Matsangaissa's death, RENAMO rebuilt its headquarters in the Gorongoza Mountains, and Dhlakama emerged as its new supreme commander and president. Once again, however, FRELIMO struck back at Gorongoza in June 1980 and captured Sitatonga base. To celebrate the victory, **Samora Moisés Machel** himself landed on Casa Banana and said, "We have broken the back of the snake."

Yet, RENAMO had not been fatally wounded. It reemerged even more determined, 17,000 men strong. It rebuilt the bases, and by 1983 it was operating in seven of the 11 provinces of Mozambique, including Inhambane in the south, and threatened Maputo City itself. The Beira-Mutare railway and its 228-kilometer (137-mile) pipeline (the so-called Beira Corridor) were paralyzed, the **Cahora Bassa** dam was neutralized through sabotage of its pylons, and electricity from Pretoria to Maputo was interrupted. At least 26 *cooperantes* had been abducted; 12 of them, including two Soviet geologists, were executed in 1982. Trains were ambushed (one derailment killed 14 people and wounded 50 others on August 9, 1982), and in December 1982 the Beira fuel depot was once again blown up, causing an estimated damage of $35 million.

The reemergence of RENAMO surprised FRELIMO, which seemed unable to stem the tide of destruction. To worsen the situation, several FRELIMO faithful, some of whom were in high positions—such as Jorge Costa, a top security officer, the ambassador to Lisbon, the first secretary at the Mozambique embassy in Harare, and the finance director in the presidency in Maputo—defected in 1982. Some joined RENAMO. To meet the crisis, FRELIMO recalled to duty some of the former guerrillas, created militias throughout the country, and distributed guns to the population. In **Sofala**, by the end of 1982, about 40 percent of the people were armed, while in the capital 30,000 men and women were organized into militias. The FPLM initiated a more aggressive campaign against RENAMO hideouts and resumed the policy adopted in 1979, when the death penalty of executing RENAMO sympathizers and captured guerrillas was introduced. In November 1982, Mozambique enlisted the active involvement and deployment of 3,000 to 6,000 Zimbabwean troops particularly along the Beira Corridor, stationed at **Chimoio**.

RENAMO, however, continued to frustrate all these efforts. At the end of 1982, the government estimated that, since the inception of their activities, the so-called armed bandits had caused damage and military expenditures in the amount of $3.8 billion and had "destroyed 840 schools, 12 health clinics, 24 maternity clinics, 174 health posts, 2 centers for the handicapped, 900 shops, and kidnapped 52 foreign technicians." RENAMO's successes were so disconcerting that in March 1983 FRELIMO's Council of Ministers declared the effort to "wipe out the bandit gangs" as Mozambique's "absolute priority." Adopting a "total strategy" against the enemy, President Samora Machel and Defense Minister Alberto Chipande initiated a diplomatic offensive to solicit financial and military assistance from the West and traveled to Britain, France, West Germany, and **Portugal**, held public executions of "traitors" as a deterrent, and liberalized the government's economic policies.

The relentless RENAMO attacks, particularly in Zambezia, Tete, and Nampula (where former SADCC projects on the Malawi-Nacala railway and roads were being severely jeopardized and constantly halted), coupled with South Africa's retaliation for Mozambique's support of the African National Congress, forced Machel to sign the **Nkomati Accord** with Prime Minister Pieter Botha on March 16, 1984. While South Africa promised to stop assistance to RENAMO, Mozambique pledged to force the ANC to evacuate its military bases from Mozambican territory. South Africa did not, however, abide by its pledge, and RENAMO seemed to grow even stronger following the signing of the accord. By 1985, its activities had spread throughout Mozambique's 11 provinces. As a result of a June 12, 1985, summit of Machel, Mugabe, and Nyerere in Harare, Zimbabwean troops and Tanzanian advisers (about 1,000) began to play an offensive rather than a defensive role in the Mozambican struggle against the insurgents.

Thus, on August 28, 1985, Zimbabwean "crack" troops, assisted by Mozambique assault helicopters, parachuted over Casa Banana, which they captured along with incriminating documentary evidence linking the South African Defense Forces, through Colonel Van Niekerk, with RENAMO. Dhlakama was not captured, however, and RENAMO's activities continued unabated (some more **cooperantes** were kidnapped), although the government subsequently claimed to have destroyed several enemy bases and killed 1,000 "rebels" during the second half of that year. The deteriorating situation in Mozambique led to the Pretoria talks between FRELIMO and RENAMO mediated by South Africa in early October 1985. The Pretoria Declaration announced an aborted cease-fire, with each side blaming the other for the failure of the parallel talks.

To the consternation of the Zimbabwean troops, Casa Banana, left to the FPLM in August 1985, fell to RENAMO forces on February 14, 1986, after RENAMO had also occupied Caia on December 18, 1985, and Marromeu (where they destroyed the sugar refinery) in January 1986. At the end of 1985, the railway from Maputo to South Africa functioned only at 33 percent of its capacity and the Swaziland line at 38 percent, while several railway bridges near the border with South Africa had been blown up by the guerrillas. RENAMO spoke of a "final offensive" against Maputo, which was under constant attack. Thus, in February 1986, FRELIMO resumed execution of RENAMO suspects. Although assistance from the West was trickling down, in March 1986 Machel signed a five-year arms pact with the **Soviet Union**, following his visit to Moscow. On April 12, 1986, government morale was restored temporarily when Zimbabwean troops recaptured Casa Banana. A few weeks earlier, however, in their attempt to recapture Marromeu, the Zimbabwean forces had lost Colonel Flint Magana, who died in a helicopter crash for which RENAMO claimed credit. In addition, RENAMO was said to have started urban "terrorism" that year, when mines were found along Maputo beaches, and bombs exploded in the capital city and Beira. To further counter RENAMO's threat, Machel, Zambian president Kenneth Kaunda, and Zimbabwean president Robert Mugabe held a minisummit in Zambia in mid-October 1986, out of which came a plan or plot, now confirmed, to overthrow the Malawi government for its alleged assistance to RENAMO. Machel's death in an airplane crash as he returned from the minisummit further complicated the Mozambican situation.

Machel had accused Malawi's president Hastings Banda of letting his country be a conduit for South African military and reconnaissance planes (which dropped reinforcements for RENAMO, particularly during the period immediately following the Nkomati Accord) and a sanctuary for rebel forces. Consequently, in December 1987, Mozambique and Malawi signed a joint security pact, the latter pledging to seal its borders to RENAMO military activities. By April 1987, some 300 Malawian troops were stationed along the Nacala-Malawi railway near the Mozambique border. Although, in 1987, the Mozambique government claimed to have slowed down RENAMO's activities considerably, RENAMO's destructive impact refuted the claim. In October 1987, RENAMO ambushed several convoy vehicles traveling from Maputo on the main highway, killing 270 people. Furthermore, its guerrillas even dared to cross the border into Zimbabwe and Zambia, causing several casualties there. RENAMO also claimed that, on December 14, 1987, some 117 FRELIMO soldiers at Caia had defected to its ranks.

In spite of the seeming victories of destruction and death, RENAMO's reputation, already suffering from accusations of terrorist tactics, was severely damaged in mid-July 1987, when the FRELIMO government announced to the world that RENAMO guerrillas had massacred 424 innocent people at Homoíne in Inhambane Province. RENAMO denied the charges and blamed FRELIMO soldiers, and requested that an independent international team be allowed to investigate the incident. The FRELIMO government refused to allow such an investigation. On December 17, 1987, FRELIMO announced a six-month amnesty, which, according to the government, had convinced some 200 guerrillas to turn themselves over by January 1988. Most likely because of the worsening situation, the presence of Eastern bloc and Cuban troops increased in Mozambique by the end of 1987 to 1,000 Soviets, 2,000 Cubans, and 500 East Germans.

Meanwhile, the internecine carnage, worsened by the drought, continued in the country, and RENAMO, whose bases were still well established on the foothills of Gorongoza, claimed to have a force of 22,000 with 30,000 more being trained. RENAMO made most rural areas and towns, including the 50-mile radius around the capital city itself, unsafe. In November 1988, it also claimed to have cut off electricity to Maputo for three days, destroyed military installations in Gurue and bridges in Gaza, burnt a railway locomotive between Mapai and Mabalane, and occupied several towns in **Manica** Province, including Vila de Junta, Vila de Rotunda, and Vila do Dondo. Simultaneously, RENAMO attempted to improve its reputation abroad by upgrading its representation in Portugal, West Germany, the **United States**, Canada, and some African states, and by facilitating direct communication with Gorongoza. Journalists were also allowed to visit Casa Banana.

Within RENAMO, however, there were two major opposing views, a development that posed a threat to the movement. One view insisted on disassociating the organization from South Africa and developing stronger ties with the West, particularly the United States. The other wished to maintain the status quo while pursuing an aggressive international campaign to counter FRELIMO's successes abroad. Observers have attributed to this internal conflict the assassination of Evo Fernandes, the movement's secretary-general, near Lisbon on April 20, 1988; the deaths of two important leaders—Mateus Lopes and João de Sousa—reportedly killed in a single-car accident in Malawi on their return from a meeting with Dhlakama in Gorongoza; and the defection of Paulo Oliveira to FRELIMO in early 1988. RENAMO spokespeople denied South African involvement at that stage: They claimed that the existence of the Nkomati Accord, coupled with MNR's sabotage of Cahora Bassa, disruption of rail transport to South Africa, and interruption of electricity from Pretoria to Maputo proved that RENAMO was acting independently from the apartheid regime and that, in fact, it was fighting both the Mozambican and South African governments. Earlier assistance from Southern Rhodesia and South Africa, however, has never been denied by RENAMO officials. RENAMO representatives claimed that the sources of assistance to the movement were the people of Mozambique and several African countries as well as some Arab states (which they never identified publicly). They further told the world community that their weapons were mainly those they captured from FRELIMO.

FRELIMO, on the other hand, increased its official contact with the South African regime, as illustrated by the September 12, 1988, summit in Songo, **Tete**, between Presidents **Joaquim Chissano** and Pieter Botha. Likewise, it accelerated contact with the West, as demonstrated by Chissano's visit to the United States in 1987 and Mozambique's acceptance of assistance and terms from the **International Monetary Fund** in 1987 and 1988. However, FRELIMO refused to directly negotiate with RENAMO, which it still considered a "gang of armed bandits and terrorists," insisting that only South Africa could speak for them.

In 1989, there were signs that FRELIMO could not win the war against RENAMO, which stepped up its activities every time the Mozambique government refused to accept the concept of a peaceful settlement. Nonetheless, hopeful signs emerged from a FRELIMO Congress. On July 31, 1989, Chissano read a "Statement of Principles" as a basis for negotiations with the "enemy." Yet, RENAMO increased its activities in the central and southern provinces, **Zambézia, Manica,** Sofala, **Gaza,** and Maputo itself, and occupied the strategic town of Luabo on the Zambezi River on August 19, 1989. The apparent successive and successful military campaigns waged by RENAMO must be seen as one of the reasons why FRELIMO decided to resume exploratory negotiations in early December 1989 and its announcement of multiparty national elections scheduled for 1991. However, because of the bickering and accusations of bad faith by the two sides, the war continued in 1990.

It ended only in 1992, and RENAMO was legalized as a political party, unsuccessfully contesting the presidential and legislative elections of 1994 and 1999, although it captured 112 seats in 1994 and, in alliance with some of the opposition, 117 of the 250 seats in 1999. Notwithstanding its tainted reputation stremming from its war tactics, RENAMO has been completely integrated into Mozambique's political life, drawing its strongest support from the central and northern provinces of the country. However, relations with FRELIMO have remained strained as a result of the 1994 and 1999 disputed elections and the personal ambitions of leaders in both parties. Bickering within RENAMO and the attempt to remove Afonso Dhlakama from leadership, thus preventing him from running as president of the country for the third time, may well result in the splitting of the party in the near future.

REVISTA AFRICANA (1881–1887). The *Revista Africana* was the first literary periodical in Mozambique, owned and operated by poet and prose writer José Pedro Campos Oliveira, at Mozambique, the colonial capital at the time. Oliveira was a Portuguese lawyer, born on the Mozambique Island in 1847.

ROADS. For its size, Mozambique has a highly underdeveloped road network. Less than 20 percent of roads are paved. Since independence, 1,734 kilometers (1,040 miles) of paved roads have been added to the existing 3,555 kilometers (2,133 miles). Following destruction and land mining that occurred during the war, road rebuilding has occurred mostly through the use of development assistance. The construction of roads in Mozambique was spurred by the introduction of the automobile at the turn of the century and the activities of the **Companhia de Moçambique** during the first decades of the 20th century. Thus, the colony had 13,516 miles of (unpaved) roads in 1930. Although the Companhia de Moçambique alone had built almost 3,000 miles of road throughout its territory, during the 1960s, road construction stagnated at 15,000 miles, of which only 2,580 miles were paved. Thereafter, the government accelerated its road construction program stimulated by increased economic activity in the colony, reaching 23,503 miles in 1974. In 1982, 330 new miles of roads were built and paved, further linking Mozambique internally and with the surrounding countries. The number of vehicles rose from 3,247 in 1930, to 25,672 in 1956, and to 85,800 in 1983, apparently to be reduced to 33,260 in 1995 and to 12,420 (*Africa: South of the Sahara*, 2002, p. 688) by 2000, most likely as a result of the war and the departure of the Portuguese settlers. The World Bank reports that, in Mozambique, there was one motor vehicle for every thousand people in 1998, which seems to imply, if correct, that only 19,000 vehicles circulated in the whole country, of course, over half of them in **Maputo**.

However, **inflation** and the constant sabotage of the communication and transportation infrastructure by **RENAMO** forced Mozambique to almost halt its road construction program during the 1980s. Many river crossings are still done by wooden bridges or ferryboats. The only vehicle bridge on the **Zambezi River** was completed in 1972 in **Tete**. Following the **Acordo Geral da Paz** and with international assistance, Mozambique has been able to build 46 roads, 2 in **Gaza**, 13 in **Manica**, 15 in Tete, 10 in **Zambézia**, and 6 in **Niassa**. Many old roads are being hastily repaired, as is the case of the Tete-Manica highway. In 2001, the government reported it had a road system that was only 16,179 miles long (from 15,000 miles in 1960), of which 3,235 or 20 percent were paved, up from 17 percent in 1990 and 19 percent in 1997. *See also* TRANSPORTATION.

RONGA. The Ronga or Rhonga people are a subgroup of the **Tonga** and inhabit parts of **Maputo**, Marracuene, Matola, Manhica, and Sabie. Both the Tonga and the Rhonga constantly defied **Portuguese** authority around Lourenço Marques during the 19th century. The Shangana, also a subgroup of the Tonga, who intermarried with the invading **Nguni**, live in Bilene, Magude, parts of Sabie, Chibuto, and Guija. The Tswa (Tsua) likewise related to the Tonga, inhabit the region that extends from the **Limpopo** to the Save Rivers and parts of Mossurize and **Sofala**. They are well known for their practice of late circumcision (ages 10 through 12) and initiation rites as well as for their practice of burying their chief inside the village, in his own house, while interring the common people in the cemetery.

ROSE-COLORED MAP (*MAPA COR DE ROSA*). A map drawn by supporters of the colonial empire and approved by the **Portuguese** government in 1877, linking Angola with Mozambique, shifting the limits of the Portuguese colonies, and attempting to carve a new empire in central Africa, which would encompass what is now Zimbabwe, Zambia, and Malawi. The map was prepared in red and printed in France in the Portuguese language. The British had always opposed such a scheme, however, claiming that the whole Macololo area was under their protection. When **Serpa Pinto** annexed the Macololo by force in 1889, the British dispatched a **British Ultimatum** to Lisbon on January 11, 1890, demanding the unconditional withdrawal of the Portuguese troops from the area. The Portuguese government capitulated, and the rose-colored map was shelved forever.

ROYAL CONCESSIONAIRE COMPANIES. The so-called royal companies were monopolistic corporations, often predominantly foreign owned and controlled, which the **Portuguese** government allowed in

Mozambique during the latter part of the 19th century in hopes of guaranteeing Portuguese sovereignty over the conquered lands, stimulating agricultural and industrial productivity, and facilitating European settlement. For a specified period of time, the companies actually enjoyed almost all rights of sovereignty.

They had exclusive rights over economic exploration and production, could set up postal and customs services; establish banks, schools, and new towns; populate their concession with Africans and Europeans; recruit labor; collect taxes; institute a police force and an army; and administer justice. Three major companies were allowed in Mozambique during the 1890s: the Mozambique Company (**Companhia de Moçambique**), the Nyasa Company (**Companhia do Niassa**), and the Zambézia Company (**Companhia da Zambézia**).

– S –

SALAZAR, DR. ANTÓNIO DE OLIVEIRA (1889–1970). Born from a peasant shopkeeper family in Vimieiro, **Beira** Alta Province in **Portugal**, on April 28, 1889, António de Oliveira Salazar wished to be a Catholic priest and entered the seminary at Viseu in 1900 but abandoned the idea and instead graduated with a Ph.D. in finance and economics from the University of Coimbra in 1918. He taught law at his alma matter, the University of Coimbra, from 1916 to 1928. Bright and highly educated for his time, Salazar was elected to the Cortes in 1921 but decided to return to the classroom as a professor after the very first session of the Assembly of the Republic. In 1928, he accepted the post of minister of finance in the military government, a position he had rejected in 1918, claiming that he was unqualified. He held this post until 1932, when he was appointed prime minister of Portugal (1932–68). He also served temporarily as minister of colonies in 1930, and, while prime minister, Salazar assumed the ministries of foreign affairs and defense from 1936 to 1944. When the liberation war erupted in the colonies in 1961, Salazar once again appointed himself minister of defense. An intelligent and extremely austere man who refused to marry or have children, he saw the rest of Europe as belittling Portugal and turned his attention overseas, thus becoming one of the principal architects of the 1933 **Portuguese constitution**, which created the so-called **Estado Novo** (New State) and the famous **Colonial Act** of 1930.

The legislation contained in the Colonial Act defined the colonies' raison d'être as sources of raw materials for the benefit of the mother country. As such, the colonies ought to have no autonomy within the empire. Salazar enforced the policy of dividing the Africans into indigenous and assimilated, even though he believed that it would take a century to assimilate an African because he was a subhuman. He endorsed forced labor, forced cultivation of such cash crops as cotton in Mozambique, inequitable use of taxes, and military recruitment of able-bodied Africans. He eliminated the foreign concessionaire companies that had received monopoly rights over certain areas of Mozambique during the 19th century.

Feared in Portugal and hated in the colonies, Salazar governed as a dictator, so much so that, when he fell off a chair at his summer residence in 1968, which led to a subsequent stroke, no one dared to tell him that President Admiral Américo Tomás had replaced him as prime minister with his longtime friend and collaborator university professor Marcello Caetano. His initial popularity, which stemmed from his handling of Portugal's finances and the economy, had evaporated by the end of World War II. Ultimately, his dictatorial style and resistance to the independence of the colonies accelerated his downfall, making Portugal a laughing stock not only in Europe but also around the world.

Salazar's ideology of authoritarianism, fascism, and anticommunism, conservative fiscal management, colonial repression, and intense nationalism was shaped by his peasant origins, his dogmatic Catholic upbringing, his admiration for Francisco Franco, whom he supported during the Spanish civil war, and Adolph Hitler, the academic environment he was associated with, and his fear that Portugal could lose its colonial possessions.

SALIM, JANFAR. Salim succeeded Twakaly Hija as sheikh of Quitangonha (1804–1817). He allied himself in 1810 with the Portuguese against Morimuno, a **Macua** leader who was accused of dealing in slaves and of threatening Mossuril. Salim, however, was playing a double game, and the **Portuguese** authorities finally arrested him in 1817 and deported him to **Inhambane**, where he died in jail.

SANTOS, MARCELINO DOS (also known as KALUNGANO, MICAIA, LILINHO) (1929–). Marcelino dos Santos, a mulatto of mixed Cape Verdian descent, is a former labor union leader, a statesman, and a poet. He studied in Maputo, Lisbon, and in Paris, at the Institut des

Sciences Politiques and L'Ecole Pratique des Hautes Etudes, Sorbonne, and was one of the first **FRELIMO Central Committee** members. From 1964 to 1988, he served as secretary for external affairs, secretary for political affairs, second party secretary, FRELIMO vice president, planning minister (1975–80), and provincial governor of **Sofala** (1983–85), with the rank of major-general. In his early years, he also lived in Algeria and Moscow and is still a Marxist hard-liner, the party ideologue, and confidant of both the late president **Samora Machel** and, distantly, of **Joaquim Chissano**. In 1986, however, dos Santos was ousted from direct governmental responsibilities. In fact, lately, he has not been a member of the Central Committee, although he has served in the Politburo. Overall, he has had virtually no power since Joaquim Chissano was elected president. Analysts interpret the ouster as a move to deemphasize the role of the hard-line ideologues, particularly in economic affairs. For a few years, he was married to a white South African.

SENA. The Sena live in Chemba, Murraça, Cheringoma, Sena, Mutarara, and the city of Beira. The Dwanwo, Chawu, Chilendje, Makate, Mambu, Mbadzo, Muwera, Nyagombe, Simboti, and Tembo are also part of this vast cluster of small ethnic groups.

SHONA (CHONA). A Mozambique ethnic group estimated to number about a million people in 1997. The Shona claim allegiance to and origin from the kingdom of **Mwenemutapa**, and some anthropologists have classified them as Karanga. Their unity was disrupted by **Nguni** invaders during the 19th century. Predominantly hunters and fishermen, the Shona are concentrated in **Manica** and **Sofala** provinces and north of the Save River. The Abarue, Banda, Chilenje, Chirumba, Chirware, Choa, Makate, Marunga, Mucato, Mwanya, Nyampisi, Nyatanza, Manhica, Mavonde, **Ndau** (who occupy **Chimoio** and parts of Manica, Mavonde, Mavita, Dondo, and vila Machado), Tembo, and **Tewe** are classified as Shona clans or subgroups. The Shona are one of the few ethnic groups that allow women to be chiefs. Some **Portuguese** anthropologists prefer to call the Shona Caranga, because they are associated with the culture of Zimbabwe and the empire of Mwenemutapa. During the 19th century, the Nguni invaders disrupted the unity of the Shona and contributed to their dispersion. Unlike the Nguni, the Shona do not practice initiation, nor do they have circumcision for boys.

SILOTA, (BISHOP) FRANCISCO JOÃO (1941–). Born in Lifidzi, Angonia, **Tete** Province, Silota completed his first priestly studies at the Zobue Minor Seminary in 1964 and then pursued his advanced philosophical and theological studies at Pio X Major Seminary in **Maputo** in 1970, at Kachebere (Malawi) Seminary in 1968, and then in England to complete his novitiate and scholastic studies. He was ordained priest of the Society of Missionaries of Africa (or White Fathers) at Lifidzi Mission in 1974, having served at the diocese of **Beira** from 1975 to 1981. In 1976, he was posted to the Barue Parish at Catandica and Inhazónia and became the director of the Diocesan Pastoral Coordination in 1978. In 1981, the Society of Missionaries of Africa sent him to Rome for further studies and, in 1984, he was posted to the diocese of Tabora in Tanzania. In March 1988, the most Reverend Silota was consecrated auxiliary bishop of Beira, with residence at Chimoio. On November 19, 1990, he would become the permanent bishop of the new Diocese of **Chimoio** with a population of close to a million and over 70,000 Catholics, scattered throughout 13 parishes.

SILVA, ANTÓNIO ALVES DA. António Alves da Silva, of Afro-**Portuguese** descent, started the Silva *prazero* family, which ruled in Maganja da Costa beginning in the early 19th century. His son, João Bonifácio Alves da Silva, succeeded him and extended his father's estate in the region until the family's "hegemony" was neutralized by Sheikh Mussa Quanto of Angoche in 1855. The Silva family remained allied to the Portuguese authorities, and its holdings acted as a buffer zone between the Swahili and the Lomwe.

SIMANGO, KAMBA (1890–1966). Born at Mashanga, on the Save River, Simango attended school at the American Board Mission Station at Mount Silinda in Southern Rhodesia and, through his connections, was able to attend Hampton Institute in the **United States**, where he received a diploma in teaching in 1919. He pursued further studies at Teachers College at Columbia University while working at odd jobs to finance his studies. Both at Hampton and Columbia, Simango assisted scholars interested in African anthropology and literature and taught **Ndau**. Scholars he met and worked with on the Ndau language of Mozambique include Franz Boas, Melville Herskovits, and Henry Junod. At Hampton, Simango sang and participated in the activities of the choir and was elected president of his senior class and the YMCA. In 1922, he married Kathleen Easmond of

Sierra Leone and, following her death, married Coussey of Ghana in 1925. Two years earlier, the Congregational Churches of Connecticut had ordained him minister.

Simango returned to Beira in 1926 after spending some time in Lisbon and Angola. He pastored briefly at the American Board station at Gogoi, near Chupangara, before being transferred to Mount Silinda Mission in Southern Rhodesia. While at Silinda, Simango was falsely accused but exonerated of having raped a colleague, a white missionary woman. Instead of reinstating him, the church turned against him and forced him to return to Mozambique and the station at Machemeje, on the Buzi River, near Beira, where he resumed his missionary activity. The Portuguese, however, refused to recognize his mission. Disgusted and afflicted by the health problems of his wife and his own, Simango left Mozambique for Accra, Ghana, where he and his wife settled. He died in Accra in 1966.

SIMANGO, URIAS TIMÓTEO. Former Protestant pastor in **Beira**, near Chupangara, organizer of a mutual aid association, and, along with Adelino Gwambe, one of the founders and first president of **União Democrática Nacional de Moçambique** (UDENAMO*)*. Simango was also one of the founders of **FRELIMO**, of which he became the vice president in 1962. Reelected vice president at the Second Congress of FRELIMO in 1968, Simango expected to accede to the presidency of the movement after the assassination of **Eduardo Chivambo Mondlane** on February 3, 1969. However, at a meeting of the **Central Committee** in April 1969, **Marcelino dos Santos** and **Samora Machel** blocked Simango's ascendancy and made him part of a triumvirate the two had conjured. Subsequently, Simango resigned his position and published a document critical of FRELIMO, titled "A Gloomy Situation in FRELIMO." He criticized the predominance of white supervisors in the Mozambique Institute, without proof accused Janet Mondlane of being a CIA agent, ridiculed FRELIMO's "scientific socialism," and charged that the movement was controlled by Mozambican southerners. His life threatened, Simango escaped to Egypt and later joined the **Comité Revolucionário de Moçambique (COREMO)**. He returned to Mozambique after independence but was arrested after he participated in an attempted coup to overthrow the transitional government. His whereabouts are still unknown.

SINDICATOS (SYNDICATES). Government organized and partially financed skill labor organizations for nongovernment employees during the colonial period. Meetings between employees and employers required the presence of a government representative, and the Mozambique Ministry of Labor and Social Welfare was called to arbitrate and make actual decisions. As a result, syndicates were created not to bargain for and defend the rights and interests of workers (especially in trade) but to provide employment, medical care, and legal assistance. Strikes were disallowed. Some 15 such syndicates existed in Mozambique, most of them in Lourenço Marques, during the 1960s and 1970s, and had about 3,000 members in 1967. Because membership required payment of a high monthly fee and completion of the third grade of elementary school, very few Africans were ever members, except for the Civil Construction Syndicates. The typical structure of a syndicate included a general assembly, a general council, and a directorate, with a president, a secretary, and three voting members.

SINGULANE, DENIS. Anglican bishop of the Diocese of Libombos, **Maputo**, Mozambique. *See also* CONSELHO CRISTÃO DE MOCAMBIQUE (CCM).

SIXTH CONGRES (FRELIMO). FRELIMO's VI Congress took place August 9–12, 1991. The congress established the basis for the fundamental political and economic changes that followed in Mozambique, both as a response to RENAMO's continued successes on the battlefield and international pressure. At the congress, several ideological changes were endorsed, including the following:

1. The FRELIMO party would no longer be viewed as the only "directing force of society" in Mozambique;
2. FRELIMO would be open to all Mozambican citizens even though it would continue to "pay special attention" to peasants and workers, who would no longer be viewed as a "revolutionary" class in Mozambique;
3. FRELIMO would respect Mozambique's regional diversity and view traditional values as an enriching patrimony of the nation; and
4. Traditional authorities (given renewed prominence by **RENAMO)** would be maintained and respected.

However, FRELIMO's basic structure would remain almost intact, namely, as the supreme organ of the party meeting every five years, electing the **Central Committee,** and leading the party between the Congress five-year intervals; the Central Committee as the elector of the party president, the secretary-general, and the Political Bureau; finally, in contrast to the past, all party organs would be elected by a secret ballot. These changes, along with the ones enacted in April–June 1991, further prepared FRELIMO for the negotiations that had already been initiated with RENAMO in 1998. *See also* CONSTITUTIONAL REFORMS. FRELIMO's new measures conformed to Mozambique's II **Constitution**, which was enacted on November 30, 1990.

SLAVERY (SLAVE TRADE). Although during the 16th century Mozambique was not a significant source of slaves to the New World, Africans in Mozambique had always been used as slaves by the northern sultans and sheikhs. Furthermore, from the 17th century on, a considerable number of slaves worked in the lands of the *prazeros*, employed as *achikunda* (soldiers) by the new lords, and performed emissary and trading functions for them. Studies have indicated that some prazeros owned as many as 25,000 slaves. The *mocambazes* (slave merchants) used the same methods as those employed by the trans-Atlantic slave traffickers, namely, kidnapping, buying, clandestine agreements with chiefs in the hinterland, and actual warfare.

Interestingly, as Pedro Gamito has noted, the structure of the prazo slave community was hierarchical. The achikunda in the prazos were normally divided into groups of 10 (the *issacas*) under a *sa'chicunda*, who was assisted by a *muscata*, all under the *mwanamambo*, or captain, who took his orders from a *bazo* (overlord). Women were also enslaved in the prazos and quite often had the same hierarchical structure as the male slaves. The *prazero* classified his slaves into the *ladino* (smart) slaves, or those who had been trained and had acquired the experience to perform their tasks well, and the *burro* (stupid; literally, donkey) slaves, the novices or those who showed no progress in the performance of assigned tasks.

During the 18th century, Mozambique began furnishing slaves for the São Tomé islands, **Brazil**, and the islands of Madagascar, Mauritius, Reunion, and Comoros. Between 1794 and 1821, according to some estimates, the number of Mozambique slaves exported from **Quelimane** and Mozambique Island alone rose from 3,807 to 15,282. For the whole colony, however, the annual number of slaves increased from 15,000 to 25,000 between 1800 and 1850, notwithstanding the fact that a Portuguese decree of 1836 had officially abolished slavery in the colonies. Governors refused to implement the decree, alleging that the settlers would not stand for it and that it would be detrimental to the economic well-being of the colony. Governor-General D. Carlos de Oyembause, the Marquis of Aracaty, simply suspended the decree on November 11, 1837.

International criticism, Lisbon's insistence, and British abolitionist efforts, however, contributed to the eventual elimination of the slave trade in the colony. In 1847, the Portuguese entered into a three-year protocol with the British, whereby the latter would be allowed to enter Mozambique ports, bays, rivers, and other areas to capture and punish slave traders, including the sultans and sheikhs, and destroy their sources of supply. As a result, a raid took place on December 21, 1847, against the sultan of Angoche.

Unfortunately, French disregard for the Portuguese decrees proved to be a major obstacle to the elimination of the slave trade in the colony. The French constantly roamed along the coast, capturing Africans or buying them from the sultans while alleging that they were taking only those Africans who volunteered to work in the sugarcane plantations on the islands of the Indian Ocean. Despite Sá da Bandeira's protest to the French embassy in Lisbon in 1855 and 1856, the French argued shamelessly that they were not enslaving the Africans but civilizing them. Between May 28, 1856, and October 17, 1857, French vessels forcibly took some 1,045 Mozambicans to the islands. The French claimed that they paid these workers between 1$120 and 1$600 a day, depending on their ages.

One of the major reasons why local Mozambican authorities were reluctant to enforce the ban on the slave trade or the capture of "workers" to the islands was that they, and the government, shared the loot. Normally, the civil authorities received between four and seven *pesos*, half of which went to the governor-general, two-thirds to the district governor, and the remainder to the customs officers, the military commanders of the garrisons, and other officials. French persistence in the slave trade resulted in an embarrassing incident in November 1857, when encouraged by the British, the Portuguese authorities seized the French vessel *Charles et Georges* at Condúcia Bay, loaded with 110 Africans bound for the islands. Its captain, Mathurin Etiènne Rouxel, was arrested and fined 500$00. Napoleon III dispatched an ultimatum demanding the release of the ship and its captain and indemnification by the Portuguese government. The Portuguese, feeling abandoned by the British, capitulated and paid the reparations—an incident that led to a temporary rupture of diplomatic relations between **Portugal** and France.

Despite the continuous efforts that led to the arrest of slave dealers during the 1860s, particularly in Angoche District, the end of the slave trade was still not in sight. The British continued to accuse the governors-general, including Governor Tavares de Almeida, of collusion with the slave traffickers. The accusations were so serious and Lisbon so dissatisfied with the governor that he was forced to resign on October 14, 1862. Only in 1877 was a serious effort made by Governor-General Guedes de Carvalho e Menezes to promulgate and enforce the 1836 decree abolishing slavery and the slave trade in the colony. However, it was not until the 1890s that, for all practical purposes, it could be said that slavery and the slave trade had been eliminated.

The Africans, of course, also contributed to the demise of the "peculiar institution" in the land. One of the reasons why the prazos did not succeed was that they experienced continuous slave revolts. When the 1888 Prazo Inquiry Commission completed its report, it noted that violence in the prazos had been the major cause of their failures. This included the resistance that the Africans maintained throughout the prazos' existence. Moreover, slave mutinies were reported at several ports. A classic mutiny occurred in January 1833 at Ibo port, when two French vessels had docked with the intent to pick up a slave cargo. The would-be victims refused to go on board and rioted. The Portuguese authorities responded violently and killed between 20 and 30 rioters, while others took refuge in the hinterland. The two French vessels sailed off empty.

Thus, although it is not possible to determine how many Mozambicans were taken as slaves to Brazil, São Tomé e Príncipe, and the islands on the Indian Ocean, it would seem accurate to say that between 1700 and 1880, an average of 8,000 to 10,000 slaves were exported yearly. Although the Lisbon authorities wanted to see the end of slavery in the colonies during the 1830s, local authorities, who were also making a profit out of this shameful trade, stubbornly refused to comply. While some authorities argued that the government did not have the means to enforce the decrees, particularly on the high seas, others claimed that, if slavery were to be abolished, no manpower would be available for the colony since, allegedly, Africans, unless forced, refused to work for anyone.

SOARES, DR. MÁRIO (1924–). Highly educated **Portuguese** intellectual and statesman, with degrees in history, philosophy, and law. A socialist in philosophy and a political activist who opposed **António Salazar's** dictatorship, Soares was arrested 12 times during the 1960s and early 1970s. During 1970–74, he lived as an exile in Paris, while teaching at the Sorbonne. He returned to **Portugal** in the aftermath of the April 1974 coup, which overthrew **Marcello Caetano's** government. Soares regrouped the Socialist Party he had cofounded in 1973 and participated in the electoral campaigns for office in the new republic. Appointed foreign minister by the **Movimento das Forças Armadas**, Soares negotiated the independence of Guinea-Bissau and signed the **Lusaka Agreement** with **FRELIMO** in September 1974, setting up a transitional government, which led to independence on June 25, 1975. As leader of the Portuguese Socialist Party, Soares eventually was elected and served as premier in 1976, 1978, and 1983–85. He assumed the presidency of the Portuguese republic in February 1986 and was reelected in 1991.

SOFALA. Mozambique east-central province dismembered from the eastern part of the **Manica** e Sofala district in 1975. Pero de Covilhã was the first **Portuguese** known to set foot in Sofala, followed by Gonçalo Vaz de Goes, who claimed to have "discovered" it on an expedition to Mombasa in 1505. Pero d'Anaia started the erection of the fort of São Caetano at Sofala, a settlement that was elevated to a *vila* (town) in 1764. Until the 19th century, Sofala was the seat of a governor or military commander. (Sofala town is also known as Nova Sofala or Chiloane.) Sofala and its city of **Beira**, the provincial capital established by the **Companhia de Moçambique** in 1891, famous for gold and ivory **trade**, provided a stimulus to the development of the whole district (now province).

Sofala has an area of 30,337 square miles and a population of 1,380,000 (1997 estimate). It borders the Indian Ocean in the east and **Tete** Province in the north. Through the port city of Beira, Sofala is linked by **railroad** and **road** to Tete Province and by paved road to Zimbabwe and **Maputo** city. Several rivers, such as the Buzi, Gorongoza, Pungue, Save, and **Zambezi**, flow through it and provide irrigation and hydroelectric power facilities. Its famous game park, Gorongoza (2,300 square miles), is potentially one of the best in Africa. Almost all Mozambique agricultural crops, such as corn, coconut, cashew nuts, cotton, and sugarcane as well as mangoes, are harvested in the province, while its soil is known to contain several minerals such as gold (famous since the 16th century and systematically mined during the 19th century). Unfortunately, Sofala Province suffered devastation through the activities of **RENAMO** and **FRELIMO** retaliatory measures against suspects' hideouts during the civil war.

SOUSA, NOÉMIA CAROLINA ABRANCHES DE (also known as VERA MICAIA). Born on September 20, 1927, she married a Portuguese while she was living in Lisbon. Noémia is considered to be the first Mozambican woman writer. Between 1951 and 1964, she worked for several journals and reviews in Mozambique, advancing the theme of African culture. Several of her articles and poems appeared in journals in the Portuguese language in Mozambique as well as in **Brazil** and Angola. Political persecution by the **Portuguese** secret police compelled her to seek refuge in France, where she has continued her literary work.

SOUTH AFRICA. As neighbors, South Africa and Mozambique have had essentially three types of relations: one friendly, during Portuguese control of Mozambique (1652–1975); another, hostile, after **FRELIMO** assumed power in Mozambique (1975–90); and the third, friendly, following the end of apartheid in South Africa in 1990. South Africa maintained a friendly relationship since 1652 when white settlers at the cape realized that a few hundred miles up north, the Portuguese had in 1498 claimed a large territory they called Mozambique. Following the 1899–1902 Boer War, which left the Union of South Africa isolated and devastated, Mozambique and its neighbor developed even closer relations and signed the **Mozambique Convention** in 1909 (later in 1926 and 1928), which allowed the **Witwatersrand Native Labor Association** (WNLA or WENELA) and two other South African companies to recruit up to 100,000 workers a year for the gold and diamond mines. However, their relation was not without major differences and tensions.

While South Africa espoused openly the policy of discrimination and segregation based on color, **Portugal** promoted a policy of assimilation and racial equality within its empire. However, because Portugal did not follow to the letter its nonracial policies and provided **Portuguese** citizenship rights only to a handful of Mozambican blacks, their racial policies overlapped in many respects. Indeed, both treated the Africans as subhumans and introduced forced labor, taxation without representation, identification passes, and labor recruitment practices that were internationally unacceptable. As the two allies faced mounting pressure from the liberation movements during the 1960s and 1970s and were ostracized at the **United Nations**, their governments clung temporarily to the popular claim that they, along with white Southern Rhodesia, were the last bastions of Western civilization in Africa and the *cordon sanitaire* against communist expansion in the African subcontinent.

Facing international criticism from many sources, the two governments maintained good diplomatic and economic relations, the latter reflected in the use of **Delagoa Bay** Harbor, the Lourenço Marques-Pretoria Railway, **tourism**, labor recruitment to the mines of the Transvaal, electric power through the **Cahora Bassa** Dam, and imports and exports, making South Africa Mozambique's second trading partner after Portugal. Mozambique's achievement of independence in 1975 presaged a new era of diplomatic tension and border conflict between the two. FRELIMO vowed to help end apartheid as well as the white regime in Rhodesia, which had issued its unilateral declaration of independence (UDI) in 1965, by openly supporting liberation movements in both neighboring countries. In retaliation, Southern Rhodesia in 1977 and South Africa since 1980 provided assistance to **RENAMO** by carrying out air and land strikes against suspected guerrilla bases in Mozambique. This forced **Samora Machel**, Mozambique's president, to sign a humiliating nonaggression pact with South Africa on March 16, 1984, pledging not to allow military bases to the African National Congress (ANC) in Mozambique. South Africa promised to stop supporting RENAMO in Mozambique. But South Africa simply ignored what it had promised to do.

However, the situation in South Africa itself was unraveling. The cost of warfare against its neighbors, especially in Angola, criticism from the West, economic problems, and even war fatigue within the white population eroded its will to defy black South Africans' quest for majority rule and normalization of relations with its African neighbors. The voice of reason began to change the views of many South African whites, including some in the Nationalist Party, such as Frederick de Klerk, who might be seen as center-conservative whites. De Klerk released Nelson Mandela from prison in 1990 and sought a modus vivendi with the ANC, which eventually resulted in the end of apartheid and the democratic election of Mandela as president of the new South Africa in 1994. This new South Africa, run by Africans, naturally sought improved relations with the new Mozambique. This period marked a new phase of equal political and economic partnership between Mozambique and South Africa, the strengthening of the **Southern African Development Community** (SADC), and it ushered in South Africa's accelerated investment in Mozambique industry, agriculture, tourism, harbor, **railroads**, and **roads**. Yet, as is the case with **Brazil** and **Portugal**, today Mozambicans ask themselves whether the relationship between the two old neighbors is that of equal partnership or still one of disguised dependency. *See also* SOUTHERN AFRICAN DEVELOPMENT COMMUNITY (SADC).

SOUTHERN AFRICAN DEVELOPMENT COMMUNITY (SADC). SADC grew out of the former Southern African Development Coordination Conference (SADCC), which had been designed to minimize apartheid **South Africa**'s hegemony on the subcontinent. Created after two meetings, one in Arusha, Tanzania, in July 1979, and another in

Lusaka, Zambia, in April 1980, by representatives from Angola, Lesotho, Malawi, Mozambique, Swaziland, Botswana, Tanzania, Zambia, and Zimbabwe (Namibia and Mauritius joined the organization during the early 1990s), SADCC's aim was to coordinate development planning and share costs of regionally beneficial projects. SADCC's areas of cooperation included agriculture, training, communications and transportation, energy, and port facilities. The introduction of majority rule in South Africa and encouragement by the members of the Preferential Trade Area emboldened the members of SADC, who in August 1992, expanded considerably SADC's mission. The newly created regional organization aims at creating a strong common market in southern Africa, promoting common values and political institutions, and protecting the environment. SADC member states have also endorsed a common defense and security pact designed to end civil and cross-border conflicts in the region. Notwithstanding this expanded noble mission, critics point to SADC's ineffective role in safeguarding human rights from the abuses of government security forces, silence in the face of rigged elections in the region, reliance on foreign aid, and inability to develop without incurring a huge external debt. Yet, SADC has attracted members that are not quite located in southern Africa, such as Seychelles and the Democratic Republic of Congo. Unfortunately, political ambitions have rocked the relations between the two most important members of SADC, namely, South Africa and Zimbabwe. President Robert Mugabe of Zimbabwe does not believe that South Africa has abandoned its hegemonic aspirations in the region and has resisted closer cooperation with the South African leadership.

Similar to its predecessor and functioning in almost the same way as the organization of African Unity, SADC heads of state and government meet once a year, while its foreign ministers meet twice a year, has a secretariat, ten sectorial coordination committees headquartered in the member states, the largest sector being transport which receives almost 50 percent of transportation funding and 50 percent of the projects. SADC holds also an annual meeting with aid donors (governments and international agencies).

SOVIET UNION (USSR, RUSSIA). As a result of the Cold War and its own history, the former Soviet Union supported virtually every liberation movement in Africa, including those movements that sprang up in the **Portuguese** colonies during the 1950s and 1960s. Yet, most of the assistance focused on military hardware and training and not on projects of great social impact. Despite the shortcomings of the relationship, Mozambique developed close ties with the Eastern European bloc, which was led by the Soviet Union, during the mid-1960s and characterized the West, especially the **United States**, as following "imperialist" policies that opposed the liberation of peoples under colonialism.

This is the reason why, following independence, the ties seemed to grow tighter between the two, evidenced in the several mutual visits and projects of assistance, including the provision of scholarships for Mozambican students to get their education in the USSR and other communist countries. In 1977, Soviet president Nikolai Podgorny visited **Maputo**, and **Samora Machel** reciprocated the visit. The two concluded several treaties, including one on Friendship, Cooperation, and Mutual Aid in 1977; one on Technical and Professional Education in February of the same year; and a five-year arms pact following Machel's visit to Moscow in 1986.

These treaties notwithstanding, the Soviet Union never became one of Mozambique's major trading partners. In fact, during the 1980s, the Soviet Union accounted for only 8 percent of Mozambique's **trade**, compared to 15 percent with **Portugal** and 23 percent with the United States. Mozambique's request for accelerated military assistance to counter South African and Rhodesian retaliations against its stance on racism and the country's support of the African National Congress, **ZANU** and **ZAPU**, and RENAMO's destructive impact, was turned down, as the Soviet Union refused adamantly to get involved in southern African affairs. With time, Mozambique statesmen and scholars also realized that the USSR and its allies would not show the same generosity after independence as they did during the liberation phase. It also became clear that most of the helicopters, vehicles, SAM missiles, and tanks provided Mozambique after independence were obsolete and no longer needed in the Soviet arsenal. Dissatisfaction with the relationship may have been one of the reasons why Mozambique never allowed the Soviets to have a naval or air base on its soil.

From hindsight, it is apparent that the degree of Soviet involvement in Mozambique was magnified by U.S. fears. It is clear now that the Soviets had already decided that southern Africa was not strategically important for their position in the world. Their debacles in Ethiopia and Somalia, where they changed sides shamelessly, were certainly a wake-up call for the communist giant. Furthermore, the period following the dismantling of the Soviet Union itself in 1991 revealed the bloc's inherent and chronic weaknesses. At present, Russia and the other former East European bloc states maintain friendly but limited relations with Mozambique. In fact, the United States exerts more influence in Mozambique today than Russia or any of its former allies.

SPÍNOLA, GENERAL ANTÓNIO SEBASTIÃO RIBEIRO DE
(1910–1998). Military officer, commander of **Portuguese** troops in Angola in 1961, and two-term military governor-general of Guinea-Bissau (1967–73), where he vowed to end once and for all the activities of the PAIGC. In 1973, he was appointed deputy chief of staff of the Portuguese Armed Forces. Out of his firsthand experiences in Angola and Guinea-Bissau, Spinola concluded that the colonial war was unwinnable and that the African colonies should be given autonomy within the **Portuguese** empire. He expressed his ideas in a book, *Portugal and the Future*, published in February 1974. As a result, he was denounced by the government and dismissed in March 1974, but his book had already caused much debate in Portuguese circles. When the **Movimento das Forças Armadas** (MFA) overthrew **Marcello Caetanos's** government on April 25, 1974, Spínola was made president of the new republic. The MFA subsequently removed him from office and allowed him to retire peacefully.

STRUCTURAL ADJUSTMENT. Two major devaluations of the *metical* took place in 1987, from MT40 to the U.S. dollar to MT200 in January and then to MT200 to the U.S. dollar in June. In 1988, further devaluations occurred to make MT620 to the U.S. dollar in October. With the devaluation of the currency costs went up, and the prices of medicine, food, and fuel increased almost fivefold. Health and education spending were cut, and the government was forced to cut food subsidies by almost four-fifths due to government spending ceilings imposed by the **International Monetary Fund** and World Bank. The income gap widened and rural incomes fell by one-third due to destabilization. By 1989, up to 70 percent of the population was living in poverty. In 2003, the U.S. dollar was worth 23,600 meticais, signifying that more people live below the poverty line today than was the case ten years ago.

SWAHILI. People of the northeastern coast of Niassa Province from Momua to Rovuma Rivers. Greatly influenced by the Arabs, the Swahili are famous traders and many of them have embraced **Islam**. The Swahili of **Niassa** Province live along the northeastern coast from the mouth of the Ligonha to the Rovuma Rivers. They are famous for their trading skills and not for their resistance to Portuguese penetration.

SWAZI. The Swazi people are considered to be a subgroup of the **Nguni** and live in Namaacha, some 25 miles from **Maputo**. They migrated from their original home, Swaziland, during the 20th century.

– T –

TAWARA. The Tawara inhabit Chicoa, Cachomba, Mague, and Changara in **Tete** Province. Known as good weavers, they consider their chiefs to be descendants of the great Mwenemutapa. The **Tonga** (not connected with the **Ronga** or the **Tonga** of southern Mozambique) live in Mungari and Mandie, near Vila Catandica and Tete city.

TEMPO. **FRELIMO's** official magazine printed in **Maputo.** As such, it reflects the government's views, although articles are often written by individuals not associated with the editing and the printing of the magazine.

TERRAS FIRMES. Until the 19th century, this was the designation of Mozambique District consisting of Mossuril Peninsula, Cabeceira Grande, and Cabeceira Pequena, about 500 square kilometers (195.3 square miles) large, with a population of about 15,000 in the mid–19th century.

TETE. The second northwestern province of Mozambique created in 1975, with an area of 38,890 square miles and a population of 1,149,000 (1997 estimate). It is composed of many of the 17th- and 18th-century *prazos* and it borders Zambia in the northwest, Malawi in the northeast and east, Zimbabwe in the south, and **Sofala** Province in the southeast. The province is known to abound in mineral resources such as coal, which has been recognized since the 18th century. Prior to the **civil war**, a Belgian company extracted coal in relatively large quantities at Moatize, although **RENAMO** had succeeded in paralyzing the mines, now being reopened. Bauxite, manganese, titanium, and gold (which attracted the Portuguese as far back as the 16th century) are also known to exist in the province. Corn, manioc, wheat, sorghum, and millet are some of its most important agricultural products.

Tete city is the provincial capital and port, located on the bank of the **Zambezi** River. Tete became a town in 1761 and a city in 1959. It is linked to **Beira** by rail and paved **road**, and to Malawi and Zambia by road. Rivers such as the Zambezi, Luia, and Luenha provide water to this extremely dry and rocky city. The area surrounding the city abounds in baobab trees (*embondeiros*) whose fruit, when ripe and dry, is edible, as well as a tree called *masau* (apple) whose little round fruit, shaped like olives, can be eaten when ripe and dry. The local population grinds the dried fruit and its seed and brew beer out of it. Eighty miles from the city of Tete stands the **Cahora (Cabora) Bassa** dam, the largest in Africa, meant to provide electricity to limited areas of Mozambique and to irrigate some of the arid areas of the province. During the 19th century, Tete was a very important commercial center, as government reports note, and traded in gold, silver, ivory, agricultural products, and slaves. Cattle raising has been successful in the province and around the dry city.

TEWE. The Tewe and the Manhica are also a subgroup of the Shona and live in **Manica** and **Sofala** Provinces. Both subgroups seem to be descendants of the Rodzi people who, led by Chief Changamire, defeated the original settlers, the Wazamoi. Manhica and Atewe main clans include the matrilineal Banda, Chilenje, Chirumba, Chiwawa, Makat, Marunga, Mwanya, Nyampisi, Nyantaza, and Tembo. Interestingly enough, among these clans, a woman could be elected chief, but she would be killed or deposed as soon as she had her first child, who, if male, would succeed her to the throne.

TONGA (THONGA). In the very distant past, the term *Tonga* meant rebel or people who sought self-government outside the more powerful established political systems of the Zimbabwe Plateau. The Caranga used the term to describe those who sought to remain outside their domination, both north and south, along the Zambezi and south of the Save Rivers, toward the **Inhambane** and **Limpopo** marshlands. Occupying only the periphery of the Zimbabwe-**Mwenemutapa** plateau states, the Tonga migrated to avoid the plateau civil strife and the dynastic rivalries or simply moved away to assert their own autonomy. Their movement accounts for the origins of such secondary states as Quiteve, **Manica**, and Sedanda, located in the east and the southeast, which were joined later by the **Barue** of north of Manica. Throughout their recorded history on the periphery of the Mwenemutapa Kingdom, the Tonga remained northwest of **Tete**, near the confluence of the **Zambezi** and the Kafue Rivers, southeast of modern Zambia.

During their early migrations from the plateau, probably in the 14th century, these **Shona** refugees formed the so-called Banamainga kingdom, which, in turn, absorbed subsequent **refugee** waves caused either by the plateau civil wars or the Portuguese onslaught of the Mwenemutapa kingdom beginning in the 17th century. The refugee influx continued well into the **Nguni** invasions of the 19th century and the Chimurenga resistance wars against Cecil Rhodes's colonial occupation during the 1890s. Other Tonga communities found along the right bank of the Zambezi River, from Tete toward the Indian Ocean, such as the Sena and the Tawara, those living south of Sedanda, and the Tonga (Bitonga) around

Inhambane, are historically known to have been stateless societies. Unfortunately, the Tonga who lived along the Zambezi Valley fell prey to the Portuguese *prazo* system from the 17th century onward. With the passing of time, the Inhambane Tonga became receptive to foreign influence and traded with the Arabs at Chibuene and Manikeni (Manikweni), two important trading stations, complete with "zimbabwes" (local stone buildings), down the coast on the Save and **Limpopo** estuaries.

However, the Tonga of the southern marshes became important middlemen in the commercial exchanges between the Zimbabwe Plateau gold merchants and the Arab traders. We know now that it was at Rio do Cobre (on the coast of Inhambane) that the Portuguese first touched the Mozambican shore on their way to India. During the 16th century, the first Jesuit missionary to the court of Mwenemutapa, Gonçalo da Silveira, and his three companions, would try to reach their destination through the land of the Bitonga (Inhambane). It was at Inhambane that the Jesuits won their first Mozambican converts.

Finally, it is interesting to note that in Tonga historiography, this ethnic group's name has seen several spellings, such as *Thonga, Bonga, Bitonga,* and *Butenga.* However, the Tonga who resided on the periphery of the plateau and fled as refugees of the Mwenemuta kingdom should not be confused with their closest neighbors, the Thonga, who are found more toward the interior or at Inhambane, or the Tsonga who lived farther south. These two ethnic groups, Thonga and Tsonga, are more culturally related to the Venda and the Sotho of **South Africa**. No one is sure of the origin of their ethnic designations.

The Tonga are the second largest ethnic group in Mozambique (2,775,000). They are an offshoot of the Zulu and have occupied the extreme south, namely, **Gaza** Province, since the 19th century. They migrated from farther south and defeated the original settlers—**Chope** and the Bitonga—during the early part of the 19th century. Once settled in Mozambique, the patrilineal Tonga lived isolated from the neighboring ethnic groups with whom they constantly battled for territory and cattle. Prior to the colonial period, they had a chief or king who wielded absolute political, religious, military, and judicial authority, although a council of elders assisted him. Affiliation to the ethnic group was determined by obedience to the chief and not necessarily by the mere accident of birth. The Tonga are known as good farmers, who also do well as merchants.

TOURISM. During the colonial period, Mozambique used to be a paradise for South African and Rhodesian white vacationers, attracted by its beaches and hotels, particularly in the south and at **Beira**. During the 1970s, Mozambique could count on 5,195 rooms in different hotels, motels, hostels, and boarding houses for its visitors. In 1972, the number of visitors reached 29,574 annually and continued to grow when Mozambique offered attractive package deals to South Africans. During the mid-1970s, some 650,000 tourists visited Mozambique yearly. In 1979, the industry continued to boom, having attracted some 986,501 tourists who spent about 108,344,000 *escudos*. Of these visitors, 63 percent were South Africans.

In 1981, however, the number fell to only 1,000 visitors. To improve the situation, the Mozambique government and **South Africa** initiated negotiations in 1984 to restore tourism to Mozambique and agreed to allow Sun International, a South Africa–based company, to explore a joint venture designed to make the Santa Carolina Island, usually known to South Africans as "the paradise island," an attractive resort area. Similar arrangements were to be made for Inhaca Island and Ponta Malongane, both extremely popular with South African whites. Due to the **RENAMO** incursions, however, tourism was at a standstill, especially for areas other than **Maputo**, during the 1980s and early 1990s. Travel from Mozambique to South Africa and Zimbabwe was relatively safe only by plane. Following the 1992 **Acordo Geral da Paz**, tourists, especially from South Africa, began returning to the country, particularly to Maputo and vicinity. **Beira**, which used to attract so many white Rhodesians and South Africans, is virtually deserted touristically speaking.

However, overall, the government claims that tourism is the fastest growing sector of the economy, which convinced the leaders to create, for the first time, a Ministry of Tourism after the 1999 elections. In fact, in 1996, U.S.$60 million were invested in the tourist industry, attracting some 550,000 tourists that year. There is a concerted effort to rehabilitate and improve the Gorongoza Park Reserve virtually connecting both South Africa's Kruger National Park with Mozambique. In addition, in 1990, South Africa, Mozambique, and Swaziland announced a $121 million investment project to open a reserve park where their less populated common borders meet, called the Lubombo Spatial Development Initiative. That year the government initiated a reserve park project of about 22,000 square kilometers (8,593.75 square miles) in the extreme north of **Niassa** Province, with 51 percent state and 49 percent private ownership. The accelerated construction of hotels, which had in 1997 some 1,200 beds, reflects the tourist industry's comeback following the long **civil war.**

TRADE. Three major features characterize Mozambique's international trade: a history of high volatility, lack of commodity diversification—agricultural and mineral primary products being by far the dominant export commodity—and export market concentration in Europe and **South Africa.** In 1994, principal exports were cashew kernels, sugar, timber, prawns, textiles and clothing, precious and semiprecious stones and mineral water; principal imports were spare parts and equipment, raw materials, and consumer goods, including food. Main trading partners are Spain, South Africa, India, Japan, Portugal for exports; South Africa, Zimbabwe, Saudi Arabia, and **Portugal** for imports.

Export earnings increased steadily from $170m in 1995 to $250m in 1999 ($390m in 2000). In 2000, exports included prawns 40 percent, cashews, cotton, sugar, citrus, timber; bulk electricity. Food exports accounted for 69 percent of merchandise exports in 1996. But both food exports and food imports are high. The main destinations of Mozambican exports in 1999 were the European Union (EU), 27 percent; South Africa, 26 percent; Zimbabwe, 15 percent; India, 12 percent; **United States**, 5 percent; and Japan, 4 percent. Imports fell from $1.02 billion in 1994 to $784 million in 1995 but rose steadily after another decline in 1996 to over $1 billion in 1999 and $1.4 billion in 2000. Manufactures imports account for over 60 percent of Mozambique's merchandise imports. In 2000, Mozambique imported mainly commodities: machinery and equipment, mineral products, chemicals, metals, foodstuffs, textiles from South Africa, 44 percent; EU, 16 percent; United States, 6.5 percent; Japan, 6.5 percent; Pakistan, 3 percent; and India, 3 percent. Mozambique has maintained trade deficits since 1980, which have averaged $500 million annually. Between 1985 and 1994, trade deficits increased significantly to reach their highest point of $767 million. In 1998, the trade balance was –$491 million.

The government has undertaken measures aimed at reducing the perennial trade deficits. In addition to the series of economic reforms that has led to the privatization of over 900 state-owned enterprises, in 1999, Mozambique launched a comprehensive tax reform program. Together with reform in the commercial code, the government has also improved transportation links to South Africa and the rest of the region, which has improved and increased foreign investments.

TRADITIONAL RELIGION. About 60 percent (even though the government cites the figure of 40 percent) of the Mozambican population still worship in the ways of their forebears, who were monotheistic. The traditionalists believe in one Supreme Being who is omniscient, almighty, and omnipresent, but who acts through intermediaries—the spirits and the ancestors. They offer him as well as the spirits and the ancestors prayer, and sacrifice. The ancestors, or the living-dead, are the guardians of the community and its morals. They are the protectors of good people and the cursers of the wicked. As part of most Bantu-speaking religious traditions, Mozambicans believe in the existence of what experts have called a "vital force" in everything that exists, humans having a higher degree of it. Among humans, traditional authorities, chiefs, for example, the sorcerer, the witch, and the medicine-man tend to have even a stronger vital force, which they use positively or negatively in society. In this context, a magician is one who is able to manipulate this force to his advantage or the benefit of others. The chief, for example, can be responsible and blamed for drought in his area, because people believe that he can do something about it.

Most Mozambicans, even when converted to Christianity, still believe in the powers of the medicine man, the sorcerer, and the witch and may practice trial by boiled oil or water, and poison. Therefore, in spite of five centuries of **Portuguese** colonialism and the work of the **Catholic Church**, Christianity did not have the desired impact on the former colony. Finally, as is common in all African societies, Mozambique traditional religion does not have missionaries or ambulant preachers who attempt to convert people who may be either traditionalists or who profess another faith. Household upbringing and noncompartmentalized instruction or practice of religion ensure that every child grows up in an environment in which religion is as much a part of one's upbringing as respect for the elders. As a result, traditional religion in Mozambique is tolerant of any foreign-introduced religion, which does not, for example, happen in the Arab countries or Israel.

TRANSITIONAL GOVERNMENT. A temporary, shared government, agreed on by the **Portuguese** government and **FRELIMO** representatives in September 1974 to allow Mozambique a smooth transition to independence, which was proclaimed on June 25, 1975. According to the **Lusaka Agreement** signed in Zambia, a **Portuguese** and a Mozambican counterpart would head each major ministry. The highest authority during the transitional government was **Joaquim Chissano**, who acted as interim prime minister until independence.

TRANSPORT. *See* PORTS; RAILROADS; ROADS.

– U –

UNIÃO NACIONAL AFRICANA DA ROMBÉZIA (UNAR) (ROMBEZIA AFRICAN NATIONAL UNION). A splinter group of Lusaka-based **Comité Revolucionário de Moçambique (COREMO)**, UNAR established its base in Blantyre, Malawi, during the late 1960s. UNAR naively believed that the **Portuguese** would willingly cede to Malawi the Mozambique region between the Rovuma and **Zambezi** Rivers in exchange for Banda's pledge not to disturb the rest of Mozambique. UNAR did receive limited protection from the Malawi Congress Party. However, the pseudonationalist movement never engaged in any guerrilla activity against the Portuguese but tried to stop **FRELIMO**'s influence in the north.

UNIÃO NACIONAL AFRICANA DE MOÇAMBIQUE (UNAMO) (MOZAMBIQUE AFRICAN NATIONAL UNION). Revolutionary movement established in Mombasa, Kenya, in 1961 by Mozambican **refugees** and workers living in Uganda, Kenya, and Tanzania. UNAMO's first president was Mathew Mmole. UNAMO moved to Tanzania the same year and merged with União Democrática Nacional de Moçambique (UDE-NAMO) and UNIÃO Nacional de Moçambique Independente (UNAMI) to form **FRELIMO** in 1962. Before moving to Tanzania, however, UN-AAMO had carried out no activity against the Portuguese. Organizational and logistical problems, exacerbated by distance, also mitigated against any realistic assault on the colonial government. (As the name suggests, MANU was modeled after TANU in Tanzania and KANU in Kenya.)

UNIÃO NACIONAL DE ESTUDANTES DE MOÇAMBIQUE (UN-EMO) (NATIONAL UNION OF MOZAMBICAN STUDENTS). Founded in Paris in 1961 by Mozambique students, UNEMO's aims were varied, namely, to foster the interests of Mozambican students; assist them in securing scholarships and enabling them to abandon the miserable life of refugees: advance the cause of Mozambique abroad, especially in academic circles; and contribute, in any way possible, in accordance with each member's conscience and means, to the elimination of colonial rule in Mozambique. Contrary to party President **Eduardo Chivambo Mondlane**'s claim in his book *The Struggle for Mozambique*, UNEMO was never a branch of **FRELIMO**, although some students, particularly those in Europe, were also FRELIMO members. In fact, some of them had been sponsored by the movement. However, the strongest and the largest section of UNEMO was based in the **United States** and had very few FRELIMO members.

Virtually all members were also convinced that FRELIMO was the only legitimate revolutionary movement in Mozambique and therefore never hesitated to advance its cause in the United States. The students did not wish to belong to a political movement, fearful that it might dictate their conduct and undermine their educational opportunities.

UNEMO met once a year and, until the early 1970s, published its magazine, *The Mozambique Bulletin*, regularly. Although the association functioned relatively well until 1973, it had been unable to resolve to everyone's satisfaction the differences between the students who grew up in Mozambique, all of whom were able to speak Portuguese, and those who grew up abroad (in such countries as Zimbabwe, Malawi, Tanzania, and Kenya) and spoke English. During the 1960s and early 1970s, all meetings were conducted in Portuguese, to the resentment of the non-Portuguese speakers. The association was dominated by Catholic ex-seminarians, a factor resented by non-ex-seminarians that became frustrated because their number was too small to influence the students' agenda. Additional differences of opinion existed as to whether UNEMO was a branch of FRELIMO. These differences, and the fact that independence came unexpectedly soon, contributed to the association's ineffectiveness and its demise in 1975.

UNIÃO NACIONAL DE MOÇAMBIQUE (UNAMO) (MOZAMBIQUE NATIONAL UNION). A **RENAMO** splinter group that emerged in 1986, with some of its members coming from the **Comité para a União Nacional Independente de Mocambique (CUNIMO).** UNAMO not only disagreed with RENAMO's alliance with **South Africa** but was also displeased that it was led by the **Ndau.** Former military chief of Africa Livre who joined RENAMO in 1982, becoming **Afonso Dhlakama**'s number one man on RENAMO's National Council in 1983, Gimo M'Phiri apparently expected to succeed General S. Henrique. Henrique died in a failed attempt to conquer Maganja da Costa in November 1986. Unexpectedly, without consulting him, Dhlakama appointed Calisto Meque as the successor to General Henrique. Following a purge of non-Ndau officials in 1987, M'Phiri, suspected by Meque of supporting a plot against Ndau leadership, seceded from the movement, along with 500 others, and began attacking RENAMO bases in **Zambézia**, killing Calisto Meque in 1988. By 1990, UNAMO's activities had weaken RENAMO temporarily and attracted much RELIMO attention as a "welcome" detractor. UNAMO's effectiveness disappeared following several meetings it held with FRELIMO officials, ending up with its acceptance of the country's 1990 **constitution.**

UNIÃO NACIONAL DE MOÇAMBIQUE INDEPENDENTE (UNAMI) (NATIONAL UNION OF INDEPENDENT MOZAMBIQUE). Revolutionary movement formed by **Tete** exiles in Blantyre, Malawi, in 1961. Its first president was José Baltazar Chagonga, whom President Hastings Banda of Malawi deported to Mozambique. After merging with **UDENAMO** and UNAMO as **FRELIMO** in 1962, UNAMI was revived in Malawi and had its headquarters (near Chileka Airport) in the home of the party's secretary-general, António Gadaga. Until 1967, despite his meager financial means, Gadaga received wholeheartedly several Mozambican refugees, many of whom were Catholic ex-seminarians who later found scholarships abroad. Malawi was not the proper place for any nationalist movement at the time, as the Portuguese could come in and out of the country almost at ease and capture nationalists. Banda also vowed to deport anyone engaged in military activity against the Portuguese government in Mozambique.

UNIÃO NACIONAL DEMOCRÁTICA DE MOÇAMBIQUE (UDENAMO) (MOZAMBIQUE NATIONAL DEMOCRATIC UNION). A revolutionary movement organized by Mozambique workers and exiles in Salisbury (capital of then Rhodesia) in 1960. It moved to Dar-es-Salaam after Tanzania's independence in an attempt to overcome the problem of mounting warfare from a white-dominated British colony. In 1962, UDENAMO merged with FRELIMO. One of UDENAMO's founders was Adelino C. Gwambe. **Urias Simango**, a pastor from **Beira**, Mozambique, headed the movement temporarily until he became FRELIMO's vice president. One UDENAMO splinter group broke away from FRELIMO and called itself Comité Secreto da Restauração (COSER) (Secret Restoration Committee). COSER subsequently established a new but ineffective UDENAMO in Cairo.

UNIÃO NACIONAL MOÇAMBICANA (UNAMO) (MOZAMBIQUE NATIONAL UNION). Initiated in 1987 by former sympathizers of **RENAMO**, UNAMO claimed to have its headquarters in **Nampula**. Its leaders are still unknown, although its director was Carlos Alexandre Rei, the same individual who directed **CUNIMO** in Lisbon. UNAMO's constitution claimed to stand for democracy and to uphold the Universal Declaration of Human Rights. One of its objectives was to end the war between RENAMO and **FRELIMO**. In 1988, the organization was nowhere recognized.

UNITED NATIONS. The United Nations has played three crucial roles in Mozambique. First was the condemnation of **Portuguese** policies in

Mozambique during the colonial period. Several resolutions were passed by the General Assembly condemning **Portugal** for its introduction of forced labor in Mozambique, its repressive political and economic policies, and its refusal to grant independence to the colony during the 1960s and 1970s. The Security Council was less successful than the General Assembly due to repeated vetoes against specific resolutions by the **United States**, Britain, and France. However, it was clear that the UN was in support of the liberation movements in the Portuguese colonies and stood firmly behind the rights of peoples under colonial rule to self-determination. The second major role played by the UN in Mozambique was the humanitarian assistance it provided to Mozambique following independence in 1975, especially during the **civil war** (1977–92), in the form of technical assistance and financial aid in education and health, as part of its effort to eliminate poverty. The UN had declared Mozambique to be among the five poorest countries in the world. The last major but most critical involvement in Mozambique was through its operation called **Organização das Nações Unidas em Moçambique (ONUMOZ)** immediately following the signing of the peace agreement between **FRELIMO** and **RENAMO** in 1992. The UN was to take the lead in the implementation of the peace process by supervising the demobilization of soldiers, the enactment of democratic reforms, and the resettlement of **refugees** and displaced Mozambicans. The repatriation of the approximately two million Mozambican refugees from the surrounding countries was the largest and the most expensive repatriation ever undertaken by the UN. In 2001 and 2002, following the devastating **floods** in the country, the UN also came to the rescue of Mozambique. *See also* ACORDO GERAL DA PAZ.

UNITED STATES OF AMERICA. Relations between Mozambique and the United States can be understood only in the context of various factors: **Portugal** and the North Atlantic Treaty Organization (NATO), the Cold War, the Vietnam War, the presence of Cuban forces in Africa, and apartheid **South Africa**. During the 1950s, it was clear that America's cordial relations with Portugal, a member of NATO, dictated its foreign policy toward Mozambique. As such, the United States opposed any liberation movement that advocated violence to achieve independence. This stance was also dictated by the need to contain communist advances in Africa, Portugal being seen at the time as the strongest bastion of Western civilization and capitalism in southern Africa. It was therefore unexpected to many observers that the Kennedy administration voted for the first time against **Portugal** at the United Nations in 1961.

However, the surprising but temporary switch in policy did not survive in Lyndon Johnson's administration, obsessed with and distracted, as it were, by the Vietnam War. Richard Nixon, who succeeded Johnson at the White House, showed more interest in southern Africa than his predecessors did, after selecting Henry Kissinger as his secretary of state. Yet, Kissinger still believed in a policy of containment of the liberation movements and, as expressed in his *National Security Memorandum* 39, the secretary of state held the view that white regimes in South Africa and Rhodesia would remain intact for the foreseeable future. Thus, he was more interested in resolving the Southern Rhodesian and South African situation peacefully in order to guarantee whites a continued predominant role in the governments of the African subcontinent.

Mozambique had, meanwhile, achieved its independence and embraced a Marxist-Leninist philosophy, which was anathema to the United States. Yet, even though still maintaining the Cold War posture, President Jimmy Carter, following a long fight with Congress, initiated a period of humanitarian assistance to Marxist Mozambique: $12.2 million in 1977 as compensation for Mozambique's revenue loss due to closure of its border with Southern Rhodesia in compliance with United Nations sanctions; and $8.7 million in humanitarian assistance in October 1977, following the visit of a Mozambique delegation to the United States that month. The visit coincided with the beginning of the civil war in Mozambique in which Southern Rhodesia and, later, South Africa, became deeply involved.

There was a shift in policy as the Ronald Reagan administration occupied the White House. The hawkish president was more determined than any of his predecessors to eliminate the so-called evil empire and its satellites from the planet. Therefore, he and his many conservative allies in Congress and within the religious Moral Majority saw with no sympathy the problems Mozambique was experiencing, which ranged from the ravages of the **civil war** to cyclical droughts and **floods**. Worsening the relations with Washington was Mozambique's expulsion of six American diplomats from **Maputo** in 1981, whom Machel accused of spying for the Central Intelligence Agency (CIA). The Reagan administration responded by cutting off all humanitarian assistance and recalling the U.S. ambassador from Maputo.

As he matured in his position as undersecretary of state for African affairs in the Reagan administration, Chester Crocker enunciated the new U.S. policy labeled "constructive engagement" in Africa, which critics considered to be nothing but "reactionary pragmatism" to save the white regimes in southern Africa. It was under such policy that Mozambique began once again to receive aid from the United States. The American ambassador returned to Maputo in 1984. At this juncture, forces inside and outside Mozambique dictated the need for the country to change its policy toward the West, especially the United States. The pressure from **RENAMO** and the United States was evident in **Samora Machel's** signing of the now infamous Nkomati Accord with South Africa that year and accepting Mozambique's membership in the **International Monetary Fund** (IMF), which provided preliminary financial assistance in 1985. Indeed, since 1983, Mozambique had begun a sustained campaign to elicit further humanitarian and military assistance from the West. It is in this context that Reagan received Machel at the White House in 1985.

At that point, Mozambique relations with the United States took a 90-degree turn toward a rapprochement, but the hawks on Capitol Hill wanted none of this as long as Mozambique followed Marxism-Leninism. When in November 1986 **Joaquim Chissano** became president of Mozambique, relations began to improve more steadily, as the Mozambique government had accepted in principle the dictates of a free market economy. As a result, Mozambique received some $1.2 billion that year from the United States. Of course, with Machel's demise, Mozambique anti-imperialist rhetoric was almost abandoned, allowing Chissano to have a "comfortable" visit to the White House in 1987. The United States supported Mozambique at the IMF, which subsequently provided it with loans of $80.9 million for 1987–89 and $50.1 million for 1989. Something else had also happened: With the collapse of the **Soviet Union** in 1991, Washington no longer saw Mozambique as a communist stronghold in southern Africa. George H. W. Bush also met Chissano and backed the idea of peace talks with **RENAMO**. It was thus that, throughout the 1989–92 FRELIMO-RENAMO peace negotiations in Rome, the United States had its own permanent representative at the talks, C. Hume, who exerted pressure on the two sides to compromise and sign a peace accord. Beginning with the Clinton administration, the United States has been a major supporter of Mozambique, providing millions of dollars annually designed to meet Mozambique's humanitarian needs, strengthen the democratic institutions, and develop and rehabilitate the country's infrastructure. Indications are that President George W. Bush will continue this policy, even though the United States' war on terrorism may divert international assistance funds from Africa.

– V –

VALENTE, MALANGATANA GWENHA. Born in Magaia, Marracuene, on June 6, 1936, Malangatana (as he is usually called) is a self-educated poet and painter. His father worked in the South African mines. To pay for his high school education, Valente worked as a *muleque* (servant) at the Lourenço Marques Club, where he met **Portuguese** architect Amâncio Guedes who "adopted" the young man and trained him as a painter. Malangatana was arrested in December 1964 and released in March 1966. His poems have appeared in *Black Orpheus* magazine (1966) and in *Modern Poetry from Africa* (1963).

– W –

WIRIYAMU MASSACRE. A village south of the city of **Tete**, Wiriyamu gained notoriety when, in 1973, the priests of the Burgos and the late diocesan priest Domingos Ferrão revealed a **Portuguese** army massacre of 400 innocent villagers suspected of cooperating with **FRELIMO.** According to Allen Isaacman, the much-publicized story "focused attention on Portuguese colonialism, generated widespread protest, embarrassed **Portugal**'s allies, and brought FRELIMO concrete financial and moral support from the World Council of Churches." The Portuguese authorities denied the incident.

WITWATERSRAND NATIVE LABOUR ASSOCIATION (WNLA, WENELA). A South African mining company authorized by the Portuguese government in 1909 and thereafter to recruit thousands of mine workers in Mozambique. *See also* MOZAMBIQUE CONVENTION.

WOMEN. As in most countries of the world, women constitute the majority of the citizens in Mozambique, accounting for close to 52 percent of the population. While the country's wars have had a toll on the men, they have also worsened the plight of women in the countryside. In spite of the many technological and social advances apparent in the country following independence, it is accurate to say that, for the overwhelming majority of women, nothing has changed substantially. Their primary roles in the household as bearers and caretakers of children, pleasers of husbands, cooks, tillers of the soil, planters, harvesters, and water and firewood fetchers, have remained the same over the decades following independence.

During the liberation war, **FRELIMO** attempted seriously to alter women's status by involving them in every aspect of the struggle, including service in the armed forces. Today, however, things seem to have regressed rather than progressed, even though presently there are three female ministers in the cabinet. When FRELIMO assumed power in Mozambique in 1975, the Organização da Mulher Moçambicana (OMM) (Mozambique Women's Organization) became active during the first years only to lose steam thereafter, rendering the condition of women no better than in other African countries. Although today there are more girls in school than 20 years ago, the overall ratio of males to females in education is still 2:1.

Distraction by the war, detraction from its goals by poor management of resources, inflationary pressures, the severity of **International Monetary Fund's structural adjustment programs**, and deteriorating **health** conditions in the country have prevented the government from implementing an aggressive affirmative action or a quota system that would elevate women's status in the country. The OMM as a branch of FRELIMO first and foremost, then as donor-dependent and a quasi–nongovernmental organization (NGO), and now again as a branch of the political party, has damaged its own standing in the country. FRELIMO's fight against *lobolo* or bride-wealth and divorce regardless of the matrilineality or patrilineality of the Mozambican societies resulted in an overall failure of women-related policies and visible discontent, especially in the northern matrilineal belt.

Therefore, notwithstanding the heightened discourse on the matter, the superficial adulation of Lurdes Mutola, an Olympian gold medal runner, and well-known figures such as **Graça Simbinen Machel**, women are still treated as second-class citizens in Mozambique, the clearest indicator being their inability to get loans and occupy business managerial positions, and their unsuccessful quest to take control of their own financial affairs both inside and outside the household. Interestingly, men have recently declared Friday a Man's Day in Mozambique (at least in **Maputo**) to allow them to stay longer hours or all night in clubs and restaurants. Yet women are not allowed to do the same, and their husbands would severely reprimand them if they tried to claim the same privileges as men.

– X –

XAI-XAI. Formerly the city of João Belo, port, town, and capital of **Gaza** Province, situated at the mouth of the **Limpopo River**, near the Indian

Ocean. It is linked with the interior by a **railroad** and with **Maputo** by **road**. Its surrounding areas, fertilized by the Limpopo, produce corn, rice, manioc, sorghum, and peanuts, and it has benefited from the cattle industry.

XICONHOCA. Popular cartoon and character invented by **FRELIMO** to represent the abuses and exploitation of the colonial period as well as the greed, corruption, and inefficiency of the postindependence bourgeois bureaucrats.

– Y –

YAO (AJAUA). About 400,000 in 1997, the matrilineal Yao or Ajaua inhabit **Niassa** (between the Lugenda and Rovuma Rivers) and **Tete** Provinces. Some live in Malawi. In the distant past, the Ajaua were hunters, but now live as farmers. They were also engaged in the slave trade, and most of them have converted to Islam.

– Z –

ZAMBEZI RIVER. The Zambezi River originates in Zambia, near the frontiers of Angola and Zaire. The fourth largest river on the continent, and also the fourth longest in the world, the Zambezi is 1,600 miles long, and serves as a border between Zambia and Zimbabwe, and flows to the Indian Ocean through central Mozambique. The river is also famous for its Victoria Falls along the border between Zambia and Zimbabwe and its two hydroelectric dams at **Cahora Bassa** and at Kariba in Zambia and Zimbabwe. Parts of the river become shallow during the dry season. However, the Zambezi is potentially deadly during the rainy season, when it swells and **floods** its banks.

ZAMBEZI VALLEY DEVELOPMENT PROJECT. An economic scheme announced by the government in 2001 to systematically explore and develop the Zambezi Valley in the sectors of fishery, agriculture, water provision, electricity, and livestock. Sérgio Vieira, **FRELIMO**'s former security chief and member of the Assembly of the Republic, has been appointed director of the project.

ZAMBÉZIA. Mozambique central province since 1975, with **Quelimane** as the provincial capital. It has a surface area of 40,544 square miles and a population of 3,202,000 (1997 estimate). Zambézia is bordered by Malawi in the west, **Nampula** and **Niassa** Provinces in the north, **Sofala** and **Tete** Provinces in the south, and the Indian Ocean in the east. It has several plateaus, the highest being the Namuli highlands (3,280 feet) and is served by several important rivers such as the **Zambezi** and its tributary, the Shire. It is endowed with a very fertile soil, capable of sustaining large crops of coconut trees (four million in 1988 extended through a 50,000-acre area), cotton, tea, sisal, corn, and cashew nuts. Minerals such as tantalum, iron, manganese, and uranium are also known to exist in its soil. Quelimane, its capital city and port, is connected to Mocuba by rail and by **road** to Malawi and Nampula Province.

ZIMBABWE AFRICAN NATIONAL UNION (ZANU). A nationalist movement led by Robert Mugabe during the 1970s, dominated by the Shona, mostly responsible for the defeat of the white Rhodesian government in 1980. Mozambique was a strong supporter of ZANU, providing military facilities to the movement and accepting large numbers of Zimbabwean refugees prior to 1980. ZANU's rival, the Zimbabwe African People's Union (ZAPU), under Joshua Nkomo, did not enjoy the same support from the People's Republic of Mozambique. The Rhodesian army retaliated frequently against Mozambique for its support of ZANU. ZANU and ZAPU have since come together to form the ZANU–Patriotic Front, but the party is in decay today, as Mugabe has become a liability rather than an asset to the country as he was during the 1980s.

ZUAVO BATTALION. Aborted African battalion formed by Governor-General Pinto de Magalhães (1851–54) to solve the problem created by the limited number of **Portuguese** soldiers in Mozambique. The governor even resorted to kidnapping Africans and requested that slave owners furnish a number of their servants and slaves to the authorities to serve in the army. However, most Africans escaped from the military headquarters, some immediately after recruitment and others once they had received the uniforms and a gun. The slave owners, on the other hand, to comply with the order, sent to the government their most incorrigible or sickest slaves. The experiment failed and was soon abandoned.

Appendix 1
Mozambique Captains and Governors

1501–1975

Sofala

Capitães-Mores

1501–1505	Sancho de Tova
1505–1506	Pedro da Naia
1506	Manuel Fernandes
1506–1507	Nunho Vaz Pereira

Sofala and Mozambique

Capitães-Mores

1507–1508	Vasco Gomes de Abreu
1508–1509	Rui de Brito Patalim
1509–1512	António de Saldanha
1512–1515	Simão de Miranda de Azevedo
1515–1518	Cristóvão de Tavora
1518–1520	Sancho de Tovar
1521–1524	Diogo de Sepúlveda
1525–1528	Lopo de Almeida
1528–1531	António da Silveira de Meneses
1531–1538	Vicente Pegado
1538–1541	Aleixo de Sousa Chicorro
1541–1548	João de Sepúlveda
1548–1551	Fernão de Sousa de Távora
1552–1553	Diogo de Mesquita
1554–1557	Diogo de Sousa

*According to sources, Serpa Pinto served temporarily as governor–general in 1899, and João de Azevedo Coutinho also occupied the position briefly in 1904.

1558–1560 Sebastião de Sá
1560–1564 Pantaleão de Sá
1564–1567 Jerónimo Barreto
1567–1569 Pedro Barreto Rolim

Mozambique

Captains-General

1569–1573 Francisco Barreto
1573–1577 Vasco Fernandes Homem
1577–1582 Pedro de Castro
1583–1586 Nunho Velho Pereira
1586–1589 Jorge Telo de Meneses
1589–1590 Lourenço de Brito
1591–1595 Pedro de Sousa
1595–1598 Nunho de Cunhão e Ataíde
1598–1601 Álvaro Abranches
1601–1604 Vasco de Mascarenhas
1604–1607 Sebastião de Macedo
1607–1609 Estevado de Ataíde

Mozambique, Sofala, Rios de Cuama, and Monomotapa

Governors

1609–1611 Nunho Álvares Pereira
1611–1612 Estevado de Ataíde
1612 Diogo Simões de Madeira
1612–1614 João de Azevedo
1614–1618 Rui de Melo Sampaio
1619–1623 Nunho Álvares Pereira
1623 Nunho da Cunha
1623–1624 Lopo de Almeida
1624–1627 Diogo de Sousa de Meneses
1628–1631 Nunho Álvares Pereira
1631–1632 Cristóvão de Brito e Vasconcelos
1632–1633 Diogo de Sousa de Meneses
1633–1634 Filipe de Mascarenhas
1635–1639 Lourenço de Souto–Maior
1639–1640 Diogo de Vasconcelos

1640–1641	António de Brito Pacheco
1641–1642	Francisco da Silveira
1643–1646	Júlio Moniz da Silva
1646–	Fernão Dias Baial
1649–1651	Álvaro de Sousa de Távora
1652	Francisco de Mascarenhas
1653–1657	Francisco de Lima
1657–1661	Manuel Corte–Real de Sampaio
1661–1664	Manuel de Mascarenhas
1664–1667	António de Melo e Castro
1667–1670	Inácio Sarmento de Carvalho
1670–1673	João de Sousa Freire
1673–1674	Simão Gomes da Silva
1674	André Pinto da Fonseca
1674–1676	Manuel da Silva
1676–1682	João de Sousa Freire
1682–1686	Caetano de Melo e Castro
1686–1689	Miguel de Almeida
1689–1692	Manuel dos Santos Pinto
1692–1693	Tomé de Sousa Correia
1694	Francisco Correia de Mesquita
1694–1695	Estêvão José da Costa
1696	Francisco da Costa
1696–1699	Luís de Melo Sampaio
1699–1703	Jacome de Morais Sarmento
1703–1706	João Fernandes de Almeida
1706–1707	Luís de Brito Freire
1708–1712	Luís Gonçalves de Câmara
1712–1714	João Fernandes de Almeida
1714–1715	Francisco de Mascarenhas
1716–1719	Francisco de Souto–Maior
1719–1721	Francisco de Alarcão e Souto–Maior
1722–1723	Álvaro Caetano de Melo e Castro
1723–1726	António João Sequeira e Faria
1726–1730	António Cardim Frois
1730–1733	António Casco de Melo
1733–1736	José Barbosa Leal
1736–1739	Nicolau Tolentino de Almeida
1740–1743	Lourenço de Noronha
1743–1746	Pedro do Rego Barreto da Gama e Castro
1746–1750	Caetano Correia de Sá

Mozambique, Zambezi, and Sofala Governors

Captains-General

1752–1758	Francisco de Melo e Castro
1758	João Manuel de Melo
	David Marques Pereira
1758–1763	Pedro de Saldanha e Albuquerque
1763–1765	João Pereira da Silva Barba
1765–1779	Baltasar Manuel Pereira do Lago
1779–1780	José de Vasconcelos e Almeida
1781–1782	Vicente Caetano de Maia e Vasconcelos
1782–1783	Pedro de Saldanha e Albuquerque
1783–1786	(junta)
1786–1793	António Manuel de Melo e Castro
1793–1797	Diogo de Sousa Coutinho
1797–1801	Francisco Guedes de Carvalho Meneses da Costa
1801–1805	Isidoro de Almeida Sousa e Sá
1805–1807	Francisco de Paula de Albuquerque do Amaral Cardoso
1807–1809	(junta)
1809–1812	António Manuel de Melo e Castro de Mendonça
1812–1817	Marcos Caetano de Abreu e Meneses
1817–1818	José Francisco de Paula Calvalcanti de Albuquerque
1819–1821	João da Costa Brito Sanches
1821–1824	(juntas)
1824–1825	João Manuel da Silva
1825–1829	Sebastião Xavier Botelho
1829–1832	Paulo José Miguel de Brito
1832–1834	(junta)
1834–1836	José Gregório Pegado

Mozambique

Governors-General

1837	António José de Melo
1837–1838	João Carlos Augusto de Oeynhausen e Gravenburg Marques de Aracaty
1838–1840	(Council)
1840–1841	Joaquim Pereira Marinho
1841–1843	João da Costa Xavier

1843–1847	Rodrigo Luciano de Abreu e Lima
1847–1851	Domingos Fortunato do Vale
1851–1854	Joaquim Pinto de Magalhães
1854–1857	Vasco Guedes de Carvalho e Meneses
1857–1864	João Tavares de Almeida
1864–1867	António do Canto e Castro
1867–1868	António Augusto de Almeida Portugal Correia de Lacerda
1869	António Tavares de Almeida
	Fernão da Costa Leal
1870–1873	José Rodrigues Coelho do Amaral
1874–1877	José Guedes de Carvalho e Meneses
1877–1880	Francisco Maria da Cunha
1880–1881	Augusto César Rodrigues Sarmento
1881–1882	Carlos Eugénio Correia da Silva, Visconde do Paço de Arcos
1882–1885	Agostinho Coelho
1885–1889	Augusto Vidal de Castilho Barreto e Noronha
1889–1890	José António de Brissac das Neves Ferreira
1890–1891	Joaquim José Machado
1891–1893	Rafael Jacome Lopes de Andrade
1893–1894	Francisco Teixeira da Silva
1894–1895	Fernão de Magalhães e Meneses
1895–1896	António José Enes
1896–1897	Joaquim Augusto Mousinho de Albuquerque
1897–1898	Baltasar Freire Cabral
1898	Carlos Alberto Schultz Xavier
1898–1900	Álvaro António da Costa Ferreira
1900	Júlio José Marques da Costa
1900	Joaquim José Machado
1900–1902	Manuel Rafael Gorjão
1902–1905	Tomás António Garcia Rosado
1905–1906	João António de Azevedo Coutinho Fragoso de Sequeira
1906–1910	Alfredo Augusto Freire de Andrade
1910–1911	José de Freitas Ribeiro
1911–1912	José Francisco de Azevedo e Silva
1912–1913	José Afonso Mendes de Magalhães
1913–1914	Augusto Ferreira dos Santos
1914–1915	Joaquim José Machado
1915	Alfredo Baptista Coelho

1915–1918	Álvaro Xavier de Castro
1918–1919	Pedro Francisco Massano do Amorim
1919–1921	Manuel Moreira da Fonseca
1921–1923	Manuel de Brito Camacho
1923–1924	Manuel Moreira da Fonseca
1924–1926	Vítor Hugo de Azevedo Coutinho
1926–1938	José Ricardo Pereira Cabral
1938–1940	José Nunes de Oliveira
1940–1947	José Tristão de Bettencourt
1947–1958	Gabriel Maurício Teixeira
1958–1961	Pedro Correia de Barros
1961–1964	Manuel Maria Sarmento Rodrigues
1964–1968	José Augusto da Costa Almeida
1968–1970	Baltasar Rebelo de Sousa
1970	Gouveia e Melo (interim governor)
1970–1971	Eduardo de Arantes e Oliveira
1971–1974	Manuel Pimentel dos Santos
1974	David Teixeira Ferreira (interim governor)
	Henrique Soares de Melo
1974–1975	Vítor Crespo

Sources: António Oliveira Marques, *História de Portugal, Vol. III* (Lisbon: Palas Editores, 1981), pp. 622–24; and David Henige, *Colonial Governors* (Madison: University of Wisconsin Press, 1970), pp. 251–53.

Appendix 2
The Mozambique Government (April 2001)

Head of State

President of the Republic and Commander in Chief of the Armed Forces: Joaquim Alberto Chissano

Council of Ministers

Prime Minister: Pascoal Mocumbi
Minister of Agriculture and Rural Development: Helder dos Santos
Minister of Culture: Miguel Costa Mkaima
Minister of Education: Alcido Eduardo Nguenha
Minister of Energy and Mineral Resources: Castigo José Langa
Minister of Environmental Coordination: John William Kachamila
Minister of Fisheries: Cadmiel Muthemba
Minister of Foreign Affairs and Cooperation: Leonardo Simão
Minister of Health: Francisco Ferreira Songane
Minister of Industry and Commerce: Alberto Carlos Morgado
Minister of Interior: Almerino da Cruz Manhenje
Minister of Justice: José Ibraime Abudo
Minister of Labor: Mário Lampião Sevene
Minister of National Defense: Tobias Joaquim Dai
Minister of Planning and Finance: Luísa Diogo
Minister in the Presidency For Parliamentary and Diplomatic Affairs: Francisco Caetano Madeira
Minister in the Presidency for Defense and Security: Almerino Manhenje
Minister of Public Works and Housing: Roberto Costley White
Minister for Women and Social Action: Virginia Matabele
Minister of State Administration: José Chichava
Minister of Higher Education, Science, and Technology: Lidia Maria Brito

Minister of Tourism: Fernando Sumbane Júnior
Minister of Transport and Communication: Tomás Salomão
Minister of Youth and Sports: José Matias Libombo

Ministry Addresses

Ministry of Agriculture and Rural Development: Praça dos Heróis Moçambicanos; telephone, 460055; fax, 460055
Ministry of Culture: Avenida Ptrice Lumumba 1217 C.P. (may change); telephone, 420068; fax, not given; telex: 6621
Ministry of Education: Avenida 24 de Julho 167, 9 Andar; telephone, 490830; fax, 492160
Ministry of Energy and Mineral Resources: Avenida Fernão Magãlhaes 34; telephone, 429615; fax, 427103
Ministry of Environmental Coordination: Avenida Acordos de Lusaka 2115, C.P. 2020; telephone, 466245; fax, 465849
Ministry of Fisheries: Praça dos Heróis Moçambicanos C.P. 1406 (may change); telephone, 460010; fax, 460145
Ministry of Foreign Affairs and Cooperation: Avenida Julius Nyerere; telephone, 492258; fax, 491460
Ministry of Health: Avenida Eduardo Mondlane; telephone, 427131; fax, 427133
Ministry of Higher Education, Science and Technology: Avenida 24 de Julho 167 (may change); telephone, 492206; fax, 492196
Ministry of Industry and Commerce: Avenida 25 de Outubro 86; telephone, 427204; fax, 421305
Ministry of Interior: Avenida Olof Palme 46/48; telephone, 420130; fax, 420084
Ministry of Justice: Avenida Julius Nyerere 33; telephone, 491613; fax, 494264
Ministry of Labor: Avenida 24 de Julho 2351, 1 Andar; telephone, 424400; fax, 421881
Ministry of National Defense: Avenida Mártires da Machava 280, 373; telephone, 493369; fax, 491619
Ministry of Planning and Finance: Praça da Marinha Popular, C.P. 272; telephone, 421303; fax, 420137
Ministry of Public Works and Housing: Avenida Karl Marx 268; telephone, 420543; fax, 421369
Ministry of State Administration: Rua da Rádio Moçambique 112; telephone, 426666; fax, 428565

Ministry of Tourism: Avenida Mártires de Inhaminga 336; telephone, 420223; fax, 431028

Ministry of Transport and Communication: Avenida Mártires de Inhaminga 336; telephone, 420223; fax, 431028

Ministry for Women and Social Action: Rua de Tchamba 86, C.P. 516; telephone, 742901; fax, 490923

Ministry of Youth and Sports: Avenida Patrice Lumumba 1217; telephone, 420068; fax, 429700

Provincial Governors (2003)

Cabo Delgado	José Pacheco
Gaza	Rosário Mualela
Inhambane	Aires Ali
Manica	Soares Nhaca
Maputo	Alfredo Namitete
Maputo City	João Baptista Cosme
Nampula	Abdul Razak
Niassa	David Simango
Sofala	Felício Zacarias
Tete	Tomás Mandlate
Zambézia	Lucas Chomera

Appendix 3
Statistical Information

Population and Area of Mozambique by Province

Province	Population 1980	1987	1997	Area (sq.km) 1987	1997
Niassa	514,000	1,109,900	764,000	82,625	129,056
Cabo Delgado	940,000	1,136,700	1,284,000	76,709	82,625
Nampula	2,402,000	1,187,000	3,065,000	68,618	81,606
Zambezia	2,500,000	755,900	3,202,000	61,661	105,008
Tete	831,000	544,700	1,149,000	25,756	100,724
Manica	641,000	2,837,900	975,000	51,606	61,661
Sofala	1,065,000	607,700	1,380,000	129,606	68,018
Inhambane	997,000	1,267,700	1,112,000	58,018	68,615
Gaza	990,000	981,300	1,034,000	100,724	75,709
Maputo Province	491,000	2,952,000	809,000	105,008	25,756
Maputo City	755,000	1,006,800	966,000	602	602

Sources: Comissão Nacional do Plano, *Moçambique: Informação Estatística*, 1980-1981, 1982; *Britanica World Data*, 1988, p. 662; Joseph Hanlon, *Mozambique: Revolution under Fire* (London: Zed Press, 1984), p. 275; Allison Butler Herric et al. *Area Handbook for Mozambique* (Washington: Government Printing Office, 1969), pp. 43-45, 48-50; *Africa: South of the Sahara* (London: Europa Publishers, 2000), p. 761.

Mozambique External Trade (million *escudos* or *meticais*)

Imports		Exports	
1969	7,481 esc.	1969	1,080.0 esc.
1971	9,636 esc.	1971	4,613.0 esc.
1974	11,741 esc.	1974	7,559.0 esc.
1977	10,568 esc.	1977	4,909.0 esc.
1980	23,200 met.	1980	11,817.0 met.
1981	25,783 met.	1981	13,115.0 met.
1982	31,573.7 met.	1982	8,655.3 met.
1983	25,517.4 met.	1983	5,286.6 met.
1984	22,903.3 met.	1984	4,060.5 met.
1986	21,937.1 met.	1986	3,198.3 met.
1995	45,436.625	1995	1,089.3 met.
1996	48,915.375	1996	1,413.1 met.
1997	1,465.5 met.		

Sources: Adapted from *Africa: South of the Sahara* (London: Europa Publishers), 1979–80, p. 708; 1983–84, p. 597; 1988, p. 713; 2000, p. 764; *Britannica World Data*, 1988, p. 662.

Mozambique's Economic Indicators

	1985	1992	1993	1994	1995	1996	1997	1998
GDP at current market prices GDP (MT bn)	192	4,757	7,829	13,415	21,267	32,093	36,693	46,137
Real GDP growth (percent)	1.0	−8.1	8.7	7.5	4.3	7.1	11.3	12.0
Merchandise exports ($mn)	77	139	132	150	169	226	230	248
Merchandise imports ($mc)	381	770	859	917	705	704	684	782
Current account balance ($bn)	−301.0	−352.3	−446.3	−467.2	−444.7	−420.5	−295.6	−476.6
Total external debt ($bn)	2.87	5.13	5.21	7.27	7.46	7.57	7.64	8.21
Debt service/export ratio (annual percentage)	34.5	22.9	32.9	31.2	34.5	26.0	18.6	18.0
Food production per capita (1989-91=100)	93.4	81.3	97.2	90.9	108.9	122.7	129.5	140.4
Foreign reserves (months export coverage)	1	2	2	1	2	3	5	5
Inflation rate (percent)	n.a.	45.5	42.2	63.2	54.4	45.0	5.5	−1.3*
Exchange rate (meticais per dollar)	43	2,517	3,874	6,039	9,024	11,294	11,544	11,875

Source: UN: *Africa Recovery*, vol. 14, 3 (October 2000): 14.

Mozambique: Select Economic and Financial Indicators (1998–2001)

(Annual percentage change, unless otherwise specified)
National income and prices

	1998	1999	2000	2001
Nominal GDP (blmt)	46,427	50,827	58,887	68,939
Nominal GDP (US$m)	3,918	4,005	3,922	4,197
Real GDP	11.9	7.3	3.8	10.4
GDP per capita	231.6	231.5	221.7	232.0
Consumer price index	0.6	3.1	12.3	5.7
Merchandise exports	6.3	10.8	15.4	119.0
Merchandise imports	7.5	46.8	−3.2	1.4
Terms of trade	5.3	−0.1	−1.5	1.5

(Annual change in percent of beginning-period broad money)

	1998	1999	2000	2001
Money and credit				
Net domestic assets	9.3	23.9	25.0	13.3
Government credit to rest of the economy	17.8	22.9	26.3	16.5
Broad money (M2)	17.6	35.1	34.0	16.0
Velocity (GDP/average M2)	5.7	5.2	4.3	4.0
Prime rate	19.6	19.6	18.4	—

(Percent of GDP)

	1998	1999	2000	2001
Investment and saving				
GD investment	23.5	32.6	29.7	27.3
Government	—	—	12.8	13.1
Other sectors	—	—	16.9	14.2
Gross national savings	11.5	15.1	15.1	16.0
Government	—	—	9.3	7.8
Gov. bud. total revenue	11.5	12.2	12.7	12.3
Total exp. + net lend.	21.8	25.2	29.1	30.0
Over. bal. before grants	−10.6	−13.4	−16.7	−17.7
Total grants	8.2	11.9	10.5	11.5
Over. bal. after grants	−2.4	−1.6	−6.1	−6.3
Domestic primary balance	−0.6	−3.5	−7.5	−7.4
Domestic bank financing	−2.3	−0.3	2.5	2.2
External sector				
Cur. ac. bal. aft. grants	−12.4	−19.2	−17.6	−8.8

(Percent of exports and non-factor services)			
	1998	1999	2000	2001
Net pres. value	538.2	202.0	163.0	150.0
External debt service (non-fin. pub. sector)				
Scheduled, before HIPC	20.0	26.1	31.3	20.2
HIPC initiative assist.				
Scheduled, after enhanced	—	—	4.4	5.8

HIPC initiative assistance (US$m, unless otherwise specified)			
	1998	1999	2000	2001
Ext. cur. ac. aft. grants	−436	−770	−690	−403
Overall bal. of payments	−204	−243	−478	−488
Gross internat. reserves	625	669	700	634
In months of imp. of goods and non-factor services	7.0	5.2	5.7	5.0
(in perc. of broad money)	82.7	76.0	70.5	56.8
Exchange rate (meticais)	12,366	13,300	16,244	—
HIPC initiative assistance				
Credit outstanding	147.2	145.4	168.5	164.3

Source: Adapted from International Monetary Fund, Press Release Index, 2001. See http//www.inf.org/external/np/sec/pr/2000/pr0073.htm

Other Mozambique Economic Indicators

	1980	1985	1986	1987	1988	1989	1990	1991	1992	1993	1994
Tea exports (1000s metric tons)	30	2	2	1	1	0	1	1	0	0	—
Cotton exports (1000s metric tons)	6	5	1	4	4	5	6	5	13	10	—
Sisal (1000s metric tons)	7	0	0	0	1	1	0	0	0	0	—
Sugar (1000s metric tons)	64	17	20	10	12	13	18	25	11	5	—
Rice yields (thousands of hectograms/hectare)	8.3	8.6	9.3	8.6	8.9	8.6	8.7	5.3	3.0	6.3	8.1
Corn	—	—	—	—	—	—	—	—	—	—	—
Cement output	—	—	—	—	—	—	—	—	—	—	—
Industrial Production	—	—	—	—	—	—	—	—	—	—	—
Cooking oil	—	—	—	—	—	—	—	—	—	—	—
Wood production	—	—	—	—	—	—	—	—	—	—	—
Construction	—	—	—	—	—	—	—	—	—	—	—

	1980	1985	1986	1987	1988	1989	1990	1991	1992	1993	1994
Industry	—	—	—	—	—	—	—	—	—	—	—
Fishing industry	—	—	—	—	—	—	—	—	—	—	—
Agricultural	110	98	101	100	99	103	08	102	85	98	—
Production index (1986=100)	—	—	—	—	—	—	—	—	—	—	—
Total external debt (millions of US$)	0	2677	3298	3635	3971	4264	4474	4486	4934	5012	5491
Debt-GDP ratio	—	—	—	—	—	—	—	—	—	—	191
Concessional long-term loans (including IMF; millions of US$)	0	362	375	334	154	165	195	123	233	154	241
GNP per capita (US$)	—	30	170	140	110	90	90	90	80	90	80
Trade balance (millions of US$)	-370	-300	-410	-390	-360	-440	-390	-310	-380	-322	-306
Overall production	—	—	—	—	—	—	—	-9.3	—	-12	—
Deficit (% of GDP)	—	15.9	22.3	15.8	16.5	13.9	18.3	—	12.3	—	11.6

Source: African Development Indicators 1996, The World Bank.

Public Education Statistics, 1997

Primary Schools by Province

Province	1° Grau (1-5)				2° Grau (6-7)			
	Schools	Students	Teach. Staff	Student/ Teacher Ratio	Schools	Students	Teach/Staff	Student/ Teacher Ratio
Total	5,689	1,745,049	28,705	60.8	336	154,482	3,965	39.0
Niassa	439	79,818	1,737	46.0	14	5,735	211	27.2
Cabo Delgado	557	121,972	2,230	54.7	22	6,657	205	32.5
Nampula	1,061	269,747	5,109	52.8	48	15,143	460	32.9
Zambezia	1,317	330,253	5,051	65.4	34	15,628	387	40.4
Tete	459	124,304	2,517	49.4	23	9,748	360	27.1
Manica	283	101,004	1,707	59.2	22	11,136	234	47.6
Sofala	303	111,179	1,980	56.2	19	12,127	316	38.4
Inhambane	465	159,838	2,340	68.3	44	16,567	352	47.1
Gaza	497	173,737	2,198	79.0	53	14,995	298	50.3
Maputo (Province)	220	130,344	1,576	82.7	19	14,786	361	41.0
Maputo (City)	88	142,853	2,260	63.2	38	31,960	781	40.9

Secondary Schools by Province

Province	1° Ciclo (8-10)				2° Ciclo (11-12)			
	Schools	Students	Teach. Staff	Student/Teacher Ratio	Schools	Students	Teach/Staff	Student/Teacher Ratio
Total	63	45,211	1,292	35.0	12	6,343	263	24.1
Niassa	4	1,694	85	19.9	1	334	16	20.9
Cabo Delgado	5	2,522	90	28.0	1	309	23	13.4
Nampula	7	4,159	142	29.3	1	583	35	16.7
Zambezia	5	3,748	76	49.3	1	382	15	25.5
Tete	6	3,124	87	35.9	1	341	18	18.9
Manica	3	2,392	80	29.9	1	201	16	12.6
Sofala	7	3,814	140	27.2	1	574	19	30.2
Inhambane	5	3,262	121	27.0	1	220	18	12.2
Gaza	6	39,040	92	42.8	1	284	16	17.8
Maputo (Province)	8	4,328	157	27.6	1	426	17	25.1
Maputo (City)	7	1,228	22	55.1	2	2,689	70	38.4

(continued)

Public Education Statistics, 1997 (continued)

Technical Education

Province	Nivel elementary				Nivel basico			
	Schools	Students	Teach. Staff	Student/ Teacher Ratio	Schools	Students	Teach/Staff	Student/ Teacher Ratio
Total	2	253	23	11	23	11,748	542	22
Niassa	0	0	0	0	2	634	30	21
Cabo Delgado	0	0	0	0	3	311	38	8
Nampula	0	0	0	0	3	795	74	11
Zambezia	0	0	0	0	2	772	22	35
Tete	0	0	0	0	3	812	61	13
Manica	0	0	0	0	1	653	22	30
Sofala	0	0	0	0	1	2,427	95	26
Inhambane	1	120	10	12.0	2	540	24	23
Gaza	0	0	0	0	2	676	29	23
Maputo (Province)	1	133	13	10.2	2	1,097	66	17
Maputo (City)	0	0	0	0	2	3,031	81	37

Public Education

Institution	1995–1996		1996–1997	
	Students	Teaching Staff	Students	Teaching Staff
Total	6,844	921	7,156	954
Universidade Eduardo Mondlane	5,200	689	5,762	711
Universidade Pedagogica	1,489	201	1,249	217
Inst. Superior Relacoes Internac.	155	31	145	26

Source: http:// www.ine.gov.mz/sector1/educa.htm

Bibliography

In comparison with the former British and French colonies, the Portuguese territories have received much less attention from social scientists and humanists, and even less from scientists. However, the situation improved dramatically immediately following the declaration of war by the liberation movements against the Portuguese government. As a result, the issues shifted from a narrow focus on Portuguese colonial motives, the relations between church and state, the "backwardness" of the Portuguese empire, and the nature of conquest and pacification, to an analysis of the impact of assimilation, taxation and forced labor, ethnic composition and social structure in Mozambique, the nature and impact of capitalism as well as Marxist-Leninist policies, and the effect of regional conflicts that have enriched as well as complicated the experiences of the people living in Mozambique.

The following bibliographic entries include mainly sources in English and in Portuguese not only because of the inadequate number of works in English but also because every center that provides academic training on Lusophone Africa in the United States requires that its students acquire a minimum knowledge of the Portuguese language for research purposes. Some French, German, and Italian materials are also listed. Ethnographic and social works and scientific studies of Mozambique (e.g., detailed geographies) are alarmingly rare, as reflected in the listings. On the other hand, history and political science students are better served at present. Also, the number of articles in periodicals has increased by leaps and bounds since the 1960s.

Four general bibliographic sources were particularly useful in the preparation of this manuscript, namely: Thyge Enevoldsen's and Vibe Johnsen's *A Political, Economic and Social Bibliography on Moçambique, with Main Emphasis on the Period 1965–1978* (Copenhagen: Centre for Development Studies); Susan Jean Gowan's *Portuguese-Speaking Africa. Vol. 2: Mozambique* (Braamfontein, South Africa: S. S. Institute of International

Relations, 1982); Colin Darch's (with Calisto Pacheleke) *World Biblio-graphical Series—Vol. 78, Mozambique* (Santa Barbara, Calif.: ABC Clio, 1987); and M. Cahen's *Documentation bibliographique d'histoire urbaine mozambicaine, 1926–1974* (Paris: University of Paris–VII, 1983). Jill Dias's bibliographic listings in the *Revista Internacional de Estudos Africanos* (vols. 1–7) are also extremely useful, along with a few others available at African Studies Centers in the United States. Equally useful is Brigitte Lachartre's listings in her recent book *Enjeux urbains au Mozam-bique* (Paris: Kathala, 2000), which also helped update some of this re-vised volume's bibliographic entries.

Aspiring researchers and scholars needing primary sources will have to visit the Arquivo Histórico Ultramarino (Overseas Historical Archives) in Lisbon, the Biblioteca da Sociedade de Geografia de Lisboa (the Library of the Geographic Society of Lisbon) in Lisbon, the Arquivo Histórico Militar (Historical Military Archives) in Lisbon, the Public Record and Foreign Offices in London, and the Arquivo Histórico de Moçambique in Maputo. In the United States, the Library of Congress and, as noted ear-lier, several African Studies Centers provide a variety of sources includ-ing works in Portuguese. For students in the American South, the Uni-versity of Virginia, Duke University, and the University of North Carolina at Chapel Hill, combined, and the University of Florida at Gainesville house excellent collections and periodicals for occasional articles and se-rious research manuscripts on Mozambique during the researcher's pre-liminary stages.

For the uninitiated, conducting research on Mozambique is therefore not an easy task, especially so if one cannot read Portuguese or has almost no background on Lusophone Africa and the colonial system that elicited such a radical response (Marxist-Leninist) from the respective revolutionary leaders, following a period of violent struggle to replace the Portuguese colonial state. Thus, where does one start?

Helpful are the general references on Africa, most notably *Africa: South of the Sahara* (Europa) and the *Encyclopedia of Africa South of the Sahara* (Scribners'), edited by John Middleton. These two references are excellent and detailed enough on economics, politics, and social themes in Mozambique. Assisted by this background, one can then venture into some of the best critical publications on history, recent politics, social is-sues confronting Mozambique, and miscellaneous themes. As noted, abundant are primary sources, which can be found in Lisbon at the Ar-quivo Histórico Ultramarino, the Biblioteca da Sociedade de Geografia de Lisboa, and the now-complete Maputo Arquivo Histórico de Moçambique. René Pélissier's volumes on Mozambique history are insightful, succint, analytical, critical, and interesting to read, and their acumen are in sharp contrast to Malyn Newitt's historical writings, including his *A History of Mozambique* (1995), which, although voluminous, is cryptic, tendentious, uncritical, and simply inaccurate in several of its assertions and conclusions. Eduardo Mondlane's *The Struggle for Mozambique* (1969) remains a classic as a quick, easy read and a succint source of information on the Portuguese colonial system. Douglas Wheeler's studies on Gungunhana provide a vivid picture of how sophisticated and proud this leader was in southern Mozambique, although Pelissier's work is still far superior.

On Mozambique politics, the recent works by Chris Alden, *Mozambique and the Construction of the New State* (2001), Anne Pitcher's *Politics in the Portuguese Empire: The State, Industry, and Cotton* (1974), Edmond Keller's and Donald Rothchild's volume on Afro-Marxist regimes (1987), and Margaret Hall's and Tom Young's *Confronting Leviathan: Mozambique since Independence* (1997), provide new insights into the state of Mozambique politics that were impossible to fathom at the time of a single-party system in the country. However, the most controversial and original work, based almost entirely on solid and sound primary sources regarding FRELIMO from its founding to the present, is João M. Cabrita's *Mozambique: A Tortuous Road to Democracy* (2000). To a certain degree, the book complements Luís Serapião's and Mohamad El-Kawas's *Mozambique in the Twentieth Century* (1979). Both Cabrita and Serapião are Mozambicans. Now that Mozambique is moving toward true democracy, books on politics and government are beginning to come out of the press, providing revisionist interpretations, even from scholars who were so pro-Mozambique government during the 1970s and 1980s that they appeared to be nothing but apologists and political advocates of the regime rather than detached and "objective" scholars.

The day-by-day peace process (1989–1992) and beyond can be followed through the accounts of the American envoy to the talks C. Hume's *Ending Mozambique's War: The Role of Mediation and Good Offices* (1994) and the United States Institute for Peace compilations of conference proceedings titled "Dialogue on Conflict Resolution: Bridging Theory and Practice" (1992). The civil war itself (1977–1992) and its causes are well covered by such authors as William Finnegan, Joseph Hanlon, Alex Vines, William Minter, and C. Geffray, and indirectly by many others. The critical issue of Mozambique refugees and their eventual repatriation resulting from the war and the role of international organizations are also well dealt with in UNHCR documents kept in Geneva. The UN volume (1995) titled *The United Nations and Mozambique (1992–1995)* is also useful for those interested in the issue of peace and reconciliation in Mozambique. See also Mario Azevedo's *Tragedy and Triumph* (2002). D. Hoile's *Mozambique: Propaganda, Myth, and Reality* (1991) as well as Carolyn Nordstrom's *A Different Kind of War Story* (1997) and Stephanie Urdang's *And Still They Dance: Women, War, and the Struggle for Change in Mozambique* constitute primers for the study of the new society in war-free Mozambique. Also, anyone interested in Mozambique's present economic conditions will be well served by looking at the various monthly updated publications of the World Bank and the International Monetary Fund. Allen Isaacman's work on cotton in Mozambique (1995), Jeanne Penvenne's study on Mozambique workers (1995), and L. Vail and L. White's volume on capitalism and colonialism (1995), as well as many others, provide a picture of colonial economic policies and labor practices and their impact on Mozambicans.

There are virtually no specialized works on religion, church and state, education and health, ethnography (see A. Rita-Ferreira), foreign relations in Mozambique, except for a few articles here and there and edited book treatises. On education and health, the *United Nations Annual Demographic Data* and World Bank reports are perhaps the only available sources of information. General works on Southern Africa, including *Comprehending and Mastering African Conflicts* (Adebayo Adebeji, 1999), *Brothers at War: Dissidence and Rebellion in Southern Africa* (Abiodun Alao, 1994), *The Dynamics of Change in Southern Africa* (Paul Rich, ed., 1994), *Prospects for Peace and Development in Southern Africa in the 1990s* (Larry Swatuck and Timothy Shaw, 1991), *A Post-Apartheid Southern Africa* (Nance Thede and Pierre Beaudette, 1993), and a few others do provide a perspective on Mozambique in the southern African context, including its role in SADC.

Africa Confidential and *Africa Research Bulletin* are current sources and a gold mine to researchers, providing critical but synoptic data on political, economic, and sociocultural issues in Mozambique and elsewhere in Africa. Finally, except for the general bibliographies on Mozambique listed earlier, the author is not aware of any other published during the 1990s. In sum, despite the existing lacunae in the historiography of the former Portuguese colonies, it is not impossible at this juncture to obtain an accurate picture of colonial and post-colonial Mozambique. Of course, the Internet is a more recent useful source of data. Check www.mozambique.mz;http://www.worldbank.org/data/countrydata/aag/moz_aag.pdf; www.inf.org/external/np/sec/pr/2000/pr0073.htm; and www.ine.gov.mz/sector1/educa.htm.

PART 1

Government Documents

Laws and Statistical Information Sources

[The authors are indebted to Brigitte Lachartre's work, from which this page of the statistical bibliography was taken.]

República Popular de Moçambique. *Lei de Nacionalidade e Constituição do primeiro governo.* 1975.
————. *Programa de 1977.* Maputo, 1977.
————. *Primeira reunião nacional sobre cidades e bairros comunais* (10 vols.). Maputo: Imprensa Nacional, 1979.
Lei 2/79: *Lei dos crimes contra a segurança do povo e do estado popular* (60 pp.). 1979.
Lei de Arrendamento, September 1979 (51 pp.).
Lei da cooperativa, March 1980 (20 pp.).
Lei do Comércio Privado, Septembee 1979 (15 pp.).
Lei de terras, August 1979 (47 pp.).
Lei 10/88: Protecção legal dos béns, materiais e imateriais do património cultural moçambicano, 1988.
República de Moçambique. Constituição da República de Moçambique, 1990.
República de Moçambique. Plano de reconstrução nacional 1994–1996. Maputo, 1996.

Assembleia Popular (People's Assembly)

Relatório sobre as Assembleias do Povo, 2as eleições gerais (45 pp.).
Regulamento interno.
Documentos, 1987 (90 pp.)

Assembleia da República (Assembly of the Republic)

Lei 13/92: Acordo Geral da paz de Moçambique.
Lei 3/94: Quadro Institutional dos Distritos Municipais.
Lei 1/95: Regimento da Assembleia da República.
Resolucao No4/95: Programa do Governo para o período 1995–1999.
Lei 9/96: Princípios e disposições sobre o poder local no texto da Lei Fundamental.
Lei 2/97: Quadro jurídico para a implementação das autarquias locais
Lei 4/97: Comissão Nacional das Eleições.
Lei 5/97: Recenseamento eleitoral sistemático para a realização de eleições e referendos.

Lei 6/97: Quadro jurídico-legal para a realização das eleicoes dos órgaos das autarquias locais.

Lei 7/97: Regime jurídico da tutela administrativa do Estado a que estão sujeitas as autarquias locais.

Lei 8/97: Organização e funcionamento do Município de Maputo.

Lei 9/97: Estudos dos titulares e dos membros dos orgãos das autarquias locais.

Lei 10/97: Criação de municípios de cicades e vilas em algumas circuncrições territoriais.

Lei 11/97: Regime jurídico-legal das finanças e do património das autarquias.

Statistical and Ministerial Documents

Comissão Nacional do Plano. January 1984: *Informação económica* (62 pp.) and *Annexes*.

————. August 1990: *Relatório do seminário nacional de população e planificação do desenvolvimento*, Série População e Desenvolvimento, Doc. No. 1 (72 pp).

————. July 1991: *Bibliografia anotada multidisciplinar sobre população e desenvolvimento em Moçambique*, Série População e Desenvolvimento, Doc. No. 4 (135 pp.).

————. July 1992: *Ilha de Moçambique: Uma população em luta pela sobrevivência e desenvolvimento*, Série População e Desenvolvimento, Doc. No. 5 (60 pp.).

————. December 1992: *Workshop sobre bases metodológicas para investigação das tendências do crescimento da população urbana em Moçambique*, Série População e Desenvolvimento, Doc. No. 6 (127 pp.).

————. November 1994: *Crescimento da população urbana e problemas de urbanização da Cidade de Maputo*, Série População e Desenvolvimento, Doc. No. 11 (85 pp.).

Conselho Coordenador do Recenseamento, 1980: *1º Recenseamento geral da população, panorama demográfico, análise nacional* (34 pp.) and *Annexos*; vol. 4: *População e Escolarização, Educação* (32 pp.); vol. 5: *População, Ocupação e Força de Trabalho* (36 pp.); vol. 6: *Habitação e condições de Vida da População* (24 pp.); vol. 10: *Projecções Demográficas*.

Direcção Nacional de Estatística. May 1993: *Inquérito demográfico nacional, composição por sexo e idade da população abrangida*, Série Inquérito Demográfico Nacional, Doc. No. 1 (42 pp.).

————. September 1993: *Relatório sobre os resultados finais do inquérito as famílias na Cidade de Maputo* (239 pp.).

————. April 1995: *Moçambique: Panorama demográfico e sócio-económico*, Série Inquerio Demográfico nacional, Doc. No. 5 (150 pp.).

Instituto Nacional de Estatística. February 1999: *II Recenseamento geral da população e habitação, resultados definitivos, 1997—Província de Maputo*.

República de Moçambique. December 1993: *Plano de reconstrução nacional, 1994–1996* (62 pp.); *Diagnóstico* (239 pp.); *Annexo Numérico* (86 pp.).
Ministério da Agricultura. April 1982: *Contribuição para o programa de cooperativação do campo.*
Ministério da Administração Estatal. December 1990, 1992: *Programa de reforma dos órgãos locais.*
———. 1993: *Relatório de actividades, program de reforma dos órgãos locais.*
———. May 1997: *Planeamento e gestão urbana em Moçambique, bases para efinição de regulamentos e procedimentos,* Instituto Brasileiro de Administração Municipal (123 pp.).
———. May 1997: *Public Administration Reform: Perspectives and Strategies* (11 pp.).
Ministério de Construção e Águas. 1992: *Departamento de Água e Saneamento, Plano de acção 1990–1992* (19 pp.) e Annexos.
Ministério das Obras Públicas e Habitação. 1979: *Projecto de Inhagóia-Nsalane* (23 pp.).
Ministério das obras Públicas e habitação e PNUD. May 1995: *Delineamento de uma política nacional de tarifação de águas para Moçambique* (125 pp.) e Annexos.
———. Direcção Nacional de Águas. 1997: *Private Sector Participation (PSP), Options and Recommendations, Halcrow* (74 pp.) and Annexes.
———. 1998: *Programa nacional de desenvolvimento do sector águas,* relatório final, Louis Berger International, Maputo, 1988.
Ministério da Indústria, Comércio e Turismo. June–July 1996: *Segundo seminário sobre o sector privado em Moçambique* (93 pp.).
Ministério do Plano e Finanças. May 1997: *Expenditure Management Reform Strategy* (10 pp.).
Secretariado de Estado da Cultura. 1984: *Estudo da valorização urbanística da baixa de Maputo, proposta* (4 pp.).
Ministério da Administração Estatal. May 1997: *Public Administration Reform: Perspectives and Strategies.*
Secretariado do Estado do Planeamento Físico-INPF. April 1984: *Plano, projecto e planeamento físico* (57 pp.).
Comissão Nacional Para os Assentamentos Humanos. 1996: *Relatório nacional sobre assentamentos humanos, Moçambique, preparado pela Habitat* (67 pp.).

General Information

Abshire, D. M., and M. A. Samuels, eds. *Portuguese Africa: A Handbook.* New York: Praeger, 1969.
Africa News. Durham, N.C.
Africa Report. New York.
Alexandro, J., and P. H. Meneses. *Moçambique: 16 anos de historiografia—focos, problemas, metodologies. Desafios para a década de 90.* Maputo: Panel Moçambicano, 1991.

António, José. *Mozambique's Economic Ties with South Africa*. Dar-es-Salaam: Centre for Foreign Relations, 1981.

Bailey, Norman A. "Testimony on Mozambique." *Issue* 5, no. 3 (1975): 14–15.

Botelho, Sebastião Xavier. *Memória estatística sobre os domínios portuguezes na Africa Oriental*. Lisbon: José Baptista Morando, 1921.

Cabral, A. A. Pereira. *Colónia de Moçambique: Indígenas da colónia de Moçambique*. Lourenço Marques: Imprensa Nacional de Moçambique, 1934.

Capela, José (pseudonym). *Moçambique pelo seu povo: Selecção prefácio a notas e cartas de Voz Africana*. Porto: Afrontamento.

Chilcote, R. H. *Portuguese Africa*. Englewood Cliffs, N.J.: Prentice Hall.

Duffy, James. "The Portuguese Territories." In *Africa: Handbook for the Continent*, ed. C. Legum et al. New York: Praeger, 1965, pp. 283–302.

———. *Portugal in Africa*. Harmondsworth, Eng.: Penguin, 1962.

———. *Portuguese Africa*. Cambridge, Mass.: Harvard University Press, 1959.

Duignan, Peter, and L. H. Gann, eds. *Colonialism in Africa, 1870–1960*. Cambridge: Cambridge University Press, 1969–1975.

Edinburgh University. Centre of African Studies. *Mozambique: Proceedings of a Seminar Held in the Centre of African Studies, University of Edinburgh, 1st and 2nd December 1978*. Edinburgh: University of Edinburgh, 1979.

Egero, Bertil. *Mozambique and Southern Africa Struggle for Liberation*. Uppsala: Scandinavian Institute of African Studies, 1985.

Fage, J. D., and Roland Oliver. *The Cambridge History of Africa*. Cambridge: Cambridge University Press, 1975–1984.

Germany (Federal Republic). "Bundesstelle fur Aussenhandels-Information." "Moçambique." In *Afrika Wirtschaftsdaten*. Cologne: Bundesstelle, 1975, pp. 23–30.

Great Britain. Geographical Section of the Naval Intelligence Division, Naval Staff, Admiralty. *A Manual of Portuguese East Africa*. London: H.M. Stationery Office, 1920.

Hanlon, Joseph. *Mozambique: The Revolution under Fire*. London: Zed, 1984.

Hedges, D. *História de Moçambique: Vol. 3. Moçambique no auge do colonialismo, 1930–1961*. Maputo: Departamento de História, EMU, 1993.

Henriksen, Thomas H. "Marxism and Mozambique." *African Affairs* 77, no. 309 (October 1978): 441–62.

Hoile, David. *Mozambique: A Nation in Crisis*. London: Claridge, 1989.

Honwana, Raul Bernardo Manuel. *Histórias ouvidas e vividas dos homens e da terra: Memórias e notas autobiográficas*. Maputo: Author, 1985.

Houser, George, and Herb Shore. *Mozambique: Dream the Size of Freedom*. New York: Africa Fund, in association with the American Committee on Africa, 1975.

Isaacman, Allen and Barbara Isaacman. *Mozambique: From Colonialism to Revolution, 1900–1982*. Boulder, Colo.: Westview, 1983.

Isaacman, Allen, ed. "Mozambique." *African Studies Association* 8, no. 1 (Spring 1978).

Jouanneau, D. *Le Mozambique.* Paris: Karthala, 1995.

Katzenellenbogen, Simon. *South Africa and Southern Mozambique.* Manchester: Manchester University Press, 1982.

Keller, Edmond, ed. *Marxist Regimes.* Denver: Rienner, 1987.

Keller, Edmond, and Louis Picard, eds. *South Africa in Southern Africa: Domestic Change and International Conflict.* Boulder, Colo.: Rienner, 1989.

Lisbon, Instituto Superior de Ciências Sociais e Políticas, *Moçambique: Curso de extensão universitária, ano lectivo de 1964–1965.* Ultramarina, Universidade Técnica de Lisboa, n.d.

Magaia, Albino. *Yo Mabalane!* Maputo: Tempográfica, 1983.

——. *Gostar de ler: Selecção de crónicas e apontamentos e comentários.* Maputo: Tempografica, 1981.

Mozambique. *Portrait of Moçambique.* Lourenço Marques: Government Printing Words (Travel and Desc), 1938.

Msabaha, Ibrahim S. R. *Confrontation and Liberation in Southern Africa.* Boulder, Colo.: Westview, 1986.

Pardal, José da Cunha. *Cambaço: Caça grossa em Moçambique.* Lisbon: Liber-Editorial, 1982.

Recently Published Articles. 1976–. Washington, D.C.: American Historical Association.

Rego, A. da Silva, T. W. Baxter, and E. E. Burke, eds. *Documents on the Portuguese in Mozambique and Central Africa,* 8 Vol. Lisbon: Centro de Estudos Históricos Ultramarinos, 1962–1975.

Secretariado Nacional da OMM. *As nossas receitas.* Maputo: Instituto Nacional do Livro e do Disco, 1981.

Segall, Malcolm. "The Communal Villages of Gaza." *People's Power in Mozambique, Angola and Guiné-Bissau,* no. 11 (January–March 1978): 12–18.

Serapião, Luís Benjamin, and Mohamed A. El-Khaswas. *Mozambique in the Twentieth Century: From Colonialism to Independence.* Washington, D.C.: University Press of America, 1979.

Spence, C. F. *Mocambique: East African Province of Portugal.* Cape Town: Howard Timmins, 1963.

Sykes, John. *Portugal and Africa: The People and the War.* London: Hutchinson, 1971.

Talbot, Stephen. "Marxism in Mozambique." *Nation* 229 (November 10, 1979): 462–63, 466. *Time out in Maputo: A Cooperante's Guide,* 2d ed. [Maputo?]: MAGIC, [n.d.].

UNESCO, International Scientific Committee for the Drafting of a General History of Africa. *General History of Africa.* Berkeley: University of California Press, 1981–1985.

U.S. Congress. *Perspectives on Mozambique.* Washington, D.C.: U.S. Government Printing Office, 1978.

U.S. Department of State. *Mozambique, Background Notes.* Washington, D.C.: Author, 1988.

Viana, Cesário Abel de Almeida et al. *Cozinha moçambicana.* Lourenço Marques: Fundo de Turismo, 1975.

Westman, Bo. *Mozambique: Land Analysis.* Stockholm: Swedish International Development Authority, 1978.

Guides, Maps, Statistics, Geography

Alpers, Edward A. "To Seek a Better Life: The Implications of Migration from Mozambique to Tanganyika for Class Formation and Political Behaviour." *Canadian Journal of African Studies* 18, no. 2 (1984): 367–83.

Anuário Estatístico, 1926/1928–1973. Lourenço Marques: Imprensa Nacional, 1929–1976.

Araújo, Manuel. *Noções elementares da geografia de Moçambique.* Maputo: Publicações Notícias, 1979.

Atlas de Portugal ultramarino e das grandes viagens portuguesas de descobrimento e expansão. Lisbon: Junta das Missões Geográficas e de Investigações Coloniais, 1948.

Atlas Geográfico. [Maputo: Ministério da Educação e Culture,] 1980–1983.

Bibliografia do ultramar português existente na Sociedade de Geografia de Lisboa. Fascículo V: Moçambique. 1970–1973. Lisbon: Sociedade de Geografia de Lisbon, 1973.

Boléo, [José de] Oliveira. *Geografia física de Moçambique (Esboço geográfico).* Lisbon: n.p., 1950.

Boletim Mensal de Estatística. 1925–1975. Lourenço Marques: Imprensa Nacional.

Botelho, Sebastião Xavier. *Memória estatística.* Lisbon: José Baptista Morando, 1833.

Brito, Raquel Soeiro de. "Ilha de Moçambique." *Geographia (Lisbon)* 6, no. 21 (January 1970): 4–21.

Carlyle-Gall, C., ed. *The Colony of Moçambique: A Territory of Vast Potentialities.* London: Mines of Africa, 1938.

Carvalho, Rosa J. B. de. "Contribuição para uma bibliografia geológica dos distritos da Beira, Tete e Vilá Pery." *Boletim do Centro de Documentação Cientifica [de Moçambique* 14, no. 4 (October–December 1971): 260–86.

Companhia de Moçambique. *Censo da população e arrolamento do ano: Ano de 1922.* Beira: Imprensa da Companhia de Moçambique, 1923.

———. *Primeiros resultados do censo da população não indígena realizado em 31 de Dezembro de 1928.* Beira: Companhia de Moçambique, 1929.

"Contribuição para uma bibliografia da região de Tete." *Boletim do Centro de Documentação Cientifica [de Moçambique]* 13, no. 1 (January–March 1970): 42–45.

Costa, Júlio Gaspar Ferreira da. *Atlas de Portugal e colónias: Descriptivo e illustrado.* Lisbon: Empresa Editora do Atlas de Geografia Universal, 1906.

Darch, Colin. "Notas sobre fontes estatísticas oficiais referentes à economia colonial moçambicana: uma crítica geral." *Estudos Moçambicanos* 4 (1983–1985): 103–25.

Delegação portuguesa de delimitação de fronteiras Moçambique-Niassalândia. Lourenço Marques: Junta das Missões Geográficas e de Investigações do Ultramar, 1956.

Dicionário de nomes geográficos de Moçambique: Sua origem. Lourenço Marques: Moderna, 1975.

Direcção de Estatística e Propaganda da Companhia de Moçambique. *Anuário estatístico do Território de Manica e Sofala, sob a administracão da Companhia de Moçambique.* Lisbon Sociedade Nacional de Tipografia, 1930–1934.

Direcção dos Serviços de Agrimensura. *Mapa das povoações criadas até 31 de Dezembro de (1959–) e sua situação legal.* Lourenço Marques: Imprensa Nacional, 1960.

Direcção dos Serviços de Economia e de Estatística Geral. *Recenseamento geral da população civilizada em 1955.* Lourenço Marques: Imprensa Nacional, 1958.

Direcção Nacional de Estatística. *Informação estatística 1975–1984.* Maputo: Comissão Nacional do Plano, 1985.

Direcção Provincial dos Serviços de Estatística. *III recenseamento geral da população na Província de Moçambique.* Lourenço Marques: Imprensa Nacional, 1969.

———. *IV recenseamento geral da população, 1970.* Lourenço Marques: Direcção Provincial dos Serviços de Estatística, 1974.

Estatísticas do Comércio Externo. Lourenço Marques, Moçambique, 1970.

Francis, Donald. "The Demography of the Portuguese Territories: Angola, Mozambique and Portuguese Guinea." In *The Demography of Tropical Africa,* ed. W. I. Brass et al. Princeton, N.J.: Princeton University Press, 1968, pp. 440–65.

Freitas António de. *A geologia e o desenvolvimento económico e social de Moçambique.* Lourenço Marques: Imprensa Nacional, 1959.

Harvey, Joan. *Statistics: Africa: Sources for Social, Economic and Market Research.* Beckenham, Eng.: CBD Research, 1978.

Indice dos rios, lagos e lagoas de Moçambique. Lourenço Marques: Direcção Provincial dos Serviços Hidráulicos, 1969.

Instituto Nacional de Estatística. *Anuário estatístico do império colonial, 1943–1961.* Lisbon: Author, 1945–1962.

Kuder, Manfred. *Moçambique: eine geographische, soziale und wirtschafliche Landeskunde.* Darmstadt: Wissenschafliche Buchgesellschaft, 1975.

Lacerda, F. Gavicho de. *Cartas da Zambézia (assuntos coloniais).* Lisbon: Tipografia do Comércio, 1923.

Livros interessando ao estudo do distrito de Lourenço Marques: Exposição promovida pelo Centro de Documentação e Informação do Banco Nacional Ultramarino com o patrocínio da Associação dos Empregados do Banco em Lourenço Marques em Julho de 1972: catálogo. Lourenço Marques: Banco Nacional Ultramarino, 1972.

Medeiros, Eduardo. "A evolução demográfica da cidade de Lourenço Marques, 1895–1975." *Revista Internacional de Estudos Africanos,* no. 3 (January–December 1985): 231–39.

Mendes, Maria Clara. *Maputo antes da independência.* Lisbon: Instituto de Investigação Científica Tropical, 1985.

Ministério dos Negócios da Marinha e Ultramar. *Anuário estatístico dos domínios ultramarinos portugueses.* Lisbon: Imprensa Nacional, 1905.

Moçambique em números. Lourenço Marques: Direcção dos Serviços de Planeamento e Integração Económica, 1973.

Portugal: Anuário Estatístico do Ultramar (anual). 1900?–.

Real, Fernando. *Geologia da bacia do rio Zambeze, Moçambique: Características geológico-mineiras da bacia do rio Zambeze, em território moçambicano.* Lisbon: Junta de Investigações do Ultramar, 1966.

"Recenseamento da população do Concelho de Lourenço Marques referido a 17 de Abril de 1904." *Boletim Oficial de Moçambique* 48, suppl. (December 1, 1904): 1–12.

Rego, A. da Silva, and Eduardo dos Santos. *Atlas Missionário português.* Lisbon: Centro de Estudos Históricos Ultramarinos, Junta de Investigações do Ultramar, 1964.

Reis, Carlos Santos. *A população de Lourenço Marques em 1894 (um censo inédito).* Lisbon: Centro de Estudos Demográficos, 1973.

Repartição Central de Estatística. "Censo da população não indígena em 2 de Maio de 1935." *Boletim Económico e Estatística,* special series, no. 13 (1936): 1–99.

Repartição de Estatística Geral. "Censo da população indígena da colonia de Moçambique." *Boletim Económico e Estatística,* special series, no. 11 (1932): 1–45.

———. *Recenseamento geral da população em 1950.* Lourenço Marques: Imprensa Nacional, 1953–1955.

Repartição Técnica de Estatística. *Censo da população em 1940.* Lourenço Marques: Imprensa Nacional, 1942–1945.

———. *Estatística Agrícola.* 1941–1972. Lourenço Marques: Imprensa Nacional, 1949.

———. *Estatística Industrial, 1947–1973.* Lourenço Marques: Imprensa Nacional, 1948–1974.

———. *Recenseamento da população não indígena em 12 de Junho de 1945.* Lourenço Marques: Imprensa Nacional, 1947.

Resumo do estado actual da Província de Moçambique dos melhoramentos de que carece, da fertilidade do seu solo e a das riquezas em que abunda, por Marques de Bemposta, II-Pasta C-32 (36 pp.). [Lisbon: Biblioteca da Sociedade de Geografia de Lisboa], 1853.

Robertson, C. L. *The Climate of Rhodesia, Nyasaland, and Mozambique.* Berlin: Gebr. Borntraeger, 1933.

Secretaria Geral da Província de Moçambique. *Recenseamentos da população e das habitações da cidade de Lourenço Marques e seus subúrbios, referidos a 1 de Dezembro de 1912.* Lourenço Marques: Imprensa Nacional, 1913.

Serviços de Agrimensura. *Atlas de Moçambique.* Lourenço Marques: Empresa Moderna, 1962.

Silveira, Luís. *Ensaio de iconografia das cidades portuguesas do ultramar.* Lisbon: Junta de Investigações do Ultramar, [n.d.].

Truão, António Norberto de Barbosa de Villas Boas. *Estatística da Capitania dos Rios de Senna do anno de 1806.* Lisbon: Imprensa Nacional, 1889.

U.S. Board on Geographic Names. *Mozambique: Official Standard Names Approved by the United States Board on Geographic Names.* Washington, D.C.: U.S. Government Printing Office, 1969.

Periodicals

Alberto, Manuel Simões. "Mouzinho e a evolução das normas de administração do ultramar." *Boletim da Sociedade de Estudos de Moçambique*, ano 25, nos. 9495 (1955): 375–93.

Annaes do Conselho Ultramarino (Lisbon). 1854–1864.

Annaes Marítimos e Coloniais (Lisbon). 1840–1846.

Boletim, Arquivo Histórico de Mocambique. 1990s–.

Boletim da Sociedade de Estudos [da Colónia] de Moçambique. Lourenço Marques, December 1931–December 1974, nos. 1176. Quarterly.

Boletim da Sociedade de Geografia de Lisboa (Lisbon). 1876–.

Boletim Geral do Ultramar (Lisbon), 1925–1961 (Also known as *Boletim da Agencia Geral das Colónias* and *Boletim Geral das Colónias*).

O Brado Africano. Lourenço Marques: Grémio [Associação] Africano de Lourenço Marques, December 14, 1918, to November 23, 1974, nos. 1–2, 544. Weekly.

O Campo. Maputo (CP 2546, Avenida Amílcar Cabral no. 214). Gabinete de Comunicação Social, June 29, 1984–. Monthly.

Combate: Órgão de informação das forças armadas de Moçambique (FPLM). Maputo: Comissariado Político Nacional das FPLM, September 25, 1981–. Weekly.

Diário de Moçambique. Beira (Rua D. João de Mascarenhas, CP 81): September 25, 1981–. Daily.

Diário do Governo 1715–. (The official *Portuguese Government Gazette*) 1953.

Domingo. Maputo: Notícias, September 27, 1981–. Weekly.

Lusophone Area Journal Studies, 1982–. (Nigeria)

Lusotopie. (1998?–).

Metical. Fax newspaper. 1999.

Mediafax. Fax newspaper. 2000.

Moçambique: Documentário trimestral. Lourenço Marques: Repartição Técnica de Estatística; Centro de Informação e Turismo, January/March 1935 to July 1961, nos. 1–105.

Não vamos esquecer! Boletim informativo da Oficina de História. Maputo: Centro de Estudos Africanos, Universidade Eduardo Mondlane, February 1983–. Irregular.

Notícias da Beira. Beira: Notícias da Beira, 1951 to September 26, 1981. Nos. 1–11, 568. Daily (from 20 August 1966).
Notícias. Maputo: Sociedade de Notícias, April 15, 1926–. Daily.
Portugal in Africa (Lisbon). 1894–. (A Catholic periodical.)
Revista Internacional de Estudos Africanos. Lisbon, 1984–.
Rumo Novo. Bi-Annual Review. 1995–. Beira: Archdiocese.
Savana, Weekly Newspaper, 1998–. Maputo and Beira.
Studia. Lisbon, Centro de Estudos Históricos Ultramarinos, 1958–1974.
Tempo. Lourenço Marques, Maputo: Tempográfica, September 20, 1970–. Weekly.
Tribuna. Lourenço Marques: Publicações Tribuna, October 7, 1962, to November 12, 1975, nos. 1–3,140.
Ultramar (Lisbon). (Journal of the Portuguese International Community.) 1960–1974.
Voz Africana. Beira: Centro Africano de Manica e Sofala, 1932 to February 15, 1975, nos. 1–556 [?].

Travel and Description

Alberto, Caetano. *A campanha d'África contada por um sargento.* Lisbon: n.p., 1896.
Anthony, Cree. *A Mozambique Sketch Book.* Oxford: Hannon, 1977.
Bernard, Frederick Lamport. *Three Years' Cruise in the Mozambique Channel for the Suppression of the Slave Trade.* London, 1848; repr., New York: Books for Libraries Press, 1971.
Bowdich, T. Edward. *An Account of the Discoveries of the Portuguese in the Interior of Angola and Mozambique.* New York: AMS, 1980.
Burton, Richard, et al. *The Lands of Cazembe: Lacerda's Journey to Cazembe in 1798; Also, Journey of the Pombeiros P. J. Baptista and Amaro José across Africa from Angola to Tete on the Zambeze; and A Resume of the Journey of Mm. Monteiro and Gamitto.* New York: Negro Universities Press, 1969.
Capelo, Hermenegildo. *De Angola à contracosta: Descripção de uma viagem atravez do continente africano [etc.].* Mira-Sintra: Europa-America, [n.d.].
Castilho, Augusto de. *A Zambézia. Apontamentos de duas viagens.* Lisbon: n.p., 1880.
Crimi, Bruno. "Tout est prêt pour le grand tour." *Jeune Afrique* 756 (1975): 35.
Davis, Jennifer. *Building Independence: A Report on a Recent Visit.* New York: Africa Fund, 1977.
Elton, James Frederic. *Travels and Researches among the Lakes and Mountains of Eastern and Central Africa.* Ed. H. B. Cotterill. London: Cass, 1968.
———. "Journal of an Exploration of the Limpopo River." *Journal of the Royal Geographical Society* 42 (June 1873): 1–49.
Erskine, St. Vincent. "Journey of Exploration to the Mouth of the River Limpopo." *Journal of the Royal Geographical Society* 39 (1869): 233–75. Also in *Proceedings of the Royal Geographical Society* 13 (1868–1869): 320–38.

Hess, Robert L., and Dalvan M, Coger. *A Bibliography of Primary Sources for Nineteenth Century Tropical Africa as Recorded by Explorers, Missionaries, Traders, Travellers, Administrators, Military Men, Adventurers and Others*. Stanford, Calif.: Hoover Institution Press, 1972.

Johnston, Sir Harry Hamilton. *British Central Africa: An Attempt to Give Some Account of a Portion of the Territories under British Influence North of the Zambesi*. London: Methuen, 1906.

Lyall, Archibald. *Black and White Make Brown: An Account of a Journey to the Cape Verde Islands and Port Guinea*. London: Heinemann, 1938.

McLeod, Lyons. *Travels in Eastern Africa, with a Narrative of a Residence in Mozambique*. London: Cass, 1971.

Mozambique, Departamento de Turismo. *Estradas e pontes de Moçambique*. Maputo: Departamento de Turismo, 1976.

Munno, Settímio. *In terra d'Africa*. Milan: Pontífico Instituto Missioni Estere, 1958.

Pereira, Francisco Raymondo Moraes. *Account of a Journey Made over and from Quelimane to Angoche in 1753*. Salisbury: Central Africa Historical Association, 1965.

Quintinha, Julião. *Oiro africano: Crónicas e impressões duma viagem jornalística na África oriental portuguesa*. 2d vol. Lisbon: Oficinas Gráficas, 1929.

Rego, Leotte do. *Costa de Moçambique: Guia de navegação*. Lisbon, 1904.

Santos, M. Emília Madeira. *Viagens de exploração terrestre dos portugueses em África*. Lisbon: n.p., 1978.

Silva, Manuel Galvão. "Diário das viagens pelas terras de Manica em 1788. In *Annais do Conselho Ultramarino*, May 1859. Lisbon: Imprensa Nacional, 1867.

Tams, George. *Visit to the Portuguese Possessions in South-Western Africa*. 2 vols. London: Newby, 1845; repr., Negro Universities Press, 1969.

Vasse, Guillaume. *Three Years' Sport in Mozambique*. London; Pitman, 1909.

Wallis, J. P. R., ed. *The Zambezi Expedition of David Livingstone, 1858-1863*. London: Chatto & Windus, 1958.

Woodhead, Cawthra. *Natal a Moçambique*. Porto: Typográphica da Empreza Literária e Typográphica, 1895.

Xavier, Alfredo Augusto Caldas. *Estudos coloniais*. Nova Goa: Imprensa Nacional, 1889.

Bibliographies and Directories

Africa Research Bulletin. 1964–. Monthly. Exeter, Eng.: Africa Research.

AIM Information Bulletin. 1976–. Monthly. Maputo: Agencia de Informação de Moçambique.

Allen, Chris. "Mozambique since 1920: A Select Bibliography." In Mozambique: Proceedings of a Seminar Held in the Centre of African Studies, University of Edinburgh, 1st and 2nd December 1978. Edinburgh: Centre of African Studies, 1979.

Anuário Católico de Moçambique. Lourenço Marques: Conferência Episcopal de Moçambique, 1961–1974.

Anuário de Moçambique. 1914–[1979]. Lourenço Marques: Bayley.

Arbeitsgruppe Dritte Welt. *Moç.: Dokumentation*. Bern: Arbeitsgruppe Dritte Welt, 1974.

Arquidiocese da Beira. *Directório Pastoral*. Beira: Arquidiocese, 1997.

Bender, Gerald J. *Portugal in Africa: A Bibliography of the UCLA Collection*. Occasional Papers, no. 12. Los Angeles: UCLA African Studies Center, 1972.

Bender, Gerald J., and Allen Isaacman. "The Changing Histiography of Angola and Mozambique." In *The Changing Direction of African Studies since 1945: A Tribute to Basil Davidson*, ed. C. Fyfe. London: Longman, 1976, pp. 220–48.

Bibliografia Científica da Junta de Investigações do Ultramar. 1960–. Annual. Lisbon: Centro de Documentação Científica Ultramarina.

Cahen, M. *Documentaation bibliographique d'histoire urbaine mozambicaine 1926–1974*. Paris: Cahen, 130 pp. Multigr., 1983 and 1985.

Catálogo dos livros com interesse para o estudo de Moçambique. Maputo: CEDIMO, 1978.

Catálogo de impressos, mapas e publicações: 1960–76. Lourenço Marques: Depósito de Impressos e Publicações, Imprensa Nacional de Moçambique, 1976.

Chilcote, Ronald H. "African Ephemeral Materials: Portuguese African Nationalist Movements." *Africana Newsletter* 1 (Winter 1963): 9–17.

———."Documenting Portuguese Africa." *Africana Newsletter* 1, no. 3 (1963): 16–36.

———. *Emerging Nationalism in Portuguese Africa 1: A Bibliography of Documentary Ephemera through 1965*. Stanford, Calif.: Hoover Institution Press, 1969 and 1972.

Chonchol, Maria-Edy. *Guide bibliographique du Mozambique: Environment naturel, developpement et organisation villageoise*. Paris: Harmattan, 1979.

Conferência Episcopal de Moçambique. *Directório Catequético Nacional*. Maputo: CEM, 1996.

Conover, Helen F. *A List of References on the Portuguese Colonies in Africa (Angola, Cape Verde Islands, Mozambique Portuguese Guinea, Sao Thome and Principe)*. Washington, D.C.: Library of Congress, 1942.

———. *Bibliography: A List of References on the Portuguese Colonies in Africa*. Washington, D.C.: Library of Congress, 1942.

Costa, Mário. *Bibliografia geral de Moçambique*. Lisbon: Agência Geral do Ultramar, [n.d.].

———. *Bibliography: A List of References on the Portuguese Colonies in Africa*. Washington, D.C.: Library of Congress, 1942.

Cunha, Rosária Silva. *Manuscritos sobre Moçambique na Sociedade de Geografia de Lisboa*. Lisbon: Gulbenkian Foundation, 1962.

Darch, Colin. "Writing and Research on Mozambique, 1975–1980." *Mozambican Studies* 1 (1980): 103–12.

Darch, Colin, and Alice Nkhome-Wamunaz, eds. *Africa Index to Current Periodical Literature*. Oxford: Zell, 1977.

Darch, Colin, and Calisto Archeleke. *World Bibliographical Series 78: Mozambique*. Santa Barbara, Calif.: ABC-Clio Press, 1987.

Dias, Jill R. "Bibliografia das publicações sobre a África de língua oficial portuguesa entre Janeiro de 1975 a Janeiro de 1983." *Revista Internacional de Estudos Africanos* [Lisbon] 1 (January–June 1984): 243–303, continued as "Bibliografia das Publicações Recentes Sobre a África de Língua Oficial Portuguesa," 2 (June–December 1984): 201–27; 3 (January–December 1985): 241–61.

Enes, António. "Lugares selectos da biblioteca colonial portuguesa." *Boletim da Agência Geral das Colónias* 1, no. 7 (August 1925): 153–62.

Enevoldsen, Thyge. *A Political, Economic and Social Bibliography on Mozambique. 1965–1978*. Copenhagen: Center for Development Research, 1978.

Facts and Reports: Press Cuttings on Southern Africa. November 1970–biweekly. Amsterdam: Holland Committee on Southern Africa.

Flores, Michel. "A Bibliographic Contribution to the Study of Portuguese Africa (1965–1972)." *Current Bibliography on African Affairs* 7, no. 2 (Spring 1976): 116–37.

Gibson, Mary Jane. *Portuguese Africa: A Guide to Official Publications*. Washington, D.C.: Library of Congress, 1967.

Gonçalves, José Júlio. *Bibliografia antropológica do ultramar português*. Lisbon: Agência Geral do Ultramar, 1960.

———. *Bibliografia do ultramar português existente na Sociedade de Geografia de Lisboa*, Fasc. IV. Angola. Lisbon, 1963.

Gowan, Susan Jean. *Portuguese-Speaking Africa, 1900–1979: A Select Bibliography. Volume 2: Mozambique*. Bloemfontein: South African Institute of International Affairs, 1982.

Heimer, Franz-Wilhelm. "Obras em língua alemã sobre a África de expressão oficial portuguesa: A colheita dos primeiros anos oitenta." *Revista Internacional de Estudos Africanos*, no. 2 (June–December 1984): 177–99.

Henderson, Robert d'A. "Portuguese Africa: Materials in English and in Translation," *Africa Research and Documentation* 11 (1976): 20–24 and 12 (1977): 15–19.

International African Bibliography: Current Books, Articles and Papers in African Studies. 1973–. Quarterly. London: Mansell for the School of Oriental and African Studies.

International African Institute. *Cumulative Bibliography of African Studies*. Boston: Hall, 1973.

Lapa, Joaquim José, and Fereri Alfredo Brandão Cro de Castro. *Elementos para um diccionário chorográphico da província de Moçambique*. Lisbon: Adolpho, Modesto, 1889.

Legum, Colin, ed. *Africa Contemporary Record: Annual Survey and Documents*. New York: Africana, 1968–1969.

Library of Congress, African Section. *Africa: South of the Sahara: Index to Periodical Literature*, 1900–. Boston: Hall, 1971–1985.

Martins, José Soares and Eduardo Medeiros. "A história de Moçambique antes de 1890: Apontamentos bibliográficos sobre os resultados de investigação entre 1960 a 1980." *Revista Internacional de Estudos Africanos* 1 (1982): 201–16.

Medeiros, Eduardo. *Bibliografia etnográfica macua*. Maputo: Universidade Eduardo Mondlane, 1980.

Ministério das Colónias. *Coimbra: Dicionário corográfico da provincia de Moçambique* Imprensa da Universidade, 1926.

Ministério dos Negócios Estrangeiros, Direcção Nacional do Protocolo. *Missões diplomáticas, consulares e representações de organizações internacionais*. Maputo: Imprensa Nacional, 1985.

Moçambique Director. Lourenço Marques: Bayley, 1952.

Moser, Gerald. *A Tentative Portuguese-African Bibliography: Portuguese Literature in Africa and African Literature in the Portuguese Language*. University Park: Pennsylvania State Libraries, 1970.

Mozambique Laws and Statutes. *Legislação sobre o tránsito em vigor na Província de Moçambique*. Lourenço Marques: Minerva Central, 1971.

———. *Contribuição industrial, código dos impostos sobre o rendimento*. Lourenço Marques, 1969.

Mussassa, Joaquim Chigogoro. "Bibliografia nacional moçambicana, 1975–1984: contribuição mestragem." Unpublished manuscript, Universidade Eduardo Mondlane, 1985.

Pelissier, René. *Africana: Bibliographies sur l'Afrique luso-hispanophone*. Orgeval: Pélissier, 1981.

"The People's Republic of Mozambique." *IDOC Bulletin* [Rome], New Series, nos. 2–3 (February–March 1978): 1–28.

Primeiro catálogo bibliográfico de Moçambique. Lourenço Marques: Imprensa Nacional, 1932.

Relatórios e artigos sobre Moçambique nas colecções do Centro de Estudos Africanos. Maputo: Centro de Estudos Africanos, 1980.

Republic of Mozambique. *Bibliografia anotada multidisciplinar de populacao e planificacao do desenvolvemento, Série População e Desenvolvimento, Doc. No. 1* (72 pp.).

Rita-Ferreira, António. *Bibliografia etnográfica de Moçambique*. Lisbon: Junta de Investigações do Ultramar, 1961.

Scheven, Yvette. *Bibliographies for African Studies 1970/75–*. Waltham, Mass.: Crossroads Press, 1977.

Sopa, António Jorge Diniz. "Catálogo dos periódicos moçambicanos precedido de uma pequena notícia histórica: 1854–1984." Unpublished manuscript, Universidade Eduardo Mondlane, 1985.

Universidade Católica de Moçambique. *Faculdade de Economia e Gestão*. Beira: Author, 2001.

Zubatsky, David S. *A Guide to Resources in the United States Libraries and Archives for the Study of Cape Verde, Guinea (Bissau), São Tomé-Principe, Angola and Mozambique.* Essays in Portuguese Studies, Essay, No. 1 International Conference Group on Modern Portugal, Mimeo (Spring 1977).

PART 2

Culture

Africa: Literatura, Arte e Cultura, July 1978–biannual. Lisbon: Africa Editora.

Alberto, Manuel Simões. "Sinopse das línguas e dialectos falados pelos autóctones de Moçambique." *Boletim do Instituto de Investigação Científica de Moçambique* 2, no. 1 (1961): 51–68.

Albuquerque, O. de. *Maxaquene (Contos).* Maputo: APPACDM de Braga, 1996.

Alpers, Edward A. "The Role of Culture in the Liberation of Mozambique." *Ufahamu* 12, no. 3 (1983): 143–89.

———. "Towards a History of the Expansion of Islam in East Africa: The Matrilineal Peoples of the Southern Interior." In *The Historical Study of African Religion,* ed. Terence O. Ranger and I. N. Kimambo. Berkeley: University of California Press, 1972.

Alves, Albano Emílio. *Dicionário português-chisena e chisena-português.* Beira: Escola de Artes e Ofícios, 1957.

Alves, P. Albino. *Dicionário etimológico bundo-português.* 2 vols. Lisbon: Silvas, 1951.

Amaral, Manuel Gomes da Gama. "O povo yao (mtundu wayao): Subsídios para o estudo de um povo do noroeste de Moçambique." Ph.D. diss., Instituto Superior de Ciências Sociais e Política Ultramarina, Universidade Técnica de Lisboa, 1968.

Andrade, Mário de, ed. *Literatura africana de expressão portuguesa: Vol. I. Poesia. Antologia Temática.* Liechtenstein: Kraus, 1970.

———. *Antologia temática de poesia africana.* Lisbon: Sá da Costa, 1979.

"Antropologia cultural: Algumas referências." *Boletim do Centro de Documentacao Científica [de Moçambique]* 14, no. 1 (January–March 1971): 56–64.

Arquivo Histórico de Moçambique. *Inventário do fim do século XVIII.* Lourenço Marques: Imprensa Nacional, 1958.

"Arte viva em Moçambique." *Cadernos do Terceiro Mundo,* no. 74 (February 1985): 87–94.

Ashton, E. O. *Swahili Grammar.* London: Longman, 1947.

Assis, António de. *Dicionário kimbundu-português.* Luanda: Argente Santos, [n. d.].

Associação Portugal-Moçambique, Delegação do Porto. *As armas estão acesas nas nossas mãos: Antologia breve da poesia revolucionária de Moçambique.* Porto: Ediçoes Apesar de Tudo, 1976.

Barker, Graeme. "Economic Models for the Manekweni Zimbabwe, Mozambique." *Azania* 13 (1978): 71–100.

Beinart, Julian. "Malangatana." *Black Orpheus* (Ibadan, Nigeria), no. 10 [196?]: 22–29.

Binford, Martha Butler. "Stalemate: A Study of Cultural Dynamics." Ph.D. diss., Michigan State University, East Lansing, 1971.

Boletim do Museu de Nampula (Museu Regional "*Comandante Ferreira de Almeida*"), nos. 1–2. Nampula, Mozambique, 1960–1961.

Burness, Donald. *Fire: Six Writers from Angola, Mozambique and Cape Verde.* Washington, D.C.: Three Continents Press, 1977.

Burt, Eugene C. *An Annotated Bibliography of the Visual Arts of East Africa.* Bloomington: Indiana University Press, 1980.

Butselaar, Jan van. *Africains, missionnaires et colonialistes: Les origines de l'Eglise Presbytérienne du Mozambique (Mission Suisse), 1880–1896.* Leiden: Brill, 1984.

Cabral, António Carlos Pereira. *Empréstimos linguísticos das linguas moçambicanas.* Lourenço Marques: Empresa Moderna, 1975.

Cardoso, Carlos. *Directo ao assunto.* Maputo: Tempográfica, 1985.

Carvalho, G. Soares de, et al. "The Quaternary Deposits and the Stone Age Artefacts of the Fluvial Terraces (Olifants' River) on the Earth-Dam Site of Massingir (Gaza Province, Moçambique)." *Memórias do Instituto de Investigação Científica de Moçambique* 10, series B (1975): 73–182.

Castro, Francisco Manuel de. *Apontamentos sobre a língua makua: Gramática, vocabulário, contos, e dialecto de Angoche.* Lourenço Marques: Imprensa Nacional, 1933.

César, Amândio, and Mário António. *Elementos para uma bibliografia da literatura e cultura portuguesa ultramarina contemporânea: Poesia, ficção, memoralismo, ensaio.* Lisbon: Agência-Geral do Ultramar, 1968.

Charrua: Revista Literária. Maputo (CP 4187): Associação dos Escritores Moçambicanos, June 1984–bimonthly.

Chatelain, Ch. W., and H. A. Junod. *Pocket Dictionary Thonga (Shangaan)-English, English-Thonga (Shangaan), Preceded by an Elementary Grammar.* Lausanne: Bridel, 1909.

Coelho, João Paulo Gorges. *Akapwitchi akaporo: Armas e escravos.* Maputo: Instituto Nacional do Livro e do Disco, 1981.

Colectivo de Trabalho. *Trabalhadores dos Caminhos de Ferro de Moçambique e estudantes da Universidade Eduardo Mondlane: A Comuna.* Maputo: Instituto Nacional do Livro e do Disco, 1979.

Conferência Episcopal de Moçambique. *Unidos na esperança pascal: Comunicados da Conferência Episcopal de Moçambique às comunidades cristãs.* Maputo: Author, 2001.

———. *Promover a cultura da vida e da paz.* Maputo: CEM, 1996.

Costa, Maria do Céu. *Evangelização.* Maputo: Nunciatura Papal, [n.d.].

Craveirinha, José. *Cela 1.* Maputo: Instituto Nacional do Livro e do Disco; Lisbon: Edições 70, 1980.

——. *Karingana ua karingana*. Maputo: Instituto Nacional do Livro e do Disco, 1982.

——. *Xigubo*. Maputo: Instituto Nacional do Livro e do Disco, 1980.

Cuenod, R. *Tsonga-English Dictionary*. Bloemfontein: Sasavona, 1967; repr., 1976.

Davies, Chaz, et al. *Tales of Mozambique*. London: Young World Books, 1980.

Departamento de Educação e Cultura. *Poesia de Combate*. Maputo: FRELIMO, 1981.

Depelchin, Jacques. "African Anthropology and History in the Light of the History of FRELIMO." *Contemporary Marxism* 7 (Fall 1983): 69–88.

Dias, J. A. Travessos Santos, et al. *Museu de História Natural: O que e o como visitá-lo*. Maputo: Universidade Eduardo Mondlane, 1979.

Dias, Jorge, et al. *Os macondes de Moçambique*. Lisbon: Junta de Investigações do Ultramar, Centro de Estudos de Antropologia Cultural, 1964–1970.

Dickinson, Margaret, ed. *When Bullets Begin to Flower: Poems of Resistance from Angola, Mozambique and Guinea*. Nairobi: East African Publishing House, 1972.

Dickinson, Ron W. "The Archaeology of the Sofala Coast." *South Africa Archaeological Bulletin* 30, nos. 119–20 (December 1975): 84–104.

Dossier Documents from a Meeting in Maputo between the Mozambican Party and State Leadership and Representatives of Religious Organizations in Mozambique, December 14–17 1982. Maputo: Agência de Informação de Moçambique, 1983.

Duarte, Maria da Luz Prata Dias Teixeira. *Fundo do Governo Geral: Inventário dos relatórios, 1906–1960*. Trabalho de diploma para a Licenciatura, Arquivo Histórico de Moçambique, Universidade Eduardo Mondlane, 1985.

—— (coordinator). *Catálogo dos instrumentos musicais de Moçambique*. Maputo: Gabinete de Organização do Festival de Canção e Música Tradicional, 1980.

Duckworth, Aidron. *Modern Makonde Sculpture*. Syracuse, N.Y.: Syracuse University, [n.d.].

Dupeyron, Pedro. *Pequeno vademecum da língua bantu na província de Moçambique, ou breve estudo da língua chi-Yao ou Adjaua, comparada com os dialectos de Sena, Tete e Quelimane e seguida d'um vocabulário da mesma língua e de Quelimane*. Lisbon: Administração do Novo Mensageiro do Coração de Jesus, [n.d.].

Eça, Filipe Gastão [de Moura Coutinho] de Almeida de. *Mosaico moçambicano. Contos e narrativas*. Lisbon: n.p., 1943.

——. *Subsídios para uma bibliografia missionária moçambicana (católica)*. Lisbon: Author, 1969.

Ehret, Christopher. "Cattle-Keeping and Milking in Eastern and Southern African History: The Linguistic Evidence." *Journal of African History* 8, no. 1 (1967): 1–17.

English-Tsonga, Tsonga-English Dictionary. Bloemfontein: Sasavona, 1978.

Ferrão, Virgílio Chide. *Norte*. Lourenço Marques: Acadêmica, 1975.

Ferraz, Maria de Lourdes Esteves dos Santos de Freitas. *Documentação histórica moçambicana*. Lisbon: Junta de Investigações do Ultramar, 1973.

Ferreira, Manuel. *No reino de Caliban II: Antologia panorâmica da poesia africana de expressão portuguesa*, 30. Volume: Moçambique. Lisbon: Platano, 1985.

———. *O mancebo e trovador Campos Oliveira*. Lisbon Imprensa Nacional-Casa da Moeda, 1985.

Filmao, E. J. *L'image de la femme dans la musique populaire urbaine à Beira (1975–1994): Musique, société et politique au Mozambique*, Mémoire de DEA, EHESS, 1995.

Forjaz, Moira, and Amélia Muge. *Muipiti: Ilha de Moçambique*. Lisbon: Imprensa Nacional-Casa da Moeda,1983.

Fortune, George. *An Analytical Grammar of Shona*. London: Longmans Green, 1955.

FRELIMO. *Terceiro Congresso*. Maputo: Instituto Nacional do Livro e do Disco, 1978.

Frente de Libertação de Moçambique (FRELIMO). *Hinos da revolução*. Lourenço Marques: Imprensa Nacional, 1975.

Fresu, Anna, and Mendes de Oliveira. *Pesquisas para um teatro popular em Moçambique*. Maputo: Tempográfica, 1982.

Fuller, Charles Edward. "An Ethnohistoric Study of Continuity and Change in Gwambe Culture." Ph.D. diss., Northwestern University, Evanston, Ill., 1955.

Garlake, P. S. "Pastoralism and Zimbabwe." *Journal of African History* 19, no. 4 (1978): 479–93.

———. "Mozambique: Excavations at Manekweni." *People's Power in Mozambique, Angola and Guinea-Bissau* 7/8 (June 1977): 10–13.

———. "An Investigation of Manekweni, Mozambique." *Azania* 11 (1976): 25–47.

Gaskin, L. J. P. *A Select Bibliography of Music in Africa, Compiled at the International African Institute*. London: International African Institute, 1965.

Gonçalves, António Carneiro. *Contos e lendas*. Maputo: Instituto Nacional do Livro e do Disco, 1980.

Grupo Cénico das Forças Populares de Libertação de Moçambique. *A sagrada família ou a crítica da crítica do javali, do camaleão, e do Xiconhoca*. Maputo: Instituto Nacional do Livro e do Disco, 1980.

Guerreiro, M. Viegas. *Rudimentos de língua maconde*. Lourenço Marques: Instituto de Investigação Científica de Moçambique, 1963.

Gunhu, António Raimundo da. "Contribuição para o estudo do povo Wayao." Ph.D. diss., Instituto Superior de Ciências Sociais e Política Ultramarina, Universidade Técnica de Lisboa, 1966.

Gwembe, (P.) Ezequiel Pedro, S.J. *Retiros de iniciação: Uma Experimentação na intercultura*. Beira: Archdiocese of Beira, 1999.

Hamilton, Russell G. *Voices from an Empire: A History of Afro-Portuguese Literature*. Minneapolis: University of Minnesota Press, 1975.

Helgesson, Alf Gustav. "The Tshwa Response to Christianity: A Study of the Religious and Cultural Impact of Protestant Christianity on the Tshwa of Southern Mozambique." Master's thesis, Witwatersrand University, Johannesburg, 1971.

Hipolito, Estevaldo. "Maputo mulher: Um filme polémico." *Cadernos do Terceiro Mundo* 80 (August 1985): 88–92.

Honwana, Luís Bernardo. *We Killed Mangy-Dog, and Other Stories.* Trans. Dorothy Guedes. London: Heinemann, 1969.

———, et al. "*A questão da cultura moçambicana.*" *África: literatura, arte e culture* 6 (October–December 1979): 69–72.

Honwana, R. B. *Memórias, Rio Tinto.* Lisbon: ASA, 1989.

Houtart, Francois. *Colonisation portugaise et discours réligieux.* Louvain-la Neuve, Belgium: Centre des Recherches Socio-Religieuses, Université Catholique de Louvain, 1978.

Inter-Territorial Language Committee for the East African Dependencies. *A Standard Swahili-English Dictionary Founded on Madan's Swahili-English Dictionary.* Nairobi: Oxford University Press, 1939.

Isaacman, Allen F. *Mozambique: The Africanization of a European Institution: The Zambesi Prazos, 1750–1902.* Madison: University of Wisconsin Press, 1972.

———. "Madzi-Manga, Mhondoro and the Use of Oral Traditions: A Chapter in Barue Religious and Political History." *Journal of African History* 14, no. 3 (1973): 395–409.

"Islam in Mozambique (East Africa)." *Islamic Literature* 15 (September 1969): 45–53.

João, Multimati Barnabe (pseudonym). *Eu, o povo.* [Lourenço Marques]: FRELIMO, 1975.

Johnston, Sir Harry H. *A Comparative Study of the Bantu and Semi-Bantu Languages.* 1919–1922. Oxford: Clarendon; New York: AMS, 1977.

Junod, Henri Philippe. *Vuthari bye vatsonga (machangana): The Wisdom of the Tsonga-Shangana People.* Bloemfontein: Sasavona, 1978.

———. *The Life of a South African Tribe.* London: Macmillan, 1927.

Katupha, José Mateus Muaria. "A Preliminary Description of Sentence Structures in the a-Saaka Dialect of a-Makhuwa." M.Phil. Dissertation, School of Oriental and African Studies, University of London, 1983.

Kuper, Hilda. "The Shona." In *The Shona and Ndebele of Southern Rhodesia.* London: International African Institute, 1954.

Langa, Alexandre, and Xidimingwana. *Grandes sucessos.* Maputo: Instituto Nacional do Livro e do Disco, 1981.

Lanham, Leonard W. *A Study of Gitonga of Inhambane.* Johannesburg: Witwatersrand University Press, 1955.

Liesegang, Gerhard. "Archaeological Sites on the Bay of Sofala." *Azania* 7 (1972): 147–59.

Lindqvist, Per-Inge. *Archaeology in Mozambique: Report on Research Work, 1982–83.* [Stockholm]: Central Board of National Antiquities, 1984.

Lopes, Policarpo. "Peuple mmeto et christianisme: Partenaires d'un dialogue." Ph.D. diss., Institut International de Catechèse et Pastorale, Université Catholique de Louvain, Belgium, 1975.

Machade, A. J. de Mello. *Entre os Macuas de Angoche.* Lisbon: Prelo, 1970.

Machel, Samora. "O combate cultural no nosso país." *África: literatura, arte e cultura,* no. 5 (July–September 1979): 554–58.

Magaia, Albino. *Assim no tempo derrubado.* Maputo: Instituto Nacional do Livro e do Disco; Lisbon: Edições 70, 1982.

Maggs, Tim. "Some Recent Radiocarbon Dates from Eastern and Southern Africa." *Journal of African History* 18, no. 2 (1977): 161–91.

Magoe, J., ed. *Moçambique, etnicidade, nacionalismo e o estado: Transição inacabada.* Maputo: Centro de Estudos Estratégicos e Internacionais, 1996.

Makavi, Gabriel. *Muambi wa Vubumabumeri.* Bloemfontein: Sasavona, 1980.

Manarte, Manuel (introduction and photographs). *Wood Sculptures of the Maconde People: Album.* Lourenço Marques: Instituto de Investigaçao Científica de Moçambique, 1963.

Margarido, Alfredo, comp. *Poetas moçambicanos.* Lisbon: Casa dos Estudantes do Império, 1962.

Marigoche, M. V. B. *A Visitor's Notebook of Chicewa.* Blantyre: Times Book Shop, [n.d.].

———, ed. "The Social and Economic Background of Portuguese Negro Poetry." *Diogenes* 37 (Spring 1962): 50–74.

Marwick, M. G. "An Ethnographic Classic Brought to Light." *Africa* 34, no. 1 (January 1964): 46–56.

Massimbe, Julieta Marta Álvaro. "A luta armada de Libertação nacional através do Museu da Revolução: Um guia." Unpublished ms., Universidade Eduardo Mondlane, 1985.

Mayoka, J. M. M. *Tuenzi wa vita v ya uhuru wa Msumbiji.* Arusha: Eastern Africa Publications, 1978.

Medeiros, Eduardo. *Bibliografia etnográfica macua: Subsídios para uma bibliografia dos estudos sociais em Moçambique.* Maputo: Faculdade de Letras, Universidade Eduardo Mondlane, 1980.

———. *O sistema linhageiro macua-lomwe.* Maputo: Faculdade de Letras, Universidade Eduardo Mondlane, 1983.

Mendes, Orlando. *As faces visitadas.* Maputo: Associação dos Escritores Moçambicanos, 1985.

———. *Lume florindo na forja.* Maputo: Instituto Nacional do Livro e do Disco, 1980.

———. *País emerso.* Lourenço Marques: Imprensa Moderna, Edição do Autor, 1975–1976.

———. *Portagem.* Maputo: Instituto Nacional do Livro e do Disco, 1981.

———. *Produção com que aprendo: Poesia e pequenas histórias.* Maputo: Instituto Nacional do Livro e do Disco, 1978.

———. *Sobre literatura moçambicana.* Maputo: Instituto Nacional do Livro e do Disco, 1982.

Missionários da Companhia de Jesus. *Dicionário cinyanja-português.* Lisbon: Junta de Investigações do Ultramar, 1963.

Moçambique: A terra e os homens. [Maputo]: Associação Moçambicana de Fotografia, 1982.

Monografia dos principais edifícios e monumentos da Ilha de Moçambique. Maputo: n.p., 1981.

Morais, João. "Mozambican Archaeology: Past and Present." *African Archaeological Review* 2 (1984): 113–28.

Morais, João, and Paul Sinclair. "Manyikeni: A Zimbabwe in Southern Mozambique." In *Proceedings of the 8th Panafrican Congress of Prehistory and Quaternary Studies, Nairobi, 5 to 10 September 1977*, ed. Richard E. Leakey and Bethwell A. Ogot. Nairobi: International Louis Leakey Memorial Institute for African Prehistory, 1977, pp. 351–54.

Moreira, Alexandre. *Practical Grammatical Notes of the Sena Language*. London: Sena Sugar Estates, 1924.

Moreira, Eduardo. *Portuguese East Africa: A Study of Its Religious Needs*. London: World Dominion Press, 1936.

Morosini, Guiseppe. "Tradizione e rivoluzione culturale in Mozambico." *Africa* [Rome] 35, no. 1 (March 1980): 43–84.

Moser, Gerald M. "African Literature in Portuguese: The First Written, the Last Discovered." *African Forum* 88, no. 4 (Spring 1967): 78–96.

———. "African Literature in the Portuguese Language." *Journal of General Education* 13, no. 4 (January 1962): 270–304.

———. *Essays in Portuguese-African Literature*. No. 26. University Park: Pennsylvania State University Studies, 1969.

———. *A Tentative Portuguese-African Bibliography: Portuguese Literature in Africa and African Literature in the Portuguese Language*. University Park: Pennsylvania State University, 1970.

Moser, Gerald, and Manuel Ferreira. *Bibliografia das literaturas africanas de expressão portuguesa*. Lisbon: Imprensa Nacional-Casa da Moeda, 1983.

Motta, Helena. *Moçambique por Eduardo Mondlane*. Maputo: Instituto Nacional do Livro e do Disco, 1984.

"Museu Histórico-Militar do colonialismo em Moçambique." *Tempo* 307 (August 22, 1976): 18–26.

Museu Nacional da Moeda. *O guia do Museu*. [Maputo]: Edições IV Congresso do Partido Frelimo, 1983.

Naguib. *Grito de Paz*. Maputo: Horizonte Arte Difusão, 1986.

Nascimento, J. Pereira do. *Diccionário Portuguez-Kimbundu*. Huila: Typographia da Missão, 1903.

Neves, Francisco de Sousa. "A poesia de Rui de Noronha." *África Literatura, Arte, e Cultura* 1 (July 1978): 17–18.

Nogar, Rui. *Silêncio escancarado*. Maputo: Instituto Nacional do Livro e do Disco, 1982.

Nurse, Derek, and Thomas Spear. *The Swahili: Reconstructing the History and Language of an African Society, 800–1500*. Philadelphia: University of Pennsylvania Press, 1985.

Ogawa, Tadahiro. "*FRELIMO vencerá*. FRELIMO will win." *The Sun* [Tokyo], no. 124 (August 1973). Tokyo: Japan Anti-Apartheid Committee, Youth Section, 1973.

Oliveira, Octávio Roza de. *Museu municipal da Beira.* Beira: Comissão Regional de Turismo, 1975.

Ouwehand, M. *Everyday Tsonga.* Bloemfontein: Sasavona, 1965.

Pacheleke, Calisto. "Relatórios da Curadoria dos Negócios Indígenas existentes no Arquivo Histórico de Moçambique, 1902–1960: inventário." Unpublished ms., Universidade Eduardo Mondlane, 1985.

Patraquim, Luís Carlos. *A inadiável viagem.* Maputo: Associação dos Escritores Moçambicanos, 1985.

———. *Monção.* Maputo: Instituto Nacional do Livro e do Disco.

Paulo, João (Borges Coelho]. *No Tempo do Farelahi.* Maputo: Instituto Nacional do Livro e do Disco, 1984.

[Pereira, Alberto Feliciano Marques]. *Museu de Arte sacra, anexo à Igreja da Misericórdia, Ilha de Moçambique,* [n.p.]: Comissão Provincial das Comemorações Centenárias de Vasco da Gama e Luís de Camões, 1969.

Pereira, António A. "Vocabulário do dialecto chi-sena." *Boletim da Agência Geral das Colónias* 62–63 (August–September 1930): 71–106.

Phillipson, D. W. *The Later Prehistory of Eastern and Southern Africa.* London: Heinemann, 1977.

Polanah, Luís. *The Saga of a Cotton Capulana (História de uma capulana de algodão).* Trans. Tamara L. Bender, with a historical introduction and notes by Allen Isaacman. Madison: African Studies Center, University of Wisconsin, 1981.

———. "O nhamussoro e as outras funções mágico-religiosas." Ph.D. diss., Instituto Superior de Ciências Sociais e Política Ultramarina, Universidade Técnica de Lisboa, 1965.

Prata, António Pires. *Dicionário português-macua.* Cucujães: Sociedade Missionária Portuguesa, 1973.

———. *Gramática da língua macua e seus dialectos.* Cucujães: Escola Tipográfica das Missões, 1960.

———. *A influência da língua portuguesa sobre o suahili e quatro línguas de Moçambique.* Lisbon: Instituto de Investigação Científica Tropical, 1983.

Preto-Rodas, Richard A. *Negritude as a Theme in the Poetry of the Portuguese Speaking World.* University of Florida Humanities Monograph No. 31. Gainesville: University of Florida Press, 1970.

Price, Thomas. *The Elements of Nyanja for English-Speaking Students.* Blantyre: Church of Scotland Mission, 1959.

Ramos, Miguel. "Une enceinte (Monomotapa?) peu connue du plateau du Songo, Mozambique." In *Proceedings of the 8th Panafrican Congress of Prehistory and Quaternary Studies, Nairobi, 5 to 10 September 1977,* ed. Richard E. Leakey and A. Bethwell Ogot. Nairobi: International Louis Leakey Memorial Institute for African Prehistory, 1980, pp. 355–56.

Rebelo, D. J. Soares. "Short Notes on an East Indian Group in Mozambique: The Ismailian Moslem Community." *Southern African Journal of Science* 58, no. 2 (February 1962): 41–44.

Ribeiro, Armando. *Gramática changana (Tsonga)*. Kisubi: Marianum, 1965.

Rita-Ferreira, A. *Groupos étnicos e história pré-colonial de Moçambique: Separata de Moçambique—aspectos da cultura Material*. Instituto de Antropologia, Universidade de Coimbra, 1986.

———. "Etno-história e cultura tradicional do grupo Angune (Nguni)." *Memórias do Instituto de Investigação Científica de Moçambique* II, Series C (1974): 1–247.

———. *Bibliografia etnológica de Moçambique, das origens a 1954*. Lisbon: Junta de Investigações do Ultramar, 1961.

Rocha, Ilídio. "Bibliografia científica de Moçambique: Linguística e literatura." *Boletim do Centro de Documentação Científica [de Moçambique]* 14, no. 2 (April–June 1971): 110–18.

Rzewuski, Eugeniusz. *Bibliografia lingüística de Moçambique: Línguas nacionais*. Maputo: Departamento de Letras Modernas, 1979.

Saba, Sebastião (pseudonym). *A noite dividida*. Maputo: Instituto Nacional do Livro e do Disco, 1981.

Sachs, Albie. *Imagens de uma revolução*. Maputo: Partido Frelimo, 1984.

Sanderson, G. Meredith. *A Dictionary of the Yao Language*. Zomba: Government Printer, 1954.

———. *The Yaos: Chiikala cha wayao*. London: Cass, 1973.

Santos, Luís Feliciano dos. *Dicionário português-chope e chope-português*. Lourenço Marques: Imprensa Nacional, 1949.

———. *Gramática da língua chope*. Lourenço Marques: Imprensa Nacional, 1941.

———. *Guia de conversação português-chope*. Braga: Tipografia Missões Franciscanas, 1953.

Saute, N., and A. Sopa, eds. *A Ilha de Moçambique pela voz dos poetas*. Lisbon: Ediçoes 70, 1992.

Schneider, Betty. "Malangatana of Mozambique." *African Arts* 5, no. 2 (Winter 1972): 40–45.

Schoffeleers, Matthew. "The History and Political Role of the M'Bona Cult among the Mang'anja." In *The Historical Study of African Religion*, ed. Terence O. Ranger and L. N. Kimambo. Berkeley: University of California Press, 1972.

Scott, David Clement. *Dictionary of the Chichewa Language, Being the Encyclopaedic Dictionary of the Mang'anja Language*. Blantyre: Christian Literature Association in Malawi, 1970.

Searle, Chris, comp. *The Sunflower of Hope: Poems from the Mozambican Revolution*. London: Allison & Busby, 1982.

Secção de Arqueologia, Instituto de Investigação Científica de Moçambique. "Arqueologia e conhecimento do passado." *Africa Literatura, Arte, e Cultura* 5 (July–September 1979): 544–51.

Secretariado de Estado da Cultura. *Ilha de Moçambique, Relatório de Moçambique*. Aarhus, Denmark: Ecole d'Architecture de Aarhus, 1982–1985.

Serra, Carlos. *Como a penetração estrangeira transformou o modo de produção dos camponeses moçambicanos: O exemplo da Zambézia (1200–1964)*. Vol. 1: Os *moçambicanos antes da penetração estrangeira*. Maputo: Núcleo Editorial da Universidade Eduardo Mondlane, 1986.

Silva, Clotilde. *Testamento 1*. Maputo: Associação dos Escritores Moçambicanos, 1985.

Silva, Raúl Alves Calane da. *Dos meninos da Malanga*. [Maputo]: Tempográfica, 1982.

Silva, Teresa Cruz. *Iron Age Research in Mozambique: Collected Preliminary Reports*. Maputo: Secção de Pré-História, Centro de Estudos Africanos, Universidade Eduardo Mondlane, 1976.

Sinclair, Paul J. J. *Some Theoretical and Methodological Aspects of Ceramic Studies in Mozambique*. Uppsala: African Studies Programme, 1986.

Sitoe, Bento. *Musongi*. Maputo: Associação dos Escritores Moçambicanos, 1985.

———. *Zambela*. Maputo: Cadernos Tempo, 1983.

Smith, Alan Kent. "The Peoples of Southern Mozambique: An Historical Survey." *Journal of African History* 14, no. 4 (1973): 565–80.

Soares, Paulo. *Música tradicional em Moçambique*. Maputo: Gabinete de Organização do Festival da Canção e Música Tradicional, 1980.

Soares, Paulo Ricardo Ribeiro. "*Produção agrícola e mão-de-obra, 1941–1960: Repertório de documentos do arquivo do Posto Administrativo de Ocua.*" Trabalho de diploma para a Licenciatura, Arquivo Histórico de Moçambique, Universidade Eduardo Mondlane, 1985.

Stout, J. Anthony. *Modern Maconde Sculpture*. London: Kegan Paul, 1966.

Streit, Robert, et al. *Bibliotheca missionum*. Freiburg: Institut für Missionswissenschaftliche Forschung, 1916.

Torrend, Júlio. *A Comparative Grammar of the South African Bantu Languages, Comprising Those of Zanzibar, Mozambique, the Zambezi, Kafirland, Benguela, Angola, the Congo, the Ogowe, the Cameroons, the Lake Region, etc.* London: Kegan Paul, Trench, Trubner, 1891.

———. *Gramática de Chisena: A Grammar of the Language of the Lower Zambezi*. Chipanga: Typographia da Missão de Chipanga, 1900.

Tracey, Hugh. *Chopi Musicians: Their Music, Poetry and Instruments*. London: Oxford University Press for the International African Institute, 1948.

Vail, Leroy, and Landeg White. "Forms of Resistance: Songs and Perceptions of Power in Colonial Mozambique." *American Historical Review* 88, no. 4 (October 1983): 883–919.

Varley, Douglas H. *African Native Music: An Annotated Bibliography*. London: Dawsons of Pall Mall, 1970.

Viegas, Jorge. *O núcleo tenaz*. Maputo: Instituto Nacional do Livro e do Disco, 1981.

Whiteley, W. H. *A Study of Yao Sentences*. Oxford: Clarendon, 1966.

[Wilson, Ralph L., and Elias Mucambe]. *Dicionário práctico português-tshwa*. Bloemfontein: Sasavona, 1978.

Woodward, H. W. "An Outline of Makua Grammar." *Bantu Studies* 2 (October 1926): 269–325.

Xiconhoca o inimigo. Maputo: Departamento do Trabalho do Partido Frelimo, 1979.
Yana. *Que venham!* Maputo: Instituto Nacional do Livro e do Disco, 1981.
Yuphuro. *Yuphuro.* Maputo: Instituto Nacional do Livro e do Disco, 1984.
Zambezi Mission, Inc. *The Student's English-Chicewa Dictionary.* Blantyre: Christian Literature Association in Malawi, 1972.

Economics

Abrahamsson, H., and A. Nilsson. *Mozambique: The Troubled Transition from Socialist Construction to Free Market Capitalism.* London: Zed, 1995.
Adamo, Yussuf et al. "Mozambican Labour to Rhodesia." *Mozambican Studies,* no. 2 (1981): 58–70.
Agronomia Moçambicana. Lourenço Marques: Instituto de Investigação Agronómica de Moçambique, January 1967–June 1974.
Almeida, António Lopes de. "Colonato do Limpopo: Contribuição da cooperativa agrícola no desenvolvimento socio-económico." Ph.D. diss., Instituto Superior de Ciências Sociais e Política Ultramarina, Universidade Técnica de Lisboa, 1970.
Alpers, Edward E. "Trade, State and Society among the Yao in the Nineteenth Century." *Journal of African History* 10, no. 3 (1969): 405–20.
Amorim, J. J. "Alguns preceitos sobre a cultura do milho e breves notas sobre a cultura da batata." Campanha de Produção Agricola Serie B, No. 54 (1954): [n.p.].
Azam, J. P., and J. J. Fauchet. "Offre de biens manufacturés et production agricole: Le cas du Mozambique." Mimeo, 131 pp., 1987.
Azevedo, Mário. "A Sober Commitment to Liberation? Mozambique and South Africa." *African Affairs* 79, no. 317 (1980): 567–84.
Barros, Alfredo Baptista. "Aspectos da produtividade da agricultura em Moçambique: primeira parte." Ph.D. diss., Instituto Superior de Ciências Sociais e Política Ultramarina, Lisbon, 1965.
Bayly, Ernest W. "The Development of Mozambique: Marked Progress Achieved in 1939—Port and Railway Extensions to Continue This Year." *African World* 150 (1949): 84–85.
Bhagavan, M. R. *Some Aspects of Industrial Development in Mozambique.* Stockholm: Swedish International Development Authority, 1977.
Blum, J. M. "Manufacturing Industries in Mozambique: Some Aspects." *Wissenschaftliche Beitrage* (Berlin, GDR), Sondernummer 2 (1976): 69–81.
Bowen, M. "Economic Crisis in Mozambique." *Current History* (May 1990): 217–28.
Bravo, Nelson Saraiva. *A cultura algodoeira na economia do norte de Moçambique.* Lisbon: Centro de Estudos Políticos e Sociais, Junta de Investigações do Ultramar, 1963.
British Overseas Trade Board. *Mozambique.* London: Author, 1977.
Brochman, Grete. "Migrant Labour and Foreign Policy: The Case of Mozambique." *Journal of Peace Research* 22, no. 4 (1985): 335–44.

Cadbury, William A. *Labour in Portuguese West Africa*. 2d ed. New York: Negro Universities Press, 1969.

Cancelas, Alexandre. "A terra e o desenvolvimento comunitário em Moçambique." Ph.D. diss., Instituto Superior de Ciências Sociais e Política Ultramarina, Universidade Técnica de Lisboa, 1965–1966.

Capela, José (pseudonym). *O movimento operário em Lourenço Marques, 1898–1927*. Porto: Afrontamento, [n.d.].

——. *O vinho para o preto: notas sobre a exportação do vinho para Africa*. Porto: Afrontamento, 1973.

Cardoso, F. *Some Experiences in Economic Development Particularly in Industry after the Fall of Colonialism in Mozambique*. Wissenschaftliche Beitrage, Supplementary Issue, 1977, pp. 111–18.

Carvalho, Mário de. *A agricultura tradicional de Moçambique: Distribuição geográfica das culturas e sua relação com o meio*. Lourenço Marques: Missão de Inquérito Agrícola de Moçambique, 1969.

Castelo-Branco, N. "Opções éconómicas de Moçambique 1975–1995: Problemas, lições e ideas alternatives." In *Moçambique. Eleições, democracia e desenvolvimento*, ed. Brazão Mazula. Maputo: Indication d'Edition, 1995, pp. 582–636.

Casting New Molds: First Steps toward Worker Control in a Mozambique Steel Factory: A Conversation with Peter Sketchley and Frances Moore Lappe. San Francisco: Institute for Food and Development Policy, 1980.

Castro, Álvaro de. "Notas sobre o orçamento de 1916–1917." *Relatórios e Informacões* 1 (1918): 127–60.

Centro de Estudos Africanos. *Cotton Production in Mozambique: A Survey*. Maputo: Universidade Eduardo Mondlane, 1981.

Cliff, Julie, Majmi Kanji, and Mike Miller. "Comments and Discussion: The Cooperative Movement in Chokwe, Mozambique." *Journal of Southern African Studies* 11 (April 1985): 295–304.

O comércio externo de Moçambique. Lourenço Marques: Câmara do Comércio de Lourenço Marques, 1968.

Committee on African Studies. *Mozambique Land Law*. Cambridge, Mass.: Harvard University Press, 1981.

Courlon (de) J. *Actividades económicas de pequena escala na área de construção e habitação*. Maputo: n.p., 1993.

Cruz, Miguel Joaquim da. "História da formação da classe trabalhadora em Manica e Sofala ao sul do Púngue, 1892–1926." Ph.D. diss., Eduardo Mondlane University, Maputo, 1982.

Cunha, Joaquim da Silva. *O trabalho indígena: Estudo de direito colonial*. Lisbon: Agencia-Geral das Colónias, 1949.

Darch, Colin. "Trabalho migratório na África austral: Um apontamento crítico sobre a literatura existente." *Estudos Moçambicanos* 3 (1981): 81–96.

Dhliwayo, Kholisile David. "External Traders in the Hinterland of Sofala, 1810–1889." Master's thesis, University of London, 1977.

Ellis, Miller W. "The Mineral Industry of Mozambique." In *Minerals Yearbook 1980*, 3: 691–95. Washington, D.C.: U.S. Government Printing Office, 1982.

"Energy Development in the People's Republic of Mozambique." In *SADCC: Energy and Development to the Year 2000*, ed. Jorge Tavares de Carvalho Simões. Uppsala: Scandinavian Institute of African Studies, 1984.

Estudo nacional de transportes: Relatório final. Copenhagen: Hoff & Overgaard; Stockholm: VIAK, 1978.

Ferraz, Bernardo, and Barry Munslow. *Sustainable Development in Mozambique*. Oxford: James Curry, Africa World Press, 1999.

Ferreira, M. Margarida Ponte. *Cotton in the Mozambican Colonial Economy: A Contribution to the Project "Cotton Production in Mozambique": A Case-Study of Development Problems and Policies*. Oslo: Norsk Utenrikspolitisk Institut, 1982.

Ferrinho, Homero. *Cooperativismo*. Lourenço Marques: Junta das Missões Geográficas e de Investigações Coloniais, 1965.

First, Ruth (pictures by Moira Forjaz). "Work-Songs and Interviews Recorded by Alpheus Manghezi." In *Black Gold: The Mozambican Miner, Proletarian and Peasant*. Brighton, Eng.: Harvester, 1983.

Fitzpatrick, J. "The Economy of Mozambique: Problems and Prospects." *Third World Quarterly* 3, no. 1 (January 1981): 77–87.

Galha, Henrique Terreiro. "Emigração indígena para o Rand: Um problema que preocupa Moçambique." Ph.d. diss., Curso de Altos Estudos Ultramarinos, Lisbon, 1952.

GAPI (Gabinete de Apoio aos de Pequena Industria). *Seminario internacional sobre o sector informal*. Maputo: Author, 1991–1992.

Geresdorff, Ralph von. "Endeavor and Achievement of Cooperatives in Mozambique." *Journal of Negro History* 45, no. 2 (April 1960): 116–25.

Gray, Richard, and David Birmingham, eds. *Pre-Colonial African Trade: Essays on Trade in Central and Eastern Africa before 1900*. London: Oxford University Press, 1970.

Grupo Urbe. *Seminário nacional de estratégias e desenvolvimento urbano e habitacional*, Dossier final. Maputo: Estatutos, November 23–26, 1992, January 1993.

Habermeier, Kurt. "Cotton: From Concentrations to Collective Production." *Mozambican Studies* 2 (1981): 36–57.

Hafkin, Nancy Jane. "Trade, Society and Politics in Northern Mozambique, ca. 1753–1913." Ph.D. diss., Boston University, Massachusetts, 1973.

Hanlon, Joe. "Does Modernisation = Mechanisation?" *New Scientist* (August 24, 1978): 562–65.

——. *Peace without Profit: How the IMF Blocks Rebuilding in Mozambique*. London: Currey, 1996.

Harris, Laurence. "Agricultural Cooperatives and Development Policy in Mozambique." *Journal of Peasant Studies* 7, no. 3 (1980): 338–52.

Harris, Marvin. "Labour Emigration among the Moçambique Thonga: Cultural and Political Factors." *Africa* 29, no. 1 (January 1959): 50–66.

———. *Portugal's African "Wards": A First-Hand Report on Labor and Education in Mocambique.* New York: American Committee on Africa, 1958.

Harris, P. *Work, Culture and Identity: Migrant Labourers in Mozambique and South Africa, c. 1860–1910.* Johannesburg: University of the Witwatersrand Press; London: James Currey, 1994.

Head, Judith Frances. "State, Capital and Migrant Labour in Zambezia, Mozambique: A Study of the Labour Force of Sena Sugar Estates Limited." Ph.D. diss., University of Durham, 1980.

Hedges, David. "Trade and Politics in Southern Mozambique and Zululand in the Eighteenth and Early Nineteenth Centuries." Ph.D. diss., School of Oriental and African Studies, University of London, 1978.

Hermele, Kenneth. *Contemporary Land Struggles on the Limpopo: A Case Study of Chokwe, Mozambique, 1950–1985.* Uppsala: Working Group for the Study of Development Strategies, Department of Development Studies, University of Uppsala, 1986.

Hogblom, Goran, comp. *Mozambique.* Uppsala: International Rural Development Division, Swedish University of Agriculture, Forestry and Veterinary Medicine, 1977.

ILO. *Informal Sector and Urban Employment: A Review of Activities of the Urban Informal Sector.* Geneva: International Labor Organization, 1990.

Isaacman, Allen. "The Mozambican Cotton Cooperative." *African Studies Review* 25, nos. 2/3 (June–September 1982): 5–26.

Isaacman, Allen, and Elias Mandala. "From Porters to Labor Extractors: The Chikunda and Kololo in the Lake Malawi and Tchiri River Area." In *The Workers of African Trade*, ed. Catherine Coquery-Vidrovitch and Paul E. Lovejoy. Beverly Hills, Calif.: Sage, 1985, pp. 209–42.

Jeeves, Alan H. "Over-Reach: The South African Gold Mines and the Struggle for the Labour of Zambezia, 1890–1920." *Canadian Journal of African Studies* 17, no. 3 (1983): 393–412.

Jenkins, Carolyn, Jonathan Leape, and Lynne Thomas. *Gaining from Trade in Southern Africa.* New York: Palgrave, 2001.

Jenkins, P. *Housing and Living Conditions in Peri-urban Areas of Maputo City.* Maputo: UNDP/UNCHS Project, 1991.

Jinadu, L. Adele. *The Social Sciences and Development in Africa: Ethiopia, Mozambique, Tanzania and Zimbabwe.* Stockholm: Swedish Agency for Research Cooperation with Developing Countries, 1985.

Katzenellenbogen, Simon E. *South Africa and Southern Mozambique: Labour, Railways and Trade in the Making of a Relationship.* Manchester: Manchester University Press, 1982.

Keller, Edmond J., and Donald Rothchild. eds. *Afro-Marxist Regimes: Ideology and Public Policy.* Boulder, Colo.: Lynne Rienner Publishers, 1987.

Konczanki, Z. A., T. M. Shaw, and J. L. Parpart, eds. *Studies in the Economic History of Southern Africa.* Vol. I. London: Cass, 1990.

Land Tenure Center. *Land Markets, Employment and Resource Use in the Peri-urban Green Zones of Maputo, Mozambique: A Case Study of Land Market*

Rigidities and Institutional Constraints to Economic Growth. Madison: University of Wisconsin Press, 1994.

Lemos, Manuel Jorge Correia de. "Fontes para o estudo do algodão em Moçambique: documentos de arquivo, 1938–1974." Unpublished ms., Universidade Eduardo Mondlane, 1985.

Lima, A. A. Lisboa. "Caminho de ferro da Suazilândia." *Boletim da Agência Geral das Colónias* 1, no. 1 (July 1925): 13–25.

Loforte, Ana Maria. "Alguns aspectos ligados á exploração da forge de trabalho migrante na Província d'Inhambane entre 1897 e 1928." Ph.D. diss., Universidade Eduardo Mondlane, 1983.

Lyne, Robert Nunez. *Mozambique: Its Agricultural Development.* London: Unwin, 1913.

Macamo, E. *Sobre o sector informal de transportes na Cidade de Maputo.* Maputo: Multigr., 1992.

———. *The Informal Sector in Mozambique as a Cross Reference for Namibia.* Windhoek: University of Nambia & Codesria, multigr, 1992.

———. *A micro e a pequena empresa em Moçambique: Alugumas reflexões.* Seminário IDIL, 1993.

Machel, S. *Produzir é aprender: Aprender para produzir e lutar melhor.* Lisbon: Nova Aurora, 1974.

Mackintosh, Maureen. "Comércio e acumulação: A comercialização do milho na Alta Zambézia." *Estudos Moçambicanos* 4 (1983–85): 77–102.

Manghezi, Alpheus. "Forced Labor by Those Who Lived through It." *Mozambican Studies* 2 (1981): 2635.

———. "The Voice of the Miner." *Mozambican Studies* 1 (1980): 75–88.

Marques, J. Montalvão. "Esboço para uma monografia agrícola do posto-sede dos muchopes e de alguns regulados do Chibuto, Moçambique." Memórias da Junta de Investigação do Ultramar, 2d series, no. 22 (1960): 7–130.

Marshall, J. *War, Debt and Structural Adjustment in Mozambique: The Social Impact.* Ottawa: North-South Institute, 1992.

Middlemas, Keith. *Cabora Bassa: Engineering and Politics in Southern Africa.* London: Weidenfeld & Nicolson, 1975.

"Mozambique." *Communal Villages: People's Power in Mozambique, Angola and Guinea-Bissau* 5 (November–December 1976): 23–35.

Munslow, Barry. "State Intervention in Agriculture: The Mozambique Experience." *Journal of Modern African Studies* 22, no. 2 (1984): 199–221.

Ndulu, Benno, and Ibrahim Elbadawi. *Economic Development in Sub-Saharan Africa.* New York: Palgrave, 1999.

Neil-Tomlison, B. "The Nyasa Chartered Company: 1891–1929." *Journal of African History* 18, no. 1 (1977): 109–28.

Nilson, Aners. *Unmasking the True Face of the MNR.* London: ECASAAMA, 1990.

O'Laughlin, Bridget. "A questão agrária em Moçambique." *Estudos Moçambicanos* 3 (1981): 9–32.

Paiva, Flávio M. Furtado de. "A obra hidroagrícola do Baixo Limpopo: medidas a adoptar para o seu desenvolvimento." Ph.D. diss., Instituto Superior de Ciências Sociais e Política Ultramarina, Universidade Técnica de Lisboa, 1971.

Pasta M-23, Vencimento do governador-geral de Moçambique anos de 1843–1844 a 1889–1890 (Sociedade da Geografia de Lisboa), [n.d.].

Penvenne, Jeanne Marie. "Chibalo and the Working Class: Lourenço Marques, 1870–1962." *Mozambican Studies* 2 (1981): 9–25.

———. "A History of African Labor in Lourenço Marques, Mozambique 1877 to 1950." Ph.D. diss., Boston University, 1982.

———. "Labor Struggles at the Port of Lourenço Marques, 1900–1933." *Review* 8, no. 2 (Fall 1984): 249–85.

———. *The Unmaking of an African Petite Bourgeoisie: Lourenço Marques, Mozambique.* Boston: African Studies Center, Boston University, 1982.

Pitcher, M. A. "Sowing the Seeds of Failure: Early Portuguese Cotton Cultivation in Angola and Mozambique, 1820–1926." *Journal of Southern African Studies,* 17 (1991): 43–70.

Plank, David N. "Aid, Debt, and the End of Sovereignty: Mozambique and Its Donors." *Journal of Modern African Studies* 31, no. 3 (1993): 407–30.

PNUD/UNCHS, and C. Butcher. *Apoio às empresas de pequena escala e micro-empresas no sector da construção no Bairro de Natite em Pemba, 1992: Portos, caminhos de ferro e transportes de Moçambique: Catálogo da esposição biblio-grafia sobre caminhos de ferro de Moçambique realizada em Nampula em Maio de 1973.* Lourenço Marques: Caminhos de Ferro de Moçambique, 1973.

Portos e caminhos de ferro: Ports and Railways. Maputo: National Directorate of Ports and Railways, 1972.

Radmann, Wolf. "The Zambezi Development Scheme: Cabora Bassa." *Issue* 4, no. 2 (Summer 1974): 4754.

Ramos, Mário Rodrigo da Fonseca. "Alguns aspectos sócio-económicos da cultura do chá em Moçambique." Ph.D. diss., Instituto Superior de Ciências Sociais e Politica Ultramarina, Universidade Técnica de Lisboa, 1965.

Report on Native Labour Conditions in the Province of Mozambique, Portuguese [East] A[frica]. *South African Labour Bulletin* 2 (July 1985): 14–27.

República Portuguesa. Colónia de Moçambique. *Legislação sobre trabalho, desem-prego e immigração.* Lourenço Marques: Imprensa Nacional, 1934.

República Portuguesa Ministério das Colónias. *Organização da comissão de me-lhoramentos do distrito de Moçambique.* Lisbon: Imprensa Nacional, 1915.

República Portuguesa. *Orçamento da receita, tabelas da despesa ordinária e extra-ordinária da província de Moçambique para o ano económico de 1918–1919.* Lourenço Marques: Imprensa Nacional, 1918.

Rita-Ferreira, António. *O movimento migratório de trabalhadores entre Moçam-bique e a Africa do Sul.* Lisbon: Centro de Estudos Políticos e Sociais, Junta de Investigações do Ultramar, 1963.

Rodrigues, Armando Lourenço. "A produção no sector indígena de Moçambique." Ph.D. diss., Curso de Altos Estudos Ultramarinos, Lisbon, 1960.

Roesch, Otto. "Reforma económica em Moçambique: Notas sobre a estabilização, a guerra e a formação das classes." *Boletim* 11 (April 1992): 5–35.

———. "Peasants and Collective Agriculture in Mozambique." In *The Politics of Agriculture in Tropical Africa*, ed. Jonathan Barker. Beverly Hills, Calif.: Sage, 1984, pp. 291–316.

———. "Socialism and Rural Development in Mozambique: The Case of Aldeia Comunal 24 de Julho." Ph.D. diss., University of Toronto, 1986.

Schaedel, Martin. *"Eingeboren-Arbeit": Formen der Ausbeutung unter der portugiesischen Kolonialherrschaft in Mosambik*. Cologne: Pahl-Rugenstein, 1984.

Schneidman, Witney. "Conflict Resolution in Mozambique: A Status Report." CSIS Notes. Washington, D.C.: Georgetown University, 1982.

Seabra, Antero Francisco de Salles Pedroso de. "Problemática das 'casas dos pescadores' em Cabo Delgado (Moçambique)." Ph.D. diss., Instituto Superior de Ciências Sociais e Política Ultramarina, Universidade Técnica de Lisboa, 1973.

Silva, Raul Ribeiro dos Santos Delgado. "O problema das oleaginosas: Posição de Moçambique." Diss., Curso de Altos Estudos Coloniais, Lisbon, 1952.

Sketchley, Peter. "Casting New Molds." San Francisco: Institute for Food and Development Policy, 1982.

———. "Forging the New Society: Steel Making in Mozambique." *Southern Africa* 13, no. 7 (September–October 1980): 2–4, 29.

Smith, Alan. "The Trade of Delagoa Bay as a Factor in Nguni Politics, 1750–1835." In *African Societies in Southern Africa: Historical Studies*, ed. Leonard Thompson. London: Heinemann, 1969.

Sogge, David. "Hammer and Hoe: Local Industries under State Socialism in Mozambique." Master's thesis, Institute of Social Studies, The Hague, 1985.

———. *Hammer and Hoe: Local Industries under State Socialism in Mozambique.* The Hague: Institute of Social Studies, 1985.

Sogge, D., ed. *Moçambique: Perspectivas sobre a ajuda e o sector civil.* Oegstgeest: GOM, 1997.

Tarp, F. "Prices in Mozambican Agriculture." *Journal of International Development* 2, no. 2 (1990): 172–208.

Thompsol, Carol. "Regional Economic Policy under Crisis Conditions: The Case of Agriculture within SADCC." *Journal of Southern African Studies* 13, no. 1 (October 1986): 82–100.

Torp, Jens Erik. *Industrial Planning and Development in Mozambique: Some Preliminary Considerations.* Uppsala: Scandinavian Institute of African Studies, 1979.

United Nations. *Cabora Bassa, G.A. Res. 2918, 2979 (XXVII)* in A/8730 (1973).

———. *G.A., A/8148/Add. 1 (1970); E/IT/1968/55 (1970).*

———. *G.A. Disaster Relief UNDRO News, September/October 1987; UNDRO/87/NL/5 (002572) (1988).*

———. *Economic Assistance (000390) A/C.2/39/SR.47 (1985); (001007) TD/B/(XXVII)I/SC.I/L.3 (1985).*

———. *Emergency Relief (000832) OEDA/86/a (1986).* (Special Report on the Emergency Situation in Africa).

——. *G.A. Family Disintegration (001609) (1988)*.

——. *G.A. Inclusion of Mozambique in the List of the Least Developed Countries. E/DEC/1988/105 (00994) (1988)*.

——. *G.A. Primary Health Care (001603) (1987)*.

Vail, Leroy. "Mozambique's Chartered Companies: The Rule of the Feeble." *Journal of African History* 18 (1976): 389–416.

Vail, Leroy, and Landeg White. "Tawani, Machambero: Forced Cotton and Rice Growing on the Zambezi." *Journal of African History* 19, no. 2 (1978): 239–63.

Vletter (de) F. *Sector Informal. Sabemos o que é e quando vemos, Suplemento Económico. Maputo*, 1993.

——. *Estudo sobre o sector informal em Moçambique (Maputo e Sofala)*. Unidade de Alívio à Pobreza. Maputo: Ministério do Plano e Finanças, 1996.

Wardman, Anna. "The Co-operative Movement in Chokwe, Mozambique." *Journal of Southern African Studies* 11, no. 2 (April 1985): 295–304.

Webster, D. J. "The Origins of Migrant Labour, Colonialism and the Underdevelopment of Mozambique." In *Working Papers in Southern African Studies*, ed. P. L. Bonner. Johannesburg: Institute of African Studies, 1978, pp. 236–79.

White, Christine Pelzer, and Alpheus Manghezi. *The Role of Cooperative Agriculture in Transforming Labour Relations and Gender Relations: Experiences from the Green Zones, Maputo, Mozambique*. Brighton, Eng.: Institute of Development Studies, University of Sussex, 1985.

Whitman, Jim. *The Sustainability Challenge for Southern Africa*. New York: Palgrave, 2001.

"Workers' Control in Mozambique." *People's Power in Mozambique, Angola and Guinea-Bissau* 10 (October–December 1977): 21–29.

World Bank. *Mozambique: An Introductory Economic Survey*. Washington, D.C.: Author, 1985.

Wuyts, Marc. "Camponeses e economia rural em Moçambique." *Reforma Agrária* [Sao Paulo, Brazil] 13, no. 6 (November–December 1983): 3–17.

——. "The Mechanization of Present-Day Mozambican Agriculture." *Development and Change* 12 (1981): 1–27.

——. *Money and Planning for Socialist Transition: The Mozambican Experience*. Aldershot: Gower, 1989.

History

AHU. *Moçambique, Relatório do Governador da Província de Moçambique, José Guedes de Carvalho e Menezes, 59-D-15, 1987*. Lisbon: Imprensa do Governo; Arquivo Histórico Ultramarino.

Alberto, Manuel Simões. "Os Angones: Os últimos povos invasores da Angónia portuguesa." *Moçambique: Documentário trimestral*, nos. 2, 3, 4 (1893).

Alberto, M. Simões, and Francisco A. Toscano. *O oriente africano português: Síntese cronológica da história de Moçambique*. Lourenço Marques: Minerva Central, 1942.

Alexandre, Valentim. *Origens do colonialismo português moderno*. Lisbon: Sá da Costa, 1979.

Alexandrino, J., and P. H. Meneses. *Moçambique: 16 anos de historiografia: factos, problemas, metodológias. Desafios para a década de 90*. Maputo: Panel Moçambicano, 1991.

Almeida, Américo Chaves de. *O problema da África oriental portuguesa: A restauração de Moçambique*. Lisbon: Tipografia Inglesa,1932.

Almeida, João Tavares de. "Relatório apresentado pelo Governador-Geral da Província de Moçàmbique à primeira junta geral, em sessão de 3 Outubro de 1859." *Anais do Conselho Ultramarino*, 1859–1861. Lisbon: Imprensa Nacional, 1867, pp. 198–203.

Almeida, Pedro Ramos de. *História do colonialismo português em África: Cronologia*. Lisbon: Estampa, 1979.

——. *História do colonialismo português em Africa: Cronologia I*. Lisbon: Estampa, 1978.

——. *História do colonialismo português em Africa: Cronologia II*. Lisbon: Estampa, 1979.

——. *História do colonialismo português em África: Cronologia III*. Lisbon: Estampa, 1979.

Alpers, Edward A. *Ivory and Slaves in East Central Africa: Changing Patterns of International Trade to the Late Nineteenth Century*. London: Heinemann, 1975.

——. "State, Merchant Capital and Gender Relations in Southern Mozambique to the End of the Nineteenth Century: Some Tentative Hypotheses." *African Economic History* 13 (1985): 23–55.

Amorim [Pedro F.]. Massano de. *Districto de Moçambique: Relatório do Governador. 1906–1907*. Lourenço Marques, 1908.

Anderson, Perry. "Portugal and the End of Ultra-Colonialism." *New Left Review* 15 (1962): 83–102; no. 16 (1962): 88–123; no. 17 (1962): 85–115.

Andersson, G. M. "The Anti-Colonial Revolution: Frelimo—A Short History." *Africa Perspectives* 1, no. 1 (1974): 12–25.

Andrade, A. Freire de. *Relatórios sobre Moçambique II, III*. Lourenço Marques: Imprensa Nacional, 1907.

Andrade, Alfredo Augusto Freire de. *Colonisação de Lourenço Marques*. Porto: Casa Editora, 1897.

Andrade, António Alberto de. *Relações de Moçambique setecentista*. Lisbon: Divisão de Publicações e Biblioteca, Agência Geral do Ultramar, 1955.

Annos, Dezoito. *Em África*. Lisbon: Adolpho de Mendonça, 1898.

Ansprenger, Franz, ed. *Wiriyamu: Eine Dokumentation zum Krieg in Mozambique*. Munich: Kaiser, 1974.

Asiwaju, A. I., et al. *Portugal in Africa*. Atlantic Highlands, N.J.: Humanities Press, 1980.

Auto do processo e da querela contra o major António Maria de Sá de Magalhães, comandante militar da Vila de Sena. Cópia [1-Pasta D-4. Rios de Sena. 17 Agosto 1853. papel 36 x fol. (Biblioteca da Sociedade de Geografia de Lisboa), 1853.

Axelson, Eric. *Congo to Cape, Early Portuguese Explorers.* London: Faber & Faber, 1973.

——. *Portugal and the Scramble for Africa, 1875–1891.* Johannesburg: Witwatersrand University Press, 1967.

——. *The Portuguese in South-East Africa, 1488–1600.* Johannesburg: Oppenheimer Institute of Portuguese Studies, 1973.

——. *The Portuguese in South-East Africa 1600–1700.* Johannesburg: Witwatersrand University Press, 1960.

Azevedo, Mario. "The Delagoa Baia Railway Dispute." *The Researcher* 9 (1981): 1–20.

Baião, R. J. "Brief Glimpses of Labor Questions in the Portuguese Province of Angola." *Trabalho* 5 (1964): 85–101.

Bandeira, Sá de. *Facts and Statements Concerning the Right of the Crown of Portugal to the Territories of Molembo, Cabinda, Ambriz, and Other Places on the West Coast of Africa.* London: Fitch, 1877.

Barratt, Charles John Adkinson. *Developments in Moçambique and Implications for South Africa: Panel Discussion on "Portugal and Africa."* Bloemfontein: South African Institute of International Affairs, 1974.

Bastide, Rober. "Lusotropicology, Race and Nationalism, and Class Protest and Development in Brazil and Portuguese Africa." In *Protest and Resistance in Angola and Brazil*, ed. Ronald H. Chilcote. Berkeley: University of California Press, 1972, pp. 225–42.

Baynham, Simon. "British Military Training Assistance in Southern Africa: Lessons for South Africa?" *Africa Insight* 22, no. 3 (1992): 218–24.

Beach, David N. *The Shona and Zimbabwe, 900–1850: An Outline of Shona History.* Gweru: Mambo, 1984.

Bender, Gerald, and Allen Isaacman. "The Changing Historiography of Angola and Mozambique." In Christopher Fyfe, ed. *African Studies since 1945.* London: Longman, 1976.

Bettencourt, José Tristão de. *Relatório do Governador Geral de Moçambique.* Lisbon: Agência Geral das Colónias, 1945.

——. *Portugal and Africa.* New York: Palegrave, 1999.

——. *Frontline Nationalism in Angola and Mozambique.* London: Currey, 1992.

Boavida, A. *Angola: Five Centuries of Portuguese Exploitation.* Richmond, Canada: Liberation Support Movement, 1972.

Boleo, Oliveira. *Moçambique.* Lisbon: Agência Geral do Ultramar, 1951.

——. *Moçambique: Pequena monografia.* Lisbon: Agência-Geral do Ultramar, 1961.

Boston, Thomas Daniel. "On the Transition to Feudalism in Mozambique." *Journal of African Studies* 8 (1981–1982): 182–87.

Botelho, José Justino Teixeira. *História militar e política dos portugueses em Moçambique de 1833 aos nossos dias.* Coimbra: Imprensa da Universidade, 1921.

Bourne, H. R. Rox. *Slave Traffic in Portuguese Africa: An Account of Slave Trading in Angola and of Slavery in the Islands of San Thome and Principe.* London: King, 1908.

Boxer, C. R. *Four Centuries of Portuguese Expansion, 1415–1825: A Succinct Survey.* Johannesburg: Witwatersrand University Press, 1965.

———. *The Portuguese Seaborne Empire, 1415–1825.* London: Hutchinson, 1969.

———. *Portuguese Society in the Tropics: The Municipal Councils of Goa, Macao, Bahia and Luanda, 1580–1800.* Madison: University of Wisconsin Press, 1965.

———. *Race Relations in the Portuguese Colonial Empire: 1415–1825.* Oxford: Clarendon, 1963.

———. "S. R. Welch and His History of the Portuguese in Africa, 1495–1806." *Journal of African History* 1, no. 1 (1960): 55–63.

———. *The Portuguese Seaborne Empire, 1415–1825.* Harmondsworth, Eng.: Penguin, 1973.

Brangança, A. de, and J. Depelchin. "From the Idealization of Frelimo to the Understanding of Mozambique's Recent History." *Review* 9, no. 1 (Winter 1988): 95–117.

Bragança, Aquino de, and Bridget O'Laughlin. "The Work of Ruth First in the Centre of African Studies: The Development Course." *Review* 8 no. 2 (Fall 1984): 159–72.

Brásio, António. *Monumenta missionária africana: Africa ocidental.* First Series, 11 vols. 1952–1971. Lisbon: Agência Geral do Ultramar (Second Series, 4 vols., 1958–).

Brazão, Eduardo. *Portugal no continente africano: A questão colonial portuguesa na segunda metade do século XIX.* Lisbon: n.p., 1935.

Cabrita, João M. *Mozambique: A Tortuous Road to Democracy.* New York: Palgrave, 2000.

Cadbury, William A. *Labour in Portuguese West Africa.* London: Routledge, 1910; repr., Negro Universities Press, 1969.

Cadernos de História: Boletim do Departamento de História da Universidade Eduardo Mondlane. Maputo: Núcleo Editorial, Universidade Eduardo Mondlane, June 1985.

Caetano, Marcello. *Depoimento.* Rio de Janeiro: Distribuidora Record, 1974.

Cahen, M. *Documentation bibliographique d'histoire urbaine mozambicaine 1926–1974.* Paris: Université de Paris, Laboratoire Tiers Monde–VII.

Cahen, M. *O contexto político-documental da investigação em história Contemporânea e imediata de África lusófona, Boletim* 17, AHM (April 1995): 125–57.

Camacho, Brito. *Moçambique, problemas coloniais.* Lisbon: Guimarães, 1926.

Cambell, H. "War, Reconstruction and Dependence in Mozambique." *Third World Quarterly* 6 (1984): 839–67.

———. "Uma campanha difamatória." *Boletim da Agência Geral das Colónias* 1, no. 2 (August 1925): 123–24.

Campos, António de, Jr. *Victórias d'África. A defesa de Lourenço Marques e as campanhas do valle do Incomáti e do país de Gaza. 1894–1895.* Lisbon: n.p., 1896.

Capão, J. "Ilha de Moçambique: Sem desenvolvimento não há conservação." *Boletim* 4 (AHM) (October 1988): 13–23.

Capela, J., and E. Medeiros. *O tráfico de escravos de Moçambique para as ilhas do Índico, 1720–1902*. Maputo: UEM, 1987.

Capela, José (pseudonym). *O imposto de palhota e a introdução do modo de produção capitalista nas colónias. As ideias coloniais de Marcelo Caetano. Legislação do trabalho nas colónias nos anos 60*. Oporto: Afrontamento, 1977.

———. *Escravatura: A empresa de saque. O abolicionismo (1810–1875)*. Porto: n.p., 1974.

Carvalho, Menezes, J. A. de. *Memória geográfica e política das possessões portuguesas n'Africa Occidental*. Lisbon: Typografia Carvalhense, 1834.

Castro, Eduardo Borges de, ed. *África oriental. Portugal em Lourenço Marques*. Porto: n.p., 1895.

Centre d'Information sur le Mozambique. *Six premiers mois d'indépendance*. Paris: Suppl. à *Libération Afrique*, 1975.

Centre d'Information sur le Mozambique. *Mozambique*. Paris: Sup. à *Libération Afrique*, 1976.

Chagas, M. J. Pinheiro. *As colónias portuguezas no século XIX, 1811–1890*. Lisbon: Pereira, 1890.

Chan, S. *War and Peace in Mozambique*. Basingstoke, Eng.: Macmillan, 1998.

Charlton, Michael. *The Last Colony in Africa: Diplomacy and the Independence of Rhodesia*. Oxford: Blackwell, 1990.

Chilcote, Ronald H. *Portuguese Africa*. Englewood Cliffs, N.J.: Prentice Hall, 1967.

Clarence-Smith, W. G. "The Myth of Uneconomic Imperialism: The Portuguese in Angola, 1836–1926." *Journal of Southern African Studies* 5, no. 2 (1979): 165–80.

Clotilde Mesquita. *Moçambique, acto de Setembro: Memórias da revolução*. Lisbon: Rua, 1977.

Coelho, Agostinho. "Província de Moçambique." Ministério da Marinha e Ultramar: Relatórios dos governadores das provincias ultramarinas." Provincias de S. Thomé e Principe e de Moçambique. Anno de 1883. Lisbon: n.p., 1889.

———. "Relatório do Governador da Província de Moçambique": Relatórios dos governadores 1872–1875, 1883 59-D-15 (Sociedade de Geografia de Lisboa): 104–15.

Coelho, João Paul. *O início da luta armada em Tete, 1968–1969*. Maputo: Arquivo Histórico de Moçambique, 1989.

Colónia portuguesa de Moçambique (A). Lourenço Marques: Imprensa Nacional, 1929.

———. *Viagens, explorações e conquistas dos portugueses: Collecção de documentos*. 6 vols. Lisbon: Imprensa Nacional, 1881.

Comité da África Portuguesa. *A crise nacional, No. 2. A colonização portuguesa*. Lisbon: Tipografia Do Comércio, [n.d.].

Correia de Lemos M.J. "Reviver a Ilha na Mafalala." *Boletim* 4 (AHM) (October 1988): 49–59.

Cortesão, Armando Zugarte. *O problema colonial português*. Lisbon: Typografia da Empresa Diário de Noticias, 1925.

Costa, António Manuel de Castro Sarmento Nogueira da. *Penetração e impacto do capital mercantil português em Moçambique nos séculos XVI a XVII: O caso de Muenemutapa*. Maputo: Cadernos Tempo, 1982.

Costa, Delfim. *Moçambique, nossa terra*. Lisbon: Lucas, 1942.

Costa [Manuel], Gomes da. *A guerra nas colónias: 1914–1918*. Lisbon: n.p., 1925.

Costa, Henrique César da Silva Barahona e. *Apontamentos para a história da guerra da Zambézia (1871–1875)*. Lisbon: n.p., 1895.

Costa, João Rodrigues Nunes da. *Do que eu vi e observei na expedição militar à Província de Moçambique, 1917–1919*. Lisbon: n.p., 1919.

Costa, Tenente Mário. *Como fizeram os Portugueses em Moçambique*. Lisbon: Premiado no Concurso de Literatura Colonial, 1927.

Covane L.A. "Lourenço Marques e o Transvaal, 1825–1928." *Boletim* 2 (AHM) (October 1987): 76–85.

Cruz, Joaquim da Sousa. *A posse da terra em Inhambane, 1885–1930: Textos e documentos seleccionados e anotados*. Unpublished ms., Universidade Eduardo Mondlane, 1985.

D'Andrade, A. Freire. *Relatórios sobre Moçambique VI*. Lourenço Marques: Imprensa Nacional, 1910.

———. *Relatórios sobre Moçambique*. Lourenço Marques: Imprensa Nacional, 1907.

D'Ornellas, Ayres. *Cartas d'África: Campanha do Gungunhana*. Lisbon: Escola Tipográfica das Oficinas de S. José, 1930.

Departamento de História, Universidade Eduardo Mondlane. *História de Moçambique*. Maputo: Tempográfica, 1982.

Descrição Geral das bocas do Zambeze com especialidade do rio Inhamisengo. Augusto de Castilho—Mocambique—18 Julho 1869—papel-7 fol. 11-5-6 (Biblioteca da Sociedade de Geografia de Lisboa).

Dias, Luiz Fernando de Carvalho. "Fontes para a história, geografia e comércio de Moçambique (Séc. XVIII)." *Anais da Junta de Investigações do Ultramar* 9, no. 1 (1954): 1-365.

Duffy, James. *Portugal in Africa*. Baltimore: Penguin, 1962.

———. *Portuguese Africa*. Cambridge, Mass.: Harvard University Press, 1959.

———. *A Question of Slavery: Labor Policies in Portuguese Africa and the British Protest, 1850–1920*. Oxford: Clarendon, 1967.

Egero B. *Moçambique: Os primeiros dez anos de construção da democracia. Estudos* 8, AHM, UEM, 1992: 272.

Egero, Bertil. "Mozambique and the Escalation of the Struggle in Southern Africa." In *Conflict and Change in Southern Africa*, ed. Douglas G. Anglin et al. Washington, D.C.: University Press of America, 1979, pp. 69–113.

Ehnmark, Anders. *Angola and Mozambique: The Case against Portugal*. London: Pall Mall Press, 1963.

Elkiss, T. H. *The Quest for an African Eldorado: Sofala, Southern Zambezia and the Portuguese, 1500–1865*. Atlanta: Crossroads, 1981.

Enes, António. *A guerra d'África em 1895: Mémorias*. Lisbon: Gama, 1945.

——. *Moçambique: Relatório apresentado ao governo.* Lisbon: Imprensa Nacional, 1971.

——. *Plano de operações em Lourenço Marques: Inhambane. II-Pasta-8 3, Abril 1895-4 fol.*

Exposition Coloniale Internationale. *Portugal: Colonie du Moçambique: Sol et climat.* Lourenço Marques: Imprimérie Nationale, 1931.

Felgas, H. A. E. *História do Congo português.* Carmona: Empresa Gráfica de Uige, 1958.

Felner, A. de A. *Angola: Apontamentos sobre a ocupação e início do estabelecimento dos portugueses no Congo.* Coimbra: Imprensa da Universidade, 1933.

Ferreira, [João Gregório] Duarte. *Relatório sobre a sublevação do xeque de Sangage.* Lourenço Marques, 1915.

Ferreira, Joaquina Maria Araújo. "Da importância da Ilha de Moçambique no período filipino." Ph.D. diss., University of Lisbon, 1964.

Finnegan, William. *A Complicated War: The Harrowing of Mozambique.* Berkeley: University of California Press, 1992.

Forjaz M., and A. Muge. *Muipiti, Ilha de Moçambique.* Maputo: Imprensa Nacional, 1983.

FRELIMO. *História da FRELIMO.* Maputo: Departamento de Trabalho Ideológico, 1981.

Friedland, Elaine A. "Mozambican Nationalist Resistance, 1920–1940." *Transafrican Journal of History* 8, no. 1/2 (1979): 117–28.

Galant, G. E. *Mozambik.* Moscow: Mysl, 1974.

Gamito, António Cândido Pedroso. "A escravatura na África oriental."*Arquivo Pittoresco* 2, no. 47 (1859): 369–72; and 2, no. 50 (1859): 397–400.

Geffray, C. *La Cause des armes au Mozambique: Anthropologie d'une guerre civile.* Paris: Karthala, 1990.

Geffray, C., and M. Pedersen. "Nampula en guerre." *Politique Africaine* 29. Mozambique: Guerre et nationalismes; Paris, 1988.

Godinho, Vitorino de Magalhães. *Documentos sobre a expansão portuguesa, 1943–56.* Lisbon: Editorial Gleba, 1960.

——. *L'économie de l'empire portugais aux IV et XVI siècles.* Paris: SEVPEN, 1969.

Gonçalves, José Júlio. *O mundo árabo-islâmico e o ultramar português.* Lisbon: Junta de Investigação do Ultramar, Centro de Estudos Políticos e Sociais, 1965.

Grilo, Velez Hugo. "Mouzinho de Albuquerque e os problemas africanos." *Boletim da Sociedade de Estudos de Moçambique* 25, nos. 94–95 (1955): 397–409.

Hamilton, Geneska Mary. *In the Wake of da Gama, the Story of Portuguese Pioneers in East Africa, 1497–1729.* London: Skeffington, 1951.

Hammond, Richard J. "Race Attitudes and Policies in Portuguese Africa in the 19th and 20th Centuries." *Race* 9, no. 2 (October 1967): 205–16.

——. "Uneconomic Imperialism: Portugal in Africa before 1910." In *Colonialism in Africa 1870–1960*, vol. I, ed. L. H. Gann and P. Duignan. New York: Cambridge University Press, 1969, pp. 352–82.

——. *Portugal and Africa, 1815–1910: A Study in Uneconomic Imperialism.* Stanford, Calif.: Stanford University Press, 1966.

Hanu, José. *Quand le vent souffle en Angola ou le dialogue pathétique du Portugal et de l'Afrique*. Brussels: Brepols, 1965.

Harries, Patrick. "Slavery, Social Incorporation and Surplus Extraction: The Nature of Free and Unfree Labour in South-East Africa." *Journal of African History* 22, no. 3 (1981): 309–30.

Harris, John H. *Portuguese Slavery: Britain's Dilemma*. London: Methuen, 1913.

Hawley, Edward A. "Eduardo Chivambo Mondlane (1920–1969): A Personal Memoir." *Africa Today* 26, no. 1 (1979): 19–24.

Hedges D., coord. *História de Moçambique, vol 3: Moçambique no auge do colonialismo, 1930–1961*. Maputo: Departmento de História, Universidade E. Mondlane, Maputo, 1993.

Henige, David P. *Colonial Governors from the Fifteenth Century to the Present*. Madison: University of Wisconsin Press, 1970.

Henriksen, Thomas H. *Mozambique: A History*. London: Collings; Cape Town: Philip, 1978.

———. "Portugal in Africa: A Non-Economic Interpretation." *African Studies Review* 16, no. 3 (December 1973): 405–16.

———. *Revolution and Counter-Revolution: Mozambique's War of Independence, 1964–1974*. Westport, Conn.: Greenwood, 1983.

———. "Some Notes on the National Liberation Wars in Angola and Mozambique." *Military Affairs* 41 (February 1977): 30–36.

Herbert, Eugenia W. "Portuguese Adaptation to Trade Patterns, Guinea to Angola (1443–1640)." *African Studies Review* 2 (September 1974): 411–23.

Hoile, D., ed. *Mozambique, 1962–1993: A Political Chronology*. London: Mozambique Institute, 1994.

Hoppe, Futz. *Portugiesisch-Ostafrika in der Zeit des Marques de Pombal (1750–1777)*. Berlin: Colloquium Verlag, 1965.

Hromnik, Cyril Andrew. "Goa and Mozambique: The Participation of Goans in Portuguese Enterprise in the Rios de Cuama, 1501–1752." Ph.D. diss., Syracuse University, 1977.

Informação de Vasco Fernandes Homem. Qui foi à conquista do Monomotapa sobre o que se passou na expedição 146-4-66 Letra do século XVI (Biblioteca da Sociedade de Geografia de Lisboa), [n.d.].

Isaacman, Allen, and Barbara Isaacman. *Mozambique: From Colonialism to Revolution, 1900–1982*. Boulder, Colo.: Westview, 1983.

Isaacman, Allen F. (em colaboracão com Barbara Isaacman). *A tradição de resistência em Moçambique: O vale do Zambeze, 1850–1921*. Porto: Edições Afrontamento, 1979.

———. *Mozambique: The Africanization of a European Institution, The Zambesi Prazos, 1750–1902*. Madison: University of Wisconsin Press, 1972.

Isaacman, Allen (in collaboration with Barbara Isaacman). *The Tradition of Resistance in Mozambique: Anti-Colonial Activity in the Zambesi Valley, 1850–1921*. Berkeley: University of California Press, 1976.

Jardim, Jorge. *Para servir Moçambique*. Lisbon: Silvas, 1959.

Jouanneau, Daniel. *Le Mozambique*. Paris: Karthala, 1995.

Kaplan, Irving. *Area Handbook for Mozambique*. Washington, D.C.: Government Printing Office, 1977.

Keith, Henry. "Masters and Slaves in Portuguese Africa in the 19th Century: First Soundings." *Studia* 33 (December 1971): 235–49.

Klein, Herbert S. "The Portuguese Slave Trade from Angola in the 18th Century." *Journal of African History* 10, no. 4 (1969): 533–49.

Labour: Forced or Free? London: Committee for Freedom in Mozambique, Angola and Guinea, Topics No. 1, [n.d.].

Lachartre, Brigitte. *Enjeux urbains au Mozambique: De Lourenço Marques à Maputo*. Paris: Karthala, 2000.

Liesegang, Gerald. "Lourenço Marques antes de 1895." *Boletim* 2 (AHM) (1987): 19–76.

——. "Dingane's Attack on Lourenço Marques in 1833." *Journal of African History* 10, no. 4 (1969).

Lima, A. A. Lisboa. "Prazos da Zambézia." *Boletim da Agência Geral das Colónias*, ano 1, No. 4 (Outubro de 1925): 56–64.

Lima, Américo Pires de. *Explorações em Moçambique*. Lisbon: Agência Geral das Colónias, 1943.

Lima, J. J. Lopes de. *Ensaios sobre a estatística das possessões portuguezas na Africa occidental e oriental: IIIi. Angola e Benguella*. Lisbon: Imprensa Nacional, 1846.

Lobato, Alexandre. *Colonização senhorial da Zambézia e outros estudos*. Lisbon: Junta de Investigações do Ultramar, 1962.

——. *A expansão portuguesa em Moçambique de 1498 a 1530*. Lisbon: Agência Geral do Ultramar; Centro de Estudos Históricos Ultramarinos, 1966.

——. *História do presídio de Lourenço Marques*. Vol. 1 (1782–1786). Lisbon, 1949; vol. 11 (1737–1799), 1960.

——. "A Ilha de Moçambique (Monografia)." *Moçambique: Documentário Trimestral* 42 (April–June 1945).

——. *Quatro estudos e uma evocação para a história de Lourenço Marques*. Lisbon: Junta de Investigações do Ultramar, 1961.

Machado, de Mello. *Entre os macuas de Angoche: História do Moçambique*. Lisbon: Prelo, 1970.

Machel S. *Le processus de la revolution démocratique populaire au Mozambique, textes du président du Frelimo, 1970–1974*. Paris: Harmattan, 1977.

Macieira, José G. "A propósito dos princípios de administração seguidos na colónia." *Boletim da Sociedade de Estudos da Colónia de Moçambique* 1, no. 4 (1932): 49–54.

Magnusson, Ake. *Moçambique*. Uppsala: Utgivaren, Nordiska Afrikainstitutet, 1969.

Manfredi, Cano. *Dominio de los esclavos negros de Mozambique*. Barcelona: de Caralt, 1975.

Martins, E. Augusto de Azambuja. "Situação militar em Moçambique." *Revista Militar* 83, nos. 3–4 (March–April 1931): 184–90.

Martins, Elísio. *Exploração portuguesa em Moçambique, 1500–1973: Esboço histórico*. Kastriep, Denmark: African Studies Editorial, 1975.

Martins, José Soares, and Eduardo da Conceição Medeiros. "A história de Moçambique antes de 1890: Apontamentos bibliográficos sobre os resultados de investigação entre 1960 e 1980." *Revista Internacional de Estudos Africanos* 1 (January–June 1984): 201–16.

Martins, Oliveira. *O Brasil e as colónias portuguesas*. Lisbon: Guimarães, 1978.

Mauro, F. *Le Portugal et l'Atlantique au XVIIe siécle, 1570–1670*. Paris: SEVPEN, 1960.

Mayo, Earl of. *"De Rubus Africanus": The Claims of Portugal to the Congo and Adjacent Littoral, with Remarks on the French Annexation*. London: Allen, 1883.

Minter, William. *Apartheid's Contras: An Inquiry into the Roots of War in Angola and Mozambique*. London: Zed, 1994.

Mondalane, E. *Mozambique: De la colonisation portugaise à la libération nationale*. Paris: Harmattan, 1979.

Mondlane, Eduardo. *The Struggle for Mozambique*. Baltimore: Penguin, 1969.

Montez, Tenente C. "Serviço nas colónias." *Revista Militar* 82, nos. 9–10 (September–October 1930): 552–59.

Moreira, J. *Os assimilados, João Albasini e as eleições, 1900–1922*. Maputo: Arquivo Histórico de Moçambique. *Estudos* 11, 1997.

Mota, A. Teixeira da. *A cartografia antiga da África central e a travessia entre Angola e Moçambique, 1500–1860*. Lourenço Marques: Sociedade de Estudos de Moçambique, 1964.

Moura, João Villas-Boas Carneiro de. *Os últimos anos da monarquia e os primeiros da república em Moçambique*. Lourenço Marques: n.p., 1965.

Mozambique. *Een yolk in beweging: Frelimo*. Amsterdam: Gennep, 1978.

Munslow, Barry. *Mozambique: The Revolution and Its Origins*. New York: Longman, 1983.

Negreiros, Almada. *Le Mozambique*. Paris: (Augustin Challamel), Librairie Maritime et Coloniale, 1904.

Newitt, Malyn. *A History of Mozambique*. Bloomington: University of Indiana Press, 1995.

———. "Angoche, the Slave-Trade and the Portuguese, ca. 1844–1910." *Journal of African History* 13, no. 4 (1972): 659–72.

———. *Portugal in Africa: The Last Three Hundred Years*. London: Longman, 1981.

———. *Portuguese Settlement on the Zambesi, Exploration, Land Tenure and Colonial Rule in East Africa*. Bristol: Barleyman, 1973.

Nogueira, da Costa I. *Contribuição para o estudo do colonial-fascismo em Moçambique. Estudo 1*. Maputo: AHM, UEM, 1986.

———. "O Arquivo Histórico de Moçambique e a Documentaçao do processo de Paz." *Boletim* 17 (AHM) (1995): 181–221.

Nogueira, João. *Socorro que de Moçambique foi a S. Lourenço contra o rei (1635)*. Lourenço Marques: Minerva Central, 1971.

Noronha, Eduardo de. *Freire de Andrade*. C. C., no. 2. Lisbon: n.p., n.d.

———. *Mousinho de Albuquerque*. Lisbon, 1934.

———. *A rebellião dos indígenas em Lourenço Marques*. Lisbon: n.p., 1894.

Noronha, Joáquim Francisco Correia de. *Memória sobre a administração dos prasos do districto de Quelimane*. Orlim: India Portuguesa, 1883.

Núñez, B. *Dictionary of Portuguese-African Civilization*. Vol. I. London: Hurst, 1981.

Oliveira, João Ferreira Craveiro Lopes de. *Os mártires da colonização portuguesa*. Lisbon, 1948.

Penvenne J. "Trabalhadores de Lourenço Marques (1870–1974)." *Antologia de Artigos*, Estudos No. 9, AHM, 216 pp., 1993.

Pereira, L. F. "Algumas notas sobre a Ilha de Moçambique: Património histórico nacional em degradação acelerada." *Boletim* 4 (AHM) (1988): 5–13.

———. "Nota sobre o comércio no norte de Moçambique em meados do século XVIII." *Boletim* 4 (AHM) (1988): 79–83.

Ponte, Bruno da. *The Last to Leave: Portuguese Colonialism in Africa: An Introductory Outline*. London: International Defence and Aid Fund, 1974.

Randles, W. G. L. *The Empire of Monomotapa from the Fifteenth to the Nineteenth Century*. Trans. R. S. Roberts. Gwelo: Mambo, 1981.

Ranger, Terence O. "Revolt in Portuguese East Africa: The Makombe Rising of 1917." In *African Affairs*, ed. Kenneth Kirkwood. London: Chatto & Windus, 1963.

Rego, António da Silva. "Portugal and Africa: A Historical Survey, 1482–1961." In *Southern Africa in Perspective: Essays in Regional Politics*, ed. C. P. Potholm and R. Dale. New York: Free Press, 1972, pp. 151–71.

———. *O ultramar português no século XIX*. Lisbon: Agência Geral do Ultramar, 1970.

———. *O ultramar português no século XVIII*. Lisbon: Agência Geral do Ultramar, 1967.

Relatório do Governador da Província de Moçambique, datado de Moçambique, 31 de Outubro de 1833 por Augusto Coelho (502 pp.).

Renamo. "Manifeste de la Résistance Nationale Mozambicaine." *Politique Africaine* (June 1988).

República Portuguesa. Ministério das Colónias. *Mousinho de Albuquerque, Moçambique, 1896–1898 II*. Lisbon: Divisão de Publicações e Biblioteca, 1934.

Rita-Ferreira, António. *Pequena história de Moçambique pré-colonial*. Lourenço Marques: Fundo do Turismo, 1975.

———. "Historia pré-colonial do Sul de Moçambique: Tentativa de Sintese." *Separata de Studia* nos. 43–44, Lisbon, 1980.

Rocha, Nuno. *Guerra em Moçambique*. Lisbon: Ulisseia, 1969.

Rodney, Walter. "The Year 1895 in Southern Mozambique: African Resistance to the Imposition of European Colonial Rule." *Journal of the Historical Society of Nigeria* 5, no. 4 (June 1971): 509–36.

Rodrigues Júnior, Manuel. *Quando se pensa nos que lutam*. Lisbon: Agência-Geral do Ultramar, 1970.

Roesch, Otto. "Peasants, War and Tradition in Central Mozambique." Conference Paper Presented in 1993. Salisbury: National Archive of Rhodesia (and Nyasaland).

Documentos sobre os portugueses em Moçambique e na Africa Central, 1497–1840. Lisbon: Centro de Estudos Históricos Ultramarinos, 1962.

Santos, Julião Vitorino. *Notas verídicas: 1911 a 1927. Apontamentos para a história colonial.* Lourenço Marques: Typografia Moderna, 1927.

Schapera, Irving, ed. *Livingstone's African Journal. 1853–1893.* 2 vols. London: Unwin, 1963.

Serra, Carlos Manuel Rodriques. *Para a história da arte militar moçambicana, 1505–1920.* Maputo: Cadernos Tempo, 1983.

Silva, José Rui de oliveira Pegado e. "A primeira carta orgânica de Moçambique (1760)." Licenciatura Dissertation, Faculdade de Letras de Lisboa, [n.d.].

Slater, M. *Mozambique.* London: New Holland, 1997.

Slavery in Portuguese Africa: Opposing Views (Containing Works by Nevinson and Monteiro). Repr., Lisbon: Metro Books, 1972.

Smith, Alan K. "The Indian Ocean Zone." In *History of Central Africa*, ed. David Birmingham and Phyllis M. Martin. New York: Longman, 1983.

———. "António Salazar and the Reversal of Portuguese Colonial Policy." *Journal of African History* 1, no. 4 (1974): 653–67.

Sociedade de Geografia de Lisboa. *Congresso colonial nacional de 6 a 10 de Maio de 1924: Teses e actas das sessões.* Lisbon: Composto e Impresso na Tipog. Papel, 1924.

Sousa, Alves de. "A África portuguesa." *Revista Militar* 31, no. 3 (February 15, 1879): 66–70.

Sousa, António Figueiredo Gomes e. "Métodos da colonização e a crise do trabalho." *Boletim da Sociedade de Estudos da Colónia de Moçambique* 3, no. 14 (1934): 37–52.

Sousa, Fernando Louro de. *Moçambique na defesa da Africa e do ultramar Português.* Lisbon: Revista Militar, 1951.

Spence, C. F. *Moçambique (East African Province of Portugal).* Cape Town: Howard Timmins, 1963.

Spinola, António de. *Portugal e o futuro.* Lisbon: Arcadia, 1974.

Theal, George McCall. *Records of South-Eastern Africa, Collected in Various Libraries and Archive Departments in Europe.* Cape Town: Struik, 1964.

Vail, Leroy, and Landeg White. *Capitalism and Colonialism in Mozambique: A Study of Quelimane District.* Minneapolis: University of Minnesota Press, 1980.

———. *Capitalism and Colonialism in Mozambique.* London: Heinemann Educational, 1995.

Venter, A. J. *Portugal's War in Guinea-Bissau.* Pasadena, Calif.: Mungo Africana Library, 1973.

Verschuur, C., et al. *Mozambique, dix ans de solitude.* Paris: Harmattan, 1986.

Villas, Gaspar de Couto Ribeiro. *História colonial.* Lisbon: Grandes Ateliers Gráficas Minerva, 1938.

Vines A. *Renamo: From Terrorism to Democracy in Mozambique.* Amsterdam: Center for Southern African Studies, London, J. Currey, 1991 (2nd.).

Vines, Alex. *RENAMO: Terrorism in Mozambique.* Bloomington: University of Indiana Press, 1991.

Wheeler, Douglas L. "African Elements in Portugal's Armies in Africa, 1961–1974." *Armed Forces and Society* 2, no. 2 (February 1976): 233–50.

——. "Gungunyana the Negotiator: A Study in African Diplomacy." *Journal of African History* 9, no. 4 (1968): 585–602.

Whitaker, Paul M. "The Revolutions of 'Portuguese' Africa." *Journal of Modern African Studies* 8, no. 1 (1970): 15–35.

White, Charles Bryant. "New England Merchants and Missionaries in Coastal Nineteenth-Century Portuguese East Africa." Ph.D. diss., Boston University, 1974.

Williams-Myers, A. J. "Mozambique: Regional Aspects of a Historical Legacy of Resistance." *Journal of Southern African Affairs* 2, no. 1 (1977): 43–60.

Wilson, K. B. "Cults of Violence and Counter-Violence in Mozambique." *Journal of Southern African Studies* (September 1992): 527–82.

Worsfold, W. Basil. *Portuguese Nyassaland: An Account of the Discovery, Native Population, Agricultural, and Mineral Resources and Present Administration of the Territory of the Nyassa Company.* New York: Negro Universities Press, 1899.

Politics

Abegunrin, Layi. "United States–Mozambique Relations since Mozambique Liberation, 1975–1980." *Lusophone Area Studies Journal* (July 1983): 4863.

Acto Colonial, Decreto-Lei No. 22: 465. *Diário do Governo*, Ia série do semestre No. 3 (April 11, 1933): 649–52.

Albuquerque, Joaquim Augusto Mouzinho de. *Moçambique.* Lisbon: Manoel Gomes, 1899.

Alden, Chris. *Mozambique and the Construction of the New African State.* New York: Palagrave, 2001.

Alexander, J. "The Local State in Post-War Mozambique: Political Practice and Ideas about Authority." *Africa* 67, no. 1 (1997): 1–26.

Almada, José d'. *Relacões de vizinhança dos portugueses com os territórios limítrofes.* [Lisbon]: Agência Geral das Colónias, 1944.

Almeida, Fortunato de. "A questão da barca 'Charles et Georges' e o Conselho do Estado." *Separata da Revista de História,* ano VI, No. 23 (June–September 1917): 207–24.

Alpers, Edward A. "The Struggle for Socialism in Mozambique, 1960–1972." In *Socialism in Sub-Saharan Africa: A New Assessment,* ed. Carl G. Rosberg and Thomas M. Callaghy. Berkeley: Institute of International Studies, University of California, 1979.

Armon, J., et al., eds. *Accord: The Mozambique Peace Process in Perspective.* London, Conciliation Resources, 1998.

Assembleia Nacional. *II plano de fomento, 1959–1964.* Lisbon: Imprensa Nacional, 1959.

Austin, Kathi. *Invisible Crimes: U.S. Private Intervention in the War in Mozambique.* Washington, D.C.: Africa Policy Information Center, 1994.

Awepa-Stae, African-European Institute. *Report of AWEPA's Observation of the Mozambique Electoral Process, 1992–1994.* Maputo: Author, 1995.

———. "As Eleições e o município exemplo de uma vila, Banda desenhada." Maputo: Author, 1997.

———. "Democracia, descentralização e eleições autárquicas: Manual de Educação Cívica para Monitores." Maputo: Author, 1997.

———. "Democracia, o município e as eleições autárquicas: Manual de educação cívica para activistas." Maputo: Author, 1997.

Axelson, Eric. "Portugal's Attitude to Nyasaland during the Period of the Partition of Africa." In *The Early History of Malawi*, ed. Bridglal Pachai. London: Longman, 1972, pp. 252–62.

Azevedo, Mario. "A Sober Commitment to Liberation? Mozambique and South Africa." *African Affairs* 79, no. 317 (1980): 567–84.

Balmes, P. "Le Mozambique." *Afrique Contemporaine* 106 (November–December 1979): 8–15.

Basilio, Francisco Xavier. "Antecedentes históricos da reforma administrativa da província de Moçambique de 1907." Ph.D. diss., Instituto Superior de Ciências Sociais e Política Ultramarina, Lisbon, 1965.

Beckett, I. "The Portuguese Army: The Campaign in Mozambique, 1964–1974." In *Armed Forces and Modern Counterinsurgency*, ed. I. Beckett and J. Pimlott. London: Croom Helm, 1977, pp. 136–62.

Berman, E. *Managing Arms in Peace Processes: Mozambique.* New York: United Nations, 1996.

Bhagavan, M. R. *Some Aspects of International Development in Mozambique.* Stockholm, Swedish International Development Authority, 1977.

Birmingham, D. *Frontline Nationalism in Angola and Mozambique.* London: Currey, 1992.

Bissio, Beatriz. "Mozambique: Las areas liberadas." *Cuadernos del Tercer Mundo* (Spanish ed.) 12 (May 1977): 31–42.

Bossen, Gerd D. "Angola and Mozambique vis-à-vis South Africa." *Aussenpolitik* (English ed.) 35, no. 3 (Third Quarter 1984): 281–94.

Botelho, José Justino. "A primeira carta orgânica de Moçambique." *Boletim da Academia das Ciências de Lisboa*, nova série a (1930): 24–32.

Botha, P. "Mozambique: The Democratic People's Revolution Fails." *Africa Insight*, 13 (1983): 1304.

Bragança, Aquino de. "O marxismo de Samora." *Três Continentes* [Lisbon] 3 (September 1980): 43–50.

Bragança, Aquino de, and Immanuel Wallerstein, eds. *The African Liberation Reader*. London: Zed, 1982.

Breytenbach, Wilhelmus Josephus. "Governmental and Power Structure in Moçambique." *Africa Institute of South Africa Bulletin* 8 (1977): 208–11.

Brionne, Bernard. "Le canal du Mozambique et la sécurité de l'Afrique du Sud." *Défense Nationale* 32 (February 1976): 125–41.

Bruce, Neil. "Angola and Mozambique: A Short Economic Survey." *Bolsa Review* 6, no. 72 (December 1972): 660–68.

———. *Portugal: The Last Empire*. New York: Wiley, 1975.

Caetano, Marcello. *Do conselho ultramarino ao conselho do império*. Lisbon: Ática, 1943.

———. *Relações das colónias de Angola e Moçambique com os territórios estrangeiros vizinhos*. Lisbon: Imprensa Nacional de Lisboa, 1946.

Cahen, M. "État et pouvoir populaire dans le Mozambique indépendant." *Politique Africaine*, no. 19: L'Afrique australe face à Pretoria. Paris: Karthala, 1985.

———. "Le Portugal et l'Afrique: Le cas des relations luso-mozambicaines 1965–1985. Etude politique et bibliographique." *Afrique Contemporaine* 137 (January–March 1986): 3–55.

———. "Mozambique: Dhlakama é maningue nice: Un ex-guerilla atypique dans la campagne électorale." *L'Afrique politique*. CEAN. Paris: Karthala, 1995.

———. "Corporatisme et colonialisme: Approache du cas mozambicain, 1933–1979." *Cahiers d'Etudes Africaines* 23, no. 4, no. 92 (1983): 383–417; 24, no. 1, no. 93 (1984): 5–24.

———. "Notes pour une lecture économique de l'Accord de Nkomati." *Estudos de Economia* (Lisboa) 6, no. 3 (April–June 1986): 421–49.

———. "Le Portugal et l'Afrique: Le cas des rélations luso-mozambicaines (1965–1985): Étude politique et bibliographique." *Afrique Contemporaine* 137 (January–March 1986): 3–55.

———. "Check on Socialism in Mozambique." *Review of African Political Economy* 57 (1993): 46–59.

Calvert, Michael. "Counter-insurgency in Mozambique." *Royal United Services Institute Journal* 188, no. 1 (1973): 81–85.

Cann, J. P. *Counter-Insurgency in Africa: The Portuguese Way of War 1961–1974*. Westport, Conn.: Greenwood, 1997.

Capão, José Armando Vidal. "Autoridades tradicionais de Magude, 1895–1975: Repertório de documentos." Trabalho de diploma para a Licenciatura, Arquivo Histórico de Moçambique, Universidade Eduardo Mondlane, 1985.

Chabal, P. "People's War, State Formation and Revolution in Africa: A Comparative Analysis of Mozambique, Guinea-Bissau and Angola." *Journal of Commonwealth and Comparative Politics* 21 (1983): 104–25.

Chilcote, Ronald H. *Emerging Nationalism in Portuguese Africa: Vol. II. Documents*. Stanford, Calif.: Hoover Institute Press, 1972.

Chimango, L. J. "The Relevance of Humanitarian International Law to the Liberation Struggles in Southern Africa: The Case of Moçambique in Retrospect."

Comparative and International Law Journal of Southern Africa 8, no. 3 (1975): 287–317.

Clarence-Smith, Gervase. "The Roots of the Mozambique Counter-Revolution." *Southern African Review of Books* (April–May 1989).

Cline, Sybil. "Renamo, Anti-Communist Insurgents in Mozambique." Washington, D.C.: U.S. Global Strategy Council, 1989.

Clough, Michael. "American Policy Options." *Africa Report* 27, no. 6 (November–December 1982): 14–17.

Coelho, César Augusto Ferreira de Castro. "As reformas de 6 de Setembro de 1961 e sua incidência político-social em Moçambique." Ph.D. diss., Instituto Superior de Ciências Sociais e Política Ultramarina, Universidade Técnica de Lisboa, 1964.

Cohen, Herman. *Intervening in Africa*. New York: Palgrave, 2000.

Colins, C. "Mozambique, Humanizing the People." *Issue* 8 (Spring 1978): 1216.

Colónia de Moçambique. *Legislação sobre Concessão de terrenos e sua tributação (1913–1942)*. Lourenço Marques: Imprensa Nacional de Moçambique, 1943.

Conferência Episcopal de Moçambique. *Diálogo, Caminho para a democracia: Carta pastoral dos bispos católicos de Moçambique*. Maputo: Author, 2001.

"A confissão da PIDE-DGS." *Cadernos do Terceiro Mundo* 38 (November 1981): 94–97.

Cornwall, Barbara. *The Bush Rebels: A Personal Account of Black Revolt in Africa*. New York: Holt, Rinehart & Winston, 1972.

Correia, Jorge. *Renamo: Resistência Nacional Moçambicana*. Lisbon: Forum Moçambicano, 1989.

Costa, Eduardo da. *Estudo sobre a administração civil das nossas possessões africanas: Memória*. Lisbon: Imprensa Nacional, 1903.

Crocker, Chester. *High Noon in Southern Africa*. New York: Norton, 1992.

Darch, Colin. "Published Documentation of the Party Frelimo: A Preliminary Study." *Mozambican Studies*, no. 2 (1981): 104–25. *Documentos base de FRELIMO, 1*. Maputo: Tempografica, 1977.

———. "Are There Warlords in Provincial Mozambique? Question of the Social Base of MNR Banditry." *Review of African Political Economy* 46/47 (1990): 34–49.

Davidson, Basil. "The Liberation Struggle in Angola and 'Portuguese' Guinea." *African Quarterly* 10, no. 1 (1970–1971): 25–39.

———. *The People's Cause: A History of Guerrillas in Africa*. Harlow, Eng.: Longman, 1981.

———. "The Politics of Armed Struggle: National Liberation in the African Colonies of Portugal." In *Southern Africa: The New Politics of Revolution*, ed. Basil Davidson et al. Harmondsworth: Penguin, 1976.

Davis, Jennifer. *The Republic of Guinea-Bissau: Triumph over Colonialism*. New York: Africa Fund, 1976.

Davis, R. *South Africa Strategy towards Mozambique in the Post-Nkomati Period: A Critical Analysis of Effects and Implications*. Uppsala: Scandinavian Institute for African Studies, 1985.

———. "*Implications for Southern Africa of the Current Impasse in the Peace Process in Mozambique.*" Bellville: University of the Western Cape, Centre for Southern African Studies, Working Paper, no. 9, 1991.

Decraene, Philippe. "Mozambique: Le voisinage sud-africain." *Révue Francaise d'Etudes Politiques Africaines* 103 (1974): 26–28.

Decreto No. 12:485, *Boletim da Agência Geral das Colónias* (October 13, 1926): 136–39.

Decreto No. 12:485, *Legislação colonial, Boletim da Agência Geral das Colónias* (November 1926): 132–57.

Department of Foreign Relations. *The Accord of Nkomati: 1984.* Pretoria: Author, 1984.

Dodson, James M. "Dynamics of Insurgency in Mozambique." *Africa Report* 12, no. 8 (November 1967): 52–55.

Donnelly, Edward. "A New Stage in the Struggle for Mozambique." *Ufahamu* 5, no. 1 (1974): 5–15.

Duffy, James. *Portugal's African Territories: Present Realities.* New York: Praeger, 1966.

Ehnmark, Anders, and Per Wastberg. *Angola and Mozambique: The Case against Portugal.* London: Pall Mall, 1963.

El-Khawas, Mohamed A. "Mozambique and the United Nations." *Issue* 2, no. 4 (1972): 30–35.

Erasmus, Gerhard. *The Accord of Nkomati.* Bloemfontein: South Africa Institute of International Affairs, 1984.

Ferreira, E. de Sousa. *Portuguese Colonialism in Africa: The End of an Era.* Paris: UNESCO, 1974.

Figueiredo, António de. *Portugal and Its Empire.* London: Gollancz, 1961.

———. *Portugal: Fifty Years of Dictatorship.* New York: Holmes & Meier, 1976.

Finnegan, W. A. *A Complicated War: The Harrowing of Mozambique.* Berkeley: University of California Press, 1992.

Foundation Friedrich Ebert. *Workshop sobre descentralização, organizado por Governo da Provincia de Nampula,* July 1994.

Freitas, João da Costa. "Movimentos subversivos contra Moçambique." In *Moçambique: Curso de extensão universitária ano lectivo de 1964–1965.* Lisbon: Instituto Superior de Ciências Sociais e Política Ultramarina, Universidade Técnica de Lisboa, [n.d.].

Frelimo. *Projecto das teses para o IV° Congreso do Partido Frelimo.* Maputo, p. 42. Relatório do Comite Central ao 4° Congresso, Maputo, 177 pp., 1983.

Frelimo III Congress, Maputo, 3–1 February 1977. *People's Power in Mozambique, Angola and Guinea-Bissau* 7/8 (June 1977): 1629.

FRELIMO Partido. *Building Socialism: The People's Answer.* Maputo: Author, 1983.

———. *Directivas económicas e sociais.* Maputo: Author, 1983.

———. *Frelimo Party Programme and Statutes.* Maputo: Author, 1983.

———. *Intervençoes dos delegados [ao 4o Congresso].* Maputo: Author, 1985.

———. *Out of Underdevelopment to Socialism: Report of the Central Committee.* Maputo: Author, 1983.

Gann, L. H. "Portugal, Africa and the Future." *Journal of Modern African Studies* 13 (March 1975): 1–18.

Gaspar, C. "*Portugal's Policies toward Angola and Mozambique since Independence.*" In *Regional Conflict and US Policy*, ed. R. Bloomfield. Boston: World Peace Foundation, 1988, pp. 40–74.

Geffray, C. "Fragments d'un discours du pouvoir." *Politique Africaine* 29. Mozambique: Guerre et nationalisme, 1988, pp. 71–87.

Gentili, Anna Maria. "Sulle origin rural del nazionalismo mozambicano." *Rivista de Storia Contemporanea* (Turin, Italy), no. 1 (1984): 70–112.

Great Britain. *Agreement between the United Kingdom and Portugal Respecting Boundaries in South-East Africa.* London: H. M. Stationery Office, 1920.

———. *Exchange of Notes between Her Majesty's Government in the United Kingdom of Great Britain and Northern Ireland and the Portuguese Government Providing for Portuguese Packerpah in the Shire Valley Project.* Lisbon, January 21; London: H. M. Stationery Office, 1953.

———. *Exchange of Notes between His Majesty'sGovernment in the United Kingdom and the Portuguese Government Regarding the Boundary between Tanganyika Territory and Mozambique, Lisbon*, May 11, 1936 and December 28, 1951. London: H. M. Stationery Office, 1957.

———. *Exchange of Notes between His Majesty's Government in the United Kingdom-and-the Portuguese Government Regarding the Delimitation of the Southern Rhodesia-Portuguese East Africa Frontiers*, London, October 29, 1940. London: H. M. Stationery Office, 1941.

———. *Exchange of Notes between the Government of the United Kingdom of Great Britain and Northern Ireland . . . and the Government of the Portuguese Republic, Accepting the Report of the Nyasaland-Mozambique Boundary Commission of the 27th of August, 1956*, Lisbon, November 29, 1963. London: H. M. Stationery Office, 1964.

———. *Notes Exchanged between His Majesty's Government in Great Britain and the Government of Portugal for the Settlement of the Boundary between Swaziland and the Province of Mozambique.* Lisbon, October 6, 1927. London: H. M. Stationery Office, 1928.

———. Mozambique Foreign Office. *Notes Exchanged between His Majesty's Government in the Union of South Africa and the Government of Portugal for the Settlement of the Boundary between the Union of South Africa and the Province of Mozambique.* London: H. M. Stationery Office, 1928.

Grest J. *Gestão urbana, reformas de governo local e processo de democratização em Moçambique: Cidade de Maputo, 1975–1990*, in *Boletim*, N°17 (AHM) (April 1995): 57–87.

Grier, Beverly, and Margaret Kinsman. *Inventory of Select Documents from the Immanuel Wallerstein Collection of Political Ephemera of the Liberation Movements of Lusophone Africa and Anglophone Southern Africa (1958–1975) on Microfilm.* New Haven, Conn.: Yale University Library. [1977].

Haight, Mabel V. Jackson. *European Powers and South-East Africa: A Study of International Relations on the South-East Coast of Africa, 1796–1856.* London: Routledge & Kegan Paul, 1967.

Hall, M. "The Mozambican National Resistance Movement." *Africa* 60, no. 1 (1990): 39–48.

Hanlon, J. *Apartheid's Second Front: South Africa's War against Its Neighbors.* Harmondsworth, Eng.: Penguin, 1986.

———. *Guia básica sobre as autarquias locais.* Maputo: AWEPA, 1997.

Hastings, Adrian. "Some Reflections upon the War in Mozambique." *African Affairs* 73, no. 292 (July 1974): 263–76.

———. *Wiriyamu.* New York: Orbis, 1974.

Henderson, Robert d'A. "Principles and Practice in Mozambique's Foreign Policy." *World Today* 34, no. 7 (July 1978): 276–86.

———. "Relations of Neighbourliness: Malawi and Portugal, 1964–74." *Journal of Modern African Studies* 15, no. 3 (1977): 425–55.

Henriksen, Thomas H. "End of an Empire: Portugal's Collapse in Africa." *Current History* 68, no. 405 (1975): 211–15.

———. "Mozambique and Angola: Revolution and Intervention." *Current History* (November 1976): 153–57.

———. "People's War in Angola, Mozambique and Guinea-Bissau." *Journal of Modern African Studies* 14, no. 3 (1976): 377–99.

———. *Revolution and Counter-Revolution: Mozambique's War of Independence, 1964–1974.* Westport, Conn.: Greenwood, 1983.

Hodges, Tony. "Mozambique: The Politics of Liberation." In *Southern Africa: The Continuing Crisis,* ed. Gwendolen M. Carter and Patrick M. O'Mears. London: Macmillan, 1979, pp. 57–92.

Hoil, D. *Mozambique: A Nation in Crisis.* London, Claridge, 1989.

———. *Mozambique: Resistance and Freedom: A Case for Reassessment.* London: Mozambique Institute, 1994.

Humbaraci, Arslan, and Nicole Muchnik. *Portugal's African Wars: Angola, Guinea Bissao [sic], Mozambique.* Dar-es-Salaam: Publishing House, 1974.

Hume, C. *Ending Mozambique's War: The Role of Mediation and Good Offices.* Washington, D.C.: United States Institute of Peace Press, 1994.

———. *The Mozambique Peace Process: The Diplomatic Record 1992–1993.* Boulder, Colo.: Westview, 1994.

Inspecção Superior do Piano de Fomento. *Relatório final da execução do I Plano de Fomento.* Lisbon: Imprensa Nacional 1959.

International Finance Corporation. *Mozambique: Administrative Barriers to Investment: The Red Tape Analysis.* Maputo: Author, November 1996.

Isaacman, Allen. "Mozambique: In Machel's Footsteps." *Africa Report* 32 (January–February 1987): 25–27.

Isaacman, Allen, and Jennifer Davis. "United States Policy towards Mozambique since 1945: The Defense of Colonialism and Regional Stability." *Africa Today* 25, no. 1 (January–March 1978): 29–55.

Kagombe, Maina D. "African Nationalism and Guerrilla Warfare in Angola and Mozambique." In *Southern Africa in Perspective: Essays in Regional Politics*, ed. C. P. Potholm and R. Dale. New York: Free Press, 1972, pp. 196–205.

Kitchner, Helen. "Conversation with Eduardo Mondlane." *Africa Report* (November 1967): 31–32, 49–51.

Kuhne, Winrich. *Sowjetische Afrikapolitik in der 'Aera Gorbatschow': Eine Analyse ihrer grundlegenden Probleme Mitte der 80er Jahre ausgehend von den Entwicklungen in Mozambique, Angola and Aethiopien.* Ebenhausen: Forschungsinstitut für Internationale Politik and Sicherheit, Stiftung Wissenschaft and Politik, 1986.

———. *Sudafrika und seine Nachbarn: Durchbruch zum Frieden? Zur Bedeutung der Vereinbarungen mit Mozambique und Angola vom Frühjahr 1984.* Baden-Baden: Nomos Verlagsgesellschaft, 1985.

Labisa, António dos Santos and Mafia de Lurdes Barata. "Breve estudo sobre a balança de pagamentos de Moçambique." In *Estudos de Economia 1.* Lisbon: Centro de Estudos Políticos e Sociais, Junta de Investigações do Ultramar, 1961, pp. 151–243.

Lacerda, Gavicho de. "A divisão da Província de Moçambique em duas, norte e sul." *Boletim da Agência Geral das Colónias* 6, no. 60 (June 6, 1930): 24–27.

Lachartre, B. "Démocratisation et municipalisation au Mozambique." *Politique Africaine* (1999): 162–69.

Legrand, J. "Logique de guerre et dynamique de la violence en Zambézia, 1976–1991." *Politique Africaine* 50 (June 1993): 88–104.

Levy, Sam. "Broken promises?" *Africa Report* 31, no. 1 (January–February 1986): 77–80.

Lobo, Rafael Carcomo de Almeida Rosa. "As autoridades tradicionais e a organização das regedorias de 1961: alguns aspectos político-administrativos na Província de Moçambique." Ph.D. diss., Instituto Superior de Ciências Sociais e Política Ultramarina, Universidade Técnica de Lisboa, 1966.

Lopes, Manuel dos Santos. "Colonato do Limpopo: Aspectos sociais do povoamento." Ph.D. diss., Instituto Superior de Ciências Sociais e Política Ultramarina, Universidade Técnica de Lisboa, 1968.

Macado, Victor de Sá. "Healing Old Wounds." *Africa Report* 31, no. 1 (January–Februrary 1986): 81–83.

Machado, Joaquim José. *Província de Moçambique, relatório sobre a administração da Província durante o ano de 1914, apresentado ao Conselho do Governo, em sessão de 2 de Janeiro de 1915.* Lourenço Marques: Imprensa Nacional, 1915.

Machel, Samora. *Building a Nation: The Enemy Within*, 53 p. 2: *Our Sophisticated Weapon.* Maputo: Instituto Nacional do Livro et do Disco, 1982.

———. *Estruturar o Partido para melhorar a vida do povo*. Colec. 15, *Estudos e Orientações* 15. Maputo: Impresna Nacional, 1983.

———. "Consolidating People's Power in Mozambique." *African Communist* 72 (First Quarter 1978): 32–49.

———. "Knowledge and Science Should Be for the Total Liberation of Man." *Race and Class* 19, no. 4 (1978): 366–404.

———. *Mozambique: Sowing the Seeds of Revolution*. London: Committee for Freedom in Mosambique [*sic*], Angola and Guinea, 1974.

———. "The People's Republic of Mozambique: The Struggle Continues." *Review of African Political Economy* 4 (November 1975): 14–25.

———. *The Tasks Ahead: Selected Speeches*. New York: Afro American Information Service, 1975.

MacQueen, Norman. "Mozambique's Widening Foreign Policy. " *World Today* 40, no. 1 (January 1984): 22–28.

———. "Portugal and Africa: The Politics of Reengagement." *Journal of Modern African Studies* 23, no. 1 (March 1985): 31–51.

———. *The Decolonization of Portuguese Africa: Metropolitan Revolution and the Dissolution of Empire*. London: Longman, 1997.

Marcum, John A. *Portugal and Africa, the Politics of Indifference: A Case Study in American Foreign Policy*. Syracuse, N.Y.: Program of Eastern African Studies, Maxwell School of Citizenship and Public Affairs, Syracuse University, 1972.

———. "Three Revolutions: Angola, Mozambique and Portuguese Guinea." *Africa Report* 12 (November 1967): 9–22.

Marsh, January. *South Africa's Undeclared War against Mozambique*. London: Mozambique Angola Committee, 1984.

Mazula, Brazão. *Mozambique: Elections, Democracy and Development*. Maputo: Manila, 1996.

Melo, Guilherme de. *Moçambique norte: Guerra e paz (reportagem)*. Lourenço Marques: Minerva Central, 1968?

Metz, Steven. "The Mozambican National Resistance and South African Foreign Policy." *African Affairs* (October 1986): 491–507.

Middlemas, Keith. "Independent Mozambique and Its Regional Policy." In *Southern Africa since the Portuguese Coup*, ed. John Seiler. Boulder, Colo.: Westview, 1980.

Miller, Joseph C. "The Politics of Decolonization in Portuguese Africa." *African Affairs* 72, no. 295 (1975): 135–47.

Minter, William. "Major Themes in Mozambican Foreign Relations, 1975–1977." *Issue* 8, no. 1 (Spring 1978): 43–49.

———. *Portuguese Africa and the West*. Baltimore: Penguin, 1972.

Moiane, José. "Reabertura da frente Tete: Oitavo aniversário." *Tempo* 283 (March 7, 1976): 24–31.

Monteiro, J. O. *Poder e democracia*. Maputo: Assembleia Popular, R.P. de Moçambique, 1988.

———. *L'administration locale au Mozambique*. DEA d'Etudes Africaines. Paris, 1991.

Morozzo, (della Rocca) Roberto. "*Sant'Egidio: La via romana alla pace.*" *Lines* 3 (1993): 69–82.

Moura, Francisco Pereira de, and Maria Fernanda Amaral. *Estimativa do produto interno de Moçambique, 1970–73–75.* Maputo: Curso de Economia, Universidade Eduardo Mondlane, [n.d.].

Mozambique. *Constituiçao/República Popular de Moçambique.* Maputo: Instituto do Livro e do Disco, 1978.

———. *Lei dos crimes contra a segurança do povo e do estado popular.* Maputo: A.P., 1979.

Mozambique (República Popular). "Principles of Revolutionary Justice: The Constitution and Other Documents on Law and State from the People's Republic of Mozambique." *Constitution.* London: Republica Popular de Moçambique, 1975.

Mozambique, Angola, and Guinea Information Centre, 1979. "Mozambique Revolution." *Dar-es-Salaam: FRELIMO,* nos. 1–61. (December 1963–June 1975).

Munslow, Barry, ed. *Samora Machel, an African Revolutionary: Selected Speeches and Writings.* Trans. Michael Wolfers. London: Zed, 1985.

Neil-Tomlinson, Barry. "The Nyasa Chartered Company, 1891–1929." *Journal of African History* 18, no. 1 (1977): 109–28.

Neuparth, Augusto. *A fronteira luso-allemã de Moçambique.* Lisbon: Typographia da Livraria Ferin, 1908.

Nilsson, Anders. "From Pseudo-Terrorists to Pseudo-Guerrillas: The MNR in Mozambique." *Review of African Political Economy* 58 (1993): 35–42.

Nkosi, Z. "The S. African Threat to Mozambique." *African Communist,* no. 60 (1975): 40–50.

Nogueira, Francisco Pedro da Veiga. *Projecto de alteração e reorganização da Província de Moçambique, 12 de Dezembro de 1916 (Tete)—12 fol. dact. 1-C19* (Biblioteca da Sociedade de Geografia de Lisbon), 1916.

Oliveira, Mário de. *Problemas do ultramar no plano intercalar de fomento.* Lisbon: Agência-Geral do Ultramar, 1964.

Oliveira, Paulo. "Os donos da 'RENAMO.'" Unpublished ms., Maputo, 1990.

Opello, Walter C., Jr. "Internal War in Mozambique: A Social-Psychological Analysis of a Nationalist Revolution." Ph.D. diss., University of Colorado, Boulder, Colorado, 1962.

Partners in Crime: The Anglo-Portuguese Alliance Past and Present. London: Committee for Freedom in Mozambique, Angola, and Guinea, 1973.

Patel, Hasu N. "Zimbabwe's Mediation in Mozambique and Angola." In *Mediation in Southern Africa,* ed. Stephen Chan and Vivienne Jabri. Basingstoke, Eng.: Macmillan, 1993, pp. 117–41.

Portugal. Ministério dos Negócios Estrangeiros. *Negócios d'África: Negoçiacões do tratado com a Inglaterra. Documentos apresentados às cortes na sessão legislativa de 1891.* Lisbon: Imprensa Nacional, 1891.

Querculus [pseudonym]. "Le Portugal et l'Afrique." *Marchés Tropicaux* 39, no. 1990 (1983): 314–62.

Radir, Michael S. "Mozambique: Non-Alignment or New Dependence." *Current History* 83, no. 83 (March 1984): 101–4, 132–35.

Rafael, Tomás Maria. "Vinte anos de finanças moçambicanas e seu reflexo na economia da colónia." Ph.D. diss., Escola Superior Colonial, Lisboa, 1949–50.

Ramalho, José. "Soviets' Nacala Takeover Tightens Indian Ocean Hold." *To the Point* 6, no. 32 (1977): 46–47.

———. "Sweden's Misplaced Missionary Zeal." *To the Point* 7, no. 20 (1978): 35.

Ribeiro-Torres, J. L. "Rural Development Schemes in Southern Mozambique." *South African Journal of African Affairs* 3 no. 2 (1973): 60–69.

S.A.C. *Como vota o cristão?* Chimoio: Diocese of Chimoio, 1998.

Samuels, Michael A. "The Nationalist Parties." In *Portuguese Africa: A Handbook*, ed. D. M. Abshire and M. A. Samuels. New York: Praeger, 1969, pp. 389–405.

Saul, J. S. "The Revolution in Portugal's African Colonies." *Canadian Journal of African Studies* 9, no. 2 (1975): 315–36.

———. *Canada and Mozambique.* Toronto: Development Education Center, 1974.

Schneidman, Whitney J. "FRELIMO's Foreign Policy and the Process of Liberation." *Africa Today* 25, no. 1 (January–March 1978): 57–67.

Seiler, J., ed. *Southern Africa under the Portuguese Coup.* Boulder, Colo.: Westview, 1980.

Serapião, Luís Benjamin. "Church and State in Mozambican Politics 1960–1980." *Lusophone Area Studies Journal* 1, no. 1 (January 1983): 67–86.

———. "Frelimo and Socialism in Mozambique." *Western Journal of Black Studies* 4, no. 1 (Winter 1980): 5764.

———. "Mozambican Foreign Policy and the West, 1975–1984." *Munger Africana Library Notes* 76 (August 1985): 1–14.

———. "Mozambique: Crisis of Political Legitimacy." *African Concord* (January 19, 1986): 7.

———. "The Preaching of Portuguese Colonialism and the Protest of White Fathers." *Issue* 2, no. 1 (Spring 1972): 34–40.

Serapião, Luís Benjamin, and Mohamed El-Khawas. *Mozambique in the Twentieth Century: From Colonialism to Independence.* Washington, D.C.: UPA, 1979.

Serra, C. *Eleitorado incapturável.* Maputo: Livraria Universitaria, UEM, 1999.

Silva, Luiz Augusto da. *Collecção de Legislação Novíssima do Ultramar: Vol. III, 1868 a 1869.* Lisbon: Imprensa Nacional, 1976.

Smith, Alan K. "António Salazar and the Reversal of Portuguese Colonial Policy." *Journal of African History* 15, no. 4 (1974): 653–67.

Somerville, Keith. "The USSR and Southern Africa." *Journal of Modern African Studies* 22, no. 1 (March 1984): 73–108.

South Africa. *Exchange of Notes between the Government of the Union of South Africa and the Portuguese Government Relative to the Mozambique Convention of September 11, 1928 as Amended on November 17, 1934 and Extended on April 21, 1939, Lisbon, May 2, 1940.* London: H. M. Stationery Office, 1941.

———. *Treaties: Convention between His Majesty's Government in the Union of South Africa and the Government of the Portuguese Republic Regarding Native*

Labor from Mozambique, Railway Matters, and Commercial Intercourse. London: H. M. Stationery Office, 1930.

"Structures of Power in Mozambique." *People's Power in Mozambique, Angola and Guinea-Bissau* 11 (1978): 22–28.

Sykes, John. *Portugal and Africa: The People and the War.* London: Hutchinson, 1971.

Teixeira, José J. "Primeira carta orgânica de Moçambique." *Boletim da Academia das Ciências de Lisboa*, 2a serie (1920): 24–32.

Terror in Tete: A Documentary Report of Portuguese Atrocities in Tete District, Mozambique, 1971–72. London: International Defence and Aid Fund, 1973.

Torres, J. L. [Ribeiro]. "Some Settlement Schemes in the Gaza District of Southern Mozambique." *South African Journal of Economics* 35, no. 3(1967): 244–55.

Transvaal. *Conversation (dated 1st April, 1909) between the Government of the Transvaal and the Portuguese Colony of Mozambique.* London: H. M. Stationery Office, 1909.

UNHCR. *Mozambique.* HCR/0028. Geneva: UNHCR, 1993.

United Nations, *G.A. Mozambique, E/CN.4/ÁC.22/RT.89, 91, 104, 106, 111, 112, 116 (1970): A/C.4/728/Add.1; A/C. /4/SR.1888, 1897.*

———. *G.A. Mozambique, ECA Res. 94 (vi) in E/3864/Rev. 1, 1964; A/AC. 109/PET.257, 277; A/ÁC.109/PET.258; A/ÁC.109/ PET 273 (1964).*

———. *G.A. Portugal, Overseas Territories, /U.N.3823, SR 1018 20 October 1960.*

———. *G.A. Self-Government A/AC.109/429, A/ÁC.109/L. 885. Note on Massacre of villagers in Mozambique (1973): E/CN. 4 /A C .22/RT .135, 136; OPI/482 (1973).*

———. *G.A. Territories under Portuguese Administration: Self-Government or Independence A/PV.2375 (1975): A/PV.2351 (1975).*

———. *Report of the Special Committee on Territories under Portuguese Administration.* a7623/Add 3 (September 25, 1969): General Assembly, 24th Session.

———. *Security Council. Report on Disputes, 16 June 1986–15 June 1987: A/42/2 (0000041) (1988).*

———. *The United Nations and Mozambique, 1992–1995.* New York and Geneva, United Nations Publications, 1995.

Vanneman, Peter. "Soviet National Security Policy in Southern Africa and the Indian Ocean: The Case of Mozambique." *Politikon* 3, no. 1 (1976): 42–50.

Venter, A. J. *Portugal's Guerrilla War: The Campaign for Africa.* Cape Town: Malherbe, 1973.

———. *The Zambesi Salient: Conflict in Southern Africa.* London: Hale, 1975.

Verdier, I., ed. *Mozambique: 100 Men in Power.* Paris: Indigo, 1996.

Vines, A. *No Democracy without Money: The Road to Peace in Mozambique (1981–1992).* London, Catholic Institute for International Relations, 1994.

———. *Renamo: Mozambique.* London: Currey; Bloomington: Indiana University Press, 1994.

———. *Renamo: From Terrorism to Democracy in Mozambique.* New York: World Press, 1995.

———. *Renamo: Terrorism in Mozambique.* 2d ed. London: Currey, 1996.

Voz da Revolução. June 1965- Dar-es-Salaam: Frente de Libertação de Moçambique and Maputo: Comité Central do Partido Frelimo, [n.d.].

Warhurst, Philip R. *Angola-Portuguese Relations in South-Central Africa, 1890–1900.* London: Longman Green for the Royal Commonwealth Society, 1962.

———. *Rhodesia and Her Neighbours, 1900–23.* Oxford: Oxford University Press, 1970.

Weimar, B. "Abstaining from the 1998 Local Government Elections in Mozambique: Some Hypotheses." Discussion paper, 25 pp., August 1998.

Weimer, Berhard. *Die Mozambiquanische Aussenpolitik, 1975–1982: Merkmale, Probleme, Dynamik.* Baden-Baden: Nomos Verlagsgesellschaft, 1983.

Whitaker, Paul M. "The Revolutions of 'Portuguese Africa.'" *Journal of Modern African Studies* 8, no. 1 (1970): 15–35.

Wuyts, Marc. "Money, Planning and Rural Transformation in Mozambique." *Journal of Development Studies* 22, no. 1 (1985): 180–207.

Young, T., and M. Hall. *Confronting Leviathan: Mozambique since Independence.* London: Hurst, 1997.

Zacarias, Agostinho. *Security and the State in Southern Africa.* New York: Palgrave, 1999.

Political Economy

Abshire, David M. "Minerals, Manufacturing, Power and Communications." In *Portuguese Africa: A Handbook*, ed. D. M. Abshire and M. A. Samuels New York: Praeger, 1969, pp. 294–319.

Akpan, Edgar. "Lights Go On in New Homes." *New African Development* 11, no. 10 (1977): 1005.

Andrews, Cyril W. *Portuguese East Africa: Economic and Commercial Conditions in Portuguese East Africa.* London: H. M. Stationery Office, 1949.

Bertulli, Cesare. *Croce e spiada in Mozambico.* Rome: Coines, 1974.

Boleo, José de Oliveira. "Aspects de l'économie du Mozambique." *Révue Française* 85 (1957).

Boletim Oficial. 13 May 1854–21 June 1975. Lourenço Marques: Imprensa Nacional, 1975.

Bonnefont de Varinary, P. de. *La Compagnie de Mozambique. Sa concession, son administration, ses résultats (1898).* Lisbon: n.p., 1899.

Bourderie, Jack. "Mozambique: L'héritage." *L'Economiste du Tiers Monde* 8 (1975): 25.

Bowen, M. "Beyond Reform: Adjustment and Political Power in Contemporary Mozambique." *Journal of Modern African Studies* 30, 2 (1992): 255–79.

Brandenburg, Frank. "Development, Finance and Trade." In *Portuguese Africa: A Handbook*, ed. D. M. Abshire and M. A. Samuels, London: Praeger, 1969, pp. 219–252.

──────. "Transport Systems and Their External Ramifications." In *Portuguese Africa: A Handbook*, ed. D. M. Abshire and M. A. Samuels. London: Praeger, 1969, pp. 320–44.

British Overseas Trade Board. *Mozambique*. London: Author (Descriptive Handbooks on Commerce), 1977.

Brito, Luís de. "Colonial Dependence and Regional Integration." *Mozambican Studies* (Amsterdam), no. 1 (1980): 23–32.

Cahen, M. "Corporatisme et colonialisme. Approche du cas Mozambicain 1933–1979. Une genèse difficile, un mouvement squelettique." *Cahiers d'études africaines* 23, no. 4 (1983).

Camacho, Brito. *Cadernos coloniais: Politica colonial*. Lisbon: Cosmos, 1936.

Campbell, Horace. "War Reconstruction and Dependency in Mozambique." *Third World Quarterly* 5, no. 6 (October 1984): 839–67.

Capela, José. *O imposto de palhota e a introdução do modo de produção capitalista nas colónias*. Porto: Afrontamento, 1977.

Carrilho, João Luís. "Sobre as principais necessidades do distrito de Tete." *B.S.G.L.*, 33a série, no. 4 (1915).

Chenu, François. "Mozambique: Offensive sur Cabora-Bassa." *Revue Française d'Etudes Politiques Africaines* 55 (1970): 20–22.

Chigono, M. F. *The State, Violence and Development: The Political Economy of War in Mozambique*. New York: Human Rights Watch, 1992.

Chissano, J. A. *Peace and Reconstruction*. Harare: Southern African Research and Documentation Centre, 1997.

Committee for Freedom in Mozambique, Angola and Guinea. *White Power: The Cunene River Scheme*. London: Author, 1973.

The Constitution of the People's Republic of Mozambique. [Maputo: Instituto Nacional do Livro e do Disco], 1980.

Cunha, J. M. da Silva. *O sistema português de política indígena: Princípios gerais*. Lisbon: Agência Geral do Ultramar, 1952.

Davidson, Basil. "Mozambique: Five Images of Progress." *People's Power in Mozambique, Angola and Guinèa-Bissau*, no. 14 (1979): 23–31.

Direccão de Estatística e Propaganda. *Anuário estatístico do território de Manica e Sofala sob a administração da Companhia de Moçambique, ano de 1930*. Lisbon: Sociedade Nacional de Tipografia, 1934.

Direcção-Geral do Comércio Externo. *Moçambique Economic Survey: Special Edition for the Independence*. Lourenço Marques Tempográfica, 1975.

Economia de Moçambique. Lourenço Marques, Moçambique: Centro Social; Beira, Mozambique: Companhia Editorial de Moçambique, December 1963–July 1974 9, no. 1. Monthly.

Egerö, Bertil. *Mozambique: A Dream Undone, the Political Economy of Democracy, 1975–1984*. Uppsala: Nordiska Afrika-Institutet, 1987.

Enevoldsen, Thyge, and Vibe Johnsen. *A Political, Economic and Social Bibliography on Moçambique, with Main Emphasis on the Period 1965–1978*. Copenhagen: Centre for Development Studies, 1978.

L'Exposition Coloniale Internationale de 1931 à Paris. *Portugal: Colonie de Moçambique et territoire de Manica et Sofala (sous l'administration de la Companhia de Moçambique).* *Instruction.* Lisbon: Sociedade Nacional de Tipografia, 1931.

Fauvet, Paul. "Roots of Counter-Revolution: The Mozambique National Resistance." *Review of African Political Economy* 19 (July 1984): 108–21.

———. "Roots of Counter-Revolution: The Mozambican National Resistance." *Review of African Political Economy* 29 (1984): 108–21.

Ferradoza, I. "Who's Afraid of Cabora Bassa?" *Portugal: An Informative Review* 29 (1972): 2–9.

Fondation Friedrich Ebert. *Movimento sindical em Moçambique: Evolução e Perspectivas.* Maputo: FFE, 1997.

Frelimo, IIIe Congrès. *Programmes et statuts. Directives économiques et sociales.* Rapport du Comité Central. Paris: Harmattan, 1977.

Frente de libertação de Moçambique. *Petition to the Special Committee for Decolonization.* Dar-es-Salaam, 1967.

Friedland, Elaine A. "The Political Economy of Colonialism in South Africa and Mozambique." *Journal of Southern African Affairs* 2, no. 1 (January 1977): 61–75.

"German Rivalry in Mozambique." *Foreign Report* 1577 (1979): 4–6.

Gifford, Tony. "Criminals into 'New Men': Penal Justice in Mozambique." *People's Power in Mozambique, Angola and Guinea-Bissau* 17 (Spring 1981): 37–43.

Green, Andrew W. "Portugal and the African Territories: Economic Implication." In *Portuguese Africa: A Handbook,* ed. David Abshire and Michael Samuels. New York: Praeger, 1969.

Green, R. *A dimensão social do ajustamento à pobreza em Moçambique: Estudo sobre o impacto social do Programa de Reabilitação économico sobre os grupos populacionais mais desfavorecidos, multigr.* Maputo: n.p., 1989.

Hafkin, Nancy Jane. *Trade, Society and Politics in Northern Mozambique, c. 1753–1913.* Boston: Boston University Graduate School, 1973.

Hammond, R. J. *Portugal and Africa 1815–1910: A Study in Uneconomic Imperialism.* Stanford, Calif.: Stanford University Press, 1966.

———. *Portugal's African Problems: Some Economic Facets.* New York: Carnegie Endowment for Peace, 1962.

Hanlon, J. *Peace without Profit: How the IMF Blocks Rebuilding in Mozambique.* Oxford: Currey, 1996.

———. *Mozambique: The Revolution under Fire.* London: Zed, 1984.

———. "Too Little, Too Late." *New Statesman* 107 (February 1984): 18.

Henriksen, Thomas. "Mozambique: The Enemy Within?" *Current History* 81 (March 1982): 111–14, 135–36.

Houk, Richard J. "Recent Development in the Portuguese Congo." *Geographical Review* 48 (April 1958): 201–21.

Isaacman, Allen, and Barbara Isaacman. "Creating a New Legal System." *Africa Report* 26 (January–February 1981): 19–22.

———. "A Socialist Legal System in the Making: Mozambique before and after Independence." In *The Politics of Informal Justice*, ed. Richard Abel. New York: Academic Press, 1982.

Jardim, Jorge. *Moçambique, terra queimada*. Lisbon: Intervenção, 1976.

Jenkins, P. *An Overview of State and Non-governmental Housing Interventions in Mozambique from Independence to 1990*. Maputo: PNUD/UNCHS, Evaluation Mission, December 1993.

Justiça Popular. November/December Maputo: Gabinete de Estudos, Ministério da Justiça, 1980.

Kalter, Joanmarie. "The Economics of Desperation." *Africa Report* 29 (May–June 1984): 19–23.

Katzenellenbogen, Simon. *South Africa and Southern Mozambique: Railways, Labour and Trade in the Making of a Relationship*. Manchester: Manchester University Press, 1982.

Leeming, F. A. "An Estimate of the Domestic Output of Angola and Mozambique." *South African Journal of Economics* 28 (June 1960): 141–54.

Lopes, José Mota. "The MNR: Opponents or Bandits?" *Africa Report* 31, no. 1 (January–February 1986): 67–73.

Machel, Samora. *A Luta contra o subdesebvolvimento, textos e documentos,* 4. Maputo: n.p., 1983.

———. "A Science Belongs to Its Creator" [an interview]. *Africa: An International Business, Economic and Political Monthly*, no. 96 (1979): 43–46.

———. *The Tasks Ahead: Selected Speeches*. New York: Afro-American Information Service, 1975.

Mackintosh, Maureen. "Economic Policy Context and Adjustment Options in Mozambique." *Development and Change* 17 (1986): 557–81.

Marshall, J. "Structural Adjustment and Social Policy in Mozambique." *Review of African Political Economy*, 47 (1990): 28–43.

Martin, David, and Phyllis Johnson. "Mozambique: To Nkomati and Beyond." In *Destructive Engagement: Southern Africa at War*, ed. Phyllis Johnson and David Martin. Harare: Zimbabwe Publishing House for the Southern African Research and Documentation Centre, 1986.

Martins, João Filipe, and Machatine P. Munguambe. *Tribunais populares*. Maputo: Ministério da Informação, 1976.

Matos, Maria Leonor Correia de. "Portuguese Law and Administration in Mozambique and Their Effect on the Customary Land Laws of Three Tribes of the Lake Nyasa Region." Ph.D. diss., University of London, 1969.

Mbwiliza, Joseph Frederick. "Towards a Political Economy of Northern Mozambique: The Makua Hinterland, 1600–1900." Ph.D. diss., Columbia University, New York, 1980.

Melo, Lopo Vaz de Sampaio e. "A campanha do Bárue de 1902." *Anuário da Escola Superior Colonial* 25 (1943–1944), 1945.

Meyens, P. "Liberation, Ideology, and National Development Strategy in Mozambique." *Review of Political Economy* 22 (October 1981): 42–64.

Miech-Chatenay, M. *Mozambique 1991: The New Phase*. Montreal; CIDMAA, 1991.

Mittleman, James H. "Mozambique: The Political Economy of Development." *Journal of Southern African Affairs* 3, no. 1 (January 1978): 35–54.

———. "State Power in Mozambique." *Issue* 8, no. 1 (Spring 1978): 4–11.

———. *Underdevelopment and the Transition to Socialism: Mozambique and Tanzania*. New York: Academic Press, 1981.

———. "Marginalization and the International Division of Labor: Mozambique's Strategy of Opening the Market." *African Studies Review* (December 1991): 89–106.

Mondlane, Eduardo (introduced by John Saul, biographical sketch by Herbert Shore). *The Struggle for Mozambique*. London: Zed, 1983.

Moorcraft, Paul. *African Nemesis: War and Revolution in Southern Africa, 1945–2010*. London: Brassey's, 1990.

Munslow, Barry. *Mozambique: The Revolution and Its Origins*. London: Longman, 1983.

Murteira, M. "Economias e sociedades em transição na África lusófona." *Lusotopie* (1995): 349–61.

Niddrie, David L. "The Cunene River: Angola's River of Life." *Journal of the American Portuguese Cultural Society* (Winter–Spring 1970): 1–17.

Novela, Orlando. *The International System and Colonial Mozambique (1848–1900)*. Dar-es-Salaam: Centre for Foreign Relations, 1948.

O'Meara, Dan. "The Collapse of Mozambican Socialism." *Transformation* 14(1991): 82–103.

Oyejide, Ademola, Benno Ndulux, and Jan Gunning. *Regional Integration and Trade Liberalization in Southern Africa*. Vol. II. New York: Palgrave, 1999.

Petrucci, Pietro. "Mozambique: La première année." *Afrique-Asie*, no. 114 (1976): 28–29.

Pitcher, Anne M. *Politics in the Portuguese Empire: The State, Industry and Cruton, 1926–1974*. Oxford: Clarendon, 1993.

Poku, Nana. *Regionalization and Security in Southern Africa*. New York: Palgrave, 2001.

Porto. *Colónia de Moçambique: Cana sacarina, monografia elaborada pela Direcção dos Serviços de Agricultura*. Lourenço Marques: Imprensa Nacional de Moçambique, 1930.

Primeira Exposição Colonial Portuguesa. *Colónia de Moçambique: Tabacco, monografia elaborada pela Direcção dos Serviços de Agricultura*. Lourenço Marques: Imprensa Nacional de Moçambique, 1934.

Principal Legislação promulgada pelo Governo [da República Popular de Moçambique]. Lourenço Marques: Imprensa Nacional, 1975.

Pringle, James. "Mozambique's Porous Front." *Newsweek* 89, no. 17 (1977): 13–14.

Rafael F. "Futuro incerto para o sector informal," *Dossier Economia* (February–March 1992): 19–38.

Rego, A. da Silva. "Adaptação missionária e assimilação colonizadora no ultramar português." *Boletim Geral do Ultramar* 34, no. 402 (December 1958): 185–213.

Relatório do Intendente da Companhia de Moçambique na Beira. Lisbon: Imprensa Nacional, 1908.

Ribeiro, José Carmona. *Sumários do Boletim Oficial de Moçambique, 1a. série, anos de 1855–1965.* Braga: Barbosa e Xavier, [n.d.].

Sachs, Albie (edited with the Assistance of the Mozambique Information Agency, AIM). *Principles of Revolutionary Justice: The Constitution and Other Documents on Law and State from the People's Republic of Mozambique.* London: Mozambique, Angola and Guinea Information Centre, 1979.

———. "Liberating the Land—Liberating the Law." In *Essays on Third World Perspectives in Jurisprudence*, ed. M. L. Marasinghe and William E. Conklin. Singapore: Malayan Law Journal, 1984.

———. "The Two Dimensions of Socialist Legality: Recent Experience in Mozambique." *International Journal of the Sociology of Law* 13 (1985): 133–46.

Saldanha, Eduardo d'Almeida. *Moçambique perante Genebra (Questões Nacionais).* Porto: Tipografia Porto Médico, 1931.

Santos, Manuel Pementel Pereira dos. *Mozambique Is Not Only Cabora Bassa.* Lisbon: Interviews published in *Diário de Notícias*, 1973.

Saul, John. *A Difficult Road in the Transition to Socialism in Mozambique.* New York: Monthly Review Press, 1985.

———. *The State and Revolution in Eastern Africa.* London: Heinemann, 1979.

———. "FRELIMO and the Mozambique Revolution." In *Essays on the Political Economy of Africa*, ed. Giovanni Arrighi and John S. Saul. London: Monthly Review Press, 1974.

Scott, Catherine. "Socialism and the 'Soft State' in Angola and Mozambique." *Journal of Southern African Studies* 26, no. 1 (March 1988): 23–36.

Sendler, Gerhard. "Zur Problematik der Seehafen Mocambiques." *Frankfurter Wirtschafts and Sozialgeographische Schriften* 26 (1977): 435–63.

Sharman, T. C. *Portuguese West Africa: Economic and Commercial Conditions in Portuguese West Africa (Angola).* London: Overseas Economic Surveys, 1954.

Sketchley, Peter. "Fishing Co-Operatives on Lake Nyasa: Seeds of a New Socialist State." *Review of African Political Economy* 24 (May–August 1982): 85–94.

Stage, Ole (assisted by Ole Norgaard). *Mozambican Development: A Bibliography Covering Social Science Literature with Emphasis on the Period after 1965.* Copenhagen: Centre for Development Research, 1982.

Swift, Kerry. *Mozambique and the Future.* London: Hale, 1975.

Sysle, Mariam. "Que cherchent Vorster et Smith?" *Afrique-Asie*, no. 150 (1977): 42–43.

Tickner, Vincent. "Structural Adjustment and Agricultural Pricing in Mozambique." *ROAPE* 53 (1992): 25–42.

Turner, Barry, ed. *Southern Africa Profiled.* New York: Palgrave, 2000.

United Nations General Assembly. *Assistance to Mozambique: Report of the Secretary-General, October 1976–June 1980.* New York: United Nations, 1980.

Uwechue, Raph. "Para Frelimo e o povo Moçambicano felicitações." *Africa: An International Business, Economic and Political Monthly* 46 (1975): 9.

Vail, Leroy. "The Political Economy of East-Central Africa." In *History of Central Africa*, ed. David Birmingham and Phillis M. Martin. London: Longman, 1983.

Vail, Leroy, and Landeg White. *Capitalism and Colonialism in Mozambique, a Study of Quelimane District*. Minneapolis: University of Minnesota Press, 1980.

Van Dongen, Irene S. "Agriculture and Other Primary Production." In *Portuguese Africa: A Handbook*, ed. D. M. Abshire and M. A. Samuels. New York: Praeger, 1969, pp. 253–93.

Vilhena, Ernesto Jardim de. *Companhia do Nyassa. Relatórios e memórias sobre os territórios pelo governador*. Lisbon: n.p., 1905.

Vletter, (de) F. *Unemployment Effects of Privatizing and Rationalizing State Enterprises*. Maputo: Ministeria do Trabalho/Gabinete de Promoção de Emprego, 1992.

Welch, Gita Honwana et al. "Transforming the Foundations of Family Law in the Course of the Mozambique Revolution." *Journal of Southern African Studies* 12, no. 1 (October 1985): 60–74.

Wheeler, Douglas Lamphier. "Gungunhana." In *Leadership in Eastern Africa*, ed. Norman R. Bennett. Boston: Boston University Press 1968.

Whitman, Jim, ed. *Migrants, Citizens and State in Southern Africa*. New York: Palgrave, 2000.

Wield, David. "Mozambique: Late Colonialism and Early Problems of Transition." In *Revolutionary Socialist Development in the Third World*, ed. Gordon White et al. Brighton: Wheatsheaf Books, 1983.

Wright, Robin B. "Mozambique: Short Term Problems, Long Term Hope." *Africa Today* 22, no. 3 (1975): 15–19.

———. *Mozambique: Six Months after Independence*. New York: Alicia Patterson Foundation, 1976.

Wuyts, M. "The Political Economy of Portugese Colonialism." *Mozambican Studies*, no. 1. Maputo: Centro de estudos Africanos, UEM (1982): 10–22.

———. "Gestão económica e política de reajustamento em Moçambique." *Estudos Moçambicanos* 8. Maputo: Centro de Estudos Africanos, UEM (1990): 97–124.

Wuyts, Marc. "The Political Economy of Portuguese Colonialism in Mozambique." *Mozambican Studies* [Amsterdam], no. 1 (1980): 1022.

———. "Mozambique: Economic Management-and Adjustment Policies." In *The IMF and the South*, ed. D. Ghai. London: Zed, 1991, pp. 215–35.

Young, Thom. "The Politics of Development in Angola and Mozambique." *African Affairs* 87, no. 347 (April 1988): 165–84.

Society

Agadjianian, Victor. "Negotiating Reproductive Change: Gender Social Interaction and Fertility in Mozambique." *Journal of Southern African Studies* 2 (June 2001): 291–309.

———. "Economic Security, Informational Resources, and Women's Reproductive Choices in Urban Mozambique." *Social Biology* 45, nos. 1–2 (1998): 60–79.

Almeida, Adelino Augusto Marques de. *Panorama de educação em Moçambique, 1973.* Lourenço Marques: Imprensa Nacional, 1973.

Almeida, Luís Moreira de. *A instrução pública em Moçambique: Sua evolução.* Lourenço Marques: Imprensa Nacional, 1956.

Alpers, Edward A. "Ethnicity, Politics and History in Mozambique." *Africa Today* 21, no. 4 (1974): 39–52.

———. "To Seek a Better Life: the Implications of Migration from Mozambique to Tanganyika for Class Formation and Political Behaviour." *Canadian Journal of African Studies* 18, no. 2 (1984): 367–88.

Amaral, Manuel Gomes da Gama. "O povo yao (mtundu wayao): Subsídios para o estudo de um povo do noroeste de Moçambique." Licenciatura Dissertation, Instituto Superior de Ciências Sociais e Política Ultramarina, Universidade Técnica de Lisboa, 1968.

"Antropologia cultural: Algumas referências." *Boletim do Centro de Documentação Científica [de Moçambique]* 14, no. 1 (January–March 1971): 56–64.

Araújo, Manuel. "Seis aldeias comunais da província de Inhambane." In *Garcia de Orta* (Lisboa), 11 (1986): 68–81.

———. "Dinámica das novas formas de redistribuição da população rural em Moçambique." *Gazeta Demográfica* (Maputo) (December 1988): 3–26.

Arnold, Guy. "Mozambique: Too Many Refugees, Too Few Skills and Far Too Little Money." *African Business*, no. 5 (1979): 1921.

Attawa, Marina. "Mozambique: From Symbolic Socialism to Symbolic Reform." *Journal of Modern African Studies* 26, no. 2 (June 1988): 211–26.

Augusto, António. *Estudos psicotécnicos.* Lisbon: Junta das Missões Geográficas e de Investigações Coloniais, 1949.

Azevedo, J. Mario. *Tragedy and Triumph: Mozambique Refugees in Southern Africa (1977–2001).* Portsmouth, N.H.: Heinemann, 2002.

———. "A Century of Colonial Education in Mozambique." In *Independence without Freedom: The Political Economy of Colonial Education in Southern Africa*, ed. Agrippah T. Mugomba and M. Nyaggah. Santa Barbara, Calif.: ABC-Clio, 1980, pp. 191–213.

———. "The Legacy of Colonial Education in Mozambique (1876–1976)." *A Current Bibliography on African Affairs*, New Series 11, no. 1 (1978–1979): 3–16.

———. *The Returning Hunter.* Thompson, Conn.: Interculture Associates, 1978.

———. "The Role of the Roman Catholic Church in the Politics and of the Colonial and Post Colonial State in Mozambique." In *Religion, State and Society in Contemporary Africa*, ed. Austin Metumara Ahanotu. New York: Lang, 1992, pp. 187–208.

Bady, A. "Les villages communitaires. Bases du pouvoir populaire Mozambicain." *Le Mois en Afrique* 215–216 (December/January 1984): 18–31.

Balmes, Pierre. "Le Mozambique." *Afrique Contemporaine*, no. 106 (1979): 8–15.

Barata, João Bernardo. *Legislação aplicável aos serviços de educação e ensino que se ministra em Moçambique.* Lourenço Marques: Minerva, 1973.

Barker, Carol. "Drugs and the Third World: The Mozambique Pharmaceutical Policy." *Lancet* (October 1, 1983): 780–82.

Barnes, Sam. *Humanitarian Aid Coordination during War and Peace in Mozambique, 1985–1995.* Piscataway, N.J.: Transaction, 1999.

Binford, Martha Butler. "Stalemate: A Study of Cultural Dynamics." Ph.D. diss., Michigan State University, East Lansing, 1971.

Binsky, Barry. *The Urban Problematic in Mozambique: Initial Post-independenee Responses, 1975–80.* Toronto: Centre for Urban and Community Studies, 1981.

Boleo, José de Oliveira. *Moçambique: Pequena monografia.* 2d ed. Lisbon: Agência Geral do Ultramar, 1966.

Bonga, Violet. *The Experience of Mozambican Refugees.* Unpublished ms. Geneva: UNHCR.

Boston, Thomas. "On the Transition to Feudalism in Mozambique." *Journal of African Studies* 8 (Winter 1981): 182–87.

Botha, Andries. "Mozambique: A Case Study on Human Freedoms." *African Freedom Annual* (1978): 125–31.

Boxer, Charles Ralph. *Race Relations in the Portuguese Colonial Empire, 1415–1825.* Oxford: Clarendon, 1963.

Braga, A. Rodrigues. "L'Afrique orientale portugaise et la maladie du sommeil." *Arquivo de Hygiene e Patologia Exóticas* 11, fasc. (30 de Abril de 1909): 192–195.

Cahen, M. "Entrons dans la Nation. Notes pour une étude du discours politique de la marginalité: Le cas de Renamo du Mozambique." *Politique Africaine* 67 (October 1997): 70–88.

"Uma campanha difamatória." *Boletim da Agência Geral das Colónias* 1, no. 2 (August 1925): 123–24.

Campbell, B. K. *Libération nationale et construction du socialisme en Afrique (Angola, Guinée Bissau, Mozambique).* Montreal: Nouvelle Optique, 1977.

Campbell, H. "War, Reconstruction and Dependence in Mozambique." *Third World Quarterly* 6 (1984): 839–67.

Capela, J. "Apontamento sobre os negreiros da Ilha de Moçambique, 1990–1920." *Boletim* 4 (AHM) (October 1998): 83–91.

Capela, José, and Eduardo Medeiros. *O tráfico de escravos de Moçambique para as ilhas do Índico.* Maputo: Universidade Eduardo Mondlane, 1987.

Casal, A.Y. "A Crise da produção familiar e as aldeias comunais em Moçambique." *Revista Internacional de Estudos Africanos* 8–9 (January–December 1988): 157–91.

Castanheira, Narciso. "Avícola E.E.: Desmascarados ladrões e infiltrados." *Tempo* (December 2, 1979): 8–13.

Centre d'Information sur le Mozambique. *Les femmes Mozambicaines: Textes de la II Conférence de l'Organisation de la Femme Mozambicaine.* Maputo. Paris 10/17 Novembre 1976.

Centro de Estudos Africanos. *A situacão nas antigas zonas libertadas de Cabo Delgado.* Maputo, 1983.

Centro de Estudos Africanos, UEM. *Avaliação socio-económica do projecto de Serviços Básics Urbanos*. Maputo: PAM—Conselho Executivo, 1985.

Chichava, J. *Participação communitária e desenvolvimento: O caso dos Grupos Dinamizadores em Moçambique*. Maputo: Assembleia Municipal, 1999.

———. *Proposta de divisão comunitaria e de organização da administração autarquica no município de Maputo*. Maputo: Assembleia Municipal, 1999.

Chonchol, M. E. *Guide bibliographique du Mozambique, Environnement naturel, développement et organisation villageoise*. Paris: Harmattan, 1979.

Christie, Lain. "Trois ans après . . . ." *Afrique* (London) 13 (1978): 34–36.

Christie, Frances, and Joseph Hanlon. *African Issues: Mozambique and the Great Flood of 2000*. Bloomington: Indiana University Press, International African Institute with James Curry, 2001.

Clerc, Andre D. *Chitlangou, Son of a Chief*. Trans. Margaret A. Bryan. London: Lutterworth, 1950; repr. Westport, Conn.: Negro Universities Press, 1971.

———. "The Marriage Laws of the Thonga Tribe." *Bantu Studies* 12 (July 1927): 75–105.

Cliff, Julie L. *Health in Mozambique: A Select Bibliography, 1950–1980*. London: Mozambique, Angola and Guinea Information Centre, 1980.

———, et al. "Mozambique Health Holding the Line." *Review of African Political-Economy* 36 (1986): 7–23.

Coimbra, Ramiro Duarte Henriques. "Bairros do caniço da cidade da Beira: Tentativa de interpretação humana." Ph.D. diss., Instituto Superior de Ciências Sociais e Política Ultramarina, Universidade Técnica de Lisboa, 1970.

Collin, Jean-Pierre. "Le Mozambique un an après l'indépendance." *Politique Étrangère* 5 (1976): 433–58.

Colónia de Moçambique. *Missão de combate às tripanosomíases: Relatório anual de 1947*. Lourenço Marques: Imprensa Nacional de Moçambique, 1948.

Conferência Episcopal de Moçambique. *Partilhar para crescer*. Comunicado da Conferência Episcopal de Moçambique às comunidades cristãs. Maputo: CEM, 2000.

———. *Para uma sã cooperação*. Comunicado da Conferência Episcopal de Moçambique às comunidades cristãs e a todo o povo moçambicano. Maputo: Author, 1998.

———. Comunicado dos bispos católicos de Moçambique às comunidades cristãs. Maputo: Author, 1998.

———. *Sinais de crescimento na fé*. Comunicado da Conferência Episcopal de Moçambique às comunidades cristãs.

Cruz, Teresa e Silva. "A IV região da Frelimo no sul de Moçambique: Lourenço Marques, 1964–65." *Estudos Africanos* 8 (1990): 127–41.

Cuidados de saúde primários em Moçambique e outros níveis de atenção de saúde. [Maputo]: Ministério da Saude, [1978].

Darch, C. "Are There Warlords in Provincial Mozambique? Question of the Social Base of MNR Banditry." *Review of African Political Economy* 46/47 (1990): 34–49.

Denghaas, Dieter, et al. *Strukturelle Abhängigkeit and Unterentwicklung am Beispiel Mozambiques*. Bonn: Wegener, n.d.

Depelchin, Jacques. "African Anthropology and History in the Light of the History of FRELIMO." *Contemporary Marxism* 7 (Fall 1983): 69–88.

Derlugyan, Georgi. "Mozambique: A Tight Knot of Problems." *International Affairs* 3 (March 1990): 103–11.

Desmaroux, Padre Félix. *Missão Santos Anjos de Quelimane, Doc. No. 6* (17 de Abril de 1893).

Dias, Jorge [and Dias, Margot]. *Os macondes de Moçambique*. 3 vols. Lisbon: n.p., 1940–1970.

———. et al. *Os macondes de Moçambique*. Lisbon: Junta de Investigações do Ultramar, Centro de Estudos de Antropologia Cultural, 1970.

Direcção Provincial dos Serviços de Estatística. *III recenseamento geral da população na Província de Moçambique*. Lourenço Marques: Imprensa Nacional, 1969.

———. *IV recenseamento geral da população, 1970*. Lourenço Marques: Direcção Provincial dos Serviços de Estatística, 1973–1974.

Dodge, Cole P., and Magne Raundalen. *Reaching Children in War: Sudan, Uganda and Mozambique*. Bergen: Sigma Forlag, 1991.

Dupeyrou, Padre Pedro. "Relatório do Reverendíssimo Superior da Missão de S. Francisco Xavier de Tumbini-Milange," Doc. No. 4, *Boletim da Sociedade de Geografia de Lisboa*, 14a série, no. 1 (1895): 655–60.

Earthy, E. Dora. "Note on the Totemism of the Ndau." *Bantu Studies* 5 (March 1931): 77–81.

———. "Of the Significance of the Body Markings of Some Natives of Portuguese East Africa." *South African Journal of Science* 21 (March 1924): 573–87.

———. *Valenge Women: The Social and Economic Life of the Valenge Women of Portuguese East Africa: An Ethnographic Study*. London: Oxford University Press for the International African Institute, 1933; repr., Cass, 1968.

"Education Policy in the People's Republic of Mozambique." *Journal of Modern African Studies* 14, no. 2 (June 1976): 331–39.

Elfferich, J. P. "Handel van portugees Oost-Afrika." *Afrika-Instituut. Mededelingen* 2, no. 11 (1949): 304–7.

Epstein, Andy, and Paul Epstein. "Health Care in Mozambique: Five Years Later." *Southern Africa* 13, no. 7 (September–October 1980): 23–24, 28.

Family Health Care, Africare. *A Review of Health Care in Mozambique: Issues, Analyses and Recommendations*. Washington, D.C.: Family Health Care Africare, 1978.

Feio, Manuel Moreira. *Indígenas de Moçambique*. Lisbon: Tipografia do Comércio, 1900.

Ferreira, Dom António Dias, Bispo titular das Thermopilas e Prelado de Moçambique. "Realtório sobre o estado religioso, moral e económico do districto de Inhambane," Doc. 5. *Boletim da Sociedade de Geografia de Lisboa*, 14a série, no. 1 (1895): 661–67.

Fondation Friedrich Ebert. *Seminário sobre a lei dos municípios realizado em Tete*, October 1995.

Fontoura, Alves. *Actas das sessões e teses: Missões religiosas em Moçambique*. *1930. 3o Congresso Colonial Nacional* (Lisbon: Tipografia e Papelaria Carmona, 1934): 20–22.

Francis, Donald. "The Demography of the Portuguese Territories: Angola, Mozambique and Portuguese Guinea." In *The Demography of Tropical Africa*, ed. W. L. Brass et al. Princeton, N.J.: Princeton University Press, 1968, pp. 440–65.

FRELIMO. *Mozambique: Du sous-développement au socialisme.* Rapport du Comité central au IV Congrès du Parti Frelimo (Maputo, 26–30 April 1983). Paris: Harmattan, 1983.

———. *Por um consenso nacional de normalização de vida: Relatório do Comité Central.* 5th Congreès, Maputo, 1989.

———. *Relótorio do Comité Central ao VI° Congresso.* Maputo: Author, 1991.

Friedland, Elaine A. *Public Policies to Improve the Living Conditions of the Poor: A Comparison of Mozambique and Zimbabwe.* Washington, D.C.: American Political Science Association, 1984.

Galvão, J. A. Lopes. "O regime da mão de obra indígena em Moçambique." *Boletim da Agência Geral das Colónias* 1, no. 3 (Setembro de 1925): 116–18.

Gaspar, M. D. C., H. A. Costa, C. R. dos Santos, R. M. Manjate, and J. Schoemaker. "*Moçambique: Inquérito demográfico e de saúde.*" Maputo: National Institute of Statistics and Calverton, Maryland, 1998.

Gasperini, Lavinia. "Direction culturelle: Éducation et développement au Mozambique." *Révue Tiers Monde* 35, no. 97 (January–March 1984): 189–204.

———. "Il sistema educativo in Mozambico: L'uomo nuovo come obiettivo." *Politica Internazionale* 10 (1980): 57–63.

Gasperini, Lavinia, and Elimar Nascimento. "Scuola e decolonizzazione in Mozambico." *Scuola e Citta* (Rome) 31, no. 4 (1980): 169–78.

Geffray, Christian, and Mogens Pedersen. *Transformação da Organização Social e do sistema agrário do campesinato no distrito de Erati.* Maputo: UEM, 1985.

Grupo, Urbe. *Programa Nacional de desenvolvimento urbano e habitacional, Proposta preliminar. Maputo:* Instituto Nacional de Planeamento Físico, 1993.

———. *Projecto de reformas dos orgãos locais, Grupo III Infraestruturas, urbanização, habitação, termos de referência dos projectos-piloto.* Maputo: Author, 1992.

Guerreiro, Manuel Viegas. *Os macondes de Moçambique.* Lisbon: Junta de Investigações do Ultramar, 1966.

Gundersen, A. "*Popular Justice in Mozambique: Between State Law and Folk Law.*" *Social and Legal Studies* 1, no. 2 (1992): 257–82.

Gunha, António Raimundo da. "Contribuição para o estudo do povo 'wayao.' Ph.D. diss., Instituto Superior de ciências Sociais e Política Ultramarina, Universidade Técnica de Lisboa, 1966.

Hamilton, R. "Cultural Change and Literary Suppression in Mozambique." *Issue* 8, no. 1 (Spring 1987): 39–42.

Hanlon, J. "Supporting Peasants in Their Fight to Defend Their Land: A Study of Land Conflict and the New Land Law." Mimeo. Maputo: 1995.

Hedges, David. "Educação, missões e a ideologia política de assimilação: História." *Cadernos de História* 1 (June 1985): 718.

Henderson, R. D'Arcy. "Marxism and Mozambique. " *African Affairs* 77, no. 309 (October 1978): 441–62.

Hiller, Padre João. *Missão de São José de Boroma: Relatório, 1893.* Res. Maço No. *3, Doc. 3o, 32* (Sociedade de Geografia de Lisboa), 1893.

Inspecção de Instrução Pública. *O ensino indígena na colónia de Moçambique.* Lourenço Marques: Imprensa Nacional, 1930.

Isaacman, Allen F. *Mozambique: The Africanization of a European Institution: The Zambesi Prazos, 1750–1902.* Madison: University of Wisconsin Press, 1972.

———. "Social Banditry in Zimbabwe (Rhodesia) and Mozambique, 1894–1907: An Expression of Early Peasant Protest." *Journal of Southern African Studies* 4, no. 1 (October 1977): 1–30.

———. "Coercion, Paternalism and the Labour Process: The Mozambican Cotton Regime, 1938–1961." *Journal of Southern African Studies* 18, no. 3 (1992): 487–526.

Jacquart, E. *Les enfants de la rue à Maputo.* Mémoire de stage, mimeo. Maputo, 1994.

Jacques, A. A. "Terms of Kinship and Corresponding Patterns of Behavior among the Thonga." *Bantu Studies* 3 (December 1929): 328–48.

Jansen, P. C. M., and Orlando Mendes. *Plantas medicinais seu uso tradicional em Moçambique.* Maputo: Ministério da Saúde, Gabinete de Estudos de Medicina Tradicional, 1983.

Jelley, Diana, and Richard J. Madeley. "Preventive Health Care for Mothers and Children: A Study in Mozambique." *Journal of Tropical Medicine and Hygiene* 86 (1983): 229–36.

Johnston, Anton. *Education in Mozambique, 1975–84: A Review.* Stockholm: Swedish International Development Authority, 1984.

Johnston, T. F. "Structure in Tsonga Music. An Analysis of Social Terms." *Journal of African Studies* 3, no. (Spring 1976): 51–81.

Jornadas de Saúde, Chongoene, 9 a 13 de Novembro de 1981. Maputo: Ministério da Saúde, [1981].

Jornal do Professor. February–March 1981—Bimonthly. Maputo: Ministério da Educação e Cultura.

Judite, Francisca, and Adolfo Casal. *Documentos de base na análise social: Leis e regulamentos sobre educação e ensino durante o período colonial, 1934–1975.* Maputo: Centro de Estudos de Comunicação, Universidade Eduardo Mondlane, 1978.

Junod, Henri. *The Life of a South African Tribe.* London: Macmillan, 1927; repr., New York: University Books, 1962.

———. *La tribu et la langue thonga.* Lausanne: Bridel, 1896.

———. *Usos e costumes dos bantos: A vida duma tribo do sul de Africa.* Vol. I. *Vida Social.* Lourenço Marques, 1974.

———. "A Contribution to the Study of Ndau Demography, Totemism and History." *Bantu Studies* 18 (1934): 175–90.

———. "Some Notes on Tsopi Origins." *Bantu Studies* 3 (July 1927): 57–73.

———. "The Mbila of the Tsopi." *Bantu Studies* 3 (July 1929): 275–87.

Kruks, Sonia, and Ben Wisner. "The State, the Party and the Female Peasantry in Mozambique." *Journal of Southern African Studies* 11, no. 1 (October 1984): 106–27.

Kuder, Manfred. *Moçambique: Geographia soziale. U. Woitschaftl Landeskunde.* Darmstadt: Wissenschaftliche Buchgesellschaft, 1975.

Kuper, Hilda. "The Shona." In *The Shona and Ndebele of Southern Rhodesia.* London: International African Institute, 1954.

Land Tenure Center. "Legal Uncertainity and Land Disputes in the Peri-urban Areas of Mozambique: Land Markets in Transition." Research Paper 121, University of Wisconsin, 111 pp., 1995.

Lazar, Carol. "A South African Girl in Frelimo Land." *Personality* (August 8, 1975): 34–47.

Leal, José Rodrigues do, and C. Walter Howard. "Campanhas antimaláricas em Lourenço Marques." *Arquivos de Hygiene e Patologias Exóticas* 3, fasc. 1 (November 15, 1910): 59–77.

Lisboa, Eugénio A. "Education in Angola and Mozambique." In *Education in South Africa,* ed. Brian Rose London: Collier-Macmillan, 1970, pp. 276–333.

Lundin, I. "Realidades sócio-culturais e modelos sócio-politicos: Um problema de democratização." In J. Magode, ed. *Moçambique: Etnicidades, nacionalismo e o estado, transição inacabada.* Maputo: CEEI/ISRI, 1996.

Machado, A. J. de Mello. *Entre os macuas de Angoche.* Lisbon: Prelo, 1970.

Machel, Samora Moisés. "Make the Information Sector an Advanced Detachment of the Class Struggle and of the Revolution." *AIM Information Bulletin,* no. 18 (Supplement) (1977), [n.p.].

Madeley, Richard et al. "The Advent of Primary Health Care in Mozambique." *Âmbio* 12, no. 6 (1983): 322–25.

Mann, Roger. "What Future for Whites?" *Africa Report* 20, no. 6 (1975): 4145.

Marchand, J. *Economie et société dans la transition libérale au Mozambique, Lusotopie: Transitions liberals en Afrique lusophone.* Paris: Karthala, 1995.

Margarido, Alfredo. "L'enseignement en Afrique dite portugaise." *Révue Française d'Etudes Politiques Africaines* 56 (August 1970): 62–85.

Marshall, J. *Education in a Mozambican Factory.* Bellville: University of the Western Cape Centre for Adult and Continuing Education, 1990.

———. *Literacy, State Formation and People's Power.* Cape Town, 1990.

Martins, Helder. "In the Words of the Minister." *World Medicine* (January 26, 1977): 22.

———. "Pharmaceutical Policy in Independent Mozambique: The First Years." *IDS Bulletin* 14, no. 4 (1983): 62–70.

Marwick, M. G. "An Ethnographic Classic Brought to Light." *Africa* 34, no. 1 (January 1964): 46–56.

Marzagão, Carlos and Malcolm Segall. "Drug Selection: Mozambique." *World Development* 11, no. 3 (1983): 205–16.

May, Jacques M., and Donna L. McLellan. *The Ecology of Malnutrition in Seven Countries of Southern Africa and in Portuguese Guinea*. New York: Hafner, 1971.

McCallin, Margaret, and Shirley Fozzard. *The Impact of Traumatic Events on the Psychological Well-Being of Mozambican Refugee Women and Children*. Geneva: International Catholic Child Bureau, 1990.

Medeiros, Eduardo. *Bibliografia etnográfica macua: Subsídios para uma bibliografia dos estudos sociais em Moçambique*. Maputo: Faculdade de Letras, Universidade Eduardo Mondlane, 1980.

———. "A evolução demográfica da cidade de Lourenço Marques, 1895–1975." *Revista Internacional de Estudos Africanos* 3 (January–December 1985): 231–39.

———. *O sistema linhageiro macua-lomwe*. Maputo: Faculdade de Letras, Universidade Eduardo Mondlane, 1985.

Meigos, Serafina. *Human Rights Problems and Prospects in Africa: A Study of the Role of Mozambican Women Organizations*. Dar-es-Salaam: Centre for Foreign Relations, 1981.

Meillassoux, C. "Entre l'état et les 'bandits armés' par l'Afrique du Sud: Les paysans ignorés du Mozambique." *Le Monde Diplomatique* (October 1985).

Mendonça, Gertrudes. "The Zone of Influence of Some Rural Health Centres in Mozambique." *Ethiopian Journal of Health Development* 1, no. 1 (1984): 41–46.

Messeca, P. *Pesquisa de campo sobre constructores informais nos bairros de Laulane Mahotas, Magoanine, Zimpeto, Matola, Libertade*. Maputo, multigr. 1993.

Mesquita, Teo. "FRELIMOS Kampf gegen moralische and materielle Korruption." *3 [dritte] Welt Magazin* 5/6 (1975): 30–31.

Middlemas, Keith. "Twentieth Century White Society in Mozambique." *Tarikh*, 6, no. 2 (1979): 30–45.

Ministry of Health, Maputo. *Report of the People's Republic of Mozambique*. Nazareth: World Health Organization, 1982.

Mitchell, Hilary Flegg. *Aspects of Urbanization and Age Structure in Lourenço Marques, 1957*. [Lusaka]: Institute for African Studies, University of Zambia, 1975.

Monreal, T. "Inquérito comportamento reproductivo da mulher moçambicana, 1987." Maputo: Ministry of Health, Eduardo Mondlane University, and UNFPA, 1991.

Moreira, Eduardo. *Portuguese East Africa: A Study of Its Religious Needs*. New York: World Dominion Press, 1936.

Mozambique: Repatriation and Reintegration of Mozambican Refugees. Geneva: UNHCR, March 1993.

"Mozambican Women's Conference." *People's Power in Mozambique, Angola and Guinea-Bissau* 6 (January–February 1977): 5–26.

Mozambique Laws and Statute. *Legislação aplicável ao ensino particular, 1973*. Lourenço Marques: Imprensa Nacional de Moçambique, 1973.

Mugomba, Agrippah. "Education in Mozambique: From Underdevelopment to Revolution." *Journal of Southern Africa Studies* 3 (October 1978): 421–32.

Mugomba, Agrippah, and Mougo Nyaggah, eds. *Independence without Freedom: The Political Economy of Colonial Education in Southern Africa.* Santa Barbara, Calif.: ABC-Clio, 1980.

Mulher Moçambicana: Boletim da OMM. Maputo: Secretariado Nacional da OMM, March 1986.

Nascimento, Elimar Pinheiro de. "A concepção da educação em Moçambique: Notas introdutórias." *Estudos Afro-Asiáticos* (Rio de Janeiro) 4 (1980): 21–41.

National Commission for Natural Disasters. "Nutritional Surveillance: Morbidity and Mortality from the 1983 Famine." *Weekly Epidemiological Record* (Geneva) 37 (September 14, 1984): 284–87.

Negrão, J. "Habitat in Rural Settlements: The Mozambican Cases." *Architecture and Development Course*, 1992.

Neves, (das) J. "Tete e o trabalho migratório para a Rodésia do Sul, 1890–1913." *Boletim* 10 (AHM) (1991): 83–103.

Niddrie, David L. "Some Recent Settlement Schemes in Angola." *Journal of the American Portuguese Cultural Society* 1 (1967): 25–31.

Nimpuno, Krisno, et al. *The Malhangalene Survey: A Housing Study of an Unplanned Settlement in Maputo, 1976.* Gothenburg: Chalmers University of Technology, 1977.

Oliveria, Martins Joaquim Pedro. *Relatório da comissão encarregada de estudar as reformas a introduzir no sistema dos prazos de Moçambique*, 1889.

Opello, W. C. "Pluralism and Elite Conflict in an Independence Movement: FRELIMO in the 1960s." *Journal of Southern African Studies* 2, no. 1 (October 1975): 66–82.

Penvenne, Jeanne. *African Workers and Colonial Racism, Mozambican Strategies and Struggles in Lourenço Marques, 1877–1962.* London: Heinemann, 1995.

———. *Making Our Own Way: Women Working in Lourenço Marques, 1900–1933.* Boston: African Studies Center, Boston University, 1986.

Pinsky, B. *The Urban Problematic in Mozambique: Initial Post-independence Response 1975–80.* Major Report No. 21, Centre for Urban and Community Studies, University of Toronto, 1982.

Pires, Edmundo Andrade. *Evolução do ensino em Moçambique nos últimos 40 anos.* Lourenço Marques: Imprensa Nacional, 1966.

Pisacane, Alfredo. "Reduction of Child Hospital Mortality in Mozambique through a Nurse Training Programme." *Annals of Tropical Pediatrics* 5 (1985): 7–10.

PNUD. *Evaluation Report of the Urban Development and Housing Programme Formulation*, Report of the Evaluation Mission. Maputo: n.p., December 1993.

PNUD/UNCHS, Butcher C. *Bairro Polana Caniço a Maputo, proposta de projecto preliminar*, 1992.

PNUD/UNCHS, Ministério da Constução e Águas. *Habitação e condição de vida nas áreas peri-urbanas da cidade de Maputo,* Projecto MOZ/86/005, June 1991.

Raikes, Philip. "Food Policy and Production in Mozambique since Independence." *Review of African Political Economy* 29 (July 1984): 95–107.

Raposo, Isabel. *O viver de hoje e ontem: Aldeia e musha.* Maputo: EMU, 1991.

"Recenseamento da população do Concelho de Lourenço Marques referido a 17 de Abril de 1904." *Boletim Oficial de Moçambique*, no. 48 supplement (1 December 1904): 1–12.

Reis, Carlos Santos. *A população de Lourenço Marques em 1894 (um censo inédito).* Lisbon: Centro de Estudos Demográficos, 1973.

Relatório da Missão de S. José de H'Langueni, por Padre Augusto Soares Pinheiro, 11-3-37-15 Fevereiro 1894 (Biblioteca da Sociedade de Geografia de Lisboa), 1894.

Relatório da Missão de S. Pedro Claver de Ricido, no Zumbo, por Padre Estevam Czimerman. Cópia 11-30-12 Marco 1893 (Biblioteca da Sociedade de Geografia de Lisboa), 1893.

Relatório da Paróquia de S. Sebastião da Ilha de Moçambique, por Padre Emílio Augusto da Esperança Machado. Cópia 30, 30 Dezembro 1893-11-3-33 (Biblioteca da Sociedade de Geografia de Lisboa), 1893.

Relatório da Prelazia de Moçambique pelo Reverendo Bispo António de Himeria, S.S.G.L., 2 de Maio de 1894. Boletim da Sociedade de Geografia de Lisboa 14, nos. 7 and 8 (1895): 568–81.

Relatório do serviço de saúde em Quelimane, relativo ao anno de 1877. Arquivos Médico-Coloniais 1, no. 1 (1890): 43–88.

Relatório sobre a câmara eclesiástica de Moçambique, por Padre Afonso Pereira II-3-35-20 Maio 1894. 20 Maio 1894-papel-11 Biblioteca da Sociedade de Geografia de Lisboa), 1894.

Repartição Central de Estatística. "Censo da populacão não indígena em 2 de Maio de 1935." *Boletim Económico e Estatística*, special series, no. 13 (1936): 1–99.

Repartição de Estatística. "Censo da população indígena da colónia de Moçambique." *Boletim Economico e Estatística*, special series, no. 11 (1932): 1–45.

Repartição de Estatística Geral. *Recenseamento geral da população em 1950.* Lourenço Marques: Imprensa Nacional, 1953–1955.

Repartição Técnica de Estatística. *Censo da população em 1940.* Lourenço Marques: Imprensa Nacional, 1942–45.

———. *Recenseamento da população não indígena em 12 de Junho de 1945.* Lourenço Marques: Imprensa Nacional, 1947.

Resende, Sebastião Soares de, Bishop of Beira. *Projecção do natal em Africa.* [n.p.], 1963.

Revista Médica de Moçambique. Maputo: Ministério da Saúde, 1982.

Reys, Lesseps José António Lourenço. *Variação humana na reposta farmacológica: Estudos de farmacogenética em Moçambique.* Doctoral Dissertation, Faculty of Medicine, University of Lourenço Marques, 1971.

Rita-Ferreira, A. *Moçambique Post-25 de Abril: Causas do êxodo da populaçao de origem europeia e asiática,* extracto Moçambique. Cultura e História de um Pais, Instituo de Antropologia, Universidad de Coimbra, 1988.

———. *Povos de Moçambique: história e cultura.* Porto: Afrontamento, 1975.

———. *Agrupamento e caracterização étnica dos indígenas de Moçambique.* Lisbon: Ministério do Ultramar, 1985.

———. *Bibliografia etnológica de Moçambique, das origens a 1954*. Lisbon: Junta de Investigações do Ultramar, 1961.

———. *"Etno-história e cultura tradicional do grupo Angune (Nguni)."* Memórias do *Instituto de Investigação Científica de Moçambique* 11, Series C (1974): 1–247.

Rodrigues, Francisco. *Os Jesuítas portugueses na África oriental: 1560 a 1759–1890 a 1910*. Porto: n.p., 1927.

Roesch, Otto. "RENAMO and the Peasantry in Southern Mozambique: A View from Gaza." *Canadian Journal of African Studies* 26 (1992): 3.

Sachs, A., and G. H. Welch. *Liberating the Law: Creating Popular Justice in Mozambique*. London: Zed, 1990.

Sachs, Albie. "Changing the Terms of the Debate: A Visit to Popular Tribunals in Mozambique." *Journal of African Law* 28, nos. 1–2 (1984): 99–108.

Saevfors, I. "Maxaquene, a Comprehensive Account of the First Urban Upgrading Experience in the New Mozambique, Human Settlements and Socio-Cultural Environments." Maputo: UNESCO, March 1986.

Samuels, Michael A., and Normal A. Bailey. "Education, Health, and Social Welfare." In D. M. Abshire and M. A. Samuels, eds. *Portuguese Africa: A Handbook*. New York: Praeger, 1969, pp. 178–201.

Sant'Ana, F. Firmino de. "Rapport d'une mission d'étude en Zambézie." *Arquivos de Hygiene e Patologia Exóticas* 3, fasc. 2 (March 31, 1912): 115–213.

Santos, João dos, Jr. *Missão antropologica de Moçambique*. Lisbon: Agência Geral das Colónias, 1940.

Santos, Joaquim. *Contribuição para o estudo da antropológia de Moçambique*. Porto: Mendonça, 1944.

Santos, Manuel Pimentel Pereira dos. "A Four Year Programme" *(Speech to Reg. Association in Mozambique)*. Lourenço Marques: Imprensa Nacional de Mozambique, 1972.

Santos, Norberto Teixeira. "Avaliação nutricional da população infantil banto (0–5 anos) de uma zona suburbana da cidade de Lourenço Marques." *Revista de Ciências Médicas* 17, séries B (1974): 1–400.

Santos, Silva, A (e). *Estudos exploratórios sobre a comunidade de "deslocados" do bairro de urbanização de Maputo*. Uma perspectiva sociológica. *Estudos Moçambicanos* (UEM) (May 1993): 79–125.

Schubert, B. *Alleviating Destitution in the Cities of Mozambique: An Attempt to Design an Effective and Efficient Urban Safetynet*. Maputo, April 1992.

Searle, Chris. *Beyond the Skin: How Mozambique Is Defeating Racism*. London: Liberation, 1979.

———. *We're Building the New School: Diary of a Teacher in Mozambique*. London: Zed, 1981.

Secretaria Geral da Província de Moçambique. *Recenseamento da população e das abitações da cidade de Lourenço Marques e seus subúrbios, referidos a 1 de Dezembro de 1912*. Lourenço Marques: Imprensa Nacional, 1913.

Segall, Malcolm. "Forward March, Left, Right? Health Care in Liberated Mozambique." *Medicine in Society* 6, nos. 2/3 (1980): 12–16.

Semin-Panzer, Ursula. "Probleme der Wirtschaftsentwicklung Mosambiks in der Transformation zum Sozialismus." *Informationsdienst Südliches Africa* 9 (September 1977): 12–18.

Serapião, Luís B. "The Influence of the Catholic Church on the Portuguese Colonial Policy." *A Current Bibliography on African Affairs* 7, no. 2 (Spring 1974): 138–18.

————. "Frelimo's Socialism in the 1980's." *Current Bibliography on African Affairs* 18, no. 4 (1985–1986): 309–18.

————. "Religion and Racism in Southern Africa: A Case Study in Mozambique." *Journal of the Society for Common Insights* 2, no. 2 (November 1978): 121–23.

————. "The Roman Catholic Church and the Principle of Self-Determination: A Case Study of Mozambique." *Journal of Church and State* 23 (Spring 1981): 323–35.

Serra, C. *Combates pela mentalidade sociológica*. Maputo: Livraria Universitária, UEM, 1997.

————. *Identidade, moçambicanidade, moçambicanização*. Maputo: Livraria Universitária, UEM, 1998.

Sheppard, Samona. "Mozambique: Progress toward Health Care for Everyone." *Journal of Health Politics, Policy and Law* 6 (Fall 1981): 520–27.

Shropshire, Denys. "The Initiation of a Doctor of the WaBarwe Tribe." *Man* 29 (December 1929): 205–6.

————. "A Kupemha Shawe of the WaBarwe Tribe." *Man* 30 (July 1930): 125–26.

————. "Midzimu Worship in a Village of the WaBarwe Tribe." *Man* 24 (May 1934): 65–67.

Sidaway, J. D., and M. Power. "Socio-spatial Transformations in the 'Post-Socialist' Periphery: The Case of Maputo, Mozambique." *Environment and Planning*. 27(1995): 1463–91.

Silva, A. J. da, and A. Condy. *Pobreza, emprego e a questão demográfica na cidade de Maputo*. Maputo: Unidade de População e Planificação, 1991.

Silva, Patrício Dias. "Relatório da epidemia de peste bubónica no Chinde na Província de Moçambique." *Arquivos de Hygiene e Patologias Exóticas* 1, fasc. 2 (December 31, 1906): 202–11.

Sistema Nacional de Educação: Linhas gerais. Maputo: Instituto Nacional do Livro e do Disco, 1985.

Sketchley, Peter. "Problems of the Transformation of Social Relations of Production in Post-independence Mozambique." *People's Power* (Winter 1979): 28–40.

Smith, Alan Kent. "The Peoples of Southern Mozambique: An Historical Survey." *Journal of African History* 14, no. 4 (1973): 565–80.

Sopa, A. *Condições de habitabilidade numa pequena povoação costeira da Africa Austral, 1892–1925*. Boletim 6 (AHM) (1989): 77–127.

Sousa, Joaquim José de. "Escola de Artes e Ofícios da Moamba." *Moçambique: Documentário Trimestral*, no. 15 (1938): 61–70.

"The Struggle to Build a Healthy Mozambique." *Mozambique Revolution* (Dar-es-Salaam) 55 (April–June 1973): 17–18.

Teyssier, S. *Etude préalable dans la périphérie de Maputo, Mozambique: Rapport de Mission.* Paris: Cimade Solidarités Internationales, June 1992.

Tickner, Vincent. "Military Attacks, Drought and Hunger in Mozambique." *Review of African Political Economy*, no. 33 (August 1985): 89–91.

UNHCR. *Mozambique: Repatriation and Reintegration of Mozambique Refugees Status Report.* Geneva: UNHCR, 20 June 1992–1995.

UNICEF/WHO Joint Committee on Health Policy. *National Decision-Making for Primary Health Care: A Study.* Geneva: World Health Organization, 1981.

United Nations. G.A. *Assistance* A/8023/Add. 3; A/AC.96/412 and Add. 1 (1970).

———. G.A. *Education* A/AC.109/L. 625/Add. 2 (Part II) (1970).

———. G.A. *Education* A/AC.109/L843 (1973).

———. G.A. *Labor* E/CN.4/AC.22/RT, 89, 91 (1970).

———. G.A. *Race Relations* (00014) A/39/18 (April 1985).

———. G.A. *South African Refugees* (000713), no. 25 (January 1986).

Urdang, Stephanie. "Pre-condition for Victory: Women's Liberation in Mozambique and Guinea-Bissau." *Issue*, 8, no. 2 (Spring 1978): 25–31.

———. "Rural Transformations: Women in the New Society." *Africa Report* 30, no. 2 (March–April 1985): 66–70.

Vail, Leroy. "Plantation Protest: The History of the Mozambican Song." *Journal of Southern African Studies* 5, no. 1 (1978): 1–25.

Vaz, Manuel. *O ensino missionário: Uma polémica jornalística de princípios de 1960.* Lourenço Marques: Notícias, Minerva Central, 1965.

Venturini, Ernesto. "La problématique de la santé mentale au Mozambique." *Psychopathologie Africaine* (Dakar, Senegal) 16, no. 3 (1980): 285–307.

Vieria, Sérgio. "A Luta Continua: The Mozambique Revolution Today." *Political Affairs* 40 (April 1981): 24–31.

Vihena, Ernesto Jardim de. "Influência Islâmica na costa oriental da Africa." *Boletim da Sociedade de Geografia de Lisboa*, 1906 (24a. série).

Vines, A. *Conspicious Destruction: War, Famine and the Reform Process in Mozambique.* New York: Human Rights Watch, 1992.

Vletter, F. (de). *O Sector informal urbano em Moçambique: Uma maioria negligenciada.* Maputo: Min. do Trabalho / Gabinete de Promoção de Emprego, 1992.

Walt, Gillian, and Julie Cliff. "The Dynamics of Health Policies in Mozambique, 1975–85." *Health Policy and Planning* 1, no. 2 (1986): 148–57.

Walt, Gillian, and Angela Melamed, eds. *Mozambique: Towards a People's Health Service.* London: Zed, 1983.

Walt, Gillian, and David Wield. *Health Policies in Mozambique.* Milton Keynes, Eng.: Open University Press, 1983.

Watts, Geoff. "Mozambique: Medicine with Politics." *New Scientists* 74 (April 1977): 70–72.

———. "What to Do When the Doctors Leave." *World Medicine* (January 26, 1977): 17–20, 25–26, 28.

Willenson, Kim, and James Pringle. "Great White Fathers. " *Newsweek* 89, no. 15 (1977): 13.

Wilson, K. B. "Cults of Violence and Counter-Violence in Mozambique." *Journal of Southern African Studies* 18, no. 3 (September 1992): 527–82.

Wuyts, M. "The Mechanization of Present-Day Mozambican Agriculture." *Development and Change* 12 (1981): 1–27.

———. "Money, Planning and Rural Transformation in Mozambique." *Journal of Development Studies* 22 (1985): 180–207.

Young, Sherilynn J. "Fertility and Famine: Women's Agricultural History in Southern Mozambique." In Robin Palmer and Neil Parsons, eds. *The Roots of Rural Poverty in Central and Southern Africa*. London: Heinemann, 1977, pp. 8–81.

Science

Aasland, Tertit. *Research in Mozambique: A Survey of the Research Sector in Mozambique with an Introduction on Norwegian Assistance to Development Research and to Mozambique*. Oslo: [NORAD], 1984.

Araújo, Manuel G. Mendes de. *Moçambique. Aspectos geográficos*. Maputo: INLD, 1982.

Awepa—African-European Institute. *Mozambique's Unnatural Disaster Persists.* 1989.

Balsan, François. *Terres vierges au Mozambique*. Paris: Plon, 1960.

Barnes, Barbara. "Flooding in the Zambezi River Valley." *Southern Africa (New York)* (1978): 28–29.

Bruton, Michael N., and Keith H. Cooper. *Studies on the Ecology of Maputoland*. Grahamstown: Rhodes University; Durban: Natal Branch of the Wildlife Society of Southern Africa, 1980.

Cahen, M. "Mozambique: Histoire géopolique d'un pays sans nation." *Lusotopie: Géopolitiques des mondes lusophones*, nos. 1–2, 1994.

Casal, A. Y. *A Crise da produção familiar e as aldeias comunais em Moçambique: Revista International de Estudos Africanos*, no. 8-9 (January–December 1988): 157–91.

Chingono, M. F. *Conspicuous Destruction: War, Famine, and the Reform Process in Mozambique*. New York: Human Rights Watch, 1992.

Chonchol, Mafia-Edy. *Guide bibliographique du Mozambique: Environement naturel, dévéloppement et organisation villageoise*. Paris: L'Harmattan, 1979.

Ciência e tecnologia. August 1980—irregular. Maputo: Ministério da Indústria e Energia; Universidade Eduardo Mondlane.

Colin, Jean-Pierre. "Le Mozambique un an après l'indépendence." *Politique Etrangère* 5 (1976): 433–58.

Construir. Maputo: Ministério das Obras Públicas e Habitação. Maputo: Faculdade de Engenharia Civil, Universidade Eduardo Mondlane, October 1979.

Cruz e Silva, Teresa. *A IV Região da Frelimo no sul de Mocambique: Lourenço Marques, 1964–65. Estudos Africanos* 8 (1990): 127–41.

Dias, J. A. Travessos Santos. *Abecedário dos mamíferos selvagens de Moçambique: Componentes de major vulto da fauna terrestre.* Maputo: Empresa Moderna, 1981.

Environmental Investigation Agency. *Under Fire: Elephants in the Front Line.* London, 1992.

Exell, A. W., et al. *Flora zambesíaca.* London: Royal Botanical Gardens, 1960.

Facultade de Arquitectura e Planeamento Fisico. *Contribuação para o Estudo do Planeamento urbano da Grande Maputo,* 1995.

Farfan, J. e Alvarinho. *Programma de abastecimento de água aos bairros periféricos das cidades de Moçambique (PAABP), Relatorio final.* Maputo, 1992.

Ferreira, Maria Corinta, and Gunderico da Veiga Ferreira. *Forest Entomology of Mozambique: Contribution for the Study of the Xylophagus Insects.* Lourenço Marques: Junta de Comércio Externo, 1951–1957.

Garcia, J. G. *Contribuições para o conhecimento da flora de Angola e de Moçambique.* Lisbon: Junta de Investigações do Ultramar, 1959.

Geffray, C. "Vivre et manger en guerre au Mozambique." In *Les spectres de Malthus,* ed. Gendreau F. Meillassoux et al. *Déséquilibres alimentaires, désiquilibres démographiques.* Paris: EDI, 1991.

Hermele, K. *Land Struggles and Social Differentiation in Southern Mozambique: Case Study of Hokwe, Limpopo, 1950–1987.* Uppsala: Scandinavian Institute for African Studies, 1988.

Instituto Nacional de Planeamento Fisico (INPF)—Conselho Executivo da Cidade de Maputo. *Plano de Estrutura: Cidade de Maputo.* Maputo: Author, 1985.

Landell-Mills, P. "Creating Transparency, Predictability and an Enabling Environment for Private Enterprise." Paper Presented at Wilton Park Special Conference, 1992.

MacNae, William, and Margaret Kalk, eds. *A Natural History of Inhaca Island, Mozambique.* Johannesburg: Witwatersrand University Press, 1969.

McDonald, David, ed. *On Borders: Perspectives on International Migration in Southern Africa.* New York: Palgrave, 2000.

McNally, T. "Adventure in Mozambique." *Outdoor Life* 129 (January 1972): 31–33.

Neeuws, Rene. *Mozambique: National Report on Socio-Economic Development and Environmental Problems.* Maputo: State Secretariat for Physical Planning, 1985.

Myre, Mário. *A vegetação do extremo sul da província de Moçambique: Contribuição para o seu estudo.* Lisbon: Junta de Investigações de Moçambique, 1964.

Pinto, António A. da Rosa, and Donald W. Lamm. "Contribution to the Study of the Ornithology of Sul do Save, Mozambique." *Memórias do Museu Dr. Álvaro de Castro* 2 (1953): 65–85; 3 (1955): 125–59; 4 (1956): 107–67; 5 (1960): 69–126.

Saul, John. "Development Studies for Social Change in Southern Africa." *Review* 8, no. 2 (Fall 1984): 173–96.

Soetre, Roald, and Rui de Paula e Silva. *The Marine Fish Resources of Mozambique*. Maputo: Serviço de Investigações Pesqueiras; Bergen: Institute of Marine Research, 1979.

Sousa, António Figueiredo Gomes e. *Dendrologia de Moçambique: Estudo geral.* Lourenço Marques: Centro de Documentação Agrária, Instituto de Investigação Agronómica de Moçambique, [n.d.].

Sousa, Mafia Inelda, and Margarida Dias. *Catálogo de peixes de Moçambique, zona sul, mais frequentemente desembarcados nos portos pesqueiros de importância do sul de Moçambique: Maputo, Inhaca, Inhambane e Inhassoro.* Maputo: Instituto de Desenvolvimento Pesqueiro, 1981.

Torres, F. Oliveira. "O cancro em Moçambique: Influência dos factores mesológicos." *Revista de Ciências Médicas* [Lourenço Marques, Mozambique] 1, série B (1969): 1–255.

Uate, Teodósio. "The Research Situation in the People's Republic of Mozambique." In *National Research Councils in Developing Countries: SAREC Seminar with Collaborating Agencies, Stockholm, Tammsvik, 16–21 January 1982.* Stockholm: Swedish Agency for Research Cooperation with Developing Countries, 1984.

UNDP/World Bank. *Mozambique Issues and Options in the Energy Sector.* New York: Author, 1987.

Waterhouse, R. *Mozambique: Rising from the Ashes.* Oxford: OXFAM, 1996.

Werger, M. J. A. *Biogeography and Ecology of Southern Africa.* The Hague: Junk, 1978.

About the Authors

Mario Azevedo was born in Mozambique and lived there until 1965, when he left as a refugee. He holds a B.A. degree in history from Catholic University, an M.A. in European history from American University, and a Ph.D. in African history from Duke University. He also has a master's degree in public health from the University of North Carolina at Chapel Hill. Azevedo is a Frank Porter Graham Professor and chair of the African-American and African Studies Department at the University of North Carolina at Charlotte. He is a well-known author and is an expert on former French Equatorial Africa, with special focus on Chad and Lusophone and southern Africa. Among his most recent books, the following stand out: *Tragedy and Triumph: Mozambique Refugees in Southern Africa* (1977–2001) (Heinemann, 2002); *Roots of Violence: A History of War in Chad* (Gordon & Breach, 1998), *Chad: A Nation in Search of Its Future* (coauthored with Emmanuel Nnadozie, Westview, 1998), and *Historical Dictionary of Mozambique* (Scarecrow, 1991). His articles have been featured in such periodicals as *African Studies Review*, *Africa Today*, *African Affairs*, *Social Science and Medicine*, *Journal of Negro History*, *Journal of Southern African Affairs*, *Journal of African History*, and *Current History*. He also has over two dozen articles in books and encyclopedias.

Tomé Mbuia João, a Mozambican by origin, completed his studies in the United States and taught at Friendship and Claflin Colleges in South Carolina before moving to Washington to work as a broadcaster in Portuguese at the Voice of America, where he has been since the early 1980s. Part of his task at the radio station is producing and broadcasting documentaries on African history, with particular emphasis on Lusophone Africa. Dr. Mbuia João holds a B.A degree in philosophy and theology from Namaacha, Mozambique; two M.A. degrees, one in international law and international relations from Catholic University, and the other in African and Latin American history from University of Illinois, Urbana-Champaign; and a

Ph.D. in African and Latin American history from Catholic University. He wrote his seminal Ph.D. dissertation (1990) on "The Revolt of Dom Jerónimo Chingulia of Mombasa (1590–1637): An Episode in the Portuguese Century of Decline."

Emmanuel Nnadozie, originally from Nigeria, is professor of economics at Truman State University, where he has taught since 1989. He received his B.A. and M.S. degrees from the University of Nigeria and a Ph.D. in development and international economics from the Sorbonne, Paris, in 1987. Professor Nnadozie worked with a World Bank Development Program in Nigeria. In 1966–1967, he was a visiting professor of economics at the University of North Carolina at Charlotte and, in 1994, a research fellow at Saint Anthony's College, University of Oxford, England. Professor Nnadozie served as president of the African Finance and Economics Association of North America for the 2001–2002 period. His scholarly works have appeared in both academic and nonacademic journals all over the world. He has written several books related to economic development, U.S.–Africa business, and investment in Africa. His books include: *Chad: A Nation in Search of its Future* (coauthored with Mario Azevedo, Westview, 1998); *Oil Boom and Socioeconomic Crisis in Nigeria* (Mellen, 1995); *African Culture and American Business in Africa: How to Strategically Manage Cultural Differences in African Business* (Afrimax, 1998); and *African Economic Development* (Academic Press/Harcourt Brace, 2003).